Creative Dimensions of Teaching and Learning in the 21st Century

ADVANCES IN CREATIVITY AND GIFTEDNESS

Volume 12

Scope:

Advances in Creativity and Gifted Education (ADVA) is the first internationally established book series that focuses exclusively on the constructs of creativity and giftedness as pertaining to the psychology, philosophy, pedagogy and ecology of talent development across the milieus of family, school, institutions and society. ADVA strives to synthesize both domain specific and domain general efforts at developing creativity, giftedness and talent. The books in the series are international in scope and include the efforts of researchers, clinicians and practitioners across the globe.

Creative Dimensions of Teaching and Learning in the 21st Century

Edited by

Jill B. Cummings
Yorkville University, Canada

and

Mary L. Blatherwick
University of New Brunswick, Canada

SENSE PUBLISHERS
ROTTERDAM/BOSTON/TAIPEI

A C.I.P. record for this book is available from the Library of Congress.

ISBN: 978-94-6351-045-5 (paperback)
ISBN: 978-94-6351-046-2 (hardback)
ISBN: 978-94-6351-047-9 (e-book)

Published by: Sense Publishers,
P.O. Box 21858,
3001 AW Rotterdam,
The Netherlands
https://www.sensepublishers.com/

All chapters in this book have undergone peer review.

Printed on acid-free paper

TABLE OF CONTENTS

KIERAN EGAN

FOREWORD

In the late 1960s I was moonlighting from my studies at Stanford by working for the IBM Corp. This was a period when IBM was expanding hugely and seemed to have money to burn. One reason the company was so successful was tied to its attention both to its employees as well as its customers. Also, at this time of selling its huge mainframe computers into companies across the world, the company attended closely to details and cutting costs where possible. I was merely a consultant working in Los Gatos and San Jose one day a week, but I learned a lot about the company one way or another, especially as one of my jobs was to write a history of IBM using the new Structural Communication programming format. The attention to employees and to detail came together one day when I met a man who had been given a significant bonus for coming up with a simple suggestion. Even in big mainframe computers, space was crucial and, of course, costs were crucial. One component fixed firmly to the frame of their new System 360 was held in place with four small screws. The creative suggestion was to fix the component onto a smaller triangular base, which ensured it was no less secure, and required only three screws and freed up a small amount of space.

IBM's motto at the time was, and still is, "THINK." Most executives had a plaque on desks or walls with THINK shouting at them all day. Well, "think" was what the creative employee did coming up with the suggestion that saved one screw and a tiny amount of space in each System 360 computer. By giving him a bonus the company was not primarily concerned with how much this innovation saved – though that was hardly irrelevant. Mainly they were rewarding and trying to stimulate the daily activity of their employees, alertness to possibilities and creativity in thinking about them as part of their corporate culture. This focus on "Creativity" is still vivid for IBM, and is highly relevant today as the Introduction to this book indicates.

Well, this may be a somewhat lumbering way to make a point about what this book is centrally concerned with. We want administrators, teachers, and students in our educational systems to be alert to possibilities and to be creative in addressing them. The IBM motto was "think" and they meant by it what we might mean by "think creatively", "think imaginatively," "think critically", etc. etc. If we were to use a Venn diagram to chart the overlapping meanings of most of the slogans used in Education for the past century we would, I am sure, find a huge overlap among them. Basically, we want people not simply to go through life in some automatic way, responding to their environments at the least challenging intellectual level required, but we want them to self-trigger their thinking into the higher level that all those slogans point towards. While learning, in particular, we want students to *think*. This simple attempt to engage students' imaginations in what they learn has also been described in endless ways, discouraging "rote-learning," (while having to carefully distinguish this from "learning by heart" which can be immensely valuable), discouraging "formal learning" (as distinct from "natural learning"—that's one of Dewey's distinctions), "filling a bucket" rather than "lighting a fire," avoiding "brain dumping," "banking," "irrelevance to students' needs," and so on. Occasionally, it can seem that there has been little educational thinking for the past century apart from struggling to come up with new metaphors for the same thing then making the same old arguments in terms of the new metaphor.

But, unfortunately, it does seem to be constantly necessary to make the case again and anew. One of the enemies of effective teaching and learning is simply the routineness of the classroom. Routine activity is one of the great enemies of creative thinking, and we are creatures who seek and rely on routine as often as possible. J. G. Bennett (in *Creative Thinking*, London: Coombe Springs Press, 1975) described what he called "The Law of Mental Declension," which stated that we perform every task at the lowest intellectual level possible. A corollary is that we try to make every task we are faced by as simple as possible as quickly as possible. Take driving a car. Initially, when we are learning to drive, we have to be extremely attentive to every movement and action. As we become more efficient we attend less and less at a conscious level until, eventually, much of our driving activity takes place at an automatic level that requires very little conscious attention. Bennett argues that this "law" operates for students in school as well, so that they will address any challenge at the lowest level possible. For many students much of the time, the greatest challenge they face is simply to be able to show the teacher they know what is going on in the classroom in case they are asked a question. Bennett uses his "law" to argue for presenting challenges that require students to attend and work intellectually at a high conscious level.

Bennett suggests that we aim to perform any task we are faced with by employing the least amount of intellectual energy possible; we strive to make every task as easy as possible, and engage it at that "Automatic" level. For other tasks, we have to be more aware, however, and so we need to remain at a "Sensitive" level of awareness and alertness to be able to handle any unexpected features of the activity at hand. For these tasks we need to be sensitive to what is going on. The next level is that at which we respond to challenges as synthetic thinkers or critical inquirers. Bennett calls this form of thinking and learning "Conscious" because we need a more complex and acute awareness of wider contexts and dimensions of the task at hand to deal with it adequately.

In classrooms, teachers ideally want Conscious learning – what in this book and in everyday discourse is usually called "creative" learning, in which new ideas and facts can be brought together with knowledge already grasped to form new combinations and spark new ideas. Using Bennett's model as a kind of heuristic, we can see the purpose of providing appropriate challenges to students, and ourselves as teachers, is what generates the degree of intellectual energy students will give to learning.

Well, this book addresses exactly this aim. The readings that follow provide a fantastic resource for administrators, teachers, and professors of education who want ideas for how to go about ensuring that classrooms much more commonly show creativity in action, and lead to greater creativity in students' thinking and behaviour, such that it becomes a habit of mind over the years and through their adulthood. The book deals with all curriculum areas, from arts to STEM, and contains a wealth of ideas for use in all grade levels. I think our schools would show a significant daily improvement if this book was a part of the library of all administrators, teachers, and professors of education and was regularly consulted.

Kieran Egan

ACKNOWLEDGEMENTS

There are many people to thank for their assistance in developing this book. It took a dedicated community of educators to whom we are thankful.

We particularly want to extend our appreciation to the contributors and authors of each of the chapters for sharing their creative ideas for teaching/learning and for their patience.

We are very grateful to Eleni Karavanidou for her attention to detail and dedication to this project. Eleni assisted with the editing process while completing her doctoral studies at the University of New Brunswick.

We also want to acknowledge the support of the team of Sense Publishers, particularly Jolanda Karada.

We are grateful to our universities, Yorkville University and the University of New Brunswick, as well as the Canadian Society for Education through Art (CSEA), for their recognition and funding support of the proofreading and final phases of publication of our book.

We are particularly appreciative of Dr. Kieran Egan, Professor Emeritus, Simon Fraser University, for his foreword explaining the significance of this work and his recommendation of this book to educators and administrators.

INTRODUCTION

Creative Dimensions of Teaching and Learning in the 21st Century will appeal to the many educators across disciplines who want to develop teaching practices that promote creative and critical thinking.

During our extensive experience in teacher education we have experienced "first hand" the need for a current and engaging scholarly text which will facilitate critical discussion of innovation in teaching, as well as share a wide range of creative approaches and practical strategies.

Creativity and critical thinking are 21st century challenges for educators. They are addressed in this book by educators who have designed and implemented solutions that have worked with learning groups at every level of education.

In the thirty-five original chapters that follow you will hear from experienced educators – mainly from across Canada and the United States. They focus creatively on conceptual and practical solutions for contexts ranging from mathematics to music; aboriginal wisdom to arts education; and, social justice to STEM. These approaches and projects facilitate deep learning connected to issues vital in education today – engagement, creativity, identity, relevance, collaborative learning, dynamic assessment, learner autonomy, multi-modal literacy, sensory learning, aesthetics, critical thinking, digital tools, teacher education, online learning, and more.

As editors, we have invited contributions by experienced educators and researchers who share their passion for teaching and learning in a collection that critically examines innovations in today's K-12 schools, post-secondary programs, and adult and community learning.

To teach creatively the educator needs to think, discuss, and act creatively. By examining, discussing, implementing and adapting the approaches presented in this book, we believe that you as educators will develop your own creative thinking and pedagogies. And your creativity and innovations will transform teaching and learning in the 21st century.

OVERVIEW OF THE BOOK

SECTION I FRAMEWORKS AND ISSUES

Chapter 1

Understanding Creativity by Philip Lambert (University of New Brunswick – UNB). Lambert explains frameworks for understanding creativity, seeing different approaches to creativity as pieces of a whole, rather than separate and conflicting points. The author addresses a question fundamental to this book: "Can we teach and learn *creativity*?"

Chapter 2

Time to Learn with Creativity in Mind by Paul Syme (UNB). The author explains temporal and spatial conditions that influence creative thinking and learning. Syme highlights that creative processes always need *space*; and discusses why these spaces need to be treated differently in our digital era. He proposes how curriculum and schooling need to be refocused to optimize creative thinking and learning in this digital age where our temporal and spatial spaces differ from previous times.

Chapter 3

Developing Creativity and Imagination by Accumulating Lots of Useless Knowledge by Kieran Egan (Simon Fraser University – SFU). Challenging the division between imagination and rationality in the curriculum, Egan recommends and explains an innovative approach, *Learning in Depth*, by which learners accumulate a great deal of detailed knowledge about a specific topic to shape the mind and fuel their creativity.

Chapter 4

Re-Imagining Relevance in Education by Gillian Judson (SFU). Judson advocates for revisiting the notion of "what is relevant in learning" in terms of "emotional" significance in order to engage students' emotional and imaginative lives in our teaching.

Chapter 5

Creative Development in Teacher Education: When You Dress Educators Up, They Need a Place to Go by Robert Kelly (University of Calgary). Kelly aims to enhance teachers' creative capacities as an underlying issue in education. This chapter explains ways to refocus teacher education to facilitate creative development.

Chapter 6

Identity Text Projects: Generating Academic Power in Multilingual Classrooms by Jim Cummins (University of Toronto – UT), Burcu Yaman Ntelioglou (Brandon University), Gail Prasad (University of Wisconsin), Saskia Stille (York University – York U.). These authors bring "identity" to the forefront as an issue for education, engagement in learning, and creativity. Their chapter examines the use of technology as an amplifier of "identity texts" to empower students from social groups whose languages, cultures, and backgrounds may have been previously devalued, often for generations, in the wider society, and to help project their identity back to them in an affirming light through their creative writing and texts.

Chapter 7

The Art of Cultivating Clever Questions to Empower Students, Improve Teaching, and Open Up the Curriculum by Samuel LeBlanc (UNB). LeBlanc discusses the benefits of asking quality questions to "flip the classroom" and produce challenging learning situations. He explains how he implements this questioning approach in the post-secondary classroom.

Chapter 8

Creative Practices in the Observation of Everyday Life: The Crack in the Door that Invites a Creative Vision by Gerald Cupchik (UT). The author explains how he provokes students in a university Social Sciences course to think critically about their discipline and the professional and cultural standards that "bind it".

Chapter 9

Back to the Garden: Coming to Our Senses by Mary Blatherwick and Jill Cummings (UNB and Yorkville University). The authors examine how sensory experiences enhance imagination, play, and creativity. They explain this through the lens of sociocultural theory-based approaches featuring sensory activities and aesthetics for enhancement of creativity in learning and teaching.

Chapter 10

Enhancing Education: Material Culture, Visual Media, and the Aesthetics of Teachers' Lives by Adrian McKerracher (University of British Columbia – UBC), Anita Sinner (Concordia University), Erika Hasebe-Ludt (University of Lethbridge), Carl Leggo (UBC), Kerri Mesner (UBC), Dustin Garnet (UBC). This chapter examines how material and popular culture communicated through the arts (film, television, literature, photography, life writing) contribute to critically advancing discourses that improve practice in teacher education.

Chapter 11

Autobiographical Creation: A Powerful Professional Development Strategy for Teachers by Antoinette Gagné, Sreemali Herath, and Marlon Valencia (UT).

Applying forms of autobiography creates multiple spaces for teachers to reflect on who they are and how this impacts their practices along the teacher education continuum.

Chapter 12

Art Matters: An Advocacy Experience for Teacher-Candidates by Elizabeth Ashworth and Kathy Mantas (Nipissing University). The importance of the advocacy of arts education is featured in this chapter. Ashworth and Mantas present Art assignments used in their teacher education courses to reach out to and promote thinking about the value of "the Arts" amongst the academic community.

SECTION II CREATIVE APPROACHES

Chapter 13

Integrating the "Human Feel" into Online Second/Additional Language Teaching Approaches by Geoff Lawrence (York U.). The author explains how educators may create engaging language learning environments in blended and online settings where connectivity amongst students becomes a catalyst for learning. Approaches and examples of e-learning strategies to build engaging language learning communities are explained.

Chapter 14

The Zone of Proximal Development and the Twin Poles of Teaching and Assessing in Vygotsky's Developmental Education by Matthew Poehner (Pennsylvania State University). Dynamic assessment brings the Zone of Proximal Development (ZPD) into focus in learning to diagnose and promote learner abilities while making use of the social dynamics within the group to change classroom practices across the curriculum. Illustrative examples from the field of second language (L2) education are discussed.

Chapter 15

Digiart and Human Rights: New Media Visual Art Integration for Teacher Candidates by Joanna Black (University of Manitoba). Black explains human rights issues in art education explored through digital technologies and activities in teacher education. She presents powerful examples of creative work bearing witness to teacher candidates' sensitivity to social challenges such as women's right to education.

Chapter 16

Card Tricks Discovery Learning and Flow in Mathematics Teacher Education by Peter Liljedahl (SFU). The author explains how to implement discovery learning to create a "flow" experience which fosters creativity in learning and teaching mathematics.

Chapter 17

Imagining Alberta's First Nations by Belinda Jamieson (UNB). Employing storytelling "re-enchants" teaching and learning. The author discusses how telling stories and aboriginal myths engage learners.

Chapter 18

The Importance of Art in Children's Writing Education by Leslie Julia Brewster (New Brunswick). Encouraging children to tell their stories with pictures before they write enhances art and writing in teaching 21st century literacies.

Chapter 19

De-Constructing Cabinets of Curiosity: Learning to Think Historically in Community History Museums by Cynthia Wallace-Casey (University of Ottawa). A series of creative activities in museums develops an active learner community of inquiry amongst middle school learners.

Chapter 20

Cultivating Creativity by Susan Galbraith (New Brunswick). Critically examining practices for developing creativity, Galbraith invites teachers to use Art as "another way of seeing" in order to bring out students' innate creative abilities in a classroom setting.

Chapter 21

STEM and a Framework for Learning by Ian Fogarty and Chris Ryan (New Brunswick). Fogarty and Ryan present an innovative assessment model for high school physics classes. In addition to bridging the gap between research and practice, their implementation of this approach highlights how 21st Century learning goals can be integrated into public education classrooms in a way that is individualized.

Chapter 22

Conceptualizing and Implementing Critical Filmmaking Pedagogies by Matt Rogers (UNB). Rogers addresses social justice issues with youth in schools through participatory filmmaking. This chapter exposes critical perspectives and issues involved in participatory film-making pedagogy. Rogers recommends questions to be incorporated to implement reflection on critical arts-based activities.

Chapter 23

European Ideas in Education by Eleni Karavanidou (UNB). Karavanidou explains an award-winning project by European school libraries working with print and digital materials to create a cross-cultural bridge between students' countries that revitalizes the love of reading.

Chapter 24

Using Experiential Learning to Engage Aboriginal Students in the Arts by Margaret Sadler (UNB). Sadler proposes a collaborative model in a multicultural classroom context where educators work alongside their students within their First Nations communities to engage all students.

Chapter 25

Web-Based Arts Education: Creativity in the Classroom by Heather McLeod (Memorial University) and Marlene Brooks (Thompson Rivers University). Aesthetic design and multimodal experiential learning are featured in this account of an award-winning online Master's course that engages graduate student participants in deep learning and professional growth.

Chapter 26

Play and Learn: Build Your Robot and Learn STEM by Ahmad Khanlari (UT). Khanlari showcases innovations in using robotics to create authentic learning environments where difficult STEM subjects become a game and students are knowledge-builders.

SECTION III EXAMPLES FROM THE CLASSROOM AND BEYOND

Chapter 27

Bringing Imagination and Literacy Circles into the Math Classroom by Sylvie Morice (New Brunswick). With the help of Egan's storytelling framework, Morice brings imagination into classrooms to successfully merge the curriculum with the interests of students and their multiple intelligences.

Chapter 28

Glyffix Play: A Modern Image-Based Form of Language Play by Dale Vandenborre (UNB). In his modern version of pictorial hieroglyphics, the author – as "A.J. Funn" – combines technology and "gamification" to wrap language play into a modern visual puzzle language where "readers" and "writers" alike communicate, enjoy, and learn creatively.

Chapter 29

Tutoring Second Language Learners within Their Zones of Proximal Development: Recommendations for Changes in University Writing Center Pedagogy by Ally Zhou and Xiaomin Hu (Oklahoma City University). An innovative pedagogical approach based on sociocultural theories of learning is explained for university writing centres and their tutoring of second language learners. This entails assessing learners' ongoing needs dynamically and incorporating graduated and contingent assistance within their zone of proximal development to help them self-regulate and to become independent writers.

Chapter 30
Assessing Creativity in the School Classroom by Robin Beyea (UNB). The author identifies gaps in old and new ways of assessing creativity, and proposes a task-specific system of assessment that incorporates both product and process, metacognitive skills, and qualitative observation.

Chapter 31
Language Acquisition through Personal Story Writing: A Learner Book Project by Lorraine Lasmanis (Waterloo). Lasmanis explains a creative project for adult learners of English as a Second Language (ESL) and Adult Literacy that empowered students to make their own course book.

Chapter 32

A Creative Process: Using Songwriting to Develop Creativity by Trevor Strong (Queen's University). An experienced musician and art-educator, the author describes techniques of song-writing for students that may unlock creativity in other domains as well.

Chapter 33

From Research Technique to Classroom Activity: Adapting Elicited Imitation as a Grammar-for-Speaking Task by Michael Busch (Saginaw Valley University). The author proposes an innovative way to make use of elicited imitation in teaching post-secondary learners of a second language. This strategy is based on research teaching methodology.

Chapter 34
Caring for the Whole Person in the EAP Classroom by Snezhana Harizanova (York U.). This educator uses *Suggestopedia*, G. Lozanov's alternative language teaching method, in a North American setting to engage the postsecondary L2 language learner holistically by taking into account facets and needs of the person that other language methods may ignore.

Chapter 35
Strategies to Engage and Transform Teacher Learners in an Online Course by Antoinette Gagné, Sreemali Herath and Marlon Valencia (UT). An online environment supports teacher learners in becoming more creative and reflective through completion of innovative activities such as blogs, videos, and cartoons dialogues that push them to "stretch" beyond their comfort zones.

PHILIP A. LAMBERT

1. UNDERSTANDING CREATIVITY

INTRODUCTION

Over 40 years ago, Paul Torrance (1970) commented that "Children are so accustomed to the one correct or best answer that they may be reluctant to think of other possibilities or to build up a pool of ideas to be evaluated later" (1970, p. 86). Despite his best efforts, and the efforts of many others, creativity scores are declining in the United States (Kim, 2011). Could North America be losing a creativity race? A race we may not even know we are in? A race that may be more important than most of us realize?

In *A Whole New Mind* Daniel Pink (2006) argues that the "advanced" world is undergoing a shift from the information age to a conceptual age and that it is inventive, creative, and empathetic people who will thrive in this new world. "The most creative among us see relationships the rest of us never notice. Such ability is at a premium in a world where specialized knowledge work can quickly become routinized work – and therefore be automated or outsourced away" (p. 135). James Kaufman and his colleagues (2008) noted in *Essentials of Creativity Assessment* that "because creativity, specifically the ability to solve problems creatively, is so universally useful, its relationship to any construct or aspect of human life is worthy of study" (p. 126). It seems to be universally acknowledged that creativity is a desired trait; it is the most used – over used? – word in LinkedIn profiles. According to Erick Schonfeld in *The Rise of the 'Creative' Class* (2011): "In a time of high unemployment when traditional skills can be outsourced or automated, creative skills remain highly sought after and highly valuable. We all want to be part of the creative class of programmers, designers, and information workers. The term used to mean artists and writers. Today, it means job stability" (in Florida, 2011, n.p.).

Most mainframe computer manufacturers disappeared in the space of about a year; the entire life cycle of the video rental business was barely more than two decades[1]; publishers of printed works have either reinvented themselves, or died; the music industry has been transformed, seemingly overnight; commonplace products, such as the thermostat and the smoke detector, are being given a new lease on life through enhanced functionality, coupled with an improved user interface and attention to aesthetic appeal, and they're commanding amazing price premiums for getting it right[2]; the once proud Canadian technology giant – Nortel – is now but a memory, and Blackberry seems destined to follow; cars are becoming entertainment centres and communication hubs that can also get you where you want to go, while

J. B. Cummings & M. L. Blatherwick (Eds.), Creative Dimensions of Teaching and Learning in the 21st Century, 1–21.

looking great doing it. "Innovate or die" isn't just a catchy slogan. It seems that everywhere you look these days the business landscape is littered with the burned-out hulks of those companies that didn't see change waves coming – even when they were tsunamis – or couldn't move quickly enough, or just weren't innovative enough. Their death and decay stands in sharp relief, starkly contrasting with their high-flying slayers; the rising stars – or, possibly, shooting stars… time will tell – of the corporate jungle. So, it should come as little surprise that an IBM survey of 1,500 CEOs from around the world found that creativity was the number one factor that had to be instilled throughout an organization in order to be successful (IBM, 2010). These CEOs valued creativity over management discipline, integrity, even over vision.

In *Rise of the Creative Class – Revisited* Richard Florida (2012) suggests that we are undergoing a change at least as dramatic as the industrial revolution:

> It wasn't just the Internet, or the rise of new technologies, or even globalization that were upending our jobs, lives, and communities, though all those things were important. Beneath the surface, unnoticed by many, an even deeper force was at work – the rise of creativity as a fundamental economic driver, and the rise of a new social class, the Creative Class. (p. vii)

But it's not just corporations and the economy that need and value creativity. The human race faces global issues unprecedented in scope, scale and complexity. Complex political, social, resource, and environmental issues demand our most creative solutions, or entire societies – if not the entire human race – may go the way of the mainframe computer. Karpova, Marckett, and Barker (2011) concluded that "Creativity becomes the focus when preparing current students and future citizens to deal with uncertainty and to adapt to continuous change both personally and professionally" (p. 53), and Csikszentmihalyi (1996) noted that "for better or for worse, our future is now closely tied to human creativity" (p. 4). Arnold Toynbee in *Is America Neglecting her Creative Minority*? said:

> This is all-important, because the outstanding creative ability of a fairly small percentage of the population is mankind's ultimate capital asset… the work of creative spirits is what gives society a chance of directing its inevitable movement along constructive instead of destructive lines. (in Taylor, 1988, pp. 112–113)

So much of what makes life worth living are creative pursuits. Csikszentmihalyi (1996) found in his research that "When people are asked to choose from a list the best description of how they feel when doing whatever they enjoy doing most… the answer most frequently chosen is 'designing or discovering something new'" (p. 108). He went on to conclude that "Even though personal creativity may not lead to fame and fortune, it can do something that from the individual's point of view is even more important: make day-to day experiences more vivid, more enjoyable, more rewarding" (p. 344). In summing up their conclusions about creative endevours Scott,

Leritz, and Mumford (2004) stated that "Few attributes of human performance have as much impact on our lives, and our world, as creativity" (p. 361). In discussing beliefs and misconceptions about creativity Sawyer (2012) noted: "Creativity is a healing, life-affirming activity. This belief is supported by the research" (p. 409).

If creativity could be the factor that keeps us all alive, and figures prominently in making life worth living, it follows that we should want more of it. But, is creativity a genetic gift bestowed upon some fortunate souls while others are left wanting, or is it something that can be nurtured in all of us? Can creativity be taught? Can it become, for each of us, an endless renewable resource that can be tapped into at any time? These are the questions that this review seeks to explore.

This review purposely took a broad view, casting a wide net in order to, perhaps, allow previous attempts at practical application to inform the theoretical. That is, to see if the research concerned with implementing creativity enhancement techniques paints enough of a picture for an existing creativity theory to emerge from the partially completed brush strokes, or if another picture may be emerging on creativity's canvas.

Challenges

"Solomon (1990), drawing from survey data, found that 25% of the organizations employing more than 100 people offer some form of creativity training" (in Scott, Leritz, & Mumford, 2004, p. 361). The perceived need for creativity has led to a proliferation of creativity enhancement programs, yet the research has not kept pace, leading to the potential for creativity "snake oil salesmen" and wasted time and resources (Puccio, Firestien, & Coyle, 2006). Some creativity enhancement methods have become quite popular, even with little research to support their use; for example, de Bono's *Parallel Thinking and Lateral Thinking* (Sternberg & Lubart, 1999, p. 5). On the other hand, many approaches that appear to offer a great deal of potential are virtually unheard of outside of academic circles, and some with great potential are rarely discussed even amongst creativity researchers.

One of the reasons that research on the enhancement of creativity has not kept pace with the rise in the number of programs may be the challenges inherent in the study of the enhancement of creativity. Particularly troublesome have been the definition of creativity and the assessment of creativity.

Definition

While most creativity researchers agree that the standard definition of creativity requires both originality and effectiveness, this definition leaves open the definition of the terms *originality* and *effectiveness*. It also does not address the question of who is to judge *originality* and *effectiveness*, or how (Runco & Jaeger, 2012).

Many creativity researchers differentiate levels of creativity by categorizing people or their creative products as either Big C or little c. But creativity is not a dichotomy, being either big or little – any more than it has three states – none, a little bit (little c), or a lot (Big C). There is a wide range of creativity unaccounted for between these dichotomies. The addition of "Pro c" and "mini c" (Kozbelt, Beghetto, & Runco, 2010) only confound the matter, resulting in more definitions of creativity. Creativity exists on a continuum (Amabile, 1996). If it were to be assigned an absolute scale from 0 to 100, 0 might represent the creativity of a rock, while 100 might represent the creativity of the primordial intelligence (or whatever conception of 'god' one may have… or whatever next best concept of the ultimate creative force one's less-than-100-on-this-creatvity-scale creative brain can come up with…) and creative theorists could spend countless hours discussing where the likes of Michelangelo, Da Vinci, and Einstein should fall on this scale – or, for that matter, where Big C, little c, pro c and mini c should land on this ultimate creativity scale. But this paper was written with more practical matters in mind. So, while I agree with Amabile's (1996) definition:

> A product or response is creative to the extent that appropriate observers independently agree it is creative. Appropriate observers are those familiar with the domain in which the product was created or the response articulated. Thus, creativity can be regarded as the quality of products or responses judged to be creative by appropriate observers, and it can also be regarded as the process by which something so judged is produced. (p. 33)

There is also value in Plucker, Beghetto & Dow's definition (2004): Creativity is "the interaction among *aptitude, process, and environment* by which an individual or group produces a *perceptible product* that is both *novel and useful* as defined within a *social context*" (p. 90).

It should be clear that, if a definition of creativity cannot be agreed on, it makes it challenging to assess. And if you can't assess creativity, how can you tell if a four-hour seminar on parallel thinking, or a two-semester course covering meta-cognition and creative problem-solving, along with other cognitive techniques and real-world exercises, actually do what they claim to do – enhance creativity?

Assessment

While there are issues related to the definition of creativity, many researchers have agreed that a creative idea or product is one which is *novel* or *original* and *useful*, *adaptive* or of *value* (Carson, 2010, p. 5). However, even if this definition of creativity is accepted, assessment remains an even more contentious issue. Torrance and Guilford have been advocates of simple tests that can be easily administered in a classroom setting and evaluated by anyone who takes the time to become familiar with the evaluation method. Other approaches have included personality inventories, biographical inventories, and behavioural tests.

Creativity research has been hampered by what is referred to as the criterion problem. "An absolute and indisputable criterion of creativity is not readily available (there is no one, single magic number or test)" (Kaufman, Plucker, & Baer, 2008, p. 53). This led Amabile (1977, 1996) to develop the Consensual Assessment Technique (CAT). The CAT consists of a number of judges, familiar with the domain in question, independently evaluating and ranking creative works.

While Amabile originally felt that the assessors did not have to be experts in the domain, they merely needed to be familiar with it (Amabile, 1977), years later she concluded that experts were required (Hennessey & Amabile, 2010). However, it seems that, in practice, CATs were being performed with domain experts all along (Kaufman et al., 2008), presumably because other researchers always felt there was a need for the assessors to be experts.

Amabile's CAT is considered one of the most effective means of assessing creativity (Kaufman et al., 2008).

This particular method has been used extensively in creativity research. Because (a) it is based on actual creative performances or artifacts; (b) it is not tied to any particular theory of creativity; and (c) it mimics the way creativity is assessed in the 'real world,' the CAT has sometimes been called the 'gold standard' of creativity assessment (Carson, 2006, p. 55).

While the CAT may mimic the way creativity is assessed in the real world, it does not mimic the way creative products are developed in the real world. The laboratory-like conditions and/or approach to these studies leaves little room for intrinsic motivation.

With respect to application of the CAT, Kaufman et al. (2008) state that "if you really don't care about the domain, then the choice of task is especially easy. You want a task that anyone can do at some level and that will not favour any group of subjects inappropriately" (p. 72). In this review of the literature, it appears that the creative efforts being asked of the participants (most often poetry writing or collage making) would typically favour groups of students inappropriately. The creative math or science student may not perform well on either of these common CAT tasks, and while some participants may be intrinsically motivated by these tasks, others would not be.

Amabile's research has indicated that extrinsic constraints tend to lower creativity scores, while intrinsic motivation tends to lead to increases in creativity. Yet there does not seem to be any CAT-based creativity research where the participants are given a choice in the task. Why not allow most (or more) participants to be intrinsically motivated by giving them choices; not just on the task performed, but also on the time when the task is completed and how long is spent on the task? Allowing for a choice in domain and choice regarding time should reduce any possible confounding effect of intrinsic motivation.

The CAT has been used with a diverse range of tasks, but Kaufman et al. (2008) conclude that "the artifacts still must be of the same kind, however (e.g., poems, or all collages, or all stories). You cannot mix different kinds of artifacts and have expert judges produce meaningful comparative ratings of creativity. (To do so would be rather like asking which is more fruity, apples or oranges.)" (p. 67). I disagree.

Of course, we can compare apples and oranges – the former tend to be red or green, while the later are usually orange. We could compare apples and oranges on many different levels: colour, acidity, texture, sweetness, growing environment, etc. Similarly, the creativity of van Gogh's *Starry Night* could be evaluated and compared to the creativity of Walker's *The Color Purple*. One may question the validity and reliability of such a survey, but the comparison is possible.

Amabile's approach can be more time consuming and challenging to implement. The studies employing this approach use simplistic creative products which may not be representative of real-world creativity, and the subject only has the opportunity to be creative in one domain, which may not be the domain in which they feel most comfortable expressing their creativity. While the Torrance Tests for Creative Thinking (TTCT) give subjects multiple ways to express their creativity, the exercises do not require real-world creativity and many authors claim that TTCTs are only tests of divergent thinking, which may be a necessary, but not sufficient, ability for creativity. The TTCT also does nothing to evaluate usefulness, or value. While Amabile's approach doesn't explicitly evaluate usefulness, there is an implied *value* when a panel of independent judges evaluates a product as creative.

Regardless of the pros and cons of various approaches, the TTCT is the most commonly used measure of creative potential. Having a history of over fifty years, it has been used in many thousands of studies and it has a norms database based on tens of thousands of subjects. It is also the basis of a large longitudinal study spanning fifty years.

Given the popularity of this approach, its evaluation categories are referred to frequently in the literature and therefore they are defined here. Torrance, Ball and Safter (2008) provide the following:

- Verbal: the verbal TTCT is composed of written responses to questions posed about an illustrated scene in the response booklet.
- Figural: the figural TTCT consists of constructing pictures based on partially completed pictures, lines, or shapes, and giving the completed picture a title.
- Fluency: "the number of ideas a person expresses through interpretable responses that sue the stimulus in a meaningful manner" (Torrance, Ball, & Safter 2008, p. 5).
- Flexibility is a measure of the subject's tendency to "break-set" or resist inertia in thinking and is scored based on the number of categories used in responses.
- Originality "is based on the statistical infrequency and unusualness of the response" (Torrance, Ball, & Safter, 2008, p. 7).
- Elaboration is a measure of the tendency to go beyond the minimum required.

Cognitive Approaches

Given the wide range of factors that have been shown, or theorized, to have an effect on creativity, it is not surprising that a multitude of programs have been developed to enhance creativity; however, the vast majority of these have been cognitive programs related to the creative process. Some of the more popular of these are reviewed here, while less common cognitive approaches, and those lacking in research studies, are briefly discussed at the end of this section.

Brainstorming

In 1938, Alex Osborn began developing techniques to enhance idea generation at his advertising firm. He had found that, on their own, individuals were not coming up with the quantity, or quality, of ideas he felt they were capable of, and that conventional meetings seemed to be hampering idea generation (Amabile, 1996; Osborn, 1952, 1963).

Osborn formalized his observations as a set of rules for an idea generation technique and coined the term *brainstorming*. Osborn (1952, 1963) published his set of rules for the now-famous technique in his seminal work *Applied Imagination*:

- Criticism is ruled out. Adverse judgment of ideas must be withheld until later.
- "Free-wheeling" is welcomed. The wilder the idea, the better; it is easier to tame down than to think up.
- Quantity is wanted. The greater the number of ideas, the more the likelihood of useful ideas.
- Combination and improvement are sought. In addition to contributing ideas of their own, participants should suggest how ideas of others can be turned into better ideas; or how two or more ideas can be joined into still another idea (Osborn, 1963, p. 156).

In 1954 Osborn founded the Creative Education Foundation and in 1955 he began a collaboration with Dr. Sidney J. Parnes, which led to the Osborn-Parnes Creative Problem-solving Process (see next section). Osborn (1963) cites many examples of success with brainstorming, but he does not cite any scientific studies that specifically focused on brainstorming, largely because he viewed brainstorming as just one step in a larger process:

> In summary, let's put group brainstorming in its place. For one thing, it is only one of the phases of idea-finding which, in turn, is only one of the phases of the creative problem-solving process. And let's bear in mind that group brainstorming is meant to be used – not as a substitute – but as a supplement. (p. 191)

On the other hand, Stein (1975, p. 37) notes that brainstorming is the most researched technique for creative problem-solving. The research clearly supports the notion that brainstorming results in more ideas than techniques that allow or encourage judgment or evaluation during idea-generation. However, in terms of the quality of ideas resulting from brainstorming, the results are less conclusive, with some research supporting brainstorming, while other research shows no improvement when applying the technique. Research has also shown that group brainstorming holds no advantage over individual brainstorming (Scott, Leritz, & Mumford, 2004; Stein, 1975), a fact which Osborn (1963) seemed to be well aware of:

> Despite the many virtues of group brainstorming, individual ideation is usually more usable and can be just as productive. In fact, the ideal methodology for idea-finding is a triple attack: (1) Individual ideation. (2) Group brainstorming. (3) Individual ideation. And, of course, each of these procedures can be far more productive if the deferment – of – judgment principle is consistently followed. (p. 191)

There are many challenges to effectively researching the premises of brainstorming. While accounting for quantity is a relatively straight forward task, determination of the quality of ideas presents challenges, such as: what is the defintion of quality, and who is the arbitor of quality. The choice of facilitator can have a large impact on the results and the degree of training or instruction provided. As noted by Stein (1975) in an introduction to his extensive review of the research regarding brainstorming (in excess of 120 pages in his two-volume examination of stimulating creativity):

> It should therefore not be surprising to the reader that studies by adherents of brainstorming support brainstorming while some other publications support it less strongly or not at all… It is insufficient to believe that the instructions as transmitted are adequate. It is important to know that the instructions have 'taken' and whether they have or not should be determined in some way other than with the same test that is used to determine the number and quality of ideas produced… It may still be that subjects who defer judgment produce more and better ideas than individuals who do not defer judgment. All that can be said is that in the studies previously mentioned and in those which shall be presented one cannot be certain that researchers were actually studying individuals who deferred judgment. And, if subjects were not deferring judgment then the researchers were not conducting a good test of brainstorming's hypotheses. (Vol. 2, pp. 38–39)

While Stein may sound, in the quotation above, like an "adherent of brainstorming", he goes on to produce a very extensive, and balanced view of the research published prior to 1975. It seems that virtually every facet of brainstorming has been studied: "Brainstorming is the most researched of all the procedures for creative problem-solving. It has been scrutinized from practically every angle and in terms of almost every variable" (Stein, 1975, p. 37); Osborn's (1963) recommended "individual-group-individual" technique has been neglected. "This tripartite sequence has not been studied. Research has concerned itself with the effects of two sequences – individual followed by group and group followed by individual" (Stein, 1975, p. 98) and the author of this paper has yet to find a study that makes any attempt to study the three-step approach. Perhaps equally surprising is Stein's (1975) comment that "Actually, little if any effort has been expended in the study and evaluation of training in brainstorming alone. Such work has usually occurred when brainstorming has been included in another procedure that has included other techniques to stimulate creativity as in creative problem-solving" (p. 138).

Creative Problem-Solving

Alex Osborn introduced Creative Problem-solving (CPS) in his 1952 book *Wake up Your Mind.* Osborn (1952, 1963) presented a revised and refined CPS model in his seminal book *Applied Imagination.* As discussed in the previous section, Osborn later teamed up with Parnes at the Creative Education Foundation where the CPS methods continue to be refined, taught and researched (Creative Education Foundation, 2013).

CPS consists of six steps arranged in three stages: *explore the challenge* consists of objective finding, fact finding, and problem finding; *generate ideas* consists of idea finding; and *prepare for action* consists of solution finding and acceptance finding. Objective finding is often based on a wish, a goal, or a dissatisfaction. Often, we may be given a vague, open-ended objective in a work situation. Fact finding is the process of collecting all available, relevant information related to the situation and may go beyond facts to include feelings, hunches, gossip, and/or assumptions. Problem finding involves exploration of the facts, a search for opportunities, reframing issues, and changing perspectives until a clear definition of a problem is arrived at. Idea generation is about brainstorming (see previous section). Solution finding includes strengthening and improving the best ideas, developing the evaluation criteria, and applying the evaluation criteria to select the most likely candidates. Finally, acceptance finding includes an analysis of what has to be done, by when, and by whom, in order to implement the solution (Creative Education Foundation, 2013). The process involves a deliberate alternation between divergent thinking and convergent thinking.

Parnes (1971) found, in a series of studies involving 350 students, that those who took the CPS course showed substantial gains in the quantity of ideas generated when compared to a control group. They also showed significantly superior quality on three tests of idea quality, greater improvement in quality in a fourth test – but not enough to be considered significant – and no superiority in a fifth measure. It was also noted that there was persistence in the effects. Parnes also noted that the CPS students showed an increase in the measure of dominance in a personality test, but did not show significant changes in measures of self-control or need-to-achieve. The dominance trait has been associated with creativity and includes characteristics such "as confidence, self-reliance, persuasiveness, initiative and leadership potential" (Parnes, 1971, p. 273).

In Torrance's (1972) survey of 142 studies he found that CPS, and variations of the model, were the most common methods used in the studies to teach children to think creatively, and it had the highest success rate, with 20 out of 22 studies reporting successful outcomes. In most studies the outcomes were determined based on the TTCT; however, several of them also focused on Guilford's alternative uses test.

Rose and Lin (1984) completed a meta-analysis of 46 studies, eight of which were based on CPS and its modifications. In their analysis, CPS showed the greatest effect size (ES = 0.63) with training reportedly explaining over 40% of the variance in scores.

Synectics

Synectics is a creativity enhancing program developed by George Prince and William Gordon, beginning in 1944. Prince and Gordon observed an individual as he talked his way through an invention process. They went on to compare their results to other individuals, then they began recording group sessions. "The Greek word Synectics[3] means the joining together of different and apparently irrelevant elements" (Gordon, 1961, p. 3).

Synectics research is based on the assumption that the creative process can be described, that such a description could be used to enhance the creative output of individuals or groups, that creative processes in arts and science are essentially the same, and the creative process employed by individuals is analogous to that employed by groups. Synectics theory is based on the hypotheses that creativity can be enhanced if people "understand the psychological process by which they operate" (Gordon, 1961, p. 6), that the emotional component of creativity is more important than the intellectual, and that it is the emotional and irrational elements that have the greatest impact on the chances of problem-solving success. Synectics seeks to make the strange familiar and the familiar strange by using metphors and analogies. Use of emotion is emphasized, for example, how it feels to be a spring (personal analogy), and judgement is deferred during idea generation. Other forms of analogy applied in Synectics include:

- direct analogy, where the characteristics of one object or process are superimposed onto another to arrive at a new or enhanced product or process;
- symbolic analogy uses images to describe the problem, or its potential solution, often in a poetic way;
- fantasy analogy "accept's Freud's wish-fulfilment theory of art, but turns it onto technical invention as well and uses it operationally." That is, wishes for the ideal product are expressed as fantastical ideas, without regard for any sorts of limitation;
- laws of physics can be ignored and magic is entertained as possible (Gordon, 1961, p. 48).

There is relatively little research published on the efficacy of Synectics training; however, Gordon (1961) did state:

> To date Synectics research has shown that it is possible to teach at least certain people to adopt certain thinking habits which will increase the probability of success in problem-stating, problem-solving situations. Also, it appears reasonable

> to expect that people with 'Synectics potential' can be identified. Further, it seems that once these thinking habits are learned they are never totally forgotten. These habits may grow hazy in the course of automatic, as opposed to conscious, employment, but they can be brought back clearly and distinctly through the formal use of the operational mechanisms at a conscious level. (p. 154)

Purdue Creative Thinking Program

The Purdue Creativity Program, PCP (later renamed the Purdue Creative Thinking Program, PCTP) was developed in 1965 by John F. Feldhusen to increase the creative potential of children in grades three to eight. The program is designed to foster verbal and visual divergent thinking skills, increasing fluency, flexibility, originality and elaboration (all measures of the Torrance Test of Creative Thinking, TTCT, or the Minnesota Tests of Creative Thinking, MTCT, as they were called at the time). It consists of 28 lessons, with each lesson consisting of a three to four-minute presentation about a creativity principle or idea for improving creativity, followed by an eight to ten-minute story about an American pioneer, followed by three or four exercises, linked in some way to the story, and designed to provide practice in the divergent thinking skills mentioned above. The lessons were originally broadcast over the WBAA radio station, but after the initial study, they were recorded and delivered by audio tape (Amabile, 1996; Feldhusen & Clinkenbeard, 1986; Feldhusen, Speedie, & Treffinger, 1971; Feldhusen, Treffinger, & Bahlke, 1970).

Feldhusen, Treffinger, and Bahlke reported that the initial research conducted using the program involved two classes, each from grades three, four and five, with six comparable classes used as a control group. After the program, students in the experimental group were found to be superior to the control group on "verbal and non-verbal originality and language achievement" (1970, p. 87). Further research included 48 classes of fourth, fifth and sixth grades. The classes were selected randomly from a population of about 100. Two classes at each grade level were randomly assigned to one of eight groups. Seven of the groups received a component, or a combination of components, of the three-component Purdue Creativity Program, and one group was the control group, being given pre and post tests only. They found support for the material, with the printed exercises being particularly effective.

Feldhusen, Treffinger, and Bahlke (1970) also discuss another study of the program, completed by Robinson, involving 66 students with 33 students serving as a control group. The result was that the experimental group "made highly significant gains on all creativity scores derived from the MTCT" (p. 90).

Torrance's (1972) meta-analysis of 142 studies aggregates the Purdue Creativity Program with the Productive Thinking Program, the Myers and Torrance *ideabooks*, and a number of other programs, under the heading of complex programs involving packages of materials. Out of 25 studies he rates 18 as being successful. Closer examination reveals that five of the studies employed the Purdue Creativity Program and all showed at least some degree of success. However, it's interesting to note that Torrance states that without the involvement of the teacher in the use of the programs, the success rate is low. Yet most of the studies conducted using the Purdue Creativity Program did not include teacher involvement. Feldhusen, Treffinger, and Bahlke (1970) even note, after reporting on three studies, that "New research is being conducted at Purdue to investigate other factors which may influence the effectiveness… including teacher involvement…" (p. 89).

Feldhusen, Speedie, and Treffinger (1971) note that, in the exercises, the need for divergent thinking – many possible answers rather than one correct answer – is stressed. They go on to give an example of one of the exercises: "Suppose that Henry Ford had not invented an automobile, and…" Hopefully their intention is not really to take creativity so far that rewriting history is considered a good thing (while he may have been responsible for designing the Model A and Model T – and some might consider him the inventor of the assembly line – he did not invent an automobile).

While Scott, Leritz, and Mumford (2004) do not present their meta-analysis of 70 research publications in a way that would allow studies involving the Purdue Creativity Program to be separated out, it is clear that they aggregated them into their divergent thinking grouping, noting that it is one of the best-known programs aimed at increasing divergent thinking. They stated that "Given the focus of creativity training on the development of creative thinking skills, it was not surprising that the largest effect sizes were obtained in studies employing divergent thinking" (p. 369). They also referred to the Purdue Creativity Program, along with the CPS, as "the more successful creativity training programs currently available" (p. 383).

Rose and Lin's (1984) meta-anlysis only included three studies that used the PCTP and they didn't fare well. The PCTP was the second poorest performing classification, out of the six groupings they analyzed.

The Productive Thinking Program

The Productive Thinking Program, PTP, was developed in 1966 by Crutchfield, Covington and Davies. It is aimed at developing creative problem-solving abilities and related attitudes in fifth and sixth grade students, and consists of 16 lessons. Each lesson presents a mystery to be solved and follows Jim and Lila Cannon as they learn to become detectives under the tutelage of their Uncle John, a science teacher whose sideline is being a detective. When indulging in his sideline, he goes by the name of Mr. Search (Trefinger & Ripple, 2013).

Torrance (1972) grouped the PTP with the Purdue Creativity Program and the Myers Torrance *ideabooks*, finding 18 of 25 studies reporting a successful outcome. In this case, success was defined as follows:

> … a score of 1 was awarded if all the measured objectives of the experiment were attained. If the experiment had a single objective, such as increasing the degree of originality of thinking, a score of 1 was still assigned. However, if

> data were presented for fluency, flexibility, originality, and elaboration and the only statistically significant gain over the control group was in originality, a score of .25 was awarded. If 10 of 20 tests of significance reached the .05 level of confidence, a score of .50 was awarded. (pp. 117–118)

Eight of the studies used the PTP. Of these, three resulted in no significant improvements over control groups, and two were rated as only partially successful. The partially successful studies showed significant differences in TTCT fluency and originality, but not flexibility or elaboration.

Rose and Lin's (1984) meta-anlysis included five studies employing the PTP. This was the worst performing group of the six groupings they analyzed. These studies showed a lack of significant improvement across all dimensions; verbal and figural; fluency, flexibility, originality, and elaboration. They even showed small negative average effect sizes for verbal fluency and flexibility – although not significant.

As with the Purdue Creativity Program, Scott, Leritz, and Mumford (2004) do not present their meta-analysis in a way that summarizes the results of individual programs. However, they did categorize the Productive Thinking Program as a divergent thinking program, so the same comments apply as in the last section.

TRIZ

"The term 'TRIZ' comes from the Russian phrase *teorija rezhenija izobretatelskih zadach,* which means the 'theory of inventive problem-solving' " (Rantanen & Domb, 2007). TRIZ was developed in the 1940s by Genrich Altshuller while he served in the Soviet Navy patent department. By analyzing thousands of patents, Altshuller came up with 40 principles that are intended to provide an objective, repeatable, engineering approach to innovation (Puccio & Cabra, 2010). TRIZ has been added to and evolved over the years and now, besides the 40 principles, it also includes 76 standard solutions, evolutionary patterns, ideal final results, and a contradiction matrix (Birdi, Leach, & Magadley, 2012). While TRIZ has been widely used in organizations, there is little research on the tools as a creativity enhancement method (Puccio & Cabra, 2010). However, Birdi, Leach, and Magadley (2012) found that 140 engineers, working for an international engineering firm, who took a one-day TRIZ workshop, increased their motivation to innovate, improved their creative problem-solving skills, increased their idea generation at work, and showed improvement in their ideas being implemented, all compared to a control group, and over an extended time period. In addition, expert ratings found that the trainees' ideas were more original, useful and persuasive.

OTHER COGNITIVE APPROACHES

Lesser-Known Cognitive Approaches

There are many other lesser-known programs and courses that rely mostly on direct cognitive methods. Many are variations of the programs discussed in the previous sections, or on combinations of them. Some are widely available. Others are unique, one-off programs available only in one location, or from one instructor. These programs span the range of effectiveness illustrated by the programs discussed in the previous sections – from not effective, like many of the implementations of the PTP that were studied, to quite effective, like many of the implementations of the CPS program that were studied (Rose & Lin, 1984; Scott, Leritz, & Mumford, 2004; Torrance, 1972).

De Bono Thinking

On the other end of the spectrum are some very popular programs that have been included in this "Others" category because of a lack of research literature. Edward de Bono's Lateral Thinking and Parallel Thinking – along with CoRT and Six Thinking Hats, which are methods for implementing his two thinking methodologies – have achieved great commercial success, with little or no research being done on their effectiveness. Sternberg and Lubart (1999) criticize de Bono and others for being primarily concerned with developing a creativity-enhancement program, while only being secondarily concerned with understanding it, and not at all concerned with testing its validity.

De Bono has written 57 books, mostly on thinking, and schools from over 20 countries have included his thinking tools in their curriculum. Yet Moseley and his collaborators note that "There is sparse research evidence to show that generalised improvements in thinking performance can be attributed to training in the use of CoRT or [Six]Thinking Hats tools" (Moseley et al., 2005, p. 139).

Cognitive Modelling

Gist studied the use of cognitive modelling as a method to enhance creativity. Cognitive modelling is similar to behavioural modelling – from Bandura's Social Learning Theory – but rather than visual observation of the behaviours of a model performing a task, cognitive modelling involves "a process of attending (or 'listening') to one's thoughts as one performs an activity and utilizing self-instructional thoughts (or 'statements') to guide performance" (Gist, 1989, p. 788). Meichenbaum, (Gist, 1989) found support for the use of cognitive modelling in improving the creativity of college students. Gist's (1989) study found that "the superiority of a training method based on cognitive modeling was impressive" and "cognitive modeling training enhanced self-efficacy" (p. 802).

NON-COGNITIVE APPROACHES

Attitude

Basadur has examined five attitude scales: Preference for Active Divergence, Preference for Avoiding Premature Convergence, Valuing New Ideas, Creative

Individual Stereotypes, and Too Busy for New Ideas. According to Basadur, Taggar and Pringle (Puccio, Firestien, & Coyle, 2006, p. 25) “unless attitudes toward divergent thinking are positive or become positive, training in creative problem-solving involving divergent thinking is not likely to result in changes in behaviour back on the job”. Basadur has shown that changes in attitude are a good predictor of gains from creativity training.

Flow

In discussing ‘flow’ – “the kind of feeling that an Olympic athlete may have when running her personal best, or a poet may have when turning a perfect phrase” – and its relationship to creativity, Csikszentmihalyi (1996) observes that:

> One obvious way to enhance creativity is to bring as much as possible of the flow experience into the various domains. It is exhilarating to build culture – to be an artist, a scientist, a thinker, or a doer. All too often, however, the joy of discovery fails to be communicated to young people, who turn instead to passive entertainment. But consuming culture is never as rewarding as producing it. If it were only possible to transmit the excitement of the people we interviewed to the next generation, there is no doubt that creativity would blossom. (p. 342)

This view seems to suggest that another form of modelling is possible, other than the cognitive modelling discussed in the previous section. While observing creative people at work may not be conducive to enhancing creativity, there may be value in learning about the thought processes and emotions of creative individuals.

Self-Statement Modification

Self-statement Modification (SSM) is a form of cognitive behaviour modification and has been successfully applied by Meichenbaum (1975) for creativity enhancement. While it was a small study of 21 subjects, the self-instructional training group showed significant increases in flexibility and originality compared to a control group and to a group who appled Gendlin’s focusing.

While SSM is considered, from the psychology point of view, a cognitive approach, from the point of view of creativity enhancement, it is viewed more as behavioural approach associated with attitudes regarding self, creativity, and the relationship between the two. Hence this method’s location here, under non-cognitve, rather than under cognitve approaches.

Domain Knowledge

Amabile (1996) argues that no creativity will take place without some level of knowledge and skill in a given domain. Further, Simonton (1999) notes that virtually all eminent creators display curiosity outside of their primary domain, giving rise to the concept of 'T' shaped domain knowledge – depth and experience in one domain, with wide breadth of knowledge across many domains – and its positive relationship to creativity. Therefore, it appears that creativity can be enhanced by developing a particular expertise, while being well informed in a variety of areas.

Metacognitive

Metacognition is, literally, cognition about cognition. Furthermore, cognition is related to all of our mental abilities, including perceiving, learning, remembering, thinking, understanding, reasoning, problem-solving and decision making. Thus, metacognition can be *thought* of (pun intended) as thinking about thinking, thinking about learning, or thinking about problem-solving. As noted by Kozbelt, Beghetto, and Runco (2010, p. 32) "Metacognitive processes are also frequently tied to creative thinking". They go on to note that tactical thinking is metacognitive, thus most, if not all, of the programs discussed in the cognitive approaches section above have a metacognitive aspect to them.

Much like SSM, metacognition has been included here, under non-cognitive approaches, because of its potential behavioural and attitudinal affects. Scott, Leritz, and Mumford (2004, p. 380), in their meta-analysis, concluded that "informing people about the nature of creativity and strategies for creative thinking is an effective, and perhaps necessary, component of creativity". Perhaps more important is the potential for metacognition to positively impact self-efficacy. Albert Bandura (1995, p. 2) defined self-efficacy as belief "in one's capabilities to organize and execute the courses of action required to manage prospective situations" Giving people the tools to be successfully creative should, as Bandura (1977, p. 193) notes, give them the "conviction that [they] can successfully execute the behaviour required to produce the outcomes".

Motivation

Amabile (1996) has written extensively about the effects of motivation on creativity. She concludes that intrinsic motivation is conducive to creativity, and that extrinsic motivation usually, but not always, has a deleterious effect. Amabile notes that the following can have a negative impact on creativity: expected reward, expected evaluation, peer pressure, surveillance, and constrained choice. These factors can all be seen to potentially affect creativity through an effect on motivation. Conversely, Amabile sees choice, control, a supportive environment, a stimulating physical environment, freedom, and play, as potential approaches to enhancing creativity.

Meditation

Fink and Neubauer (2006) found that more original creative problem-solving responses are associated with alpha synchronization, which has been associated with wakeful relaxation, whereas convergent tasks produce alpha desynchronization. Since meditation is known to produce alpha synchronization, it has long been hypothesized that meditation could increase creativity, but Krampen (1997), in his literature review, found inconsistent effects from long-term relaxation or meditation programs. However, Krampen's study on the short-term effects of relaxation exercises showed consistent, significant improvements in both divergent and convergent thinking.

Ostafin and Kassman's (2012) two studies, of a total of 157 participants, found that mindfulness training improved insight, but not non-insight problem-solving.

Discussion

Most of the literature reviewed seems to answer *yes* to the question "can creativity be taught?" "The overall results of this meta-analysis suggest that training does affect creativity" (Rose & Lin, 1984, p. 22). "Taken as a whole, these observations lead to a relatively unambiguous conclusion. Creativity training works… it was found that training stressing the cognitive processing activities commonly held to underlie creative efforts, specifically the core processes identified by Mumford et al. (1991), was positively related to study success… problem finding, conceptual combination, and idea generation, proved to be the most powerful influences on the effectiveness of training" (Scott, Leritz, & Mumford, 2004, p. 382). "It does indeed seem possible to teach children to think creatively" (Torrance, 1972, p. 132).

While these researchers seem to be emphatic regarding the virtues of creativity training, the results presented in the literature showed a great deal of inconsistency. Even CPS, the most consistently highly-rated program, was not consistently successful. Other programs ranged from mostly successful, to mostly not successful, and to inconclusive due to lack of data. This inconsistency suggests a need for caution when it comes to the practical application of programs intended to enhance creativity, and that further research is needed.

The definition of success regarding creativity enhancement interventions remains problematic, as does a lack of theories on what goes wrong when these programs don't work. The answers may be hidden in the long list of non-cognitive approaches to enhancing creativity.

A Complex Systems Theory of Creativity

Perhaps, within all these cognitive programs, there is more going on than just cognitive skills training – as suggested by Scott, Leritz, and Mumford (2004), who noted that confluence models were effective across criteria, and that motivational and personality approaches were positively related to performance.

Amabile (1996) has long argued for a componential theory of creativity, suggesting that domain knowledge, creativity skills, and intrinsic motivation must coincide in order for there to be creativity. And Csikszentmihalyi's (1996) systems approach to creativity argues that creativity has as much or more to do with culture than with an individual's personality, skills, abilities, or motivations.

I would argue that Amabile's componential model does not go far enough, while Csikszentmihalyi's systems approach goes off on what is effectively a tangent. That is, Amabile's model does not take into consideration environmental factors, except for considering how they may impact motivation, and it does not consider other factors of the individual such as alpha-coherence or self-efficacy; while Csikszentmihalyi's approach tends toward the realm of innovation (creativity implemented) and is concerned only with "Big C" creativity.

I propose that the all-encompassing view – the essential view – is to see creativity as a complex, with respect to the individual, operating within a complex environment. It also seems reasonable to imagine that these complex systems – the individual, other individuals, the sociocultural-political environment, and the physical environment – may react to changes non-linearly. That is, a small change in a factor, or system, could have a large effect on the observed end result – degree of creativity, in this case – while a large change in another factor, or system, may have minimal impact, or vice versa. Not only that, but a factor initially having a large impact as a result of a small change, may have declining impact as the size of the change increases – and vice versa. With many factors at play within several interacting systems, it would seem that the application of complexity theory will be needed to approach an understanding of creativity.

From domain knowledge to motivation, personality, knowledge of creativity tools, attitude, physical environment, social environment, cultural environment, and political environment, there seems to be little doubt that what impacts creativity is multifaceted, making the study of what might be called one small sub-factor[4] challenging, to say the least. How could we ever expect to see the impact of a brief seminar instructing students on how to come up with more ideas by applying the four rules of brainstorming to show up through the "noise" of other factors? There are just too many moving parts, with inconsistent relationships, and inconsistent impacts.

In *The Wisdom of Crowds*, Surowiecki (2005) illustrates that, in many situations, the average answer given by a crowd of people is often more accurate than that of any one expert. He explains how the right level of diversity, independence, and decentralization are required for crowds to live up to their potential. These three conditions correlate well with the five control parameters – which determine whether an organization will operate at the edge of chaos in the "space for novelty" – proposed by Stacey (1996, p. 179) in his complex systems theory of creativity within organizations: "the rate of information flow, the degree of diversity, the richness of connectivity, the level of contained anxiety, and the degree of power differentials". If creativity does indeed operate as a complex system – following the principles of complexity theory – this would suggest that it is impossible to accurately predict the long-term outcome of various interventions, but it doesn't mean we should give up. It merely means that a holistic approach is required in order to fully understand creativity and its enhancement. Informing that holistic approach will require large sample sizes, with a large number of factors under consideration, along with multivariate statistical analysis. Or perhaps extensive qualitative research could go further in completing the picture of creativity that is still sorely fragmented and incomplete after over six decades of research. Regardless of the research approach taken, a complete theory of creativity would serve to light the way.

Even in the face of all these challenges, this literature review found that most studies showed creativity enhancement efforts have had a positive effect on creativity, but much remains to be done to explain what is going on when we attempt to enhance creativity, and to improve the consistency of results – or at least to make them more consistently positive, given that complexity theory would suggest we can never expect consistency.

NOTES

1 Blockbuster, which became the largest video rental chain, was launched in 1985, but didn't become commonplace until around 1990. They filed for bankruptcy in 2010 (Phillips & Ferdman, 2013).
2 See, for example, www.nest.com/ca/
3 More accurately, the word *Synectics* is a hybrid word with Greek roots. (Editor's note).
4 For example, ideation could be considered a sub-factor within the cognitive-creativity complex, intrinsic motivation could be considered a sub-factor within the social-psychology of creativity complex and existence/effectiveness of a mentor might be thought of as a sub-factor within the creativity-supporting-environment complex.

REFERENCES

Amabile, T. M. (1977). *Effects of extrinsic constraint on creativity* (Doctoral Dissertation). Stanford University, CA.

Amabile, T. M. (1996). *Creativity in context.* Boulder, CO: Westview Press Inc.

Bandura, A. (1977). Self-efficacy: Toward a unifying theory of behavioral change. *Psychological Review, 84*(2), 191–215.

Bandura, A. (1995). *Self-efficacy in changing societies.* Cambridge & New York, NY: Cambridge University Press.

Birdi, K., Leach, D., & Magadley, W. (2012). Evaluating the impact of TRIZ creativity training: An organizational field study. *R&D Management, 42*, 315–326.

Carson, S. (2010). *Your creative brain.* San Francisco, CA: Jossey-Bass.

Creative Education Foundation. (2013, November 23). *A little history.* Retrieved from http://www.creativeeducationfoundation.org/about-cef/a-history-of-cef/

Csikszentmihalyi, M. (1996). *Creativity: Flow and the psychology of discovery and invention.* New York, NY: HarperCollins.

Feldhusen, J. F., & Clinkenbeard, P. R. (1986). Creativity instructional materials: A review of research. *The Journal of Creative Behavior, 20*(3), 153–182.

Feldhusen, J. F., Treffinger, D. J., & Bahlke, S. J. (1970). Developing creative thinking: The Purdue Creativity Program. *Journal of Creative Studies, 4*, 85–90.

Feldhusen, J. F., Speedie, S. M., & Treffinger, D. J. (1971). The Purdue Creative Thinking Program: Research and evaluation. *NSPI Journal, 10*(3), 5–9.

Fink, A., & Neubauer, A. C. (2006). EEG alpha oscillations during the performance of verbal creativity tasks: Differential effects of sex and verbal intelligence. *International Journal of Psychophysiology, 62*(1), 46–53.

Florida, R. (2012). *The rise of the creative class: Revisited.* New York, NY: Basic Books.
Gist, M. E. (1989). The influence of training method on self-efficacy and idea generation amoung managers. *Personnel Psychology, 42*, 787–805.
Gordon, W. J. (1961). *Synectics: The development of creative capacity.* New York, NY: Harper & Row, Publishers.
Hennessey, B. A., & Amabile, T. M. (2010). Creativity. *Annual Review of Psychology, 61*, 569–598.
IBM. (2010, May 18). *IBM 2010 global CEO study: Creativity selected as most crucial factor for future success.* Armonk, NY: IBM.
Karpova, E., Marckett, S. B., & Barker, J. (2011). The efficacy of teaching creativity: Assessment of student creative thinking before and after exercises. *Clothing and Textiles Research Journal, 29*(1), 52–66.
Kaufman, J. C., Plucker, J. A., & Baer, J. (2008). *Essentials of creativity assessment.* Hoboken, NJ: John Wiley & Sons Inc.
Kim, K. H. (2011). The creativity crisis: The decrease in creative thinking scores on the Torrance tests of creative thinking. *Creativity Research Journal, 23*(4), 285–295.
Kozbelt, A., Beghetto, R. A., & Runco, M. R. (2010). Theories of creativity. In J. C. Kaufman & R. J. Sternberg (Eds.), *The Cambridge handbook of creativity* (pp. 20–47). New York, NY: Cambridge University Press.
Krampen, G. (1997). Promotion of creativity (divergent productions) and convergent productions by systematic-relaxation exercises: Empirical evidence from five experimental studies with children, young adults, and elderly. *European Journal of Personality, 11*, 83–99.
Meichenbaum, D. (1975). Enhancing creativity by modifying what subjects say to themselves. *American Educational Research Journal, 12*(2), 129–145.
Moseley, D., Baumfield, V., Elliott, J., Gregson, M., Higgins, S., Miller, J., & Newton, D. (2005). De Bono's lateral and parallel thinking tools. In D. Moseley (Ed.), *Frameworks for thinking a handbook for teaching and learning* (pp. 133–140). Cambridge, UK: Cambridge University Press.
Osborn, A. F. (1952). *Wake up your mind: 101 ways to develop creativeness.* New York, NY: Scribner.
Osborn, A. F. (1963). *Applied imagination: Principles and procedures of creative problem-solving.* New York, NY: Scribner.
Ostafin, B. D., & Kassman, K. T. (2012). Stepping out of history: Mindfulness improves insight problem-solving. *Consciousness and Cognition, 21*, 1031–1036.
Parnes, S. J. (1971). Can creativity be increased? In G. A. Davis, & J. A. Scott (Eds.), *Training creative thinking* (pp. 270–275). New York, NY: Holt, Rinehart and Winston, Inc.
Pink, D. H. (2006). *A whole new mind: Why right-brainers will rule the future.* New York, NY: Penguin Group USA.
Plucker, J. A., Beghetto, R. A., & Dow, G. T. (2004). Why isn't creativity more important to educational psychologists? Potentials, pitfalls, and future directions in creativity research. *Educational Psychologist, 39*(2), 83–96.
Puccio, G. J., & Cabra, J. F. (2010). Organizational creativity: A sysytems approach. In J. C. Kaufman & R. J. Sternberg (Eds.), *The Cambridge handbook of creativity* (pp. 145–173). New York, NY: Cambridge University Press.
Puccio, G. J., Firestien, R. L., & Coyle, C. M. (2006, March 01). A review of the effectiveness of CPS training: A focus on workplace issues. *Creativity and Innovation Management, 15*(1), 19–33.
Rantanen, K., & Domb, E. (2007). *TRIZ, simplified new problem-solving applications for engineers and manufacturing professionals.* New York, NY: Auerbach Publications.
Rose, L. H., & Lin, H.-T. (1984). A meta-analysis of long-term creativity training programs. *The Journal of Creative Behavior, 18*(1), 11–22.
Runco, M. A., & Jaeger, G. J. (2012). The standard definition of creativity. *Creativity Research Journal, 24*(1), 92–96.
Sawyer, R. K. (2012). *Explaining creativity: The science of human innovation.* New York, NY: Oxford University Press.
Schonfeld, E. (2011, December 14). *The Rise of the 'Creative' Class.* Retrieved from http://techcrunch.com/2011/12/14/creative-class/

Scott, G., Leritz, L. E., & Mumford, M. D. (2004). The effectiveness of creativity training: A quantitative review. *Creativity Research Journal, 16*(4), 361–388.

Simonton, D. K. (1999). *Origins of genius: Darwinian perspectives on creativity.* New York, NY: Oxford University Press.

Stacey, R. D. (1996). *Complexity and creativity in organizations.* San Francisco, CA: Berrett-Koehler Publishers, Inc.

Stein, M. I. (1975). *Stimulating creativity.* New York, NY: Accedemic Press Inc.

Sternberg, R. J., & Lubart, T. I. (1999). The concept of creativity: Prospects and paradigms. In R. J. Sternberg (Ed.), *Handbook of creativity* (pp. 3–15). New York, NY: Cambridge University Press.

Surowiecki, J. (2005). *The wisdom of crowds.* New York, NY: Knopf Doubleday Publishing Group.

Taylor, C. W. (1988). Various approaches to and definitions of creativity. In R. J. Sternberg (Ed.), *The nature of creativity* (pp. 99–121). Cambridge, England: Cambridge University Press.

Torrance, P. E. (1970). *Encouraging creativity in the classroom.* Dubuque, IO: W.C. Brown Co.

Torrance, P. E. (1972). Can we teach children to think creatively? *The Journal of Creative Behaviour, 6*(2), 114–143.

Torrance, P. E., Ball, O. E., & Safter, H. T. (2008). *Torrance tests of creative thinking streamlined scoring guide for figural forms A and B.* Bensenville, IL: Scolastic Testing Service, Inc.

Trefinger, D. J., & Ripple, R. E. (2013, November 24). *Programmed instruction in creative problem-solving.* Retrieved from http://www.ascd.org/ASCD/pdf/journals/ed_lead/el_197103_treffinger.pdf

Philip A. Lambert
University of New Brunswick

PAUL SYME

2. TIME TO LEARN WITH CREATIVITY IN MIND

INTRODUCTION

The philosopher R. G. Collingwood defines creative expression as "an activity of which there can be no technique" (1967, p. 111). Collingwood speaks to creativity as an unconscious process where we work through experiences, memories, and media to reveal that which was previously unknown. Creative processes need space – not necessarily physical though always temporal – for the subconscious to operate and make connections outside of rational or analytical thought. Where I live and teach in Nova Scotia, time is optimized to serve accountability and student achievement. The development of creativity and innovative problem-solving is scheduled to occur in designated periods and certain subjects. It is reasonable, therefore, to question if such conditions sufficiently develop the child towards meeting the challenges of a society under the influence of digital environments.

A Modern Education System

Nova Scotia aims to meet the needs of 21st century learners while attempting to address flat-lining and falling scores in math and literacy through their *Action Plan for Education, 2015. The 3R's: Renew, Refocus, Rebuild* (Nova Scotia, 2015). The Ministry affirms that "we need to be accountable and we need to see real, tangible results" (p. 5) to be achieved by strategies built on four pillars. The first two of these pillars are particularly relevant to this paper. The first one is to "build a modern education system", a regrettable pillar considering, as I will argue, that modernity is obsolete. In the second pillar the Ministry of Education aims to "make the curriculum more streamlined, coordinated, and innovative" (p. 18) where, while promising more hands-on learning activities and access to modern technology, they are "laser-focused" on improving literacy and math. Math, in particular, will see more common assessments, increased time and mentors in the early years, class size caps with time doubled, and it will be compulsory for every student through grade twelve (pp. 18–23). Such efforts will impact the space, time, and autonomy afforded to student self-determination. Creativity, on the other hand, is presented as belonging among "innovation, creativity, problem-solving skills" (p. 160). It is addressed only in response to those interested in entrepreneurship and the arts and not as a core

J. B. Cummings & M. L. Blatherwick (Eds.), Creative Dimensions of Teaching and Learning in the 21st Century, 23–35.

value or need of 21st century economy. The framework provides little evidence that creativity and innovation are understood or valued.

Like many political institutions of the modern era, the government of Nova Scotia seems to be unaware that the systems that have shaped the modern era, particularly the dependable and abstract order of the clock, are having to now share space with or be pushed aside by the non-linear, personalized, and divergent spaces provided through digital media. The digital age strips bare the necessities of time and space as defined in the modern age. Where the modern era had shaped a citizenry to value its logical order, similarly, the digital age is fashioning people to seek a new order – one that I will argue echoes creative thought. It remains to be seen if we are ready to embrace the trials and possibilities of the digital age through a society with sufficient capacity for "creative achievement [as] reflected in production of useful, new ideas or products that result from defining a problem and solving it in a novel way within a particular cultural context" (Zimmerman, 2009, p. 386). Regardless, change is before us and all stakeholders in education will feel its effects. Marshall McLuhan's *Laws of Media* (1988) should help reveal the best route as it aids in illuminating and comparing the nature of time in modern and digital learning environments and the potential for creativity among them.

Time Shapes us

As products of the Modern Age we find comfort in order as well as excitement about some degree of chaos. Modernity reinforces order through its industrial foundations of machinery, the clock, and its capacity to convert phenomena to something observable and measurable. Modern education continues to socialize youth through the pedagogical primacy of numeracy and literacy, maintaining order through a kinship with the alphabet and the clock's sequence while marginalizing the apparent disorder of creative thought processes. Now, in the Digital Age, our social and pedagogical priorities are challenged to reflect a new network-based society and an explosive list of social, political, economic and environmental concerns globally. Our "network society" (Castells, 2001) is intensifying our retribalization into a global village (McLuhan, 1962), where we nurture connections beyond conventional space and time, sharing information and experiences in a non-linear, non-sequential manner. In the network society, we step outside of our orderly boxes to find others, entertainment, meaning, and insight from divergent patterns that often echo processes of creative thought.

Though a product of modernity's order, public schools are challenged to chart a meaningful course that reflects the current and future needs of students in a context of shifting dynamics. The urgency for us to resolve this challenge is heightened by greater forces than longstanding competition with private and charter schools. Schools now have to contend with the growing efficacy of digital learning environments such as Massive Open Online Courses (MOOCs). If Harvard Business School's Clayton Christensen is correct, thanks to MOOCs "fifteen years from now more than half of the universities [in America] will be in bankruptcy" (The Economist, 2014). Without charting a meaningful path for the 21st century, as the steamship sank wood, wind and sail, so too may be the destiny of modern schools. Finding a fruitful course for schools should include critical inquiry into our relationship with new media – how we shape them and how they shape us.

From Machines to Clouds – A Turbulent Shift

We do not need to look far to witness the volatility in our shift from a largely industrial society to one dominated by electronic and digital media. Marshall McLuhan (1969) noted that this shift "is a highly traumatic process, since the clash … creates a crisis of identity, a vacuum of the self, which generates tremendous violence – violence that is simply an identity quest, private or corporate, social or commercial." He traces the fuel for this conflict to the implications of change. Literacy itself is threatened by a "future, [where] we could imagine a cyberspace with less or no alphabet – an online communication system comprised in part or entirely of speech" (Levinson, 2004, p. 51).

School leaders struggle with the place of smart phones and other Wireless Mobile Devices (WMD's) as useful tools for learning or weapons of mass distraction. As these devices have become extensions of most students and teachers we need to assume that they are here to stay and their presence will only swell. We would be well-served to determine when these devices aid learning and when they hinder it. Furthermore, if we believe that creativity is important in the lives of students, we need to know the pace of these devices in our current and changing pedagogy and media landscape.

Seeking Insights through the Laws of Media

The Laws of Media (McLuhan, E. & McLuhan, M., 1988) provide us with a useful instrument to assess the connection between our media and their effects on such things as time, space, schools, and creativity. They are designed to expose patterns and deliver insight into a medium's potential impact on the world. The laws assert that with the arrival of an archetype, such as a new tool or concept, a human element is *extended.* Simultaneously something else is rendered *obsolete*, a previous idea or media is *retrieved* or *released* to serve a new function, and when pushed to the extreme, the media's effect is reversed.

The Laws of Media teach us that *clock time,* for example:

- *enhances* efficiency and order allowing us to synchronize such things as events, machines and labor. It favours the reasoning capacity of our brain's left hemisphere – work;
- *obsolesces* organic time as given to us by the sun, tides and the stars – allows us to disconnect from nature and leisure;
- *retrieves* the abstract nature, linearity and order of literacy and chronology; and

- *reverses creative human expressiveness* – as we use time to enhance efficiency we disconnect ourselves from nature and the frailty of our humanity. And, as we increase reliance on our brain's left hemisphere, we diminish our brain's creative capacity (pp. 166–167).

The Laws of Media might find that laptops and other wireless mobile devices *enhance* our ability to share information that engages multiple senses and provides greater illusions of connectedness and fantasy. They also *enhance a sense of belonging* through messaging, blogging, chats, avatars, etc. When pushed to their extreme, they *reverse* what is "real" to being irrelevant. We can spend our days divided among various physical, temporal, or virtual spaces. Direct experiential learning as well as direct human interaction are removed. We become detached from our physical selves and we can separate from our obligatory tribes in exchange for new ones. This does retrieve the notion of tribes but now we can choose new ones – tribes by choice through shared interest. This obsolesces our need for local communities, one-way mass-media communication and traditional purveyors of education where teachers and broadcasters are obsolete as content mediators.

A probe into the Nova Scotia Action Plan for Education, 2015 (see Figure 1) observes effects of the province's aim to enhance efficiencies and literacies at the expense of other ways of knowing. This retrieves the idea of the industrial bureaucracy, discouraging holistic learning while also resisting change that, in turn,

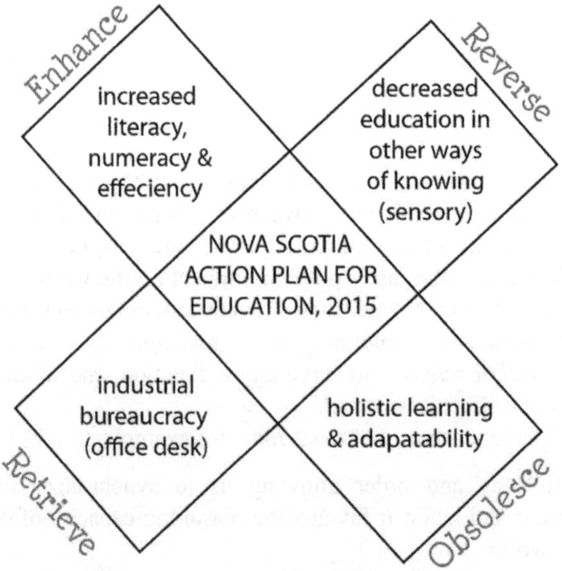

Figure 1. Nova Scotia Action Plan for Education, 2015 a learning focus Laws of Media tetrad

counters adaptability. With the times changing so rapidly, it would be wise to weigh our hopeful gains against the expense of apparent trade-offs. Time itself is worthy of investigation for its implications for our shift from industrial modernity to the immergence of digital media.

Time

Time may be known in many ways – by the sky, the seasons, our appetite, plant growth, and so on. Marie Webb, a young artist who is touched with Downe's Syndrome does not mark time with a clock, but rather by moving from one celebration to the next. As her mother explains, "Marie's internal clock is not numerical; the days and months are punctuated with the associated events and celebrations. As one birthday ends, another one begins" (Sheppard, 2013, p. 49). Her notion of time is central to her artwork. Where most of us might allow our lives to be ordered by work Webb's life is consumed with family, friends, faith and celebrations – all of which she documents and expresses through drawing.

Webb's time, along with other organic or rhythmic concepts of time, highlights what is central to this paper: that how we behave prioritizes our lives since the onset of the modern industrialized age is not inherent to our chromosomes and genetics. Figure 2 models where we have invented a concept of time and space to echo the machine, replacing nature and God. And importantly, the digital age is causing time to shift again.

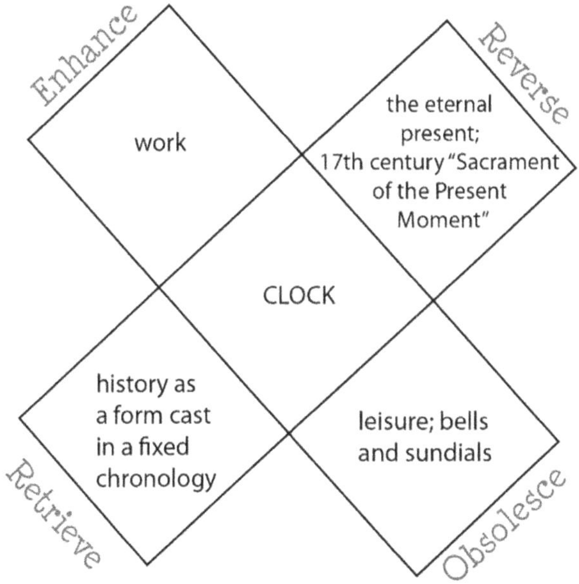

Figure 2. Clock from McLuhan (1988, p. 166)

Time as a medium is inseparable from recent dominant technological and communication paradigm shifts. Our sensory dominance has also moved in step.

Tribal people were oral communicators, and though all senses were equal, time came from the sun and stars. The invention of the alphabet and literacy catapulted sight to the top of our senses and time followed literacy's abstract form. Gutenberg's printing press of the Renaissance brought us to the machine age and the mechanical clock. This clock soon became portable spreading a concept that all could be made "visual, abstract and uniform", and making way for the printing press and the press led us to the industrial revolution and modernity (Adam, 2003, p. 62; McLuhan, 1964, p. 138). Through its abundance, we then became numb to time's effects and thus allowed it to shape most aspects of our daily lives. And, where we invented the clock to order our lives, borrowing from Lewis Mumford, Neil Postman (1986, p. 11) observed that after the 14th Century the clock made us "time-keepers, and then time-savers, and now time-servers".

Clock time shaped modernity to accelerate and expand the primacy of rational, sequential and abstract thought.

Abstract, machinic, invariable, and linear time – a disciplining time that would rationally arrange the social world, and rhythm it to synchronize with a universal and cosmological order – was at the very heart of what was to become modernity. And its introduction was revolutionary (Hassan, 2011, p. 13).

Electricity extended acoustical space with the telephone. Radio and television shows gave us entertainment to set our watches by. Now in the digital age, time is moving towards irrelevance and our media are connecting us with each other while numbingly integrating with all of our senses.

Sensory Spaces

Our WMD's are unique extensions of us in that they interface with our tactile, acoustical and visual sensibilities. We interface with these devices through touch in a way that each touch is relatively invisible – our entire tactile field is diminished to the smooth nothingness of glass (providing the irony for Apple Computer's concept of the *iPod "Touch"*). As we connect and disconnect from a surface we disrupt order and encourage play. As such, touch is not connectedness, it is not constant: it is linking through intervals.

Though mainly visual tools, WMD's seem to allow us to simultaneously enter multiple virtual spaces, qualities McLuhan & McLuhan identify as particular to acoustical space. Acoustical spaces, like the tactile, obsolesces the connected and, unlike visual spaces, the space is not linear or static (see Figures 3 & 4). Sight allows us to fixate on a focal point and sound delivers an entire space. As such, visual space is fixed while acoustical space is ubiquitous.

WMD's trick us – in them we lose sight of the fact that an image is not on a surface, it really occurs in our mind. Like our mind's kluge-like structure, in WMD's, time

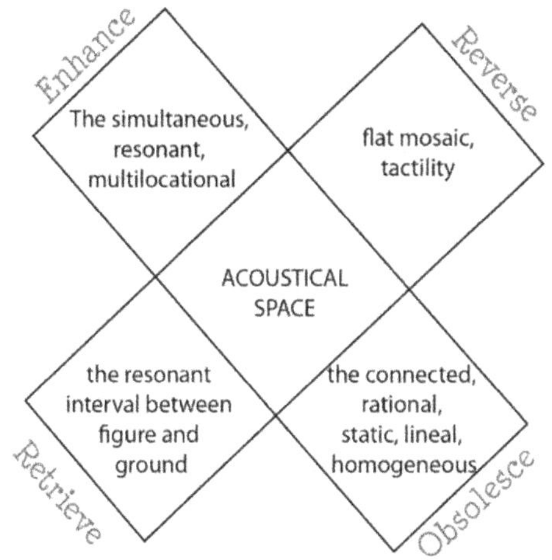

Figure 3. Acoustical space from McLuhan & McLuhan (1988, p. 160)

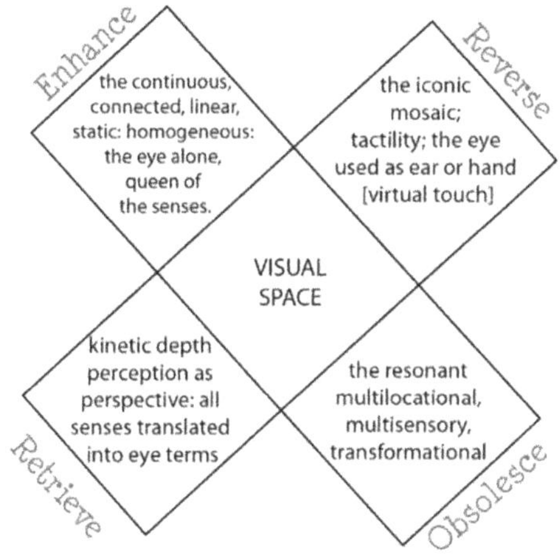

Figure 4. Visual space from McLuhan & McLuhan (1988, p. 205)

is disjointed, rearranged, unpredictable and irrational. In these spaces, our rational self lets us believe we are actually connecting to various spaces. In this delusional space, the irrational sensibility of the WMD interface sets us up to lose track of time and place. As we flow in and through virtual and physical spaces performing tasks in both, the flows collide and mingle in our minds. Each space offers its own notion of time. When they mix together our ability to keep pace with a rhythm becomes increasingly elusive and irrelevant. As such, the primacy of clock time and physical spaces are disputed in the digital age.

Space of Flows

Much like gazing out the window, with WMD's our attention flows from physical space to virtual ones found behind glass. The content of digital media and our network society gives us the power to construct temporal spaces, expanding where we live and learn. For Manuel Castells "space organizes time in the network society" (2010, p. 79), a space he calls the "space of flows". In the space of flows, our connection to diverse and distant physical spaces is achieved through circuitry, satellites and nodes or intersections. Castells suggests these spaces are "asymmetrically organized around the dominant interests specific to each social structure" (pp. 79–90). Our near seamless interconnectedness is the source of our retribalized sensibilities. Consider how each of us are connected at least as much by shared interests on line as we are by our neighbors. It is through this seamless convenience that we lose one ground and way of thinking for another – shifting our consciousness. As charted in Figure 5, we can see how the space of flows might be known through the laws of media. Note that as a social structure the space of flows retrieves our notion of extra sensory perception while as a thought process it recalls Sigmund Freud's "dream logic" (Gelernter, 2010). And while we obsolete physical spaces we also push aside rational and sequential thought. We need to consider what increased time in the space of flows does to the interests, values, and the conceptions of students.

Time, Space and the Creative Mind

"Joy, creativity, the process of total involvement with life I call *flow.*" Here, Mihaly Csikszentmihalyi (1990, preface) sees a state of flow in creativity because creativity is a space and time where someone is fully immersed or lost in their activity. Form and meaning result from the collision and interplay of otherwise unrelated forms. Like surrealist art and jazz music, creative solutions have long been held to come from the juxtaposition of disparate concepts or remote associates via serendipity, similarity,

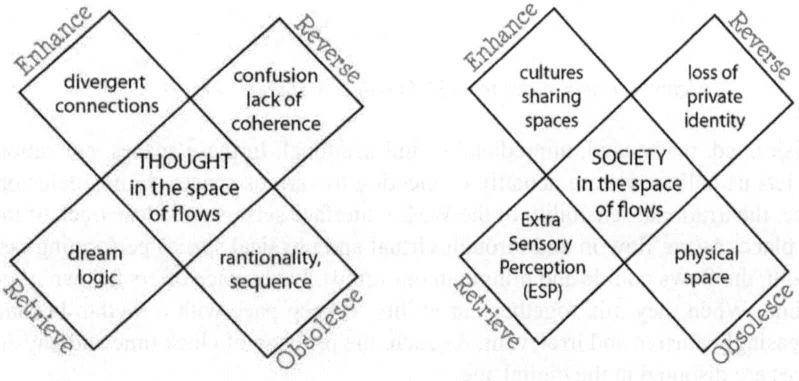

Figure 5. Space of flows in the Laws of Media: Society and Thought

or mediation (Mednick, 1962). Neuroscientists John Kounios and Mark Beeman (2009) followed Mednick's observation to find the *eureka* moments or creative incidents in the brain and found it manifest as distinct bursts of gamma energy in the participant brains' right hemisphere (RH). As such, dream logic and the audio-tactile spatial illusion spaces that WMD's nurture, while not making people creative, people creative, appear to echo creative processes where connections and novel ideas are made of otherwise loosely connected disparate concepts. Alternatively, the qualities that define the clock share ground with literacy and numeracy and other tasks performed in the left hemisphere (LH) including such conscious constructs as linear reasoning, logic, words and numbers, details, analysis and sequence. As a unified system, we may search our LH to solve analytical or factual problems and we rely on our RH to help us solve novel problems. We do a lot to train students to solve problems based in fact, and little to tackle the novel.

A Creative Pedagogy for New Times

With schools, for the most part, curricular and pedagogical changes remain modest – we teach and they are to learn in a system that guides us to solve problems through LH or logocentric thinking. Our curricular priorities and structure conflict with an audience who may be poised to more effectively solve problems creatively. With this imbalance, school reform should offer students a schooling program that nurtures the 4Cs: creative thinking, curiosity, critical thinking and collaboration, at least on par with the traditional 3Rs of reading, writing, and arithmetic. Reaching this equilibrium requires us to critically observe our students' learning and media ecologies.

As the "space of flows" (Castells, 2010) suggests, our global destinies are interwoven. Until recently, a child's world did not extend far beyond the physical spaces where they lived. Today's youth reside between their physical world and the temporality of cyberspace. By and large, adults are adapting to the new environment that our students were born into – they are the natives while we are the tourists. Students need to be equipped with relevant tools to gain control over *their* world, not the one we have known.

Inasmuch as the student's gaze shifts its fix from the board at front of the room in exchange for the personalized small screen, simultaneously classrooms no longer have to be fixed in time and space. Where modernity delivered textbooks and videos, our digital media offers students global connectivity. Students can know their world through a variety of interfaces and processes, such as conversations, games, and other expressive works. With WMD's our classrooms are fractured, multidirectional, and asynchronous – more acoustical. This can be embraced for its potentials or resisted for its distractions. While the WMD experience is more akin to a dream than to an essay, exchanging ordered logic for hyper-logic, when focused on a critical or creative task, the creative thinker may feel at home in these environments (Carr, 2010, p. 119).

Consider Marcel Duchamp's "Fountain" (1917). A readymade art form, "Fountain" was a urinal reoriented 90 degrees on its back and signed "R. Mutt, 1917".

Duchamp's Fountain, though initially rejected and ridiculed (Saltz, 2006), later became the archetype for other artists to follow – where found objects placed in a foreign context offer us another way to realize new meaning from the form. "Fountain" exemplifies the type of creative idea that is or was alien to the rational order of modernity. For those steeped in LH thinking, such RH ideas and the experiences that nurture them may appear irrelevant or inaccessible, but to others they offer deep meaning. Recognizing this, we need to be cautious of a hemispheric hegemony where creative thinking and processes continue to be marginalized.

Sir Ken Robinson's notable TED Talk, *Do Schools Kill Creativity?* (2006) and his companion texts *The Element* (2009) and *Out of Our Minds* (2011) have challenged public education systems to put their money where their mouth is to assess current practices and reorient schooling towards nurturing whole brain thinkers – to do things differently.

Where people like Sir Ken Robinson aim to normalize and promote creative thinking, they do so in a largely antithetical schooling culture. We may rhetorically say that we want to encourage creativity, however our industrial hangover begs to differ. Our fixation with accountability, numeracy and literacy achievement data, timetables, subject-based departments, classrooms with student desks facing *Smart boards* that draws students to buttress the teacher's authority at the front of the room reinforce to modernity's order. Our conflict is internalized. Pulled in opposing directions we want schools to uphold the objectives of our industrial heritage while priming students with the savvy and sensitivities to succeed in the 21st century economy where creativity is a core skill (Florida, 2011; WEF, 2016). When we fail to see the contradiction, we increase the odds of employing strategies that exacerbate the problem.

For this reason, we should seriously probe whether efforts to enhance the 3Rs are exposing a reverse situation where schools will persist in killing creativity. Like Nova Scotia's *Time to Learn Strategy* (2002) that guides all school timetables and subject exposure, their *Action Plan for Education, 2015, The 3R's: Renew, Refocus, Rebuild* makes no claim nor provides evidence to address the concerns over creative development expressed by Robinson and Florida. Also missing is evidence of appreciation for the breadth and depth of digital media's impact on learning. The learning and media ecology shaping our world and our students appears to be happening independently of our government's optimistic remedies and faith in achievement data. The Minister is on target to achieve their first pillar to "build a modern education system" but, as we move beyond modernity to less predictable and increasingly dynamic times, we could do more to build a school system that mobilizes resources and curriculum to address the nature of the digital age. To this end, we could consider a range of approaches, such as:

1. *As digital media reroute time and space, can we steer it towards creative learning?*

   It should be noted that though WMDs draw the users' attention from physical spaces towards ones which may echo or mirror creative processes, we should remain critical of claims that suggest WMDs are a panacea for the lack of student engagement and creativity in teaching and learning. The various effects of their often seductive and engaging interface, deserves critical observation and consideration. Having said that, in their capacity to free us from the necessity of logocentric schedules and processes, to connect us to more people and spaces, and in their access to information and experiences, lay opportunities to reshape schooling. For teachers, allowing time and space for creativity is a worthy pursuit, as it is worth exploring how we might embed it to reshape or *flip* when, what, and how students learn, as well as the fundamental teacher-student relationship. Since learning is about making connections and creativity is the making of connections between disparate concepts, creative thinking has the potential to deepen understanding within all content areas. Along with opening new spaces and (non)sequences, digital media also offer audio-tactile sensory expriences to complement the visual. As classes need not persist in segregating music and movement from math or science from art, desks need not be in sequence to buttress the teacher's supremacy. In this new order, teachers will make better coaches than bosses.

The digital age offers opportunities to fashion our learning ecology's structures and strategies to suit more student-centered learning. Whether we own it or not, students will continue to augment their learning through such media and the more they augment without us, the less relevant we become. Also, if we insist on using new media to do old things we risk reinforcing linear teaching and antiquated priorities where students will use the device to escape from teachers through distraction. The lesson here is (a) if teachers do not ensure their relevance to students in a digital world, teachers may be displaced and (b) the implications are for public education systems most everywhere.

2. *Make time for life in learning.*

To achieve *eureka* moments where juxtapositions are made and new archetypes are invented, the space of time needs to be opened in schools. Actively seeking answers through conscious and linear processes will only lead to calculated solutions whereas creative solutions flourish in less rigid spaces. Time to play, relax, and distract the mind are needed if the subconscious is to arrive at unexpected, creative insights. If what Daniel Pink shares in *Drive* (2011) is true, that motivation comes from a combination of autonomy, mastery, and purpose, then affording time for students to follow their own interests and develop their own queries with us there. To offer skills to master, engages and empowers students to own and drive their learning.

3. *Employ strategies that encourage creative inquiry.*

While embedding more sensory and arts-based strategies throughout schooling is a good place to start, I wish to leave you with one strategy to enhance creativity in learning. Consider the Laws of Media as an instrument of creative inquiry. This is particularly apparent when probing our memories and experiences for retrievals. A retrieval rings true when patterns of how one tool relates to and impacts us echoes a previous form. Finding such patterns often means tasking our subconscious to seek out and juxtapose lexical and semantic information from among a range of histories and experiences. Typically, when a retrieval is found after a long inward journey, it presents itself as an *aha* moment where awareness comes in a flash – the result of a creative process. Arriving at novel solutions grows from allowing for the unfettered flow and connecting of memories and ideas, hunting for retrievals is one such exercise. My recalls tend to come when I am relaxed, happy, and void of conscious thought, often in the shower.

4. *Nourish the senses.*

   If increased achievement and student engagement are the primary goals of a good curriculum, we would reach more students if we involve more of their senses. We have explored that with the onset of literacy our visual sense had dominated and largely pushed aside the development of other senses. In spite of this, we have not done enough to lead students to think critically about the visual text and other sensory phenomena. Though the visual arts and media studies do this, they are often marginalized or taught without the experience to lend critical insights into visual text where, as is, students will remain numb and susceptible to visual persuasion.

   And, though schooling favours sight over the other senses, our priorities and structures reinforce this tradition. We might try to rebalance this by providing opportunities where students learn through tactility, movement, voice and sound. We can, for instance, employ devices like movement and voice in many disciplines beyond the arts, technology and physical education. By increasing the breadth and frequency of sensory experiences we might grow opportunities where students can know things "inside-out" (visceral knowing) or by the "palm of their hand" (tactile knowing) rather than just "the back of their hand" (visual knowing) or the "sound of their own voice" (acoustical knowing).

   It is through the thoughtful and aware integration of digital media and sensory experiences that we further engage students. Along the way, we may also activate more centers of the brain, give new dimensions to a subject, and overall heighten each student's capacity to learn. Fundamentally, the attention we pay to the shifts born of the digital age will define schooling in the 21st century.

REFERENCES

Adam, B. (2003). Reflexive modernization temporalize. *Theory, Culture & Society, 20*(2), 59–78.

Carr, N. (2010). *The shallows: What the internet is doing to our brains*. New York, NY: W.W. Norton & Company.

Castells, M. (2001). Epilogue: Informationalism and the network society. In P. Himanen (Ed.), *The hacker ethic and the spirit of the information age* (pp. 155–178). New York, NY: Random House.

Castells, M. (2010). *The rise of the network society: The information age: Economy, society, and culture* (Vol. 1). Chichester: John Wiley & Sons Ltd.

Christensen, C. (n.d.). *Disruptive education.* Retrieved March 29, 2016, from http://www.claytonchristensen.com/key-concepts/

Collingwood, R. G. (1967). *The principles of art.* London: Oxford University Press.

Csikszentmihalyi, M. (1990). *Flow.* Toronto: Harper Collins.

Florida, R. (2012). *The rise of the creative class-revisited.* New York, NY: Basic Books.

Gelernter, D. (2010). Dream logic, the internet and artificial thought. *The Edge.* Retrieved March, 29, 2016, from https://www.edge.org/conversation/david_gelernter-dream-logic-the-internet-and-artifical-thought

Hassan, R. (2011). *The age of distraction: Reading, writing, and politics in a high-speed networked economy.* Edison, NJ: Transaction Publishers.

Kounios, J., & Beeman, M. (2009). The Aha! moment: The cognitive neuroscience of insight. *Current Directions in Psychological Science, 18*(4), 210–216.

Levinson, P. (2004). *Digital McLuhan: A guide to the information millennium.* New York, NY: Routledge.

McLuhan, E., & McLuhan, M. (1988). *Laws of media: The new science.* Toronto: University of Toronto Press.

McLuhan, M. (1962). *The Gutenberg galaxy.* Toronto: The New America Library.

McLuhan, M. (1964). *Understanding media.* New York, NY: McGraw-Hill.

McLuhan, M. (1969, March). The playboy interview: Marshall McLuhan. *Playboy Magazine.* Retrieved from http://www.digitallantern.net/mcluhan/mcluhanplayboy.htm

Mednick, S. A. (1962). The associative basis of the creative process. *Psychological Review, 69,* 220–232.

Nova Scotia Department of Education and Early Childhood Development. (2002). *Nova Scotia time to learn strategy.* Retrieved from http://www.ednet.ns.ca/files/ps-policies/instructional_time_guidelines_p-6.pdf

Nova Scotia Department of Education and Early Childhood Development. (2015). *Action plan for education, 2015. The 3R's: Renew, refocus, rebuild.* Retrieved from http://www.ednet.ns.ca/files/2015/Education_Action_Plan_2015_EN.pdf

Pink, D. (2009). *Drive: The surprising truth about what motivates us.* Toronto: Penguin group.

Postman, N. (1986). *Amusing ourselves to death.* Toronto: Penguin Group.

Robinson, K. (2006). Do schools kill creativity? *TED talks* (video) Retrieved from http://www.ted.com/talks/ken_robinson_says_schools_kill_creativity.html

Robinson, K. (2009). *The element: How finding your passion changes everything.* Toronto: Penguin Group.

Robinson, K. (2011). *Out of our minds.* Chichester: Capstone Publishing Ltd.

Saltz, J. (2006, February 21). Idol thoughts: The glory of *Fountain*, Marcel Duchamp's ground-breaking "moneybags piss pot". *The Village Voice.* Retrieved from http://www.villagevoice.com/2006-02-21/art/idol-thoughts/

Sheppard, D. (2013). *Magic in her hands.* Halifax: Art Gallery of Nova Scotia.

The Economist. (2014, June 28). *The digital degree.* Retrieved March 29, 2016, from http://www.economist.com/news/briefing/21605899-staid-higher-education-business-about-experience-welcome-earthquake-digital

WEF (World Economic Forum). (2016). *The future of jobs employment, skills and workforce strategy for the fourth industrial revolution.* Retrieved March, 20, 2016, from http://www3.weforum.org/docs/Media/WEF_Future_of_Jobs_embargoed.pdf

Zimmerman, E. (2009). Reconceptualizing the role of creativity in art education theory and practice. *Studies in Art Education, 50*(4), 382–399.

Paul Syme
Acadia University

KIERAN EGAN

3. DEVELOPING CREATIVITY AND IMAGINATION BY ACCUMULATING LOTS OF USELESS KNOWLEDGE

INTRODUCTION

Human experience in early childhood involves emotional vividness, openness to experience, and imaginative fertility. Children are then given into the care of school systems that were designed for an industrial age, and these systems, despite the heroic efforts of many teachers and administrators within them, tend to impose literalness, homogeneity, accumulation of much irrelevant knowledge, and desiccated forms of rationalism, which at least discourage and often stifle effective learning, imaginative engagement, and creativity. Children are raced through a curriculum which they sample only superficially, and rarely to the point that their imaginations become involved with the contents and the genuine wonders of knowledge.

That is too stark a way of putting it, of course, though the messy outlines of schooling practices do display prominent features that align with this simplification.

One troubling feature of that way of putting it, though, is that too many people see imagination and the accumulation of knowledge and development of reason as somewhat at odds with each other: we are encouraged to fight for greater success in mastering basic knowledge and skills, on the one hand, or greater creativity and freedom of expression and exploratory learning on the other. As though these can be represented as alternatives in any sane view of the world; as though developing one's reasoning abilities infringes on or is inhibited by encouraging development of creativity and imagination.

It is useful to bear in mind that all the knowledge in the curriculum is a product of someone's hopes, fears, passions, or ingenuity. If we want students to learn that knowledge in a manner that will make it meaningful and memorable, then we need to bring it to life for them in the context of those hopes, fears, passions, or ingenuity. The great agent that will allow us to achieve this routinely in everyday classrooms is the imagination, and the imagination is a great spur to creativity in any field.

Put this way we can see imagination as necessary for conveying knowledge meaningfully, and, reciprocally, accumulating knowledge as necessary for engaging the imagination. And while it is hard not to conclude that hopes, fears, passions and ingenuity are not very evident in most current teaching practice nor in programs that prepare teachers for work in classrooms, nevertheless this way of putting it aligns better with Wordsworth's insight that "*Imagination … is Reason in her most*

J. B. Cummings & M. L. Blatherwick (Eds.), Creative Dimensions of Teaching and Learning in the 21st Century, 37–45.

exalted mood." So if we hope to bring richer meaning, and hopes, fears, passions, and ingenuity into the classroom, we need to have both accumulating knowledge and reason and imagination working together.

I have begun, then, by suggesting that a common, if somewhat subdued, assumption in educational thinking that influences daily practice is that there is a kind of tension between teaching to encourage creativity and imagination, on the one hand, and encouraging knowledge accumulation and rationality, on the other. We have inherited this division in educational thinking from a long history, a prominent part of which includes the Progressivist program, whose rhetoric emphasized a conflict between what they represented as the traditional emphasis on teaching irrelevant, ornamental, and useless knowledge contrasted with the new and progressive emphasis on teaching relevant skills and processes that prepared students for the world around them (Egan, 2002). I want to disrupt further this division too many people seem still to take for granted by recommending a new way to approach developing imagination in learning about the world; exemplified by a new program that aims to develop imagination and creativity by the route of accumulating a great deal of detailed and "useless" knowledge about a specific topic.

Learning in Depth

If one begins to study the imagination or creativity in detail, one quickly learns that these potent intellectual abilities are not like the kind of mind-wandering and idle fancy they are sometimes associated with. One realizes that the more one knows about something the easier it is to be imaginative about it, and creativity in any field follows deep knowledge about that field. And furthermore, and further conflicting with common assumptions today, the imagination can work only with what we know. It can't work with the contents of the library or the Internet. It is common to hear educators say that what is important is to know how to find knowledge as one needs it, rather than load up one's memory with all kinds of knowledge that may prove to be useless. But ignorance and vaguely grasped general knowledge provide no stimulus for the imagination; richness of detailed knowledge stored in the mind is what gets imaginations up in the morning. You can't imagine or be creative with what you don't know, regardless of how skilled you might be in finding out knowledge you need. If your imagination is not working with knowledge, you don't know what you need, and your mind remains idle.

Well, yes, this also simplifies the spurs to imagination and creativity, but much less so than the casual assumption that developing imagination is in some way at odds with accumulating knowledge. It seemed to me that we needed to introduce into the curriculum a simple program that would be devoted to enabling children to accumulate lots and lots of knowledge about something. The program I have suggested (Egan, 2011) is starkly simple and can be described in a single paragraph:

"Learning in Depth" (LiD) begins, ideally, soon after children begin schooling. It starts with a ceremony in which each child is given a specific topic. The plan is that they will build a portfolio on that topic for the whole of their school career. Topics might include apples, bees, fish, the circus, railroads, water, birds, the solar system, and so on. For an hour each week children can work on their topics, supported by teachers. They can also work on their topic at home, helped by parents or other caregivers. By the end of their schooling, each child will be an expert on something; each child will know almost as much about her or his topic as anyone on earth.

Given our normal experience of schooling, and the assumptions about children and learning conditioned by current schooling, the LiD program might at first seem odd, to say the least. Most educators, when they first hear it described, tend to immediately think of reasons why it will not or cannot work. They think children will quickly get bored; they assume children will also lose motivation because the LiD work is not graded; teachers are already overwhelmed with pressures and new programs and certainly don't need to take on a new and peculiar addition to the curriculum; they think it is too complicated to organize; and many other reasons are given for not trying it.

A much smaller number of teachers take to LiD with great enthusiasm, and set about implementing it in their own classrooms. The first implementations were in two schools in British Columbia during the 2008–2009 school year. In one school, in Langley, a teacher decided to try out LiD after she heard it described in a university class she was taking at the time. It should be said that she did so in the face of not a little skepticism, and worse, from some of her fellow teachers. In the following year, six other teachers in the school began the program in their classes, and in the next year there were eleven teachers implementing it. What did those other teachers see that made them go from dismissive skepticism to becoming enthusiastic implementers themselves, within a year or two? They saw a class of students who were showing huge enthusiasm to learn about their individual topics, also bringing to school materials for their fellow students to help them build their portfolios, coming to school with special energy on the day they had their one hour time slot set aside for LiD, talking to their parents and siblings about what they were learning, accumulating knowledge from libraries, papers and magazines, the Internet, drawing, tracing, talking with adults, including other teachers, etc. The first Langley teacher, who has been teaching for around 30 years, said: "I have never experienced the kind of questions and interactions I now have with my students … I have never experienced these kinds of conversations with children" (Linda Holmes, Imaginative Education Research Group, 2014). The second teacher who began the program in 2008–2009, in Victoria, summed up his experience after a year simply with "The kids love it!" (David Futter). One of Mr. Futter's "underperforming" pupils, aged twelve, refused to consider any topic other than skateboarding. The teacher persuaded him to take on "the wheel" as a topic – by the end of the year the student was studying the physics of balance, surface resistances, and so on. A teacher in Oregon wrote: "The Learning in Depth project has brought to our students a completely new relationship to learning that has been surprising in its depth and quality. After seeing Learning in Depth at work in our school community, I know this has been a critical, missing element. It has proven to be everything we imagined (and much more we didn't) when we heard about [it initially]" (Sheri Dunton, IERG, 2014).

The program was designed to begin in the first years of schooling, but already there are implementations somewhere in every year of schooling, including the final year or so in high schools. Even more unexpectedly, the program has engaged many students who are often resistant to learning, or are considered "at-risk", and has given them something that is theirs that they can pursue in their own way.

My aim here is not to discuss the LiD program at length, or to respond to the objections some have made to it. It may be enough to mention that within the past few years the program is being implemented in scores of schools in British Columbia and in a smattering of schools across Canada and the U.S., and in schools in at least a dozen other countries. In nearly all schools where the program has been introduced many children quickly become enthusiastic about their topics, and within a few years their portfolios are unlike anything children have ever produced in the history of schooling. The three small-scale research studies conducted so far, all report very positive results about student engagement, teacher satisfaction, lack of administrative difficulties, and the disconfirmation of predictions that the program will die out due to student boredom and the absence of the stimulus of grading ("Boredom is a product of ignorance, not of knowledge" was a conclusion). For more details about the LiD program, the IERG website may be explored.

Imagination and LiD

The caricature of "traditional" teaching and learning presented in the powerfully influential works of Herbert Spencer (1897, 1927) and John Dewey (1916) invoke an image of ornamental and useless knowledge being crammed into reluctant students on the belief that somehow knowledge of Latin or whatever would do their minds some good, even though it might be practically useless. The caricature was earlier developed by Rousseau when he introduced his own even more powerfully influential view of education in his peculiar novel/thesis about Émile (1762). The target of all of them was the creative originator of the tradition that has shaped our cultural life in ways too subtle and complex and massive for us to now untangle; Plato for better or worse is a part of our minds. We are the intellectual slaves of dead scribblers, and few have enslaved more people over a longer time than Plato.

Plato believed that accumulating a lot of specific kinds of knowledge did something good for the mind. He also believed – which is largely ignored in modern treatises on education – that this had to go along with the acquisition of courage and a bunch of other virtues. Two things have happened in educational thinking that influence the way we read Plato today. First is forgetting all that inconvenient stuff about virtues; second is the articulation of psychological theories of development.

Talk of virtues in education makes most people metaphorically squirm; talk of psychological development is taken as obvious and beyond question. As I don't enjoy squirming, I too will ignore virtues, but I do want to question the dominance of ideas about psychological development. The plausibility of the LiD project fits uncomfortably in a world where those ideas are taken as true.

Those ideas became dominant in educational thinking also as a result of Rousseau's fantastic rhetorical power. He proposed that the mind has its own natural process of development, to whose stages educators needed to conform their methods of teaching. This view has been given a more modern form in the work of that most Rousseauian of psychologists, Jean Piaget. These notions of a spontaneous psychological developmental process largely displaced Plato's ideas. Plato does have a highly articulated developmental scheme built into the *Republic*, but it is an account of stages of increasing epistemological precision and clarity of understanding. Plato believed that accumulating increasing amounts and clarity of a specific curriculum of knowledge, along with the appropriate intellectual disciplines and virtues of character, is what develops the mind.

To indicate the distinction crudely, today most people recognize the advent of "abstract" forms of thought in mid or later teen years in terms of psychological development, such as Piaget's account of how "formal operations" *develop*. Plato characterizes the development of "abstract" thinking as a product of learning sufficient amounts of particular kinds of knowledge. He believed that knowledge by itself did things to the mind, rather than that the mind itself goes through some spontaneous process as we grow older. For Plato, the mind is made up of what we know; for Rousseau the mind, like the body, goes through a process of growth determined by its own nature, as long as it has appropriate and sufficient interactions with our environment. Again, this is obviously too simple a way of putting it, but it captures enough of the distinction to allow me to indicate why it makes sense today to propose a program focused purely on the accumulation of "useless" knowledge as important for education.

Minds and Bodies

The human mind remains a mysterious country to its possessors. We expand our understanding of it by using metaphors and analogies. So we ask, "What is the mind like?" The trouble is that the human mind is unlike anything else we know. Rousseau and Herbert Spencer, and modern educational researchers, took quite literally the answer that the mind is like the body; or, rather, researchers and those who rely on them in Education misjudged the degree of metaphor involved in thinking of the mind in terms derived from thinking about the body.

Spencer wrote: "We must compare mental phenomena with the phenomena most like them… The phenomena which those of Mind resemble in the greatest degree are those of bodily life" (1897, pp. 292–293). Using such an analogy, has led to all kinds of biological notions being imported into thinking about the mind and its development. The mind's "growth" became a focus of effort in education; knowledge became thought of as "food" for mental "growth" by Spencer and Piaget and many others; and the belief took hold that the mind goes through its own spontaneous process of development, with major changes at specific stages.

If we think of minds as like bodies we are inclined to see knowledge as subservient – as food – to a supposedly distinct process of mental development. But there is a problem with this simplistic view, as stated by Paul Hirst (1974):

> To acquire knowledge is to learn to see, to experience the world in a way otherwise unknown, and thereby come to have a mind in a fuller sense. It is not that the mind is some kind of organ or muscle with its own inbuilt forms of operation, which if somehow developed, naturally lead to different kinds of knowledge. It is not that the mind has predetermined patterns of functioning. (p. 40)

Hirst's argument is that one simply cannot locate and describe some underlying process of cognitive development. What has been considered a process of psychological development, Hirst suggests, is simply a by-product of the kind and amount of knowledge we have learned. If there are regularities to be seen in our development, they are produced by the regularities of our having socialized children and having taught them certain forms of knowledge at regular times. Jerry Fodor (1985) has similarly given reasons to doubt "that there is such a thing as cognitive development in the sense that developmental cognitive psychologists have in mind" (p. 35; see also Fodor, 1983). And Hirst and Fodor are hardly alone in the growing skepticism that the forms of psychological assumptions that have undergirded American psychology for some time are sound. Hence, the increasing attractiveness to many of the ideas of Lev Vygotsky and his socio-cultural psychological bases.

In the currently dominant view, derived in significant degree from Herbert Spencer (1928), the educator's task is to recognize that "there is a sequence in which the faculties spontaneously develop, and a certain kind of knowledge which each requires during its development; and that it is for us to ascertain this sequence, and supply this knowledge" (pp. 52–53). What the good teacher has to do, then, is "to guide the intellect to the appropriate food" (p. 68). The teacher thus becomes like an environmental aide, or, using Spencer's metaphor, like a domestic servant to the master-program of development inherent in the child's mind.

If we try to look at the developmental process without the body metaphor shaping our perception, one prominent objection to current theories stands out vividly. Knowledge just doesn't seem to have the same relation with the mind that food has with the body; knowledge constitutes the mind in a way that food doesn't constitute the body. The body has its own pre-programmed developmental process to go through, and as long as it receives a sufficient variety of foods it will follow that program; the experiences one has and the things we learn become parts of our mind in a clearly different way. (And this isn't to say that the analogy has no validity, just that it is only an analogy and has commonly been taken as establishing greater similarity between the two processes than is warranted.)

Time to recognize that the emperor is sartorially a tad deficient, we might conclude. But it isn't that easy. The difficulty I find in suggesting problems with Piaget's theory, even though inadequacies might be conceded in point after point, is that it has become the lens through which most people in education see children's development. It is what most educators think about development *with*, and consequently they find it very hard to think *about* its adequacy.

If, instead, we take a Vygotskian approach to development, we cease to look for some underlying spontaneous process within physical and cultural environments whose role it is to support some unfolding ontogenesis. Rather, we will see development in terms of "a system of psychological functions corresponding to the entire system of symbolic means available in a given culture" (Kozulin, 1998, p. 16). From a Vygotskian perspective, our intellectual abilities are not "natural" but are sociocultural constructs. They are not forms of intellectual life that we are programmed in some sense to bring to realization; there is no naturally preferred form of human intellectual maturity. We are not designed, for example, to move in the direction of "formal operations" or abstract thinking or whatever. These forms of intellectual life are products of our learning to use particular cultural tools invented in our cultural history. And the knowledge generated in our cultural history is what can generate for each of us the cognitive toolkits that become part of the furniture of our minds as we learn the content of the curriculum. The trick is to acquire that knowledge in the context of human hopes, fears, passions, and ingenuity that can give it meaning.

Well, this has been a rapid gallop across some huge ideas. My aim can hardly be to demonstrate their adequacy in so small a space; instead I want simply to suggest that the reasons we have been led to think about knowledge as educationally less important and generative than supporting psychological development and such processes and skills as "critical thinking," "inquiry," "communication," and, yes, "creativity" might not be good reasons. Part of the problem comes from suggesting the division in the first place – for which we can thank Rousseau – seeing development and creativity as processes distinct from knowledge. In a sociocultural view, they are not distinct; one picks up cognitive tools while learning the knowledge created in one's cultural history. The idea that one can separate out processes of "critical thinking" from whatever one is to critically think about, or that one can be creative in some generic sense apart from what one is being creative with, begins to look a bit absurd. It is, nevertheless, an absurdity that seems to dominate much educational thinking today.

Useless Knowledge

One of the products of progressivism has been a sense that the opposite of education is not ignorance. Progressivism, as a general movement, grew from a recognition that much stored or "banked" or "rote-learned" knowledge did not an educated person make. So that bathwater was thrown out. Along with the bathwater went a number of babies. One of them was the importance of knowing something in depth, and learning much by heart, to the education of the imagination. My undergraduate students, as a result of the great educational purging of "rote-learning," know by heart only the words of an occasional pop song or, for some few of them, the words of a prayer. The rest is silence. Their minds are generally deficient in the fuel that drives imaginations. They have been taught that they are skilled in "learning how to learn" and how to "think critically" and all the other processes and skills that have displaced actually knowing things.

The "ornamental" curriculum that Spencer and Dewey derided as largely useless for the lives modern students were to lead is indeed full of things most students will not *need* to know. Why do we teach most students how to divide fractions or have them learn how to prove that alternate interior angles of a parallelogram are congruent? When will they ever need such knowledge, especially in the days of sophisticated calculators that can generate the answer in response to our spoken question.

In the face of this general consensus I want to offer two scenarios. The first is of a seven-year-old girl who has been studying bees as her LiD topic for three years. It might be too much to say she is obsessed with bees, but she has developed a formidable expertise from working on her portfolio for one hour each week during school time, and more time outside school. She recently finished a study of bees' anatomy, which resulted in her annual presentation where she had a very large scale model of a cross-section of a bee. She is going on now, she has decided, to study the collapse of so many bee colonies and see what she can discover from the various theories about the causes. She might then, she says quietly, try to work on solutions to this potential catastrophe.

The second is of a teacher who describes a rather odd man who is digging a pit in the courtyard of a building in North Africa two thousand years ago, because he wants to measure the circumference of the earth. He knows that 500 miles to the south of the building there is a town where, during the summer solstice, the sun casts no shadow, but it does cast a shadow in Alexandria where he lives. The man then fixes an upright stick in the pit, held firmly in place with struts at the top. Exactly at the solstice, he measures the angle the sun casts on the upright stick. Considering that the rays of the sun are parallel wherever they strike the earth, and knowing that alternate interior angles of a parallelogram are congruent, Eratosthenes calculates that the circumference of the earth is 25,000 miles. The teacher has arranged with a school 1,500 miles to the south that they will conduct a similar experiment on the next summer solstice.

What knowledge in these two scenarios is useless? The girl may, indeed, not be the one to solve the problem of bee colony deaths, and maybe all the students who learn how Eratosthenes worked out the circumference of the earth will not make practical use of the theorem. Neither of them has been taking lessons in critical thinking or learning how to learn.

Everything is wonderful – if only you know enough about it. The problem with the experience of most children in our schools is that they gallop through a curriculum and never learn anything more than superficially, even though everything can be made vividly meaningful if learned in the context of people's hopes, fears, passions, and ingenuity. And worse, they hardly ever will learn enough about anything for it to engage their imaginations.

CONCLUSION

We have given up too easily, and with no evident benefits, on Plato's insight that knowledge of specific kinds can shape the mind and give it greater power. The LiD program gives a hint of what is wrong with educational thinking that has become enthralled with simplistic notions about accumulating lots of "useless" knowledge. To see classes of students sprawled on floors, building models, drawing, adding sections to their portfolios with great enthusiasm astonishes many of their teachers. This is ungraded work on often randomly allotted topics about which the students a few months earlier knew nothing nor had any interest in, and here they are within months engaged, within years proud of their accumulating expertise and knowledgeable about how little they know about their topic and what they want to study next about it. The more they know about their topics the more imaginatively they pursue new knowledge and the more creative they are enabled to be about it.

REFERENCES

Dewey, J. (1916). *Democracy and education.* New York, NY: Macmillan.

Egan, K. (2002). *Getting it wrong from the beginning: Our progressivist inheritance from Herbert Spencer, John Dewey, and Jean Piaget.* New Haven: Yale University Press.

Egan, K. (2011). *Learning in depth: A simple innovation that can transform schooling.* Chicago, IL: University of Chicago Press.

Fodor, J. (1983). *The modularity of mind: An essay on faculty psychology.* Cambridge, MA: MIT Press.

Fodor, J. (1985). Précis of 'The modularity of mind.' *The Behavioral and Brain Sciences, 8,* 1–42.

Hirst, P. (1974). *Knowledge and the curriculum.* London: Routledge and Kegan Paul.

Imaginative Education Research Group (IERG). (n.d.). *Learning in depth program.* Retrieved from http://ierg.ca/LID/

Kozulin, A. (1998). *Psychological tools: A sociocultural approach to education.* Cambridge, MA: Harvard University Press.

Spencer, H. (1897). *The principles of psychology* (3rd ed., 2 vols). New York, NY: D. Appleton.

Spencer, H. (1928). *Essays on education, etc* (Introduction by Charles W. Eliot [1910]). London: Dent.

Kieran Egan
Simon Fraser University

GILLIAN JUDSON

4. RE-IMAGINING RELEVANCE IN EDUCATION

INTRODUCTION

Educational relevance. If we had the ability to look into the brains of practicing teachers we'd see this notion rolling steadily through cells in the frontal lobe. Looking for relevance allows us to *interest* our students. It allows us to coerce them into learning something new or, at least, something the powers-that-be consider important for them to know. If we stopped brain-watching and instead listened into a typical seminar for pre-service teachers on curriculum and planning, we would also encounter this term. It is the plight of the teacher to help students *connect* with topics. Faced with this task, looking for relevance seems like the logical thing to do. By connecting students with something – by "hooking" them as teachers so often call it – we assume that we are more likely to be able to teach them and that they, in turn, will be more likely to learn.

This chapter commits some educational heresy. I want to argue that this conception of relevance is not as useful for learning as we think it is. Looking to relevance and feeling confident that it, in conjunction with the kinds of objectives-based approaches to curriculum planning that run rampant in our schools, is most important is actually a recipe for educational disaster or, in the very least, boredom (but isn't boredom in the classroom synonymous with educational disaster?). Following a brief discussion of the pedagogical limitations of relevance I will indicate, with an example, how we might more successfully engage students in learning.

Some Limitations of Relevance

There are at least four problems with looking for "relevance" as a means of engaging students in learning.

First, looking for the relevance of a topic in relation to the students' lived experiences connects back to the widespread belief in education that we should start with what students *know* in order to engage in learning. I would hazard a bet that many students are in fact tired of what they *know*, of their daily experiences and would much rather encounter and envision for themselves other possibilities. In short, relevance doesn't allow us to begin with what students can imagine as being possible.

Second, the notion of relevance often seems to be defined in utilitarian terms. So, for example, we encourage students to learn something because it will serve

J. B. Cummings & M. L. Blatherwick (Eds.), Creative Dimensions of Teaching and Learning in the 21st Century, 47–57.

a particular social purpose; it will help them to participate in the workforce (the "get a job" argument), be an active and responsible citizen (the "Canadians should know something about the history of Canada" argument), or appropriately interact with their peers (the "learn this skill and you will be a better communicator/friend/reader/writer" argument). My point is not that these reasons are totally unimportant, but more that the utilitarian significance of a topic is not necessarily something that engages students on an emotional level. Indeed, some of the future-oriented reasons we associate with relevance have little immediate importance to students. In order to connect with students of any age we must think about topic in emotional terms; the emotional significance of a topic is a means of engaging the imagination of the child.

Third, the conception of relevance we often talk about in education isn't easily found when it comes to some topics. Consider, for example, mathematical concepts or historical knowledge. How does one apply relevance to particularly abstract topics without somehow compromising the complexity of the topic? (I'm thinking algebra here!) How does one teach historical topics such as Ancient Civilizations when relevance is the guide? Sure, one could identify the different ways in which Algebra infuses students' daily lives or we could trace the influence of certain features of the Roman Empire through to the governance we have today. The problem is that both of these ideas dilute something of the ingenuity of the mathematical concept and the vividness of the historical era. The challenge for teachers is to engage students in meaningful and memorable ways while maintaining, as much as possible, the wonder inherent in the topic itself.

Fourth, seeking relevance connects to the widely-held belief that good teaching requires "hooking" students. The idea of connecting students with a topic is not the problem; indeed, the necessity of this connection is what I'm arguing for. The problem with thinking about how to "hook" a student – besides the obvious image that evokes of some poor student hanging limply from a line like fish out of water or, perhaps less gruesome, some poor kid with a large cane hooked around its neck – is the belief that this is an *initial* requirement for learning. One "hooks" the students and then one gets on with teaching. This kind of thinking fails to acknowledge that all learning requires emotional and imaginative engagement. Engagement – defined here as when we feel some emotional connection in response to a topic and, often, our ability to imagine possibilities is evoked – lies at the heart of learning. So rather than a hook, we are seeking to create learning experiences that engage students' emotions and imaginations in more profound and long-lasting ways.

Think for a moment about a really memorable learning experience you had in your elementary or secondary school years – perhaps an activity you did. What was it? What knowledge was gained through this experience? What we tend to most often remember from our past educational experiences are those times when we were most emotionally and imaginatively engaged. Unfortunately, many things we learned in school are not memorable for us. Take this a step further, teachers, and you have your reality check: without engaging your students' emotions and imaginations in learning, much (if not *most*) of what you teach your students will be forgotten.

Of course, the human memory has its limits. My point is that even if your teacher managed to teach you something long enough for a test – and if you manage the same for your students – it is unlikely you will recall that information today. It may have been "relevant" at the time, but not memorable.

This chapter introduces a new approach to dealing with the age-old problem we face as educators: *How do we make the knowledge we are teaching our students meaningful for them?* We live in an age when there is no shortage of sources of information and technologies for accessing knowledge. Increasingly it seems educators are discussing the importance of teaching students how to access this information. The technologies might be new and, certainly, the scope of access students have to information is colossally greater than it once was but our problem remains: how do we make the knowledge we are teaching students meaningful? What good is the information on the internet if we don't have a way to remember it? If we want to resolve this problem – or, at least, have a fighting chance of addressing it – we need to re-imagine the notion of "relevance" in terms of emotional significance. With emotional significance as our aim, we will shape the topics we teach in ways that employ the main features of our students' emotional and imaginative lives. Doing so offers us a means of dealing with the limitations we started with:

1. Looking for emotional significance in a topic allows us to connect to students' imaginations; we begin with what they can imagine about the world as opposed to what they already know.
2. The emotional significance of a topic reflects something all students can share immediately with a topic and with each other in the classroom; all topics can be taught in ways that bring out emotional dimensions. Leaving students *feeling* something for the topics they are learning is, in some ways, the greatest kind of connection we can hope for.
3. We can connect students with all topics of the curriculum if we look at topics as stories to tell as opposed to inert bodies of knowledge. So, like the reporter sent out to get "the story" on something happening in the community, we do not create a fiction when we teach the curriculum, but we ask ourselves what *the story* is. By answering this question for any topic in the curriculum – whether mathematical concept, historical event, scientific principle – we create an emotional connection, a context through which students can share, with the topic and those people involved in it, a common human emotion. They finish a lesson or unit *feeling* something for what they are learning.
4. When educators plan their units with students' emotional and imaginative lives in mind, they put the "hooks" away. No more dangling fish. Instead, teaching is framed in an emotional context from the start. The ways students learn about topics employs features of their imaginations that they already use to experience the world around them. So, teachers of young children shape their topics in story-form that evoke abstract oppositions, and that contain vivid images evoked from words, jokes and humor, rhythms and patterns, and metaphor. Teachers of older

students shape their topics in story-form that reveals what is heroic about the knowledge, its human dimensions, its wonder and its weird, wild and wonderful features. These are all examples of learning tools students are using to make sense of the world around them everyday, everywhere.

Now it is time for some explanation and demonstration. Following a very brief introduction to the basic principles of *Imaginative Education* I will walk through an example of an imaginative approach to teaching about the Roman Empire, a topic most children learn as part of the social studies curriculum in the late elementary or early secondary school years. I've chosen this example for two reasons. First, this was a topic I taught for many years as a social studies teacher. At the time, I thought my teaching was engaging and interesting for students. Beyond seeing with my own eyes that my students were having a good time, their test scores indicated that they were learning something. I realize now that while they may have learned it for a while and many had fun in the process, I was unsuccessful in making the topic memorable over the long run. I had the pleasant – or rather unpleasant – experience of meeting one of my students a few years ago. She had been in my class for social studies 8, 9, and 10 and was by all standards a good student. I took the opportunity to ask her what she remembered from her three years of social studies in my class. After an awkward silence, she said, "Not much." I pushed the issue a little and said, "Come on, what about the Roman Empire, remember what we learned about the rise and fall of Rome?" She answered simply, "We studied the Roman Empire? Really?"

My fear is that this is typical of a lot of what students are learning in schools. When I taught about the Roman Empire I worked toward my objectives and included "fun" activities that would keep students active during their learning. Now I realize that I failed to frame the topic in any emotionally significant way; with some additional reading on my part it didn't take long to create the example I share here. The second reason I've chosen to include this topic is because teachers often find it hard to find "relevance" in relation to historical topics. This example indicates how a typical 13-year-old kid in a suburban school in British Columbia might leave *feeling* connected to a topic *more* ancient than their teacher – the Roman Empire.

Introduction to Imaginative Education: A Few Terms

At the core of what is meaningful for human beings everywhere is emotion. The aspects of the world that are meaningful to us, whether in the social group, family or culture, evoke our emotions and imagination. It is crucially important, therefore, that students are emotionally engaged in the learning process. But what is it that emotionally engages children? How are their imaginations engaged? These are questions that Egan (1992, 1997, 2005, 2007) explores in detail and that he integrates into an educational theory called Imaginative Education (IE).

IE pairs a theoretical understanding of the imagination's role in learning (Egan, 1997), with a comprehensive practical discussion of how to engage imagination in learning (2005). Of central importance for this work are Egan's (1992, 1997) insights into how students' imaginations engage differently in the world as they acquire oral, written and increasingly theoretical uses of language. These different forms of language provide them with "sets" of learning tools or what Egan calls, following Vygotsky (1962, 1978), "cognitive tools" that shape specific imaginative understandings of the world. IE may be described as a "cognitive tools" approach to learning; it is centrally concerned with employing in teaching the culturally-based learning tools that come along with language in order to most effectively engage students' emotions and imaginations in learning. Cognitive tools (for example, story/narrative, jokes, metaphor, extremes of experience and limits of reality, and collections) are "little factories of understanding" (Hughes, 1988, p. 12); they are tools that come along with language that help us to learn the knowledge with which they are tied up in emotionally engaging ways.

Let's get on with an example. Have you noticed how children from about age 7 or 8 through about 15 are fascinated by the kind of extremes and limits of reality one finds in the *Guinness Book of World Records*? Or how they tend to idolize sports stars, musicians, actors or activists? All of these characteristics are dimensions of the literate imagination; they are cognitive or learning tools that shape a Romantic understanding of the world. For someone with Romantic understanding the world is full of wonder; one can "turn on" this fascination with the wonderful aspects of the world. Everything can be seen in terms of a heroic human quality; it is through a personal association with a transcendent human quality that students become imaginatively engaged. Whether the precision of a mathematical formula or the strength of a worm, every topic we teach has something heroic about it that we can employ to engage students.

Let's consider now how some of these tools can come together to shape a unit on the Roman Empire. My aim is to evoke the overarching context you could use to make this topic emotionally significant for your students. Therefore, I only suggest possible activities rather than delineate these in any degree of specificity. Moreover, as a "snap shot" kind of look at IE, I've only focused on some main tools that accompany literacy and which shape what we call Romantic Understanding. A comprehensive outline would also include an articulation of how learning tools that come along with oral language and the body could be engaged to make the learning meaningful as well as, for older students, consideration of more theoretical features of the topic.

A Detailed Example: Using Cognitive Tools to Teach about the Roman Empire

This section follows a few steps that can guide you in incorporating cognitive tools in teaching. These steps are organized as templates and are readily downloaded from the following website: http://www.ierg.ca/teaching.

1. Identifying "heroic" or transcendent qualities

What heroic human qualities are central to the topic? What emotional images do they evoke? What within the topic can best evoke wonder?

Identifying heroic qualities:

- Main heroic quality: organizational effectiveness
- Alternative(s): ingenuity

Images that capture the heroic quality: You might begin by describing for your students a scene in which the blood-soaked battle grounds of yet another Roman victory are juxtaposed with people building roads, bridges and aqueducts, elections being held, senators battling in wars of words, tribunals engaged in legal disputes that invoke the Justinian Code, students sitting in schools, and young boys training for military service. We will want to help students to visualize the great organizational strength of Rome as a heroic quality. In other words, we want them to understand that in addition to military fortitude, maintaining Rome as a political giant was facilitated by administrative organization and a physical infrastructure in terms of government, law, education, military, and architecture.

2. Organizing the content into a narrative structure

2.1. Initial access

What aspect of the topic best embodies the heroic qualities identified as central to the topic? Does this expose some extreme of experience or limit of reality? What image can help capture this aspect?

Exotic/extreme content that best embodies the heroic quality: During this era, feats of incredible engineering skill were performed with only the most basic tools. We might discuss Roman achievements as characters in the story of Roman power – a result of great organizational and military might. For example, we could describe Roman roads – well-built, stone-covered roads, laid on proper foundations that ran to every corner of the Roman Empire. (Some historians suggest that they were the best roads in the world for at least a millennium. Some are still in use today.) These reliable roads (passable in all weathers) allowed the Romans to control their territories and supported trade that, in turn, brought in taxes. Sooner or later all towns and cities of the empire were connected by an elaborate road system, which meant that from any place within the empire you could travel to Rome by road – leading to the famous phrase "All roads lead to Rome". (In all, about 53,000 miles of roads were built by the Romans.)

Rivers were no match for Roman engineers. In order to easily re-supply their troops located beyond the great Rhine and Danube rivers the Romans built enormous bridges. Julius Caesar famously constructed a bridge across the Rhine in only 10 days. Trajan built a huge bridge across the Danube into Dacia. The Roman aqueducts facilitated the growth of large cities and towns. While most aqueducts ran underground, across valleys and rivers the aqueducts were elevated on a bridge of stone arches that enabled the water to flow at a constant rate. The water channels within the aqueducts were always covered in order to shield the water from the sun and to avoid possible poisoning by an enemy. (Of course, before aqueducts were built, sources of water had to be detected. They detected underground water sources in various ways including lying face downwards on the ground, chin on hands, just before sunrise. Places where vapor could be seen emerging from the ground identified water sources. They would also place bronze bowls overnight in holes in the ground. If the bowl had condensation in it in the morning, there was underground water.)

2.2. Structuring the body of the lesson or unit

How do we organize the material into a narrative structure to best illustrate the heroic qualities? Sketch the story, ensuring that the qualities will be made clear by the narrative.

Sketch the overall structure of the lesson/unit: The Roman Empire was a massive, ingenious organizational achievement. Each organizational dimension of the Roman Empire has roots in the human context. We must situate each aspect, then, within the human dimension; associating each aspect with its source in the hopes, fears and passions of individual human beings. It may be useful to build our narrative in pieces – like a recipe for success if you will. We could investigate various dimensions in terms of their structural and organizational contributions to the Roman Empire. Each piece, whether the military, government, infrastructure, education or whatever, represents a character, of sorts, in the story of Rome's unmatched organizational power. Importantly, we should encourage students to do profiles or provide biographies for individuals they believe were central to the realm they investigated.

So, we might begin by introducing the unsung heroes of Roman power and success: the roads, bridges and aqueducts. Each of these features of Roman infrastructure contributed in significant ways to military success and to governmental organization. For example, the roads and bridges allowed the army to travel quickly and efficiently. Moreover, it was much easier to reinforce the troops or bring extra supplies when the roads reached into the farthest corners of the empire and, because made of stone and placed on solid foundations, were passable year-round. The roads and bridges allowed communication across the empire that facilitated governmental stability and cohesion. The aqueducts brought water to large towns and cities, thereby facilitating their expansion.

We will want to tell the stories, too, of the people involved in their construction. Take, for example, the placing of milestones every 1000 paces on the Roman roads. These milestones measured from the "golden milestone" or *milarium aurum* near the Temple of Saturn in Rome. To ensure accurate placements, the Romans employed a machine invented and built by Archimedes, a Greek inventor and mathematician. It was the first odometer. (It was a chariot with a wheel that would revolve 400 times over the distance of one mile. A peg on the inside rim of the wheel was tied to a gear with 400 teeth. On the 400th revolution of the wheel the machine would drop a pebble into a cup indicating that a mile had been traveled.)

Next, we might focus on the governmental structure as another character in our story of the heroic infrastructure. The Roman constitution outlined the legal rights of citizens (which covered everyone except women, slaves and resident aliens). There was a great sense of patriotism among the Roman people. The Republic was supposed to be a government of checks and balances so that no one man or group could seize power. However, in reality, Roman families had an immense amount of influence – possibly more than the political process outlined in the constitution. (Alliances, marriages, divorces, adoptions, and assassinations could make or break a family's path to political power in the Roman world. By 100 B.C. the influential families were so powerful that it was nearly impossible for a man to become a consul whose ancestors had not also been consuls.)

And then there was the army – what might at first seem like the biggest hero in our story of Roman success. The Roman army was, indeed powerful due to the extreme discipline of the troops and the innovative battle techniques used. However, a central message in our story might be how the army relied on the unsung heroes – each contributed an important piece to the power of Rome. (For every soldier who marched along a Roman road, one hundred people carrying paper walked – carrying, that is, the intellectual tools that governed the empire.)

2.3. Humanizing the content

What aspects of the narrative best illustrate the human emotions in it and evoke a sense of wonder? What ideals and/or challenges to tradition or convention are evident in the content?

What content can be best shown in terms of hopes, fears, intentions or other emotions? Emperor Justinian achieved lasting influence for his judicial reforms, most importantly, the *Corpus Juris Civilis*, a uniform rewrite of the Roman law that still informs the legal system of many modern states. If it weren't for the revision of law made by his uncle Justin I allowing the intermarriage of people from different social classes, he wouldn't have been able to marry Theodora, the love of his life and greatest supporter. She had started as a stage performer and was twenty years younger. Perhaps he would have reformed that law himself? Despots do things like that.

We can focus on the most outrageous emperors like Nero (who most say was insane) or the most famous such as Julius Cesar. What were their hopes and fears? What was unique about them? By the way, did you know that Julius Caesar was highly superstitious? He insisted on using the same horse in battle – one that had hooves cloven into five parts such that they looked like toes. Julius Caesar is also said to be one of the first people in history who was able to read silently – nearly everyone until the later Middle Ages spoke as they read. Caesar learned to read silently so no one could overhear the messages or plans he was reading.

Consider how we might humanize our teaching of the census. Not only was it a very thorough process in which the citizens of Rome were counted every five years, but it was also a process that supported a Roman sense of civic pride. One might introduce Marcus Aemilius Scaurus, one Roman politician in charge of the census. Every five years, each male Roman citizen had to register his wife, children, extended family, slaves and riches to the Roman census. Should he fail to do this, his possessions would be confiscated and he would be sold into slavery. Throughout the entire republican era, registration in the census was the only way that a Roman could ensure that his identity and status as a citizen were recognized. Primarily the census served to count the number of citizens and to assess the potential military strength and future tax revenue. It also transformed the city into a unified political and military community. To the Roman citizens, the census was one of the cornerstones of their civilization; it made them a *populus*, a people, capable of collective action. To bring forth the emotional dimensions further, we might look more closely at the roles of the two censors responsible for compiling the lists. The men given these roles were appointed for their proven integrity and authority. It was their role to scrutinize each man, carefully evaluating his riches and his rank and placing him in his rightful place within the civic hierarchy of Rome. The censors looking into a man's public and private lives, might decide to move a citizen a few rungs down the social ladder if he had, for example, turned a blind eye to his wife's adulteries, committed perjury, fathered no children, appeared on the stage (actors were held in contempt by Roman society) or failed to cultivate his land properly.

2.4. Pursuing details

What parts of the topic can students best explore in exhaustive detail?

List those aspects of the topic that students can explore exhaustively: If we build our narrative as described above, students may individually or in groups become experts on an aspect of the empire in terms of its organizational structure and how this piece contributed to the overall empire. Encouraging students to focus their investigations on the human angle of these stories will help to locate the administrative might of the empire within the realm of human emotion with which students can most readily relate. One group might, for example, look at the role and power of government officials. In Latin there are two different words to describe a person's power: *potentia* for personal power and *potestas* or political power. Holding power in Rome was not comparable to political positions in the modern Western world insofar as Roman magistrates were dictators. Moreover, while today's governments separate the powers of the political rulers of the country (executive), the politicians making laws (legislature), and the judges who apply the law in the courts (judiciary), this was not the case in ancient Rome. All such powers rested with the highest magistrates, the consuls. But these elected consuls were not the only powerful figures in Rome. Other offices such as those of the *praetors*, *aediles* or *quaestors*, allowed their holders to make their own laws, oversee their enforcement, and to prosecute and punish anyone who failed to abide by them. As well, we will want our students to consider how the structure or process of organization they have explored in detail contributes to the overall power of Rome.

3. Concluding

How can one best bring the topic to satisfactory closure? How can the student feel this satisfaction? How can we evoke a sense of wonder about the topic?

Concluding activities: At the time, it was quite inconceivable that Roman power would end. But, of course, our story of the Roman Empire does come to an end. What happened? As we investigate the structural strength and the administrative power behind the Empire at its peak we might also keep our attention turned to what looked like "cracks" in the structure; that is, the foundational weaknesses, which with time led to the downfall of Rome. In so doing students can gain a sense of the multiple dimensions contributing to both success and failure. What students can marvel at certainly are the possibilities that existed for the Empire at its peak, as well as what can happen to a seemingly invincible superpower. What connections could be made with superpower nations of the modern world?

Students might also build portfolios that describe in various formats the structural ingredients of Rome around which we have based our teaching – each revealing the "recipe" for Rome's success. These portfolios would include the expert research they conducted and profiles of the people most representative of that dimension etc. They could reflect on the ingenuity of organization in the Roman Empire and what happened to these when the walls came crumbling down (so to speak). What can be learned from the Roman example in terms of organizational strength and potential threats to that strength? How can role-play be employed to assess student learning? What crazy emperors might students become?

FINAL REMARKS

So, there you have it: one serving of educational heresy, iced with a new kind of educational thinking and topped off with a unit overview in which the search for emotional significance is employed to engage students. You are now in the process of digesting, I hope, a unit outline in which features of students' emotional and imaginative lives – indeed, tools that help them to think and make sense of the world around them – are employed to shape a topic. My hope is that you've found this chapter and its contents emotionally engaging. (In other words, no indigestion but, rather, an interest in learning more.) It was written with emotional significance in mind; to learn more about the learning tools I've employed in writing it (e.g., the story-form/narrative, mental imagery, humor [she says hopefully], identification of heroic qualities, humanization of meaning, revolt and idealism) visit the Imaginative Education Research Website. Check out the lessons and units. Explore some of the many examples provided. Learn more about – and join if you wish – NIET (A Network of Imaginative Education Teachers) – www.ierg.net

REFERENCES

Egan, K. (1992). *Imagination in teaching and learning: The middle school years.* Chicago, IL: University of Chicago Press.

Egan, K. (1997). *Educated mind: How cognitive tools shape our understanding.* Chicago, IL: University of Chicago Press.

Egan, K. (2005). *An imaginative approach to teaching.* San Francisco, CA: Jossey-Bass.

Egan, K. (2007). Imagination, past and present. In K. Egan, M. Stout, & K. Takaya (Eds.), *Teaching and learning outside the box: Inspiring imagination across the curriculum* (pp. 3–20). London & Ontario: The Althouse Press.

Hughes, T. (1988). Myth and education. In K. Egan & D. Nadaner (Eds.), *Imagination and education* (pp. 30–44). New York, NY: Teachers College Press.

Vygotsky, L. (1962). *Thought and language*. Cambridge: MIT Press.

Vygotsky, L. (1978). *Mind in society: The development of higher psychological processes.* Cambridge: Harvard University Press.

Gillian Judson
Simon Fraser University

ROBERT KELLY

5. CREATIVE DEVELOPMENT IN TEACHER EDUCATION

When You Dress Educators up, They Need a Place to Go

INTRODUCTION

The Need for Creative Development in Teacher Education

The need for creativity and innovation as an integral part of 21st century skills in education has been widely espoused by numerous government jurisdictions and private organizations, notably Alberta Education's Inspiring Education (2010) initiative along with the Partnership for 21st Century Skills (P21) (2009) in the United States and the international Organization for Economic Cooperation and Development (OECD, Ananiadou & Clario, 2009). This is often presented in the context of the 4C's of creativity and innovation, critical thinking and problem-solving, collaboration and communication in a networked, interconnected and interdependent transdisciplinary world (Bocchi et al., 2014). Creativity and innovation are viewed as essential for future students and teachers to deal with increasing complexities of higher education while enhancing creative design practice to enable increased economic and social innovation for emerging and future problems at a variety of levels.

Applied educational work in the field of creativity and innovation requires a clear and common vocabulary derived from comprehensive research resources such as Sternberg (1999), Piirto (2004), Kaufman and Sternberg (2006, 2010), Runco (2007), Starko (2010) and Beghetto and Kaufman (2010). A most concise and accessible definition of creativity is Lubart's (2000), who defines this concept as a sequence of thoughts and actions that leads to novel, adaption production. Runco (2007) defines innovation as the application of creative practice where ideas are introduced and applied to a situation that benefits a job, process, organization or the development of a product.

The epicenter of the transformation of educational culture to embrace creativity and innovation lies with a transformation of the professional culture (Kelly, 2012). This implies that teacher education programs nationally and internationally have to embrace a transformation that builds understanding and practice around creativity and innovation into the educational mainstream in a meaningful way. This goes beyond offering traditional courses, lectures and workshops that are about creativity where participants are placed largely in the role of consumers of information. Pink (2005) talks of how we have moved from the information age to the conceptual age. Ideas are the currency of contemporary learning with creativity as the engine (Kelly & Leggo,

J. B. Cummings & M. L. Blatherwick (Eds.), Creative Dimensions of Teaching and Learning in the 21st Century, 59–68.

2008). A primary educational challenge is not so much obtaining and accessing information but rather equipping educators and learners with a creative disposition to apply and grow this information in innovative ways across the discipline spectrum.

This has informed the design and development of the Creative Development in Educational Practice graduate certificate program at the University of Calgary. It is one of many program options for educators as part of the Interdisciplinary MEd program at the Werklund School of Education at the University of Calgary. The principal focus of this ten-month program is on enhancing the creative development of educators through first-hand research, engagement and documentation of longitudinal, creative practice. This is supported in a highly collaborative environment of idea generation and prototyping. A fundamental understanding here is that the educator must engage in creative practice to grow their own creative capacity and depth of understanding of creative development, in order to educationally enable the creative development of learners.

Understanding Creative Development

Creative development represents the growth of one's creative capacity from our natural disposition of intuitive/ adaptive creativity to encompass the ability to engage in self-instigated, sustained creative practice characterized by recurrent iterations of idea generation and experimentation and prototyping over time (Kelly, 2012). As one develops creative capacity, creative confidence (Kelley, 2013) increases to the point where a higher level of creative capacity is reached as one gains the ability to engage in increasingly more sophisticated, sustained creative practice.

The term "intuitive/adaptive creativity" refers to small "c" creativity or the everyday creativity that we engage in as a part of daily living (Csikszentmihalyi, 1995, 1996). This could apply to cooking, daily problem-solving or improvising when one shows up for work unprepared or when one requires a spontaneous response when faced with an unusual dilemma. We are innately imbued with this disposition that gives everyone the potential to develop creative capacity to higher levels of complexity. Consciously applying the principles of creative development in educational practice can ensure this potential is realized. In this context, creative development is viewed as important to the fabric of mainstream education as more traditional developmental strands such as literacy and numeracy.

The increase in a person's creative capacity leads to an enhanced ability to collaboratively engage in increasingly more complex sustained creative practice requiring deeper and broader iterations of idea generation and prototyping. This is accompanied by more substantial demands of critical and analytical thinking to sort through alternatives against the backdrop of growing discipline complexity. Being able to sustain engagement in this creative dynamic over a considerable period of time is one of the benchmarks of creative maturity.

Sustained creative practice can be characterized as falling into three general categories that are closely interrelated: inventive, involving the creation of original work across the disciplines; innovative, involving the redesign or modification of an existing form, product or system usually associated with business and industry; and interpretive, involving redesign, modification, evolution, or interpretation of existing work or forms often associated with the arts (Kelly, 2012). Figure 1. illustrates the practical, theoretical basis for creative development that informs the foundation of the Creative Development in Educational Practice program for educators. The eight developmental strands that collectively constitute this construct are collaborative development, research/investigative development, self-instigative development, generative development, experimentational/prototyping development, critical thinking/analytical development, discipline complexity development and creative sustain development. These eight interwoven developmental strands form the basis for instructional design considerations for the Creative Development program as well

Figure 1. Creative Development (adapted from Kelly, 2012)

as the basis for assessing growth and development of creative capacity of participants in the program.

THE CREATIVE DEVELOPMENT STRANDS

Collaborative Development

Leadbeater (2008) contends that collaborative creativity is essential for contemporary creative practice. To understand collaborative development one must understand the difference between the concepts of collaboration, cooperation and compliance. Nelson (2008) describes the concept of collaboration as the connection and actions among a group of people who freely give and accept ideas by bringing depth, breadth and interest in the entire solution-finding process. This allows the group to communicate on multiple diverse levels. He sees collaboration as purposeful amplification of fellow group members and their ideas.

The concept of cooperation implies group members do jobs or tasks that are parts of a whole alongside each other without necessary interactive cohesiveness of idea exchange and support. In this context, there is reliance on the parts coming together to create the form that was the focus of the task. Compliance implies that all participants acquiesce to a predominant command and control structure for the completion of the task.

Creative environments require lots of stimuli and a culture where all ideas are validated and all involved are free to share ideas and to experiment. True collaborative environments enable this and are an essential foundational element to systematic creative development.

Self-Instigative Development

Self-instigative development involves the transition from extrinsic motivation to the development of the capacity to initiate an intrinsically motivated creative exploration that is intellectually and emotionally of personal meaning and relevance (Kelly, 2012). Participants have a higher potential to engage in sustained creative practice over time when intrinsically motivated (Pink, 2009).

Research/Investigative Development

Sustained creative practice requires constant sources of fuel. This requires research and a disposition of constant investigation where any stimuli or input is kept in play to fuel sustained creative practice.

Generative Development and Experimentational Development

The closely related strands of idea generation and experimentation are both generative practices. Vast quantities of ideas are essential in greasing the creative process

(Sweeney, 2004). Smith (1998) contends that idea generation is the indispensable core of creativity. As creativity involves making something new or novel (Piirto, 2004), creative practice involves going from thought to form through prototyping and experimentation. In sustained creative practice, there is a perpetual flow of idea generation and resultant prototyping as thoughts materialize into experimental forms through recurrent cycles of divergent and convergent thinking and production (Kelly, 2012; Kelly & Leggo, 2008; Kelly, 2005).

Discipline Complexity Development

Sustained creative practice and corresponding increases in creative capacity are built upon increased growth in understanding of relevant discipline complexities. Gaining more complex understandings of discipline areas is perhaps most meaningful to learners when in the creation of emotionally and intellectually relevant original work through engagement in creative practice.

Critical/Analytical Thinking Development

Critical/analytical thinking development involves developing the capacity to source and assess the constant stream of thought and form resolutions for a given problem for their potential to resolve the problem. Astute comparative analysis is essential for convergence on a solution or a short set of potential solutions in sustained creative practice.

Creative Sustain Development

Creative sustain development represents the capacity to embody the rigor and perseverance necessary to engage in recurrent iterations of idea generation and form experimentation over extended periods of time. The concept of creative sustain is problematical for many entering the field of creative practice who have largely been immersed in a culture characterized by the early closure of ideas and expedient solutions counter opposed to the breadth and depth of sustained practice.

Designing for Creative Development in Teacher Education

The conceptualization, design and implementation of the Creative Development in Educational Practice graduate program at the University of Calgary takes into consideration some of the fundamental tenets of longitudinal creative development. There has to be a space where each participant can engage in longer-term creative practice around a personal passion area in order to experience recurrent rounds of collaborative idea generation and prototyping.

The design of the Creative Development in Educational Practice program is centred on the notion of a cohesive, longitudinal developmental program superimposed over a four-course structure. The Creative Development in Educational Practice program is based on the following rationale (Kelly, 2012):

- Developing the creative capacity of an educator is optimally accomplished through long-term engagement in creative production that is emotionally and intellectually relevant to the participant.
- All educators and students at every level of education in every discipline should be creating original work. Original work in this context is described as new or novel, adaptive production relevant to the previous, personal production of each educator and learner (Starko, 2010).
- Creative development applies to all discipline areas.
- A positive, collaborative educational environment is essential in enabling creative development.
- Creative practice applies to interpretation and instructional design of mandated curriculum as well as the production of original work beyond curriculum content.
- Creative development is based on eight interwoven developmental strands: collaborative development, self-instigative development, research/ investigative development, generative development, prototyping/ experimentational development, discipline complexity development, critical/ analytical thinking development and creative sustain development.

Program Structure

The cornerstone of this four-course developmental program is the overarching Personal Creative Development Project that is launched out of course # 1 – *Creative Development: An Introduction* at the beginning of the program, landing in course # 4 – *Instructional Design and Assessment for Creative Development*, ten months later at the end of the program. This is the primary platform for longitudinal, first-hand research and engagement in creative practice. This ultimately leads to a growth in creative capacity while providing an intimate understanding of sustained creative practice that can be applied to teaching practice. Creative work is deliberately focused on personal themes outside of an individual's educational practice to enable a fresh lens on creative growth that is not impeded by biases or entrenched habits from a typical work routine (Kelly, 2012). Any field is fair game for these creative development projects. They range from writing plays or books of fiction, non-fiction or poetry to starting businesses to initiatives of social or entrepreneurial innovation. The first course in this program launches this project after establishing a trusting, collaborative environment fueled by contemporary creativity and creative development theory and vocabulary and small scale, collaborative, creative design challenges.

The second course, *Creativity in Communication*, expands collaborative and independent creative experience to the field of communication with a focus on creative writing. This also fuels the *Personal Creative Development Projects* of many participants who focus on creating original written work. Course 3, *Creative Development across the Disciplines*, expands understanding of creative development into the maths, sciences, humanities, arts, as well as economic and social innovation further fueling the *Personal Creative Development Projects* while providing teaching practice ideas in these areas. Course 4, the final course, *Instructional Design and Assessment of Creative Development*, sees the completion, presentation and research analysis of the *Personal Creative Development Projects*. This research is applied to the educational practice of each participant through the creation of instructional design strategies and tactics and assessment regimens to systematically enable longitudinal, creative development of all learners across disciplines.

Creative Development Program Prototyping Design Considerations, Strategies and Tactics

The growth and development of the Creative Development program over its first few years and into its present iterations embodied the very creative dynamic that the program was about in that it was a living, evolving prototype. This entails constant redesign and adjustments as new issues and problems arise as the program unfolds through a diverse range of participants over time. The following are some of these design considerations and responses that influenced the evolving design of the Creative Development program.

1. *Transitioning into a learning culture of open collaboration.*
   Sharing ideas and giving ideas does not come easily for many as traditional educational cultures are often characterized by a preoccupation with competition, privacy and ownership of ideas. This is counter-intuitive to a collaborative culture of creativity where participants are required to openly give and accept ideas in a positive, highly social environment. The transition into this way of doing brings considerable anxiety to participants until they get used to and learn to trust that it will eventually bear considerable creative fruit.
   The program design response to this is to create a status-less class environment (Sweeney, 2004). This involves creating a learning culture where all ideas are unconditionally accepted and added to in the spirit of Nelson's (2008) concept of plusing where all ideas are validated and added to. Once a positive, status-less culture is established, the collaborative idea generation and prototyping of ideas flourishes.
2. *Transitioning from Extrinsic Motivation to Intrinsic Motivation*
   Many who come into post-secondary educational environments often expect traditional assignment structures generated by the instructor involving research reading and reporting. This type of structure inherently relies on extrinsic motivation, as it is largely instructor-driven. Transitioning participants through self-instigative development into the initiation and execution of personally meaningful, intrinsically motivated long-term creative explorations is a considerable program

challenge. The program design response to this challenge is to invest considerable time in metaphorical self-inventories of discovery personal passion areas of participants. An accompanying response is to also work on giving participants permission to engage in these passion areas where they initially didn't perceive themselves as being able to create. This goes as far as enabling participants to give themselves permission to create where they had never imagined or been enabled before.

3. *Learning to Create a Pre-Inventive Structure to get Creative Practice Started*
A primary learning challenge for participants in the *Creative Development* program was learning how to create a pre-inventive structure that describes their creative intentions in a manner that enables them to move their work forward. A pre-inventive structure is basically a design brief that describes the goals and parameters of a potential creative exploration (Finke et al., 1992). A good pre-inventive structure allows enough room for exploration and play while providing enough structure and focus to prevent creative efforts from floundering from the paradox of choice. The character of the pre-inventive structure will vary from student to student, depending on the level of creative development of the individual (Kelly, 2012). The program design response to this is to walk educators through increasingly more complex, collaborative design challenges as a group to demonstrate how an effective pre-inventive structure is created before they move on to create their own.
4. *Managing Assessment Anxiety*
Assessment anxiety seems to be ever present in most classes. Many participants have a fear of comparison with others and a fear of the prospect of being measured by the instructor. This negative disposition is certainly not conducive to the development of a highly collaborative, creative culture in a status-less environment. If these fears are not dealt with from the onset, inventive momentum of any kind will be difficult. The primary program strategy to counter this is to move the conversation with the student away from discussion of grades to a dialogue about the creative work that they are engaged in. Specific tactics involve using cooperative-reflective assessment where specific, insightful developmental questions are co-developed with the student leading to a cooperative, highly dialogic assessment that focuses on the development of the student's work. Assessment in this context is nurturing and non-threatening and an integral part of the collaborative creative educational environment.
5. *Maintaining Inventive Momentum in the Virtual Space between Physical Class and Meeting Times*
Sustained creative practice requires lots of stimuli to maintain inventive momentum. This is the fuel that sustains creative practice when one is in an environment where there is a constant bombardment of new ideas. In an intense, social environment of scheduled class time this is easy to accomplish with class-based generative experiences and the invaluable casual conversations among participants that occur over lunch, coffee and other short time spaces between

scheduled course work. When the time spaces between physical meetings become weeks and months, a challenge arises of maintaining a high-stimuli, inventive environment in virtual space amongst group participants. The primary tactic in response to this challenge is to place everyone in a group discussion board in virtual space to constantly post all ideas and prototyping examples for plusing. This is a positive, open, constantly changing, generative environment. Another tactic is to conduct all interactions, student to student and instructor to student using vehicles such as Skype, where faces can be viewed to experience a deeper form of listening making it easier to maintain the social/ emotional connection amongst group members established during physical class meetings. Regardless, periodic physical meeting times are essential to reboot this process as the phenomenon of diminished returns presents itself in extended virtual time spaces.

CONCLUSION: CONTINUED PROTOTYPING AND EXPERIMENTATION

The Creative Development in Educational Practice graduate program continues to evolve through constant experimentation and prototyping. What emerged from past Creative Development program participants was a need for associated programming to continue the creative work and research that past cohort members had started. This has led to the design and development of a sister program entitled *Design Thinking for Educational Innovation*. Design thinking in this context is viewed as a derivative of classic creativity stage theory (Osborn, 1963). The programs are differentiated through each having a unique emphasis. The *Creative Development* program focuses on longitudinal engagement in creative practice and the increase of creative capacity of each participant. The *Design Thinking* program applies design thinking and design practice to diverse problem-solving contexts across the professional teaching spectrum relevant to each participant's educational practice. The *Design Thinking for Educational Innovation program* is a prototype…and yes, it will evolve into components that haven't been discovered yet. Engaging in creative practice in pursuit and discovery of outcomes unknown is always so exciting. It is of paramount importance that these programs live and embody what they are about.

REFERENCES

Alberta Education. (2010). *Inspiring education.* Edmonton: Alberta Education.

Ananiadou, K., & Claro, M. (2009). *21st century skills and competencies for new millenium learners in OECD countries* (OECD Education Working Papers No. 41). Paris: Organization of Economic Cooperation and Development, OECD Publishing.

Beghetto, R. A., & Kaufman, J. C. (Eds.). (2010). *Nurturing creativity in the classroom.* New York, NY: Cambridge University Press.

Bocchi, G., Cianci, E., Montuori, A., Trigona, R., & Nicolaus, O. (2014). Educating for creativity. *World Futures: The Journal of New Paradigm Research, 70*(5–6), 336–369.

Csikszentmihalyi, M. (1995). *Creativity.* New York, NY: Harper Collins.

Csikszentmihalyi, M. (1996). *Creativity: Flow and the psychology of discovery and invention.* New York, NY: Harper Collins.

Finke, R. A., Ward, T. B., & Smith, S. M. (1992). *Creative cognition: Theory, research and applications*. Cambridge: MIT Press.
Kaufman, J. C., & Sternberg, R. J. (Eds.). (2006). *International handbook of creativity*. New York, NY: Cambridge University Press.
Kaufman, J. C., & Sternberg, R. J. (Eds.). (2010). *The Cambridge handbook of creativity*. New York, NY: Cambridge University Press.
Kelley, T. (2013). *Creative confidence: Unleashing the creative potential within us all*. New York, NY: Crown Business.
Kelly, R. W. (2005). Idea generation: Fueling the creative process. *BCATA Journal for Art Teachers, 47*(2), 4–10.
Kelly, R. W. (2012). *Educating for creativity: A global conversation*. Edmonton: Brush Education.
Kelly, R. W., & Leggo, C. D. (Eds.). (2008). *Creative expression, creative education: Creativity as a primary rationale for education*. Calgary: Temeron Detselig.
Leadbeater, C. (2008). *We-think: The power of mass creativity*. London: Profile Books.
Lubart, T. I. (2000–2001). Models of creative process: Past, present and future. *Creativity Research Journal, 13*(3–4), 295–308.
Nelson, R. (2008). Learning and working in the collaborative age. *Edutopia* [Video]. Retrieved from http://youtu.be/QhXJe8ANws8
Osborn, A. (1953). *Applied imagination*. New York, NY: Charles Schribner.
Partnership for 21st Century Skills. (2009). *Learning for the 21st century, A report and mile guide for 21st century skill*. Washington, DC: United States Department of Education.
Piirto, J. (2004). *Understanding creativity*. Scottsdale, AZ: Great Potential Press.
Pink, D. H. (2005). *A whole new mind*. New York, NY: Riverhead Books.
Pink, D. H. (2009). *Drive: The surprising truth about what motivates us*. New York, NY: Riverhead Books.
Runco, M. A. (2007). *Creativity: Theories and themes: Research, development and practice*. San Diego, CA: Elsevier Academic Press.
Smith, G. (1998). Idea generation techniques: A formulary of active ingredients. *Journal of Creative Behaviour, 32*(2), 107–133.
Starko, A. J. (2010). *Creativity in the classroom* (4th ed.). New York, NY: Routledge.
Sternberg, R. J. (Ed.). (1999). *Handbook of creativity*. New York, NY: Cambridge University Press.
Sweeney, J. (2004). *Innovation at the speed of laughter*. Minneapolis, MN: Aerialist Press.

Robert Kelly
University of Calgary

JIM CUMMINS, BURCU YAMAN NTELIOGLOU,
GAIL PRASAD AND SASKIA STILLE

6. IDENTITY TEXT PROJECTS

Generating Academic Power in Multilingual Classrooms

INTRODUCTION

The premise of this paper is that students will engage actively with literacy only to the extent that such engagement is identity-affirming. In this regard, creative writing and other forms of cultural production assume particular importance as *expressions* of identity, *projections* of identity into new social spheres, and *re-creation* of identity as a result of feedback from and dialogue with multiple audiences. This re-creation of identity through the production of what we have termed *identity texts* (Cummins & Early, 2011) assumes particular importance in the case of students from social groups whose languages, cultures, religions, and institutions have been devalued, often for generations, in the wider society. Students invest their identities in the creation of these texts which can be written, spoken, signed, visual, musical, dramatic, or combinations in multimodal forms. The identity text then holds a mirror up to students in which their identities are reflected back in a positive light. When bilingual students from marginalized social backgrounds write in both their home language (L1) and the school language (L2), the identity text validates their bilingualism as a personal and academic asset and challenges the widespread societal prejudice that devalues their linguistic talents.

Similarly, when students share identity texts with multiple audiences (peers, teachers, parents, grandparents, Internet-connected partner classes, the media, etc.) they are likely to receive positive feedback and affirmation of self in interaction with these audiences. Although not always an essential component, technology acts as an amplifier to enhance the process of identity text production and dissemination.

The power of identity text production to transform identities has been demonstrated in several projects conducted during the past decade. We sketch four examples to illustrate the process and outcomes of identity text projects.

Dual-language book creation by newcomer students. The New Country (Figure 1) is a 20-page English/Urdu book written and web-published by three the Grade 7 Pakistani-origin students in the Greater Toronto Area. Kanta and Sulmana had been in Canada since Grade 4 but Madiha had only recently arrived and her knowledge of English was minimal. Reflections on the process of writing the story by Kanta and Madiha illustrate the profound impact that identity text creation can

J. B. Cummings & M. L. Blatherwick (Eds.), Creative Dimensions of Teaching and Learning in the 21st Century, 69–76.

Figure 1. The new country
(http://www.multiliteracies.ca/index.php/folio/viewGalleryBook/8/42/0)

have on students' sense-of-self and academic self-confidence (Cummins & Early, 2011).

> *Kanta:* My first language is Punjabi, my second language is Urdu, and my third language is English. Madiha had come just about a month before Ms. Leoni told us to do the story so we were just talking about the difficulties she faced and the difficulties we had faced since we were immigrants also. Then we started talking about why not write about the differences between one country and the other, about all our differences, what was going through me when I came here, what Sulmana saw when she came here and how it was for Madiha, so that's how we came up with the idea to write the story about our three experiences.
>
> How it helped me was when I came here in Grade 4 the teachers didn't know what I was capable of. I was given a pack of crayons and a coloring

book and told to get on coloring with it. And after I felt so bad about that – I'm capable of doing much more than just that. I have my own inner skills to show the world than just coloring and I felt that those skills of mine are important also. So when we started writing the book [The New Country], I could actually show the world that I am something instead of just coloring. And that's how it helped me and it made me so proud of myself that I am actually capable of doing something, and here today [at the 2005 Ontario TESL conference] I *am* actually doing something. I'm not just a coloring person – I can show you that I am something.

Madiha. I am proud of The New Country because it is our story. Nobody else has written that story. And when we showed it to Ms. Leoni she said it was really good. She said, "It's about your home country, and family, and Canada, it's all attached, that's so good." I like that because it means she cares about our family and our country, not just Canada. Because she cares about us, that makes us want to do more work. My parents were really happy to see that I was writing in both Urdu and English; my mother was happy because she knows that not everyone has that chance.

Digital technology as a cognitive and affective amplifier. Our second example derives from a collaborative project involving school-based educators/researchers (Jennifer Fannin and Mike Montanera) and university-based educators/researchers (Burcu Yaman Ntelioglou and Jim Cummins) (Ntelioglou, Fannin, Montanera, & Cummins, 2014). The participating school was an inner-city elementary school with large numbers of English language learners (ELLs) in the Greater Toronto Area. The student body included a recent wave of Roma students and some of these students were experiencing significant language, literacy and social challenges. Students in two Grade 2–3 mixed classes were introduced to several forms of digital technologies and multilingual pedagogies to create instructional approaches that would support students' academic engagement in general, and literacy engagement in particular. We wanted to connect learning with students' funds of knowledge and create opportunities for them to invest their plurilingual identities into creating academically relevant literacy artifacts.

Lala [pseudonym, shown in Figure 2] was a Roma student who spoke very little English. One of the sub-projects in which she participated involved VOKI, an application that allows students to create an avatar that incorporates various attributes that they themselves choose (e.g., appearance, language, accent, etc.). The focus of this sub-project was to explore the extent to which this kind of technological support might encourage all students, including the recently arrived Roma students who were early-stage English language learners and reluctant readers, to engage with literacy. The significance of this kind of technologically supported identity text creation was that students could represent aspects of their current identities and also project aspects of their imagined identities in their new country into the avatars they created. They were encouraged to use their home languages as well as English as

Figure 2. "Lala" engaged in creating avatars using VOKI (Photo taken by Burcu Yaman Ntelioglou)

they created their avatars and decided on the information their avatars were going to share in the digital space. Students reacted enthusiastically and used both their home languages and English to talk and write about their avatars.

Students as co-researchers of their own plurilingualism. The series of studies summarized in this section is based on both the identity text construct and the Council of Europe's elaboration of the construct of *plurilingualism* to refer to the dynamically integrated and intersecting nature of bilingual and plurilingual individuals' linguistic repertoires, which include unevenly developed competencies in a variety of languages, dialects, and registers (Coste, Moore, & Zarate, 2009). The research examined the implications for classroom practice of moving away from the predominant monolingual instructional paradigm towards a plurilingual paradigm that would encourage all students to draw on and expand their plurilingual and pluricultural communicative repertoires (Prasad, 2013).

During the four to six month intervention in each of the five participating schools located in both Canada and France, students documented their plurilingual and pluricultural experiences: they took digital photos of their literacy practices at school and at home and classified them by theme to analyze the linguistic landscape around them and to reflect collaboratively on the implicit and explicit language policies operating in different spaces. Using a variety of modalities such as reflective drawing, plurilingual writing and collage, students represented their plurilingualism by creating a range of individual and collective identity texts. For example, during the plurilingual multimodal book-making, students from different language backgrounds were purposely grouped together, in order to help them make connections between different languages, as well as the language(s) of instruction in the school.

Thus, in the multimodal book published by students in Montpellier, each student wrote a brief physical self-description in French, English (a foreign language), Occitan (a regional language) and their home languages (Figure 3). At the end of the process, the teacher and students began to recognize similarities and differences among all the languages that were included in the book.

As a follow-up, because students had all included their age in each language, we decided to create a table of numbers from 1 to 10 in all the languages represented in the project (Figure 4). This enabled all students to benefit from the cultural and linguistic resources that were part of their classroom community. Students' metalinguistic awareness deepened as they compared their personal home languages to the languages of instruction at school and the collective languages of their peers. They expressed pride in their home languages and cultural practices and became curious about the linguistic diversity in their classroom. Students in the four Toronto-based case studies informally made similar observations of similarities and differences across languages based on their plurilingual books. Examples of the various creative multimodal plurilingual activities carried out through this exploratory inquiry can be viewed on the project website: www.iamplurilingual.com

Digital film: Room 217 makes a school garden. Documentary filmmaking has a long tradition of bringing light to hidden stories. These films harness the power of visual communication to help audiences see and think differently about the experiences of others, often raising critical social questions. Drawing on these

Figure 3. Example of a multilingual self-portrait from students in Montpellier

	1	2	3	4	5
français	un	deux	trois	quatre	cinq
occitan	un	dos	tres	quatre	cinc
anglais	one	two	three	four	five
espagnol	uno	dos	tres	quarto	cinco
italien	uno	due	tre	quarto	cinque
turc	bir	iki	uç	dört	bez
albanais	një	dy	tre	katër	pesë
arabe	١	٢	٣	٤	٥
	waahid	eeth-nayn	thalaatha	arba'a	khamsa

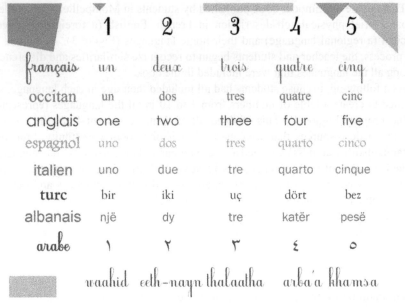

Figure 4. Extract from table comparing numbers in different languages

potentials of documentary film to facilitate students' expression, projection, and re-creation of identity, the project described here brought filmmaking to a multilingual, multicultural third-grade class in an urban school (Stille, 2013).

As part of the social studies curriculum, the children in the class were learning about urban and rural communities. The students summarized characteristics of their own school community and they identified (lack of) access to nature as an important issue. Many of the students' families had a great deal of experience in farming and agriculture in their countries of origin. Students described growing dates and pomegranates, taking care of chickens, and sifting rice by hand with their mother. However, they had few opportunities to draw upon their knowledge and experience of farming and agriculture in their new Canadian home.

To address the disjuncture between students' experiences in these different contexts, the classroom teacher, I (Saskia Stille), and the students decided to create a school garden, and to document and share the experience of doing this work by means of a digital film, called *Room 217 Makes a School Garden*. The setting for the garden was one of several courtyards at the school. The students documented the creation of the garden using digital film and photography, and we used iMovie software to produce the digital film from this footage as illustrated in the Figure below.

The students were involved in every stage of creating the film: they decided what events to record, they held the camera, and conducted interviews with one another. They also chose which footage of themselves to include in the film, selecting clips and adding voiceover narration of the scenes if they wished. Finally, the teacher and I assembled these clips into the final product, constructing a narrative to run through the film and connect the clips into a whole.

A core theme running through the film was the children's perception that they were making a difference in the world through their work. For instance, one student commented: "We are making a garden because we want to make the world a better place." As they shared the film with other students, teachers, and administrators at the school, the students harnessed the potential of digital film to tell their story, to make visible their unique identities, and to connect school curriculum with the realities of their migration experience.

Curriculum Significance

The significance of this kind of identity text project in diverse societies characterized by differential status accorded to languages, cultures, religions, and identities is that it creates a space within which the devaluation of community identity in the wider society can be actively challenged in the interactions between teachers and students. Numerous research studies demonstrate that societal power relations exert a highly significant influence on the academic engagement and achievement of marginalized group students (Canadian First Nations represent an obvious example). The implication is that reversal of this process demands instruction that affirms students' and communities' identities, thereby challenging the operation of coercive relations of power. Although most of the students in the projects we have described have not experienced the degree of marginalization of First Nations communities, their languages and cultures have typically not been reinforced positively within the school context. Identity text work that legitimates students' languages and cultures

Figure 5. Screen shot from iMovie software used to create digital film

represents a powerful instructional strategy for teachers and students to engage with broader societal power relations by simultaneously fostering literacy engagement and identity affirmation.

REFERENCES

Coste, D., Moore, D., & Zarate, G. (2009). *Plurilingual and pluricultural competence. Studies towards a common European framework of reference for language learning and teaching.* Strasbourg, France: Council of Europe Publishing.

Cummins, J., & Early, M. (2011). *Identity texts: The collaborative creation of power in multilingual schools.* Stoke-on-Trent, England: Trentham Books.

Ntelioglou, B. Y., Fannin, J., Montanera, M., & Cummins, J. (2014). A multilingual and multimodal approach to literacy teaching and learning in urban education: A collaborative inquiry project in an inner city elementary school. *Frontiers in Psychology, 5*, 1–10.

Prasad, G. (2013). Plurilingual children as co-ethnographers of their own language and literacy practices: An exploratory case study. *Language & Literacy: An e-journal, 15*(3), 4–30.

Stille, S. (2013). Making an edible school garden with multilingual children: Engaging linguistic, cultural, and community resources. In S. V. Chappell & C. J. Faltis (Eds.), *The arts and emergent bilingual youth: Building critical, creative programs in school and community contexts* (pp. 52–59). New York, NY: Taylor and Francis.

Jim Cummins
University of Toronto

Burcu Yaman Ntelioglou
Brandon University

Gail Prasad
University of Wisconsin-Madison

Saskia Stille
York University

SAMUEL LEBLANC

7. THE ART OF CULTIVATING CLEVER QUESTIONS TO EMPOWER STUDENTS, IMPROVE TEACHING, AND OPEN UP THE CURRICULUM

INTRODUCTION

Legions of students have been taught by this maxim: "There are no stupid questions." Yet in requiring students to write down questions built on course content, we see that some questions are indeed better than others. Such a call to student imagination, innovation, and reflection opens up the curriculum, revives educators, and aligns perfectly with critical thinking, as well as democratic education. In what I propose here there is a strong reversal of roles between the teacher and the student in order to open up the curriculum, foster dialogue, and generate authentic learning.

The practice of requiring students to ask carefully crafted questions is described here along five axes. First, I discuss the origin of the practice, the logic behind it, and sketch its pedagogical uses. Second, I present the instructions associated with the practice, as I do in my classes. Third, I go through a description of the implementation of the practice. Fourth, problems and shortcomings of the practice are addressed. Finally, I contextualize the practice in curriculum theory to show its empowering and virtuous qualities. As such, this chapter reflects a decade-long discussion with my students, who have generated over 7,000 questions, all of which I have answered with the pleasure of pushing them to inquire and explore content beyond the usual boundaries.

What Is It about Asking Questions?

Asking questions is by no means original, and by promoting this activity, I am by no means unique. At the birth of Western philosophy, Socrates was already on his merry – if pestering – way towards asking intelligent questions in Athens. Rarely content with what he was told, he prodded, quizzed, charmed, enlightened, and annoyed fellow citizens. Questions, always more questions, that is, until that fateful day in 399 BCE, when his questioning would be forcefully silenced.[1] What *is it* about asking questions?

Jump to 1999, at McGill University. As an undergraduate student in philosophy, Professor Marguerite Deslauriers introduced us to her formal requirement of asking

J. B. Cummings & M. L. Blatherwick (Eds.), Creative Dimensions of Teaching and Learning in the 21st Century, 77–89.

intelligent questions in an advanced feminist theory class. The task, in outline, was fairly simple: read up to 100 pages of assigned philosophical texts for the up and coming Monday, and have half a page, single-spaced questions prepared for the class. There were 10 questions in all. Forego the assignment once; fail the class. Throughout the term, Sunday afternoons were spent rereading, thinking, drafting, struggling, and questioning. Occasionally, philosophical despair crept in; Socrates' fate did not seem so bad after all. Yet I, like the others, survived. But more than that, I became an avid questioner, and a proponent of this method – in and outside of university. What follows is thus both a defence of the merits of this approach to learning, and a tribute to Professor Deslauriers.

Now, a common challenge of teaching is convincing students to read the assigned material prior to attending class (or sometimes reading at all). As most educators will recognize, the exercise of reading the prescribed material provides an important first contact with the content, so as be able to hit the ground running when class starts. The common, albeit not only, strategy to encourage reading is to have students to summarize articles or chapters. Beyond reading, it does fulfill some pedagogical functions like learning to paraphrase or grasping the essential elements of the text. Yet it can also become repetitive, and exasperating for students and educators (especially in large groups). So why not look elsewhere?

The practice of requiring students to ask questions based on course content is a transparent strategy to entice them to read. Reading does not, however, suffice. In order to ask a proper question, as it is shown in the next section, the student must engage with the material. To make it clear at the outset that this practice is not superficial, I tell my students that, contrary to the enthusiastic credo that there are no dumb questions, some are better than others, and whisper that *there are actually some dumb questions*. Of course, this is no secret. There are some inconsiderate and vile questions, such that asking *good* questions demands work, thinking, and reading.

Pedagogically, when I state this to my students, I couch it so as not to offend the shyer ones, or those with little self-esteem. To this end, I give example of my thoughtless questions, such as "When will the *live* broadcast be aired?" ("Now") or "When will the sunset scene be filmed?" ("At sunset," replied my boss). Then, I provide some quick, context-specific questions to highlight that they need not be sophisticated in order to be clever. So, for example, upon hearing professors and dignitaries at the London School of Economics flaunt their knowledge, just after the world economic collapse of 2008, Queen Elizabeth II asked: "Why did nobody notice it?" (Pierce, 2008). Context and clarity go a long way. Then, I ask students to think of their idol, and what question would they put to them. This gets them probing. Surely, if it's President Obama or Canadian astronaut Chris Hatfield, it would not be an off the cuff, "Is it difficult to do your job?" Or if it were the young education activist Malala Yousafzai, asking, "Do the Taliban hate you?" would be of limited interest. Of course they are difficult jobs, very few make it so far; of course it does, the group tried to assassinate her. If that does not engage them, I invite them to imagine what would be the last question that they would put to their father or mother.

The first point that needs to be made is that intelligent questions require some background. For the present topic, background knowledge is provided by the content of the curriculum. In a science class, asking an intelligent question to Hatfield requires that one knows, for example, that he was the first Canadian to manage the International Space Station. Here, the student, much like a reporter, can go in different directions. She can field political, ethical, or technological questions. The student thus controls content – for a period of time – and tries to push the boundaries of everyone's knowledge.

The second point touches on the reflective component of asking intelligent questions. Requiring students to take time to think about their question invites them to imagine possible answers. This encourages attentive reading, and critical thinking. Quite often, when asking students how they dealt with the exercise, they talk of the frustration of finding their questions too easy to answer. The personal exploration invites students to better understand the matter at hand, locate unexplored themes, and find out where confusions may emerge or the role of a given concept. When personal exploration is not enough, many of my students have reported using their roommates, partners, parents, or friends as sounding boards. Occasionally, after chatting with students, or upon meeting new students, and even parents, I have been told stories of dinner time or weekend outings that were stimulated by the questions my students were trying to work out.

Finally, if Socrates and Deslauriers have taught us one thing, it is the fecundity of asking questions. For my purposes, the challenge is to build on the students' natural tendency to question, and have them deliberately ask intelligent questions that belong to them, as well as potentially radiate beyond the classroom. So how does one harness this skill that is common, rewarding, difficult, social, and risky?

How to Ask a Good Question?

Over the past decade, my instructions have evolved from just requiring students to write a question based on the forthcoming readings, to the detailed explanations below. Because I have often taught to large groups (up to 80 students), and a variety of courses (in philosophy, economics, and political sciences), these instructions are conceived to be applicable to various contents, without sacrificing the spirit of asking quality questions.

How to Ask a Question?

For this course, students must submit original written questions. These questions draw on the readings given by the date on the course calendar. They are to be delivered prior to 11:00 PM, on the evening before the course material will be formally covered.

- The question must be submitted via the course online support platform (D2L, Clic, Blackboard, etc.) under penalty of having a grade of 0% otherwise.
- The question must be submitted using the Word template provided for this class.
- The topics correspond with the readings given on the course calendar date.
- There will be 10 questions to do, each worth 2.5% of the final grade.
- Any form of plagiarism will be reprimanded according to university policy.

One week after the questions have been handed in, a student will be chosen to briefly present his or her question and outline a response (verbally).

General example of the assignment:
In the *Theaetetus*, Plato recounts an anecdote about Thales. We learn that Thales: "was struggling to know what is happening in the sky, and he paid no attention to what was in front of him and his feet" (Plato, *Theaetetus*, p. 183). Plato adds that someone laughed at the lofty philosopher, so that distinction is being made between theoretical and practical knowledge. If this distinction is valid, how does one determine what is worth knowing?

Elements sought to assess the question:
- Understanding of the passage quoted (noting that the issue is not settled elsewhere in the text given to read).
- The question attempts to clarify thinking, or show a contradiction, or sends us towards new thinking avenues.
- The question is well stated, in clear language.
- The question is accurate, does not take the form of, "What do you think about…"

Learning objectives:
- Develop an ability to compose clear, concise, and specific questions.
- Become comfortable with the quotation-writing format.
- Explore the implications, assumptions, and gaps of an argument or conclusion.
- Validate the complete reading of the text.
- Invite students to reveal his or her philosophical concerns.
- Develop a philosophical language, and critical thinking with regard to the theory.

I answer and comment on every question submitted, touching along the way conceptual and grammatical issues. Anonymized student questions will be made available to all, via the online platform in a PDF document, as a testimony of the vast possibilities, styles, and explorations attached to each reading.

In the same way that educators are trained to give life to a course curriculum, I now turn to the implementation of this practice. As we shall see, some initial guidance is required, since what appears like a straightforward exercise to the educator can be quite destabilizing for the students. Asking questions often leads to more questions.

Grading, Commenting, and Class Dynamics

Throughout the years, the worth of each question has varied between 1 and 4%, and the number of questions between 5 and 10. The challenge has been to strike the right balance to incite students to feel free to explore, be daring, and imaginative, without falling into fanciful or flippant questions. Thus, 1% did not prove enough to generate the seriousness sought for the exercise in general, while more than 3% curtailed their imagination and fostered overly conservative questions.

Once the motivational elements are set in place, a schedule is developed. This is justified by the pedagogical importance of keeping up with the readings, as well as the general value associated with learning to plan ahead, and organize one's workload. Some diligent students read a couple of chapters at once, and submit their questions a few days ahead of time, while most wait towards the end of the allotted time. To those that tend to wait, I warn them that the quality of the work generally suffers. Moreover, if they undergo a surprising computer glitch or are disturbed otherwise, I recall that they had more than one week to complete the assignment. The relatively small penalty of not submitting a question on time is thus, and also, an occasion to teach the importance of preparedness, as well as cultivating prudence with regards to the contingencies of life.

The means by which questions are submitted have also evolved over time. At first, pen and paper sufficed to deliver the assignment on class day. Now, a carefully crafted Word computer template provides the desired unity, clarity, and flexibility that is especially necessary for large groups. The template simply consists of having to fill in the name, the topic, the relevant pages, and the question number. While this may seem pedantic, I always have a few students who read the wrong chapter, and are thus not adequately prepared for the up and coming class. Furthermore, some chapters are more suited to the assignment than others, and are chosen in consequence.

Once students understand this, and have done the readings, they are well prepared to embark on this intellectual adventure. This is usually quite destabilizing at the outset. Some students quote an overly long excerpt, allowing little place for their question; others report always finding an answer to their question; some simply feel that their questions are not up to par; and others cannot stop writing. At one end of the spectrum, I instruct students that a one-line question is generally insufficient. This habit of some students is dealt with by requiring a quote from the text. Then, I further explain to them that the excerpt needs to be paraphrased, much in the same way that a quote is used in an essay, or explicitly linked to the final question. At the other end of the spectrum, the template tempers inspired students to focus on quality, rather than quantity. From questions that were one-liners, to those that reached a full single-spaced page, I settled on a limit of 500 characters (roughly 90 words).

The main attractiveness of the word limit is to compel students to think about their words and sentences. For, once a certain degree of proficiency in the course content and question asking was reached, many did become quite verbose and wrote exceedingly. While this is laudable in some contexts, it does not fulfill the pedagogical aim of asking quality questions; rather, it reinforces the tendency to ramble on, generate confusion, and become a commentary instead of a question. Now, with the 500-character limit, filler is cut to a minimum, words are – hopefully – chosen for their specific meaning, and sentence structure has to be as clear as possible. I also explain to my students that this ability is transferable to the term essay required for my class (or any other), where clear and concise writing is praised. Finally, the length is not too daunting, such that the exploratory nature of the assignment is kept alive.

So, apart from my example, what does the assignment look like? I have chosen a question taken from one of my third-year philosophy class in epistemology (the field associated with analysing the nature, limit, and content of knowledge). We had an excerpt of Wittgenstein's *On Certainty* (1998) to analyse, and this was a student's question:

In the text, *On Certainty*, Wittgenstein shows that knowledge depends upon the circumstances, and that these circumstances change without people "knowing." He says: "One may be wrong even about 'there being a hand here'. Only in particular circumstances is it impossible. "Even in a calculation one can be wrong – only in certain circumstances one can't" (p. 6). Does this importance of context necessarily lead to relativism? And, if our knowledge depends on the context, how can we find universal truths?[2]

I'll invite the reader to assess the quality of this question, or questions to be precise, with the guidelines provided in my instructions. In doing this mental exercise, it is important to keep in mind that the material has not yet been covered in class, so grading the question needs to reflect possible specific misunderstandings for which the student should not be faulted. Blatantly false or hastily construed understandings, however, should be discouraged. On the whole, the question above is a good specimen.

My numerical grading is always accompanied by a worded answer to the question, which is usually of the same length as the question. This is admittedly a time-consuming task, but it has numerous benefits. First, it allows me to develop individual relationships with students, something that attenuates the anonymity of large groups. Second, I can correct language use, quotation formatting, and best of all misunderstandings. Third, I often reply with another question, in order to invite students to dig deeper into the matter, as a qualitative testimony of the value of their work.

Up to now, mainly the student and I share the fruits of the labour of the assignment. The next step involves selecting a question to have it read aloud in class. This is usually a factor of stress for students, and understandably so, especially when it is a single voice in a class of 80. However, because public speaking is so critical, and particularly when one has a probing question to ask, I insist upon this oral practice, which is done in the safe setting of our classroom. Also, I supply a paper copy of the question to the student, and simply ask that she read – seated at her place – in a clear, loud, and composed voice so that everyone can hear. Results vary according to many factors. Shyness, pride, stress, humility, uncertainty, arrogance, humour have all appeared at one moment or another during these mini performances. I do not hesitate to ask students to reread their question if its content was not communicated properly.

In general, my choice of the question depends on its propensity for discussion, whether it has coincided with similar interrogations by other students, or if it captures a theme that was difficult to understand and that we should review. I also pay attention to who is in my class. White male students tend to be more vocal, such that I vary my choices to ensure that women, and international students also be heard. This is also transparently inclusive, and curtails some problems in curriculum conception (an issue to which I return in the final section).

While having administered this exercise over 10 years, and amassed numerous stories, I will simply share one that I tell my students to illustrate the transformative nature of the exercise, and to embrace the challenge. A few years ago, in my third-year History of Economics class, I had a particularly shy student who was performing very well in a group of 30. This, obviously, also showed itself in the questions assignment. Aware of her timid nature, I asked her if it was all right that I chose her to read her question in the next class. It was not an issue of improving upon the quality of her written work, but rather getting her to voice her intelligence. Without protest, she discreetly nodded an OK. When the next class came, she was mentally prepared, yet anxious, as I handed her the question to read aloud. In conjuring up the courage to loosen up her vocal chords, we could hear the slight sound of the ruffling sheet of paper in her trembling hands. A few seconds later, once she started to voice her words, the timidity subsided. This led to a thought provoking discussion. After that she became a vocal – *very* vocal as I like to amusingly remind my student – participant in our class, to everyone's benefit for the rest of the semester.

If this student's progress captures the ongoing nature of the class, my requirement of having students ask questions stresses upon the process of learning. Since the weeklong delay between receiving the questions, grading them, and covering the material, it is useful to see the questions as a means to review the material. Depending on the class's reaction to the question, I take from 10 to 15 minutes to explore and debate the matter with them, while writing their responses on the board. This reinforces the need for quality questions because the better they are, the more the class benefits. Students can thus take partial ownership of the value of their learning, tweak the direction of the curriculum content, and confront their ideas.

The semi-public and collective nature of the exercise still leaves open the possibility of exploiting at an even greater level the potential of the questions submitted. For, beyond my one-to-one interactions with each student, and the collective exploration of *a* question, there are still numerous questions that remain in the shadows. In time, through reflection, and having asked feedback from my students, I decided that I would start sharing the questions in a common document. Using the questions supplied in template form (which assures uniformity of format),

I quickly create a document for each series of questions (so 10 documents for the term), where the names of the students are removed. This document, made accessible to all, has numerous benefits. First, it shares the thoughts, knowledge, concerns, and proficiency of fellow classmates. Second, because of its open-ended nature, those that consult it obtain a broader picture of what we are learning. Third, it sets a standard with which students can discretely compare themselves, and modify their approach accordingly. Fourth, the questions themselves can inspire students, as it has, to choose to answer a particular question for their term essay. Finally, I use this to drive the point home concerning the impact of plagiarism, since the submission of a question based on plagiarised content (which has happened) has broader ramifications, because it is being shared with every student. It can create falsely high standards to which some students may aspire.

In closing this section, I will note that one of the amendments to this practice that I have been entertaining concerns sharing the questions at another level. Inspired by the work of Venkantesh (2012), who studies the dynamics of online communities, and incorporates some of these practices in his masters-level classes, he makes sharing and transparency very appealing pedagogical strategies. In these terms, Venkatesh renders available, under certain circumstances, both the essays of past students (who have accepted his request), as well as his grading of the assignments. Accused of giving away the answer, Venkatesh replies that he also evolves with his grading practice, such that his students cannot be content with replicating a previously submitted work (with which Venkatesh is obviously acquainted). In my context, this would entail providing students with the previous cohorts' work, and my comments. On the positive side, this would provide students with a rich heritage of past questions, and comments with regards to their course. On the negative side, it could stifle some reflection and exploration. The value of arriving at a question that is one's own is not only reflected in the final written assignment, but also in the thought process associated with getting there. By offering previously submitted questions, the students would lose the occasions to possibly end up with a similar – and valid – question to one that was previously submitted. Furthermore, it could make the assignment too daunting. Students would not only be confronted with their own internal questions, but the multitude of those submitted by others before them. Finally, I would need to suppose that most, or all have read the previous questions in order to properly assess their degree of background knowledge in this context.

This section has illustrated many nuances, complexities, benefits, and possibilities derived from implementing this practice. From the introduction of the practice to its completion by students, having students craft quality questions in a class setting is a higher order process. While setting the stage is time consuming, it paves the way for greater student engagement, the development of good scheduling habits, and the production of questions that deepen the value of the curriculum's content. So if everything is so clear, what could possibly go wrong?

"So, When Will You Send Us the Question?"

Given all the precautions and supplementary explanations that I provide with regards to this practice, it may surprise some to find out that the process is not without its hiccups. Here, I present the six most pressing challenges.

The first problem is attitudinal. The greatest hindrance to the installation of the practice is lack of attention in a "culture of distraction" (Jackson, 2008, p. 17). Between cell phones and indifference, there are enough details that can slip through to warrant a re-explanation of the whole assignment. It is not uncommon, especially in large groups to have students ask, "So, when will you send us the question?" Besides not having listened in class, this type of question also echoes the unfamiliarity of the request. For the most part, students are drilled from their tender age in primary school to become question-answering-machines. To be able to answer many questions is a sign of authority, of expertise. Yet, asking intelligent questions can also be a sign of authority, or expertise, which is usually the task of the educator. So this invitation to question should not surprisingly lead to some confusion.

The second problem is technological. Earlier on, this was not an issue when pen and paper, or printed assignments were accepted for the assignment. And yet, that had its series of challenges too. While pen and paper questions were delivered late (for whatever reason), printed assignments would occasionally fall prey to printer breakdown or ink depletion. The electronic method is more congenial for submitting the assignment, and allows me to create the collective documents with all the questions. It is also environmentally friendly. Think of my 80 students in a class with 10 questions each; in other words, that amounts to 800 pages of eventual paper waste per semester. Nevertheless, electronic submissions can face problems of computer or template compatibility. These kinks should be dealt with at the beginning of the term, by setting up a troubleshooting task to ensure that everyone can technically do the assignment.

The third problem is psychological. Some students dread being called upon, even to the point of not submitting any question. For clinical reasons or otherwise, I have had students approach me to deal with this issue. Judging whether a student can be excused from the public part of the practice is made on a case-by-case basis. However, the value of the common discussion, and their potential contribution to it should not be discounted. Simply reading a question can lead toward dominating one's fear of public speaking.

The fourth problem is mathematical. These questions may represent up to 25% of the final grade. It has happened that some students had decided that the work was just not significant enough. Then, when the grades came in after the final exam, negotiations began. At one end of the spectrum, it can seem cruel to point out that a student's failure is the result of not having handed in a few questions because he couldn't be bothered. At the other end, some students want to have their grade rounded up; but here again, a few questions were not submitted. In both cases, students ask if they can resubmit. To this, I answer that equity would require that I offer the same opportunity to every student, which I cannot do. The value of doing each question must be stressed.

The fifth problem is ethical. As in many classes, plagiarism is a fact of today's teaching burden (Hersey, 2013; Pecorari, 2013). Despite explanations, encouragements to the contrary, and warnings, questions submitted with plagiarised content have crept into these assignments. The most subtly crafted process belonged to a student who groomed me into thinking that his writing was getting better with each question, while in reality, he was slowly introducing copied content into his assignment. Diligence is required.

The sixth, and last problem is dispositional. In the same manner that plagiarism is an attempt to shirk work, some students will try and get away with reading only a page or two of the required readings. Knowing what is being taught, and having the content fresh in the educator's mind deals fairly well with this problem. If a student asks a question, and there is an air of familiarity because the author has answered it elsewhere in the assigned reading, the task is to find that sentence. Once located, I simply quote it, and penalize accordingly for lack of effort, diligence, or attentiveness.

So if these problems exist, why bother using the practice? The answer lies in part in the next section, where the theory backs the practice. I will point out, however, that that question is only of value, because the chapter has been read so far.

The Education, Politics, and Philosophy behind the Need to Question

This section secures a place for the cultivation of quality question asking to guard against the aberrant uses of the curriculum, and foster authentic learning. The first part draws attention to the main critiques of curriculum use and the importance of critical thinking. The second part argues for educator and student engagement in the spirit of intellectual, democratic, and virtuous learning.

From Rousseau (1961) to Noddings (1983, 2003), including Dewey (1929), Freire (1970), and Jackson, P. W. (2005), many thinkers have, and continue to voice concerns surrounding the uses and abuses of curricula. As a conduit of knowledge, Carr (2009) aptly captures the impact of the uncritical reception of the curriculum when he says:

> in the light of feminist and other critical theory, it is now evident that traditional academic curricula have fostered, whether by accident or design, a range of prejudices of race, class, gender, sexuality—often in the name of "objective" truth—in school subjects as diverse as history, science, literature, art and religious education. (p. 286)

This is a result, amongst other things, of a top down approach to knowledge sanctioning and delivery, as well as its acceptance by many unquestioning (Apple, 1979, p. 14) administrators, educators and students.

Now, the contemporary push for educating for critical thinking has certainly helped many to avoid passive submission to the curriculum. Key thinkers like Siegel (1989) argue forcefully for the development of critically thinking students at large, because "Critical thinking [...] speaks to virtually all of our educational endeavors. It provides both important goals for our educational efforts and direction for the achievement of those goals" (pp. 27–28). This approach tries to give back some power and control to students over what they are taught. In relation to Carr's (2009) assessment, critical thinking goes a long way towards building a renewed connection between the student and what s/he is being taught. For, according to Siegel (1989), "education aimed at the promulgation of critical thinking is nothing less than education aimed at the fostering of rationality and the development of rational persons" (p. 21) and *rational persons do ask questions*.

Those that fear questions tend to want to hide something. Question asking is deeply political, potentially disruptive, and decidedly personal. In relation to the curriculum that embodies educational and societal goals, the introduction of mandatory question asking can be seen as heretical and confrontational. To a certain extent, it is. The fact that curriculum content will come under the intelligent and probing minds of students can create an air of mistrust. However, in the spirit of transparency, rigour, and love of learning, questioning should not be feared, but embraced.

The second part of this section calls attention to impacts of this willful embracement of an open, and thoughtful dialogue surrounding curriculum content. On one side, by explicitly valuing students' questions through this type of assignment, educators further demonstrate their desire for student flourishing. The assignment creates an intellectual and emotional space for students to explore, imagine, and be innovative with regards to their learning in an open and self-affirming way. Students gain control in a way that retrenches passivity in learning. Questions tackle head on what Whitehead (1967, p. 1) feared most in education; that is the transmission of "inert ideas." Finally, inducing students to voice their questions belongs to the grander objective of cultivating dynamic citizens for modern democracies. To take democracy seriously is to take asking questions seriously.

On the other side, the challenges incurred by educators require a certain degree of fortitude. Because questions can be disruptive (Locke, 1894, pp. 11, 452), humility is an important intellectual virtue to call upon. Not knowing can be embarrassing, especially when questions reveal inadequate practices, or pernicious teachings. When questions show their full power, the curricula itself can be jeopardized. Indeed, thinkers from Rousseau to Apple have done so. But, why is it the privilege of the learned, and not also of the learners to forcefully ask these questions? Quite often, student questions entail more research. Occasionally, they demand the revision of some of ideas, and the modification of some content. Finally, they prompt more questions. The educator's willful invitation of student questions represents partnered disposition towards mutual learning. Education is an ongoing process for both, not to be hindered by the limits, biases, and rigidity of the curriculum, but propelled by them.

In closing, I refer to recent work in the field of virtue epistemology, or intellectual excellences to draw attention to the general values associated with asking carefully crafted questions. Building on the research of Roberts and Wood (2007), as well as Baehr (2011), Watson (in press, p. 6) offers a nuanced and meticulous description of the virtue of inquisitiveness, giving particular attention to question asking. For the present purposes, I simply refer to Watson's depiction of the role of inquisitiveness whereby "not only should the inquisitive person be characteristically motivated to ask questions but their questioning should be directed towards the common goal of the intellectual virtues; improving epistemic standing," (p. 3) that is improving "everything that she knows, understands or truly believes." These are the philosophical underpinnings that explain how, and justify why asking questions is fundamental to learning.

The objective of this final section has been to argue for the inclusion of question asking as part of an educational, political, and philosophical agenda. In the first instance, question asking was set in relation with the existing practice of fighting against received notions and uncritical thinking. Rather than hiding behind the brick wall that the curriculum can represent, this invitation to question shows faith in the idea of treating and nurturing students as rational persons. In the second instance, the philosophical or epistemological justification served to go at the root of learning. The active nature of asking questions invites students to engage with their learning in a way that makes them more responsible for the breadth and level of understanding of what they are being taught. Finally, as far as asking questions may come from one voice, the way in which the assignment is conceived entails that it becomes a collective journey, which bodes well socially, politically, and intellectually.

CONCLUSION

Asking questions is about taking ownership. From my initial philosophical and university encounters with this practice, I have sought to describe the process of requiring students to ask quality questions. My experience has shown the complexities and benefits of the practice, to the point of defending it here as a genuine pedagogical practice to embrace. From the personal to the social, asking probing questions is a skill that students can develop in an intellectually virtuous way that contributes to democratic life. Finally, based on this reading, I cannot help but wonder, what carefully crafted question would you want to put to me?

NOTES

1 See Plato, *Apology* (2005).

2 The student has given me written consent to allow for the inclusion of his question in this text.

REFERENCES

Apple, M. (1979). *Ideology and curriculum*. London: Routledge & Kegan Paul.
Baehr, J. (2011). *The inquiring mind: On intellectual virtues and virtue epistemology*. Oxford, UK: Oxford University Press.
Carr, D. (2009). Curriculum and the value of knowledge. In H. Siegel (Ed.), *The Oxford handbook of philosophy of education* (pp. 281–299). Oxford & New York, NY: Oxford University Press.
Dewey, J. (1929). My pedagogic creed. *Journal of the National Education Association, 18*(9), 291–295.
Freire, P. (1970). *Pedagogy of the oppressed.* New York, NY: Herder and Herder.
Hersey, C. (2013). The business of online plagiarism in post-secondary education. In J. Herrington, A. Couros, & V. Irvine (Eds.), *Proceedings of world conference on educational media and technology 2013* (pp. 749–756). Victoria, Canada: Association for the Advancement of Computing in Education.
Jackson, M. (2008). *Distracted: The erosion of attention and the coming dark age.* Amherst, NY: Prometheus Books.
Jackson, P. W. (2005). The daily grind. In D. J. Flinders & S. J. Thornton (Eds.), *The curriculum studies reader* (pp. 93–102). New York, NY: Routledge Falmer.
Locke, J. (1894). *An essay concerning human understanding: Collated and annotated, with prolegomena, biographical, critical and historical* (Vol. 2, A. C. Fraser, Ed.). Oxford, UK, Clarendon Press.
Noddings, N. (1983). The false promise of the Paideia: A critical review of the Paideia proposal. *Journal of Thought, 18*(4), 81–91.
Noddings, N. (2003). The aims of education. In N. Noddings (Ed.), *Happiness and education* (pp. 74–93). Cambridge, UK: Cambridge University Press.
Pecorari, D. (2013). *Teaching to avoid plagiarism: How to promote good source use.* Maidenhead, Berkshire, UK: McGraw-Hill Education, Open University Press.
Pierce, A. (2015, November 5). The Queen asks why no one saw the credit crunch coming. *The Telegraph UK.* Retrieved from http://www.telegraph.co.uk/news/uknews/theroyalfamily/3386353/The-Queen-asks-why-no-one-saw-the-credit-crunch-coming.html
Plato. (2005). Apology. In E. Hamilton & H. Cairns (Eds.), *The collected dialogues of Plato, Including the letters* (pp. 3–26). New York, NY: Pantheon Books.
Plato. (2005). Theaetetus. In E. Hamilton & H. Cairns (Eds.), *The collected dialogues of Plato, including the letters* (pp. 845–919). New York, NY: Pantheon Books.
Roberts, R. C., & Wood, J. W. (2007). *Intellectual virtues: An essay in regulative epistemology.* Oxford, UK: Oxford University Press.
Rousseau, J.-J., Richard, F., & Richard, P. (1961). Émile*, ou, De l'éducation.* Paris: Garnier Frères.
Shaikh, K., Venkatesh, V., Thomas, T., Urbaniak, K., & Gallant, T. (2011). A manifesto for technological transparency in the age of Web 2.0. *Canadian Issues Spring,* 87–90.
Siegel, H. (1989). The rationality of science, critical thinking, and science education. *Synthese, 80*(1), 9–41.
Venkatesh, V. (2012, November 12). Heavy metal forums and online learning. *From Spark by CBC.* Retrieved from http://www.cbc.ca/spark/full-interviews/2012/11/19/vivek-venkatesh-on-heavy-metal-forums-and-online-learnign/
Watson, L. (in press). Why should we educate for inquisitiveness. In J. Baehr (Ed.), *Educating for intellectual virtues: Applying virtue epistemology to educational theory and practice.* Retrieved from http://philosophyofquestions.com/publications/
Weiss, L., McCarthy, C., & Dimitriadis, G. (Eds.). (2006). *Ideology, curriculum, and the new sociology of education: Revisiting the work of Micheal Apple.* New York, NY: Taylor & Francis.
Whitehead, A. N. (1967). *The aims of education.* New York, NY: Free Press.
Wittgenstein, L. (1998). *On certainty.* In G. E. M. Anscombe & G. H. von Wright (Eds.), *The collected works of Ludwig Wittgenstein* (Electronic Edition, Vol. 13, D. Paul & G. E. M. Anscombe, Trans.). Charlottesville, VA: InteLex Corp.

Samuel LeBlanc
University of Moncton

GERALD C. CUPCHIK

8. CREATIVE PRACTICES IN THE OBSERVATION OF EVERYDAY LIFE

The Crack in the Door That Invites a Creative Vision

Universities have changed over the past forty years that I have been teaching. We see more and more hybridized course offerings that build bridges across various disciplines. The same kind of process is evident in the hiring practices of research-oriented departments of psychology. In "the old days" we hired new faculty either in social/personality/developmental, cognitive/learning, or physiological psychology. Nowadays, to get a job in social psychology at a major university in Canada your "brand" has to sound something like "neuro-cognitive-social" or you will not get anywhere near a short list.

The same goes for prospective graduate students who need to fit the narrowly defined, programmatic, and grant-driven interests of faculty. What is shaping this change in the academic landscape and how does it impact creativity? Do we put the blame on "globalization" which, in this case, has to do with eliminating barriers (read as "redundancy") between structures for the purpose of enhancing efficiency? Is this a reflection of modernity with an emphasis on cutting-edge problem-solving? Or, as one of my recently nearly retired colleagues, said to me a couple of years back: "Gerry. It's no longer about ideas. It's all about toys."

I am not writing this piece from the perspective of a neo-romantic, anti-science humanist or some other kind of curmudgeon who is long in the academic tooth. Quite the opposite. My goal, as a researcher, is to link the sciences with the humanities and integrate mainstream theories about emotion and aesthetics in a complementary manner (see Cupchik, 2016). But this article is not about me or other professors as researchers. Rather, my focus is on creative teaching and learning practices which help my students find niches in an age of globalization that is sustained by the internet. And who are these students? The sample space of students at these universities has changed radically over the years. As I like to tell my colleagues from universities in the United States and Europe, "I teach more students with more first language backgrounds and from more places than you have ever seen or heard of!" And I should add the simple demographic fact that, in many cases, they are the first generation in their families to enter a university. This places an extra burden on their shoulders. So what can I do to help these students when only a generation ago, and no doubt still today, their parents were told that they could not get this or that job because they "lacked Canadian experience".

J. B. Cummings & M. L. Blatherwick (Eds.), Creative Dimensions of Teaching and Learning in the 21st Century, 91–98.

Here is my prescription for helping students overcome the hidden boundaries of globalization and ethnic or racial provenance. My approach reflects a combination of what we called "gorilla theatre" back in the 1960s and plain old pragmatic wisdom from the Eastern European towns from which my parents came to Canada in the 1920s. It might even be considered radical and subversive if my colleagues ever heard about it. Fortunately, students who take the class that I am about to describe are in their fourth year. If they were to unleash a little too much reflective and mindful criticism, they would never make it to graduate school. After all, we can be honest enough to admit that professors don't take lightly to criticism about the "paradigms of truth" which lie at the heart of their successful research careers.

The course titled "Critical analysis in social psychology," which I have taught for more than twenty-five years, involves one part reflective consciousness and another part diplomatic smoothness. It bears noting that I have both assessed the efficacy of this course (Cupchik, 1993), and have also lectured (as in "proselytized") about its potential virtues at a wonderful conference on *Narrative Matters* at Acadia University (Cupchik, 2006). The last thing that I (or they) need is to teach students to think in a creative (i.e., reflective and cutting-edge) manner only to have them flush themselves down the proverbial professional toilet for appearing too critical.

I am going to begin by describing the "creative" goals of the course which exist at two levels. The surface level has to do with understanding the history of social psychology which recapitulates the long-running battle between some who focus on the individual and others who emphasize group processes. With the increasing hegemony of cognitive science, which I consider to be equivalent, methodologically speaking, to behaviourism clad in empirical camouflage, individual processes have tended to (but don't have to) be examined in a laboratory setting, whereas group processes are associated with seemingly more liberal approaches in the human sciences (e.g., ethnomethodology). While the battle between quantitative and qualitative researchers has been acrimonious, it need not be so. A wise sociologist at the University of Toronto once said that "qualitative data hide in the error term of the analysis of variance." This implies that the two kinds of data are complementary. In the end, it is a matter of appreciating the dynamic interaction between understanding individual cases involving qualitative narratives and a search for causal explanations using quantitative data (Cupchik, 2001).

A deeper level of understanding involves experiencing the world in a direct way as a precondition for saying anything about it. This means that one should orient toward phenomena in the lived-world; enter these phenomena *before* theorizing about them. An appropriate metaphor involves holding phenomena with an outstretched arm and interposing the lenses of investigation with the other so that underlying processes are brought into focus rather than being distorted through the introduction of biases, values, and illusions. This fits with a Taoist perspective: "To understand the meaning or significance of a thing, one must become the thing, harmonize one's consciousness with it and reach the mental attitude which brings knowledge without…intellectual deliberation" (Levenson & Schurmann, 1971, p. 126). This strategy feeds back into the laboratory setting, encouraging students to be more critically reflective about quantitative methods which are taken for granted. Sophisticated equipment, so highly valued in our laboratory culture, can provide valuable data relating neural structure to mind and culture (Wang, Mo, Vartanian, Cant, & Cupchik, 2015). But it remains essential that situations and tasks examined in the laboratory are "ecologically valid," meaningfully representing events that occur in the lived-world.

The assignment in question for the twenty-five students in the class is deceptively simple. They have to pick a phenomenon in the social world and find four people each of whom provides two concrete episodes which illuminate the underlying processes. Sounds easy, right? Wrong. Just picking a phenomenon can be challenging. Students generally choose topics that are personally meaningful even though at first this might not be evident. This year, the topics included, for example: "Chinese parents' attitudes about their homosexual children" (in China); "Exploring forgiveness in inter-racial and inter-caste relationships"; "Coptic identity in Egypt and Canada"; "Identity and first generation Jamaican immigrants"; and "Meaningful relationships with god, religion, and spirituality." When students finally hear all the topics during a final class discussion about the projects, they feel pride in what they have accomplished and respect for each other's brave efforts. As you can imagine, given the seriousness of the topics, finding respondents is challenging because students might find people with relevant experiences who don't want to talk about them lest bad memories return. Thus, while this topic may be liberating for students, even the first steps can be difficult. The next task is to record and transcribe these interviews. The most interesting phase of the project involves interpreting the episodes and integrating insights into a coherent theory.

And then comes the *pièce de resistance* when I tell them that if I see the word "hypothesis" or even one word of psychology, I will fail them. I must confess to experiencing a certain malicious sense of glee because most courses that they take in psychology at our university are framed in a discursive space that involves operationalizing concepts, hypothesis testing, and verification. This generally elicits some nervous laughter but students realize that I mean business and expect them to take creative intellectual risks. Now you know what I mean by giving them a subversive task with a gorilla-theatre leitmotif. After writing their theory section, and only then, do students search for four articles in the mainstream literature which address their topic, however tangentially. They compare their approach and findings to those by established researchers. These papers, written in a single term, range in length from about 40 to more than 100 pages.

Finally, students write an epilogue in which they reflect back on their experiences and can say anything they like such as "I don't give a shit if you like my paper. I love it!" (I gave the student a bonus half grade) and this was a paper in which the student interviewed Italian grandmothers who are the backbone of the family and never really learned to speak English even after being in Canada for more than 25 years. The interviews were transcribed in Italian with translation. I sent the paper to Franco Vaccarino who was the Principal of the University of Toronto at Scarborough (now President of the University of Guelph). Needless to say, as a *Siciliano*, he loved the paper. When the principal of a college can relate to this kind of paper that explores cultural experiences, you know that something is working nicely.

How does this particular approach to a course in psychology relate to the notion of "creative practices" and the goals of this book? The particular assignment is not crucial. Rather, the underlying goals and process of engagement between teacher and student and between student and his or her worlds, both personal and academic, as well as with each other, are crucial. I should point out that, a number of years ago, I conducted an assessment to determine the efficacy of the assignment given the goals of the course (Cupchik, 1993). At the last moment, I realized that students should be invited to propose questions of their own. These questions were most efficacious at predicting their grades in the term paper. The most important question had to do with how easy or difficult it was for the student to articulate his or her own thoughts. Students who were generally searching for wisdom, comfortable with new methods, and found it easy to express their thoughts received the highest grades. In other words, they could adapt to the grounded nature of the course assignment. Clearly, students who lived through this demanding assignment implicitly understood what was important in shaping their learning experiences at the various stages of performing it.

Where is the creativity in all of this? There are different kinds of answers to that question and it all depends on how we define creativity. I think of it as a disposition to open the mental gates wide and to look for novel relations among disparate elements or ideas. The opening of these mental gates applies just as readily to the teacher as it does to the student. Here is an excellent example of the challenge that we face when grading assignments such as the one that I give my students about lived-world experiences. This morning I graded a sixty-four page paper titled "Meaningful Relationships with God, Religion, and Spirituality: A Search for Meaning" (Agbaba, 2015). I, of course, anticipated a reserved account of life experiences and views related to this very serious topic. Then I encountered the following answer by Respondent #4 to the question: "Why do we even ask [ourselves] about the search for meaning?" I believe the appropriate thing to do here, as a responsible professor and author, is to warn you that *reader discretion is advised* because the answer has a "salty" (i.e., profanity-laced) aspect, albeit a wise and wonderful one:

> Asking why you search for meaning is a lot like asking why you remove your pants before you shit. Because it leaves a f…ing mess if you don't. You have to make sense of the world.
>
> Searching for meaning is that which you have to do because, if you don't search for meaning, you just get in the way of yourself. Because all of your instincts, all of your implicit drives will get in the way of each other if you don't orient them towards a particular cause. (Agbaba, 2015)

Now your sensibilities may be slightly offended by his choice of words but you must admit that this twenty-three year old respondent captured the essence of an ethical search for meaning in life. This is what I mean by opening the mental gates to the unexpected. Of course, along with the other excellent interview material, I had to give the student an "A" for the paper.

Creative activity always takes place in the midst of a fundamental binary – originality versus conventionality. Accordingly, a person can develop an idea, image, narrative, and so forth that is so novel no one can understand it. This might be because the ideas are not expressed clearly or that the context to which these ideas pertain is not defined. It is incumbent upon the original thinker (or artist) to help audiences situate their work in a meaningful context even if the group is select (such as fellow members of an artistic group). Eventually, the principles of transformation that determine the creative value of the world should be formalized even though they were intuitive at the outset. This implies that we cannot be creative without taking the audience into account. Thus, creative people who are successful must somehow appreciate their relations to conventional communities with whom they may wish to communicate. Pragmatically speaking, we want our students to be creative because this may eventually help them get jobs. Creativity in an applied sense means viewing a problem from a fresh perspective and this reorientation enables the person to arrive at a novel and useful solution.

Now let's return to my students' assignments. Before we even begin to think about the assignment, my students need to learn to situate themselves in the creative process. To facilitate this, I find it helpful to make a distinction between psychology as a *discipline* and as a *profession.* Of course this applies just as readily to being an artist, author or whatever. A *discipline*, in psychology at least, encompasses three domains; *phenomena*, *method*, and *theory*. The term *social phenomena* refers to structured events that recur and can be observed by members of a social group. This is a cultural concept because groups and individuals can observe the same event and interpret it in radically different ways. We have to go no further than the motto "spare the rod and spoil the child" to realize that abusive practices in one community are abhorred by another. Students have to cultivate "acts of noticing" to carefully observe events in their social worlds. The term paper that I discussed earlier encourages students to immerse themselves in the lived-worlds of others. Whether we are thinking about refugees, homeless people, or street musicians, the best way to understand their lives is to be concretely among them, listening to them rather than theorizing abstractly from the outside.

A similar kind of process is observed in the art studio. If one wants to paint a still-life, then one must enter it in all possible ways, noticing composition, colours, shadows, shapes, textures, and so forth. The greater the number of viewpoints that we can adopt, the deeper our appreciation of both life experiences and aesthetic events. In this context, creativity involves adopting new perspectives or placing things in new contexts so as to awaken ourselves and others to relational meanings which have not been considered.

This brings us to the problem of method which all too readily is treated as the mere application of technique. The problem here is that the word "technique" implies something that is conventional. In order to create new techniques of investigation or expression, it is essential to peer beneath the surface of technique and discover the assumptions that are taken for granted. The historian of psychology Kurt Danziger (2000) states that "methodology is not ontologically neutral" (p. 332). By this he means that every method takes for granted, is predicated on, certain assumptions about the world. In order to create a new method, we have to understand the older ones so that we can appreciate their limitations and the sense in which ours is in fact original. What does it offer a community of practitioners as a new way to engage in "acts of noticing" or express meanings and feelings? Thus, we need to engage in complementary acts of observing (i.e., noticing) the world and testing out our ideas in order to determine whether or not they are efficacious.

If we observe the world in an original way, using creative and disciplined methods, then our understanding or theory about the underlying phenomena will be meaningful. A meaningful theory in everyday life determines what is real for us and therefore how we interact with our worlds and shape them. Thus, phenomena, theory, and method are fully integrated in everyday life. We orient around what is taken as "real". Accordingly, creative practices are relevant to all aspects of a discipline. They enable us to observe our worlds in new ways so that events are interpreted through fresh eyes and formalized. This applies equally to abstractions in science that can only be inferred (e.g., particles) as well as to ways of artistically rendering or depicting the everyday world (e.g., Cubism).

Ultimately, this process is all about relationships between us and the social, physical, and organic worlds within which we are embedded. This is an important point to consider because creative acts define new ways of relating to and understanding these worlds. However, professions place very powerful constraints on both students and experienced practitioners to limit criticism of the dominant paradigms (Kuhn, 1962). Scholars who question accepted assumptions about the world are marginalized from the mainstream and, as we all know, may have difficulty finding a job. It is for this reason that those who propose revolutionary paradigms can be burned both literally and figuratively. This is equally true in science and the arts. The term Impressionism, that is so readily taken for granted in the twenty-first century, was conceived of as a derogatory reference in the 1870s to artworks that were sketch-like and contravened the accepted emphasis on realistically painted historical themes.

Students who are creative can benefit from a deep understanding of their position relative to the mainstream so that they can beat it at its (or their) own game. Heightened consciousness about one's own position relative to a mainstream group is essential for survival in this day and age. It makes for a nice story to read about the great artistic or scientific genius who was appreciated *after* he or she was dead. But you wouldn't want to be in their position and I don't advocate it for my students. The reality of professional jealousy is something that we have all confronted. This is not to say that I am recommending placating the mainstream by watering down one's ideas. I just want to prepare my students so that they are fulfilled in the end. Appreciating the complementary nature of conventional and creative pressures places the student in a position to succeed and pass on ideas to young and aspiring creative students. The sooner students understand the nature of professions as power structures that are fundamentally conventional, the better off they are when it comes to survival. Of course, life is not a game but creativity certainly has a playful aspect and the highly creative but naive student rarely gets the job. We hear about them or remember them from undergraduate days as creative friends who never quite made it. The question is: Did they have someone to wake them up so that they understood (even relished) their position on the fringes of their disciplines, scientific or artistic? The answer is usually "No. They were loners."

Those of us who have survived in academia with tenured positions (what a friend once called "the last aristocracy") should realize that we have a responsibility to foster creative practices in teaching and learning so that the next generation can enjoy the blessings of our lives. One way to accomplish this, I would suggest, is to help situate them in the various worlds they might inhabit. This implies that the way forward is to abandon one's sense of isolation and to at least appreciate one's position relative to the mainstream. When we understand the history of our discipline or *métiers*, we are in a better position to consolidate a sense of personal identity and to join with others in common cause to establish the value of creative thinking and practices. My favourite year in Picasso's career was 1901. As I visit museums around the world, I continually run into works from that year when he systematically embodied the styles of his predecessors before launching out on his own unique path.

I guess that, in the end, I am advocating a form of mindfulness training that combines an appreciation of the antecedents of our disciplines while situating ourselves in relation to the power structures that surround us. Please don't consider this a cynical statement. I realized early on in my career that we might be considered paranoid when asking fundamental questions about hidden assumptions and power structures. But, when we get tenure and are promoted to Full Professor, we are seen as "politically astute" (I expect readers to silently giggle to themselves, having survived long enough to actually be interested in reading my little piece.). I actually gave a lecture, not unlike this essay, to the Social Area Group that I organized at the University of Toronto back in 1980 around the time that I received tenure. I recall, in the haze of time, that the department Chair rolled his eyes when I presented my ideas about uncovering hidden assumptions. Being a psychologist with longish curly hair (which I recall fondly) and a beard (in other words, an almost *bona fide* "hippie"), I visited his office the next day to inquire about the meaning of his "rolling of the eyes response". After all, I am a psychologist! He dismissed it as not having had any real meaning because he was just joking around. I guess that this was true in the end. Getting tenure has a way of curing these kinds of sensitivities, doesn't it?

What's the point of this reminiscence and how is it relevant to theme of this book? The simple idea is this. If we want our students to win, in other words, enjoy creative careers, then they have to beat the mainstream at its own game. This is accomplished by mastering the discipline in a fully reflective manner. They need to appreciate the phenomena that are accepted by the dominant group and the paradigms to which they are committed both theoretically and methodologically. They also need to be able to apply the techniques that are considered *de rigeur* in the discipline. And, of greatest importance, they should know and understand the history of the ideas, methods, and techniques that preceded them. This requires an abandonment of ego that is so challenging for rebellious youth and in many cases for their teachers. When we appreciate the contributions of those who came before (and especially of those who have been forgotten…many of them women) and situate ourselves in the social structure, we can better see the crack in the door that invites a creative vision. In my own little corner of the world, I remind my students that, when they choose the phenomenon for their paper and interview their respondents about critical life episodes, they are in a position to have insights as deep as many established scholars. We do well to remember the advice of Goethe about the importance of always maintaining a sense of humility and an appreciation of ironies in life (Sepper, 1998). This is just as important 200 years later and I suggest that it lies at the heart of fostering "creative practices."

REFERENCES

Agbaba, M. (2015). *Meaningful relationships with God, religion, and spirituality: A search for meaning* (Unpublished manuscript). University of Toronto, Toronto.

Cupchik, G. C. (1993). Observing the social world. *Canadian Psychology, 34*(2), 166–175.

Cupchik, G. C. (2001, February). Constructivist realism: An ontology that encompasses positivist and constructivist approaches to the social sciences. *Forum Qualitative Sozialforschung/Forum: Qualitative Social Research, 2*(1). Retrieved from http://qualitative-research.net/fqs/fqs-eng.htm

Cupchik, G. C. (2006). Personal narratives and the hidden metaphors of life. *Narrative Matters*. Acadia University, Wolfville, Nova Scotia.

Cupchik, G. C. (2016). *The aesthetics of emotion: Up the down staircase of the mind-body*. Cambridge, UK: Cambridge University Press.

Danziger, K. (2000). Making social psychology experimental: A conceptual history, 1920–1970. *Journal of the History of the Behavioral Sciences, 36*(4), 329–347.

Kuhn, T. (1962). *The structure of scientific revolutions*. Chicago, IL: University of Chicago Press.

Levenson, J. R., & Schurmann, F. (1971). *China: An interpretive history from the beginnings to the fall of Han*. Oakland, CA: University of California Press.

Sepper, D. L. (1998). *Goethe contra Newton: Polemics and the project for a new science of color*. Cambridge, UK: Cambridge University Press.

Wang, T., Mo, L., Vartanian, O., Cant, J. S., & Cupchik, G. C. (2015). An investigation of the neural substrates of mind wandering induced by viewing traditional Chinese landscape paintings. *Frontiers in Human Neurosciences, 8*(1018), 1–10.

Gerald C. Cupchik
University of Toronto at Scarborough

MARY L. BLATHERWICK AND JILL B. CUMMINGS

9. BACK TO THE GARDEN

Coming to Our Senses

> But you know life is for learning
> We are stardust
> We are golden
> And we've got to get ourselves
> Back to the garden
> (from lyrics to "Woodstock", Joni Mitchell, 1968)

> We as creative beings should take care not to lose sight of our sensory ways of knowing. We need to take care not to replace sensory ways of knowing with technologically driven ways of knowing in an increasingly technology-driven world.
> (Carroll & Kop, 2016)

INTRODUCTION

Online information, the Internet, Google and numerous other search engines, YouTube, TV, cell phones, MOOCs,[1] digital and other information resources multiply day by day, moment by moment. Our information world constantly expands and becomes more instantaneous. Yet at the same time as we come closer to sources of knowledge, we are becoming more removed from the experience of our sensory worlds that excite and shape our imaginations and increase our creative capacities.

Our lives are transformed through creativity and innovation. Creativity is a process of forming new connections and conceiving something new or unusual, while innovation is usually thought of as the application of this process (Pink, 2006). Without creativity, learners, teachers, the public in general, become performers of repeated lives, ideas, and solutions. While routine is comfortable, creativity and innovation expand our thinking and our possibilities. Daniel Pink (2006) explains that creativity is a process in which changing routines and making new connections is central. Pink notes that to survive in the 21st century: "We'll need to supplement our well-developed high-tech abilities with abilities that are high concept and high touch" (pp. 51–52). High concept skills require the abilities "…to create artistic and emotional beauty, to detect patterns and opportunities, to craft a satisfying narrative, and to combine seemingly unrelated ideas into novel invention" (pp. 51–52).

J. B. Cummings & M. L. Blatherwick (Eds.), Creative Dimensions of Teaching and Learning in the 21st Century, 99–106.

These abilities to make new connections are enabled and enhanced by what we perceive through our senses – sight, touch, taste, sound and smell. The senses are grounded in human experiences, which are foundational to the development of how we think and feel. As technology and information expand, we risk "losing touch" with our sensory worlds and these feelings and thoughts. We need to ensure that learning does not become a process devoid of elemental sensory experiences that shape our abilities to see and combine patterns, imagine possibilities and make connections; and, to form the language and metaphors that help connect us to our historical-cultural knowledge and traditions. It is essential for us as human beings, learners, and teachers to learn about our physical and aesthetic worlds filled with rich sensory possibilities for connecting and making meaning.

In this paper, we examine the significance of sensory experiences, and their importance for enhancing creativity. Sensory experiences are fundamental to developing ways of thinking and learning, and cultivate the imagination and mindfulness, which help forge new connections. We explain how sensory experiences, aesthetic awareness, play, and mindfulness may be viewed by educators through the lens of sociocultural theories of learning as activities that shape or mediate creative development. This conception of learning via sensory experiences and play describes how the creative process of gaining regulation over skills, knowledge, and imagination can take place (Vygotsky, 1986, 2004).

Creative Development

Many researchers (Csikszentmihalyi, 1996; Greene, 1979; Robinson, 2011; Sawyer, 2006) have suggested that the development of creativity can be ignited through enhanced sensory and aesthetic awareness. Both forms of awareness relate to the ability to decipher and convey meaning through the senses. In the words of Maxine Greene (1979):

> To learn through the use of our senses is to open oneself to altogether new visions, to unsuspected experienced possibilities. It is to become personally engaged in looking from an altered viewpoint, on the materials of one's own lived life, and in imaginatively transmuting (from a fresh standpoint) the fragments of the presented world. (p. 187)

Learning through the Senses

Learning through the senses might seem to be a basic starting point as it takes place naturally as children explore their environment. However, in our daily lives we are often too preoccupied with routines to take in the details of our surroundings. We are increasingly removed from the real world of senses as the "distancing effect" of literacy, technology and other information resources separate us from immediate and direct experiences. This has been explained by Vygotsky and sociocultural educators

(Bodrova, 2008; Vygotsky, 2004) as the result of the increasing development of academic literacy and the immersion of children in the world of information accompanied by their decreasing creative play in the natural world of imagination. Sir Ken Robinson (2011) argues that public school education, with its emphasis on conformity and the "one right answer approach to learning" has also been a major cause for the decrease in students' levels of creativity.

The need for curriculum, teaching, and learning teacher education programs to embrace creative explorations through sensory awareness has therefore become urgent in a world that is increasingly emphasizing the need for creative problem-solving, innovation and invention. Sir Ken Robinson (2011) stresses that the delivery and memorization of information can no longer be the best means for learning and developing minds in a world that requires conceptualization and creativity.

Re-Imagining Education

Egan (2008) and the Imaginative Education Research Group (www.IERG.ca) have elaborated a conceptual framework for imaginative learning with specific concepts and sample lessons that encourage teachers, administrators, and curriculum makers to "roll up their sleeves" and re-imagine education. Egan (2008) has explained this process as beginning with the development of sensory or somatic understanding via language play using humor, nursery rhymes, riddles, and songs with our youngest learners. These activities evoke excitement and giggles engaging both the senses and emotions (Egan, 2002), and develop early literacy knowledge and skills through sight, sound, feeling connections.

Egan asserts that these sensory activities engage the emotions of the child and enhance imagination; opening it to new possibilities. Anyone who has played the "Itsy Bitsy Spider" song/game https://www.youtube.com/watch?v=xwKX6m2tCR4 recently with a preschooler knows the sensory involvement, language learning, and excitement this song evokes. This type of sensory engagement develops the child's imagination through visualization, and the child feels the nursery rhyme not only "in his/her head, but through his body and in her/his heart". This action song develops the child's imagination, preparing the mind for basic literacy (rhyme, rhythm, sounds, images, words, sentences) through images evoked by the sounds and physical movements. It also engages the child's excitement for learning through play. Involving the senses in early literacy development has long been a practice with preschoolers as they sing, draw, act out songs and rhymes. Effective preschools have sensory activities planned throughout the day.

The Role of Play

Such sensory activities are akin to the capacity for "play" that Pink (2006) urges us to develop at any age. "Play", Pink explains, involves humour, joyfulness, exploration, stress reduction, and a freeing up of the spirit of invention that fuels creativity. Facilitating sensory engagement through play ignites one's imagination, ability to see connections, and desire to innovate.

Play involving sensory experiences offers educators a valuable means for engaging students in activities that develop awareness and initiate exploration. Many educators, including Greene (1979) and Robinson (2011), point out that there is a need to encourage the use of play to allow learners to externalize their own imaginings through various forms of expression. Play can be a strategy for teaching any age level. If understood as activities that are planned and encouraged, play-based sensory activities enhance imagination and creativity by engaging learners' minds and stimulating their senses.

Play-based sensory activities can also be used in the education of older students if we plan and implement age appropriate activities and content. Language play for high school students might involve creating word games, puzzles, chants, raps, poetry, images, videos and songs. Older students are inspired by such sensory rich experiences, just as early learners are fascinated by the world around them when first encouraged to experience it through their senses. Students of all ages awaken to new meanings of their world through activities that encourage them to focus, imagine, create and reflect.

These sensory awareness activities could include experiences in the natural world through field trips and encounters with environmental sites, workplaces, habitats, museums, and galleries. Experiencing the work of artists through engaging and sometimes play-based activities can excite the senses through the discovery of color, forms and textures. The same is true of music with its range of melodies, patterns and sounds. The arts and aesthetics as learning through the senses can form the basis for enriching sensory activities in school and outside.

The Mindfulness Connection

According to Langer (1997), to learn through our sensory experiences and aesthetic responses requires a form of "re-attention" and mindfulness. She points out that such mindfulness can be defined as a state of being in which one achieves intense presence – "awakeness" to the present. We learn to focus by using our senses, taking the time to actually notice, and think critically while we observe, listen, touch, feel and taste the world in which we live. Greene (1979), Pink (2006), and Tsai (2012) have discussed how humans develop images of their world along with knowledge and new understandings when they refocus their attention and experience the world directly, ask questions and make new connections – all parts of a creative process.

This need for greater awakeness or mindfulness is discussed by several theorists including Schutz (1967), who points out that refocusing our attention allows new thoughts and insights to be formed. The mindful approach to living generates a flow of actions, which are characterized by the continuous creation of new categories, openness to new information, and an implicit awareness of more than one perspective. By living, feeling, observing, listening and sensing in this state it is possible to see connections and be more receptive to creative possibilities. The imagination is awakened to multiple ways of knowing and learning through mindfulness and is able to make new connections between experiences and ideas.

Sociocultural Theories of Learning

Sociocultural theorists (Bruner, 1979; Egan, 2002, 2008; Vygotsky, 1986; Wertsch, 1999) explain that learning is developed and regulated by humans through their use of activities, tools, resources, and ideas that "mediate" or shape and develop mind. These resources and activities include sensory experiences. Language, images, concepts, ideas, skills and thinking strategies are mediated by the use of these tools, activities, and resources, which the learner uses in developing his/her regulation of a learning activity and its goal. These resources include tools such as pencils, books and web sources, which are ideal for exploring a wide range of interpretations, ideas, concepts and philosophies. Through these means teachers and learners can awaken to new perceptions, questions, associations amongst ideas, and knowledge that stimulate creativity and innovation (Egan, 2008).

These social theories of learning explain the development of imagination differently from the generally accepted theories of experiential learning based on conceptions of learning according to set stages of development (Egan, 2002; 2008; Vygotsky, 1986; Wertsch, 1999). Egan (2002) explains the fallacy related to stage theories of development, that is, that learning proceeds from the simple to the complex. Stage theories of development fail to recognize that learning through arts-based, sensory activities is not a simple but a complex task that requires a mind full of imagination; not "simple at all" (Egan, 2002).

Furthermore, stages of development do not always regularly appear in children at innate, specified stages; rather they develop through the use of activities and tools according to a much more expandable developmental path than progressivist educators like Spencer and Dewey expounded (Egan, 2002, 2008). We know that various children develop different abilities at different stages in their lives according to the conditions, resources, and mentoring that they experience. For example, we have all had the experience of a younger child in a family learning a song and words to that song because of the child's exposure and practice of that song while playing with an older sibling. We have seen the early inventiveness of children at play in their own contexts – inventing new forms of transport from their experiences with climbing trees, watching clouds and animals or inventing a song based on the sounds and rhythms they hear around them.

These experiences are often scaffolded or supported by a more experienced mentor – in many instances the teacher or instructor – who provides modelling, experience, and assistance in the types of processes and thinking that shape the learner's development and learning (Bodrova, 2008; Tsai, 2012; Vygotsky, 2004). We argue that these sociocultural explanations should be offered to teachers as a significant re-starting point in their thinking about learning and creativity. These explanations give us the means to examine sensory activities and the arts as consciously enacted activities whereby learners develop and gain regulation of imagination, literacy skills, and knowledge. As well, instructors and teachers as the mentors who support, model, and lead students' creative and sensory experiences need practice and education in these types of imaginative activities and experiences.

Such theories of learning recognize the social nature of learning in that tools, skills, concepts, ideas and strategies are learned within a social context or construct that give knowledge a social meaning and perspective. Sensory activities and conceptions of creativity are not universal in their delivery – what is appreciated, valued, taught, and meaningful varies from context to context and school system to school system, from family to family, according to the times and conditions (Egan, 2006; Vygotsky, 2004). For example, in the recent quest for excellence in Science, Technology, Engineering, and Math (STEM), North American schools may have moved away from the arts and aesthetics to put more time and resources into STEM activities. We maintain that this trend needs to be rethought. We need to engage and develop the imaginations of learners through sensory activities in both the arts and sciences. We encourage educators to place more value on the use of sensory activities for enhancing creative development.

The Role of the Imagination

Melvin Rader (1974), in his article "The Imaginative Mode of Awareness", described imagination as having two phases – the attentional and elaborative. In the attentional phase, we "grasp the object in its full qualitative richness and imaginative fecundity" (p. 136). The elaborative phase is a more active one; it transforms the object by imaginative vision. He states that imaginative experience is often proceeded by heightened sensory and aesthetic awareness and it is this knowledge that provides moments of clarity that enable transformation and learning to take place. This explanation is akin to Egan's explanation of the development of imagination and knowledge through the development of various types of understanding from somatic/sensory understanding, mythic or story understanding, and romantic, philosophic, and ironic understanding. Each involves an encounter with knowledge, dialogic or reflective thinking, and emotional engagement and experience of the knowledge – whether it be through sensory experiences, story, romance, concepts, philosophy, or ironic contrast (Egan, 2002, 2008).

We encourage educators to facilitate opportunities for sensory experiences to happen – in the classroom and outside – both through observation and direct experience and through reflective moments in which students re-experience these sensations while talking and thinking about these experiences, writing, listening to others, and doing numerous other dialogic and reflective activities. Thus, learners develop the ability to gain control of their learning and to understand these sensations in their lives and the world around them. As educators, it is our job to create spaces and opportunities where students can be open to new knowledge and imaginings through sensory activities. By cultivating an atmosphere that encourages students to think in new ways, educators instill curiosity about the world and encourage creative development. Students also need the time and space to be mindful of and reflect on the richly layered nuances and deeper meanings of what they have experienced and created. This contemplative space is where insights can occur and creativity begins.

CONCLUSION

In the current climate that demands the ability to think creatively and innovate, enhancing sensory and aesthetic awareness can provide a re-starting point for developing more creative approaches to teaching and learning. In "Landscapes of Learning", Greene (1979) quotes Piaget, stating that "the principal goal of education should be to create men and women who are capable of doing new things, not simply repeating what other generations have done – men and women who are creative, inventive and discoverers", who have minds which "can be critical, can verify, and not accept everything they are offered" (p. 80). For Greene, the curriculum is a means to providing aesthetic and creative opportunities "for the seizing of a range of meanings for persons to be open to the world, especially today" (p. 169). This, she points out, happens when educators enhance qualitative awareness, release imagination, and free people to see, shape and transform (Greene, 1979, p. 193).

In appeals to reawakening creativity, (Csikszentmihalyi, 1996; Egan, 2008; Robinson, 2011) stress the need for greater understanding of how the imagination works as a rich repository for sensory memories and images that foster learning and creativity. Sensory experiences can be implemented in teaching and learning activities as conscious tools to develop emotional engagement, awareness, knowledge, and reflection in our curricula. They awaken the imagination and associations that stimulate creativity and innovation. Sensory activities and experiences therefore are essential tools and resources for creative development.

Understanding creativity and how it relates to sensory awareness, the imagination, play and mindfulness are needed to help revitalize the educational process. We need to provide opportunities for both teachers and students to use their imaginative powers through sensory activities. In this way they will experience the world through a state of heightened awareness and emotional engagement that enables them to respond aesthetically through words, images, movement, and sound. It is through greater sensory engagement that creative development can begin. This is what we mean by "getting back to the garden" (our apologies to Joni Mitchell, 1968). Although we may have added a new layer of meaning to this expression, sensory awareness and engagement are powerful tools for awakening learners' imaginations and creativity. We maintain that "coming to our senses" is important for developing creative and critical thinking within students and teachers alike.

NOTE

[1] Massive Open Online Courses.

REFERENCES

Bodrova, E. (2008). Make-believe play versus academic skills: A Vygotskian approach to today's dilemma of early childhood education. *European Early Childhood Education Research Journal, 16*(3), 357–369.

Bruner, J. (1979). *On knowing essays for the left hand.* Boston, MA: Harvard University Press.

Carroll, F., & Kop, R. (2016). Colouring the gaps in technology enhanced learning: Aesthetics and the visual in learning and analytics. *International Journal of Distance Education Technologies, 14*(1), 92–103.

Csikszentmihalyi, M. (1996). *Creativity and the flow and psychology of discovery and invention.* New York, NY: Harper Collins.

Egan, K. (2002). *Getting it wrong from the beginning: Our progressivist inheritance from Herbert Spencer, John Dewey, and Jean Piaget.* New Haven: Yale University Press.

Egan, K. (2006). *Teaching literacy: Engaging the imagination of new readers and writers.* Thousand Oaks, CA: Corwin Press.

Egan, K. (2008). *The future of education: Reimagining our schools from the ground up.* New Haven: Yale University Press.

Greene, M. (1979). *Landscapes of learning.* New York, NY: Teacher's College Press.

Langer, E. (1997). *The power of mindful learning.* Cambridge, MA: Perseus Books.

Pink, D. (2006). *A whole new mind.* New York, NY: Riverhead Books.

Rader, M. (1974). The imaginative mode of awareness. *The Journal of Aesthetics and Art Criticism, 33*(2), 131–137.

Robinson, K. (2011). *Out of our minds.* Chichester, England: Capstone Publishing Ltd.

Sawyer, R. (2006). *Explaining creativity.* Oxford: Oxford University Press.

Schutz, A. (1967). *The problem of social reality*, Collected papers 1. The Hague: Martinus Nijhoff.

Tsai, K. C. (2012). Play, imagination, and creativity: A brief literature review. *Journal of Education and Learning, 1*(2), 15–20. Retrieved from http://dx.doi.org/10.5539/jrl.v1n2p15

Vygotsky, L. (1986). *Thought and language.* Cambridge, MA: The MIT Press.

Vygotsky, L. (2004). Imagination and creativity in childhood. *Journal of Russian and East European Psychology, 42*(1), 7–97.

Wertsch, J. (1999). *Voices of the mind: A sociocultural approach to mediated action.* Cambridge, MA: Harvard University Press.

Mary L. Blatherwick
University of New Brunswick

Jill B. Cummings
Yorkville University

ADRIAN MCKERRACHER, ANITA SINNER,
ERIKA HASEBE-LUDT, CARL LEGGO,
KERRI MESNER AND DUSTIN GARNET

10. ENHANCING EDUCATION

Material Culture, Visual Media, and the Aesthetics of Teachers' Lives

> The aesthetic imagination is the primary mode of knowing the cosmos, and aesthetic language the most fitting way to formulate the world.
> (James Hillman, from *The Force of Character and the Lasting Life*)

INTRODUCTION

In order to provoke discussion about the importance of creative practices in education, our group of six researchers investigates contemporary and historic portrayals of teachers through integrative methods of visual arts, digital media, and creative nonfiction.[1,2] By braiding the different strands of our inquiry, we address how material and popular culture, communicated through the arts – film, television, literature, photography, life writing, and other sources (archival and current) – contribute to critically advancing discourses that promise to improve practice in teacher education. Through arts-based methods that examine both practices and material objects, we are confronting our concerns for the potentially impoverished conditions surrounding human knowledge and human relationships. We question the ways in which the material culture we are immersed in both constrains and empowers us to live and work well with each other and to improve learning conditions and life in schools and society.

First Braid: Creative Practices and the History of Art Education

In this braid we explore our emerging creative methods of practice as an approach to studying the history of art education. As researchers, we interrogate stories as starting points for inquiry in archives, making the relationship between stories and archives a forum in which the staging of the event of knowledge, as Rogoff (2011) suggests, is the historical moment. Our research practices are concerned with life writing, in which we weave stories about the lives of teachers and students in-between the synergistic interplay of material culture, geographic location and perhaps most importantly, in the dialogue surrounding archival inquiry that inscribes research practices (Garnet, 2012; Sinner, 2013). Through stories we seek a means to generate, expand and

J. B. Cummings & M. L. Blatherwick (Eds.), Creative Dimensions of Teaching and Learning in the 21st Century, 107–115.

advance discourses to bring visibility to the everyday moments underway in schools past and present, and to more broadly conceive of historical understandings by rethinking stories as interactive encounters, rather than as static, descriptive practices for our students. As part of our evolving methods we strive to cultivate an awareness of collective memories and the characterization of teachers and students through oral stories, institutional documents, school newsletters, photographs, curriculum, teaching schedules, maps, architectural plans and much more. By attending to archival practice, in which the "ability to produce stories" as Arendt (1958, p. 97) stated, is a way to "become historical" in a contemporary context, we seek to open a vital conversation about developing innovative approaches to teaching and learning that bring to the fore imaginative thinking about the history of art education in new ways.

Stories about the lives of teachers and students are sources of information that can operate to document methods, protocols and procedures, and through life writing also disclose researcher subjectivity, extending Grumet's (1990) position that "narratives of educational experience challenge us to listen to stories and to hear the resonance in the distant orchestration of academic knowledge" (p. 323). In this case, we share Sue's story as an exemplar of creative practice that braids oral histories and archives, and demonstrates our approach to inquiry in the history of art education. Sue's story encapsulates the journey of a lifelong learner who graduated from both the high school generalist and specialized art program, and the adult education program at Central Technical School (CTS), where she continues to volunteer today. Sue has contributed to the artistic community at CTS for over forty years and works closely with Dustin in his teaching practice. Sue described her student experience in the 1950s:

> The teachers that I had here were exceptionally brilliant. This goes for Mr. Dawson Kennedy, who was my design teacher. I was just inspired by him. The way he taught – and what he did for the students. A lot of times he would help us one-on-one. He would come around, and he would sit with us, guide us, and show us and, explain to us how it's done. I could tell he took pride in developing people.

For Dustin, her enthusiastic account immediately linked to an interview with another former student from the 1960s, Canadian painter Harold Klunder, who also remembered Mr. Kennedy:

> He was a real tough nut. If you didn't get it in on time he'd be on your case, and you'd get really low marks. And lettering – he was fanatical. You know, spacing had to be done a certain way. And everything was done with designer colors. It's hard to imagine now that anyone works like that, but, it was good experience. And maybe I learned a bit from him because he was so hard-nosed.
>
> As Dustin describes:

> There was a good chance I may not have followed up on Dawson Kennedy. As a result of my interview with Sue, I went back to the interview with Harold,

and then into the archives to see if there was a more complex story to be found on this teacher. What I found in the archives was an extensive amount of objects and documents that showed Dawson Kennedy was a major force in the art department, something I did not know, despite working here since 2005. This layer I may not have otherwise explored or at least understood without the connections of Sue and Harold.

As researchers of life stories, we believe the connectedness woven between archives, time, the character of the schools, and our lives as artists, teachers and researchers, provides a means to access and formulate critical questions. Doing research as a creative practice leads to new possibilities within historical research, indeed "the poetics of the archive is a poetics of recollection, of re-membering, in which all truths are provisional and subject to revision" (Voss & Werner, 1999, p. ii).

It is this interrelatedness between archives, storytellers and researchers that we are most interested in developing further, extending this approach to post-secondary and secondary classrooms alike in an effort to advance curriculum and pedagogic processes that provide an alternate educational project to our learners, regardless of age. Indeed, when we construct stories like Sue's, Harold's, Dawson Kennedy's and our own in relation to archives, it is akin to Benjamin's (1968) position that "the traces of the storyteller cling to the story the way the handprints of the potter cling to the clay vessel" (p. 92). Historical understandings within art education then are part of the accountability and responsibility of scholarship for the public good, as well as a foundation of quality education for the teacher education students, graduate students and high school students we work with in our teaching and researching lives.

Second Braid: Inciting New Conversations in a Curriculum of Film

In our research we are investigating the pedagogical implications of narrative depictions of educators and youth in films. Even though there are more than one thousand (mostly Hollywood produced) films about life in schools, education scholars have paid relatively little attention to the popular and influential curriculum of film. While we note the valuable textual research already undertaken around various filmic tropes in education (for example, the heroic teacher, the bad teacher, and the teacher as buffoon – see, for example, Farhi, 1999; Breault, 2009; Bulman, 2002, 2005; Dalton, 2004), we want to move beyond these more obvious analyses – indeed, to ask different questions. One such question that arises with great resonance for us throughout this research project is, quite simply, "*what is this film good for*?" This question opens up possibilities for looking at stories in films, especially those that are often overlooked, silenced, or marginalized, in order to pay attention to an expansive range of evocatively exciting interpretations and pedagogical implications. In response to the question, "*What is this film good for*?", we suggest that an investigation of pedagogy and curriculum in film needs to *instigate,* to *indecent*, and to *inspirit.*

The curriculum of film needs to *instigate* conversations about teachers' and learners' formation, identities, and bodies. Like De Castell (1993), we are interested in films that challenge traditional redemptive stories by exploring more dangerous narratives, especially in films that challenge stereotypes of teachers' identities (Backus 2009), in order to explore more nuanced and ambiguous portrayals of the lived experiences of educators (Burant, 2011; Brie & Torevell, 2007). Like Dalton (2004), we are intrigued by how filmic portrayals serve to make teachers' and students' differences, disabilities, and even their bodied selves, invisible. We want to highlight films that instigate conversations about the ways their bodies are disciplined and shaped by filmic portrayals (Hughes-Decatur, 2011). Films like *Bang Bang You're Dead* (2002), *Dead Poets' Society* (1989), and *The Emperor's Club* (2002) offer fascinating springboards for such conversations.

Representations of pedagogy and curriculum in film also need to *indecent* our understandings of teachers' and learners' sexuality and spirituality. Here, we look to queer theologian Althaus-Reid's (2002) notion of "indecenting" as a verb – that is, to actively transgress theological, political, and cultural structures by moving towards the margins of Christian decency, and making explicit the interwoven nature of theology, sexuality, and politics. We're interested, like Dalton (2004) and Keroes (1999), in the ways that teachers' and learners' sexuality, queerness, and desire are portrayed in films, as well as, like Keller and Glass (1998) and Steinberg (2000), in the ways that gayness is mainstreamed to make it more palatable to popular film audiences. We are also interested in the *indecenting* of Christian spirituality in films about schools, teachers, and students – whether by problematizing Christianity's influence in Hollywood economics (see, for example, Rosin, 2005), or by looking at the relationship between spiritual experiences in the church and in the movie theatre (see, for example, Johnston, 2000; Graham, 1997). Like Beck (2005), Brie and Torevell (2007), and Christian (2004), we are fascinated by the debates and ambiguities that filmic portrayals of Christianity and schools raise. Two exemplary resources for complex analyses of sexuality and spirituality in film include *Saved!* (2004) and *Loving Annabelle* (2006) – two films that we explore in greater depth in another essay (Leggo & Mesner, in print).

Finally, the curriculum of film needs to *inspirit* our notions of teachers' and learners' lived experiences. We recognize, like Shaw and Nederhouser (2005), the affective power of films in shaping teachers' meaning-making processes, and like Grant (2002), we want to make more effective use of popular films in teacher preparation and education. Moreover, we seek films that will inspirit a more complex and artistically evocative analysis of pedagogical issues (see, for example, Burant, 2011). Like Dalton (2004), we seek films that stretch the boundaries of educational conformity and that inspirit prophetic educational leadership. Perhaps at its heart, and *because* the curriculum of film can engage the heart, we sense that films can inspirit our hopes and vocations with artistic possibilities that are more aesthetic than anaesthetic – a sense that gives us tremendous hope for our educational institutions.

Here, we might look to aesthetically (if not financially) rich films like *Rabbit-Proof Fence* (2002) and *Whale Rider* (2002).

As our research continues, we are instigating challenging and enlivening conversations, indecenting our understandings of spirituality, religion, and sexuality in filmic portrayals of educators' and students' lives, and inspiriting our creative-critical perspectives by attending to the curriculum and pedagogy of film. In so doing, in returning to our original question, "*What is this film good for?*", we find the value, not in the answers, but in inciting more questions in response. In our research, we are imagining a curriculum of film as a way for opening up possibilities for more creative and critical pedagogy.

Third Braid: Life Writing, Art Making, and the Aesthetics of Teaching in Cosmopolitan Times

Our final braid investigates the pedagogical potential of narrating teachers' lives and looks at the way in which the aesthetics of storytelling offers unique opportunities for understanding one's self in relation to others. By encouraging teachers to reflect on their own experience, we explore life writing as a cosmopolitan ethos for our time. In our work with teachers in different graduate cohorts,[3] we explore how life writing constitutes an engagement with difference and affinity, with human values and ideas as well as aesthetic notions that we articulate to the world and that the world awakens in us (Bly, 2001; Pinar, 2009). We suggest that in this way life writing is a creative and empathetic *wordly* practice, one that is urgently required the face of the rapid change and increasing diversity of education in the 21st century. In these times of globalization, "crises of pedagogy," and proliferation of "great untruths" (Smith, 2006), which are often characterized by human disconnectedness, mental anguish, and spiritual impoverishment, teachers and students together are challenged to enter into a worldly conversation that enables them to develop a new ethos of care, an ethical advocacy for a more equal and just society.

Our work contributes to the growing research on life writing (see Chambers, 2004; Chambers, Hasebe-Ludt, Leggo, & Sinner, 2012; Chambers, Hasebe-Ludt, Donald, Hurren, Leggo, & Oberg, 2008; Eakin, 2004; Hasebe-Ludt, 2010; Hasebe-Ludt, Sinner, Leggo, Pletz, Simoongwe, & Wilson, 2010; Jolly, 2001; Richardson, 2001; Richardson & St. Pierre, 2005; Sinner, Leggo, Irwin, Gouzouasis, & Grauer, 2006), and emphasizes the literary aspects of composing a story of one's experience. In order to expand understandings of the range of forms these life narratives can take, we turn to examples from contemporary literature and creative non-fiction that illuminate new possibilities for seeing oneself in relation to others. We believe that this ability to see oneself as another, to see that "I" is simultaneously "he" or "she" to someone else, is foundational to a cosmopolitan ethos that allows different worldviews to coexist in what Pinar (2004, 2009) calls "a complicated conversation" as part of a "cosmopolitan education." For example, our recent research examines a form that South African Nobel-laureate J. M. Coetzee calls "*autre*biography", which blurs lines between fact and fiction by positioning the autobiographical main character in third person, often employing the present tense and utilizing free indirect speech (Cheney, 2009; Coetzee, 1992; see also Coetzee, 1998, 2002, 2009). This alternative to conventional forms of narrating the self varies the "pact" that is made between reader and author (Lenta, 2003) and offers the life writing practitioner new opportunities to reflect on their experience in relation to others. Similarly, we draw on Portuguese poet Fernando Pessoa's notion of *heteronyms* – multiple writing personalities each with unique aesthetic tastes, political orientations and biographies that he used to explore different perspectives, attitudes, and ideas. Through one of those heteronyms (of which Pessoa reportedly had a whopping 72), Pessoa (1991, p. 62) expressed that had "created various personalities" within himself and that he was "the living stage across which various actors pass acting out different plays". Embracing Pessoa's concept of heteronyms gives license to the life writer to examine not only their life story but their life *stories*, making room for the way that each person is a place for the refraction and convergence of multiple selves. Our third example looks at the narrative structure of *The Savage Detectives* (2007) by Chilean-Mexican Roberto Bolaño, in which the story of a semi-fictional main character (called "Arturo Belano") is told in the form of 52 monologues by the people that knew him. By framing the protagonist's experience in the form of these first person but externalized narrators, the story of one man's life becomes inextricably caught up in the events, attitudes, and perceptions of those around him.

Through these three literary models and others like them, our research explores the ways in which diverse forms of storytelling can open up new ways of understanding the self and inspire a "pedagogy of the imagination" (Calvino, 1995). By examining how one's life is implicated in the lives of many others, one glimpses the extent to which experience can be viewed from multiple perspectives. This practice of qualitative, arts-based inquiry is a pedagogical strategy for reflecting on and expanding the limits of storytelling so that new ways of understanding the self in relation to others can be engaged. Life stories as original literature of the self, and other world/worldly literature, are forms of truth telling, and repositories of important and often neglected or suppressed historical and sociocultural and place-specific knowledge (King, 2003). They reach out from self to other/world/cosmos across genealogies, times, and places; reading and writing narrative literature of this kind, both fiction and nonfiction, then becomes "a type of world-making activity that enable us to imagine the world" (Cheah, 2012, p. 138). It becomes a kind of "visceral cosmopolitanism" (Nava, 2007) played out in our small worlds of schools, neighbourhoods, and backyards, through our feeling, thinking, and acting in a community of human relations engaged dialogically in "a collective, creative endeavor, beyond the individual" (Werbner, 2012, p. 162). We suggest that this practice of writing and rewriting the self is integral to ethical considerations of living well with others, based on a foundation of reflection, relation, and imagination.

Closing

Considered together, these three approaches to research – archival, cinematic, and literary – offer unique and important creative arts-based practices to educational research. It is our hope that they will inspire further investigation of the pedagogical potential of working closely with the aesthetics of teaching and teachers' lives.

NOTES

1 We gratefully acknowledge support from the Social Sciences and Humanities Research Council of Canada (SSHRC) through the grant, "Portrayals of Teachers' Lives: Investigating Teacher Education Through Popular Culture and Digital Media as Arts Education". Dr. Anita Sinner is principal investigator; Dr. Erika Hasebe-Ludt and Dr. Carl Leggo are co-investigators. Adrian McKerracher, Kerri Mesner, and Dustin Garnet are doctoral researchers on the project.

2 A version of this paper was presented at The Canadian Society for Studies in Education (CSSE) annual conference in Victoria, BC, on June 4, 2013.

3 *Urban Learner* MEd cohorts at the University of British Columbia and *Literacy in Globalzized Canadian Classrooms* MEd cohorts at the University of Lethbridge.

REFERENCES

Althaus-Reid, M. (2002). *Indecent theology: Theological perversions in sex, gender and politics*. New York, NY: Routledge.

Arendt, H. (1958). *The human condition*. Chicago, IL: University of Chicago Press.

Backus, S. (2009). Freshman comp tantrums. *Chronicle of Higher Education, 56*(5), B24–B24.

Beck, B. (2005). Has anybody here seen my old friend Jesus?: Christian movies in a Christian country. *Multicultural Perspectives, 7*(1), 26–29.

Benjamin, W. (1968). The storyteller: Reflections on the works of Nikolai Leskov. In W. Benjamin (Ed.), *Illuminations* (H. Arendt, Ed., H. Zohn, Trans., pp. 83–110). New York, NY: Harcourt, Brace & World.

Bly, C. (2001). *Beyond the writers' workshop: New ways to write creative nonfiction*. New York, NY: Anchor Books.

Bolaño, R. (2007). *The savage detectives* (N. Wimmer, Trans.) New York, NY: Picador.

Breault, R. (2009). The celluloid teacher. *Educational Forum, 73*(4), 306–317.

Brie, S., & Torevell, D. (1997). Moral ambiguity and contradiction in *Dead Poets' Society*. In C. Marsh & G. Ortiz (Eds.), *Explorations in theology and film* (pp. 167–180). Malden, MA: Blackwell.

Brooks, K. (Director). (2006). *Loving Annabelle* (Motion picture). USA: Big Easy Pictures; Divine Light Productions.

Bulman, R. (2002). Teachers in the 'hood: Hollywood's middle-class fantasy. *Urban Review, 34*(3), 251–276.

Bulman, R. (2005). *Hollywood goes to high school: Cinema, schools, and American culture*. New York, NY: Worth.

Burant, T. (2011). More than just dance lessons. In E. Marshall & O. Sensoy (Eds.), *Rethinking popular culture and media* (pp. 238–243). Milwaukee, WI: Rethinking Schools.

Calvino, I. (1995). *Six memos for the next millennium*. Toronto, ON: Vintage Canada.

Caro, N. (Writer). (2002). *Whale rider*. USA: Henderson Valley.

Chambers, C. (2004). Research that matters: Finding a path with heart. *Journal of the Canadian Association for Curriculum Studies, 2*(1), 1–19.

Chambers, C. C., Hasebe-Ludt, E., Leggo, C., & Sinner, A. (Eds.). (2012). *A heart of wisdom: Life writing as empathetic inquiry*. New York, NY: Peter Lang.

Chambers, C., Hasebe-Ludt, E., Donald, D., Hurren, W., Leggo, C., & Oberg, A. (2008). Métissage: A research praxis. In J. G. Knowles & A. L. Cole (Eds.), *Handbook of the arts in qualitative research: Perspectives, methodologies, examples, and issues* (pp. 141–153). Los Angeles, CA: Sage.
Cheah, P. (2012). What is a world? On world literature as world-making activity. In G. Delanty (Ed.), *Routledge handbook of cosmopolitan studies* (pp. 138–149). London, UK: Routledge.
Cheney, M. (2009, December 7). Intentional schizophrenia: J. M. Coetzee's autobiographical trilogy and the falling authority of the author. *The Quarterly Conversation.* Retrieved August 18, 2013, from http://quarterlyconversation.com/intentional-schizophrenia-j-m-coetzees-autobiographical-trilogy-and-the-falling-authority-of-the-author
Christian, T. (2004, May 28). Snarky '*saved!*' shows a little mercy. *Washington Times*. Retrieved from http://www.washingtontimes.com/news/2004/may/27/20040527-092559-3098r/?page=all
Coetzee, J. M. (1992). *Doubling the point: Essays and interview* (D. Attwell, Ed.). Cambridge, MA: Harvard University Press.
Coetzee, J. M. (1998). *Boyhood: Scenes from provincial life.* New York, NY: Penguin Books.
Coetzee, J. M. (2002). *Youth.* London, UK: Vintage.
Coetzee, J. M. (2009). *Summertime: Scenes from provincial life.* London, UK: Harvill Secker.
Dalton, M. M. (2004). *The Hollywood curriculum: Teachers in the movies*. New York, NY: Peter Lang.
Dannelly, B. (Director). (2004). *Saved!* (Motion picture). USA: MGM.
De Castell, S. (1993). Introduction. *Canadian Journal of Education, 18*(3), 185–188.
Eakin, P. J. (2004). *The ethics of life writing*. Ithaca, NY: Cornell University Press.
Farhi, A. (1999). Hollywood goes to school: Recognizing the superteacher myth in film. *Clearing House, 72*(3), 157–159.
Ferland, G. (Director). (2002). *Bang bang you're dead* (Motion picture). USA: Showtime.
Garnet, D. (2012). Unknown and Hidden: The Toronto district school board education archive. *The Canadian Review of Art Education, 39*, 48–63.
Graham, D. J. (1997). The uses of film in theology. In C. Marsh & G. Ortiz (Eds.), *Explorations in theology and film: Movies and meaning* (pp. 35–43). Malden, MA: Blackwell.
Grant, P. A. (2002). Using popular films to challenge preservice teacher's beliefs about teaching in urban schools. *Urban Education, 37*(1), 77–95.
Grumet, M. (1990). Retrospective: Autobiography and the analysis of educational experience. *Cambridge Journal of Education, 20*(3), 321–326.
Hasebe-Ludt, E. (2010). A lovesong to our pluriverse: Life writing as cosmopolitan *motherwise* text. *Transnational Curriculum Inquiry, 7*(2), 39–46.
Hasebe-Ludt, E., Sinner, A., Leggo, C., Pletz, J., Simoongwe, F., & Wilson, L. (2010). These tensioned places of teaching: Life writing in precarious cosmopolitan times. *Creative Approaches to Research, 3*(2), 21–38.
Hillman, J. (1999). *The force of character and the lasting life.* New York, NY: Ballantine Books.
Hoffman, M. (Director). (2002). *Emperor's club* (Motion picture).USA: Beacon.
Hughes-Decatur, H. (2011). Embodied literacies: Learning to first acknowledge and then read the body in education *English Teaching: Practice and Critique, 10*(3), 72–89.
Jolly, M. (Ed.). (2001). *Encyclopedia of life writing: Autobiography and biographical forms.* Chicago, IL: Fitzroy Dearborn Publishers.
Johnston, R. K. (2000). Evangelicalism. In A. Hastings, A. Mason, & H. Pyper (Eds.), *The Oxford companion to Christian thought* (pp. 217–220). Oxford: Oxford University Press.
Keller, J., & Glass, W. (1998). In & out. *Journal of Popular Film & Television, 26*(3), 136.
Keroes, J. (1999). *Tales out of school: Gender, longing, and the teacher in fiction and film.* Carbondale, IL: Southern Illinois University.
King, T. (2003). *The truth about stories: A native narrative.* Toronto, ON: Anansi Press.
Leggo, C., & Mesner, K. (in print). Surprising representations of youth in *Saved!* and *Loving Annabelle.* In A. Ibrahim & S. Steinberg (Eds.), *Critical youth studies reader.* New York, NY: Peter Lang.
Lenta, M. (2003, May). J. M. Coetzee's "Boyhood" and "Youth". *English in Africa, 30*(1), 157–169.
Nava, M. (2007). *Visceral cosmopolitanism: Gender, culture and the normalization of difference.* New York, NY: Berg.

Noyce, P. (Director). (2002). *Rabbit-proof fence* (Motion picture). Australia: Rumbalara Films.
Pessoa, F. (1991). *The book of disquiet* (M. Jull Costa, Trans.) New York, NY: Serpent's Tail.
Pinar, W. F. (2004). *What is curriculum theory?* Mahwah, NJ: Lawrence Earlbaum.
Pinar, W. F. (2009). *The worldliness of a cosmopolitan education: Passionate lives in public service.* New York, NY: Routledge.
Richardson, L. (2001). Getting personal: Writing-stories. *International Journal of Qualitative Studies in Education, 14*(1), 33–38.
Richardson, L., & St. Pierre, E. (2005). Writing: A method of inquiry. In N. Denzin & Y. Lincoln (Eds.), *Handbook of qualitative research* (3rd ed., pp. 959–978). Thousand Oaks, CA: Sage.
Rogoff, I. (2011, July). The implicated. In Keynote address at the 2011 *International Visual Sociology Association Annual Conference*, The University of British Columbia, Vancouver, Canada.
Rosin, H. (2005). Can Jesus save Hollywood? *Atlantic Monthly, 296*(5), 161–168.
Sameshima, P. (2006). *Seeing red: A pedagogy of parallax* (Unpublished doctoral dissertation). University of British Columbia, Vancouver, BC.
Shaw, C. C., & Nederhouser, D. D. (2005). Reel teachers: References for reflection for real teachers. *Action in Teacher Education, 27*(3), 85–94.
Sinner, A. (2013). Archival research as living inquiry: An alternate approach for research in the histories of teacher education. *International Journal of Research and Method in Education, 36*(3), 241–251.
Sinner, A., Leggo, C., Irwin, R. L., Gouzouasis, P., & Grauer, K. (2006). Arts-based educational research dissertations: Reviewing the practices of new scholars. *Canadian Journal of Education, 29*(4), 1223–1270.
Smith, D. G. (2006). *Trying to teach in a season of great untruth: Globalization, empire and the crises of pedagogy*. Rotterdam, The Netherlands: Sense Publishers.
Steinberg, S. R. (2000). From the closet to the corral: Neo-stereotyping in *In & Out*. In S. Talburt & S. R. Steinberg (Eds.), *Thinking queer: Sexuality, culture, & education* (pp. 153–159). New York, NY: Peter Lang.
Voss, P. J., & Werner, M. L. (1999). Toward a poetics of the archive: Introduction. *Studies in the Literary Imagination, 32*(1), i–viii.
Weir, P. (Director.). (1989). *Dead poets society* (Motion picture). USA: Touchstone.
Werbner, P. (2012). Anthropology and the new ethical cosmopolitanism. In G. Delanty (Ed.), *Routledge handbook of cosmopolitan studies* (pp. 153–165). London, UK: Routledge.

Adrian McKerracher
University of British Columbia

Anita Sinner
Concordia University

Erika Hasebe-Ludt
University of Lethbridge

Carl Leggo
University of British Columbia

Kerri Mesner
Arcadia University

Dustin Garnet
Central Technical School Art Centre

ANTOINETTE GAGNÉ, SREEMALI HERATH AND MARLON VALENCIA

11. AUTOBIOGRAPHICAL CREATION

A Powerful Professional Development Strategy for Teachers

> It is the supreme art of the teacher to awaken joy in creative expression and knowledge.
>
> (Albert Einstein)

INTRODUCTION

A great deal has been written about autobiographical writing and how it can support the initial and continued development of teachers (Alvine, 2001; Carter & Doyle, 1996; Contreras, 2000; Edwards, 2009; Jaatinen, 2001; Raya, 1999). In this article, the focus is on an assignment requiring teacher candidates or graduate students in education to create a teaching and learning autobiography in a genre or format they believe will "stretch" them. A description of the project is provided in the appendix.

Since the late 90s, there has been an increase in the number of studies investigating various aspects of the *self* among language teachers. These include a focus on the emotions (Benesh, 2012), values (Crookes, 2009; Johnston, 2003), cognition (Borg, 2006), autonomy (Brumfit, 2001), narratives (Johnson & Golombek, 2002; Edge, 2011), and experiences (Senior, 2006) of teachers. The knowledge base for teachers has also been reconceptualized to include the knowledge of self (Freeman & Johnson, 1998; Turner-Bisset, 1999).

In the first chapter of *The Courage to Teach* (1997), Parker Palmer captures the rationale for autobiographical creation in teacher preparation and development:

> Teaching, like any truly human activity, emerges from one's inwardness, for better or worse. As I teach, I project the condition of my soul onto my students, my subject, and our way of being together. The entanglements I experience in the classroom are often no more or less than the convolutions of my inner life. Viewed from this angle, teaching holds a mirror to the soul. If I am willing to look in that mirror, and not run from what I see, I have a chance to gain self-knowledge – and knowing myself is as crucial to good teaching as knowing my students and my subject. (pp. 2–3)

J. B. Cummings & M. L. Blatherwick (Eds.), Creative Dimensions of Teaching and Learning in the 21st Century, 117–129.

Teaching Context

The autobiographical creation is an assignment which Antoinette has embedded in a range of initial teacher education and graduate courses for language teachers of English, French and other languages including Spanish, Mandarin and Korean. These pre-service and in-service teachers work across levels including primary, secondary and adult education as well as college and university. They also teach within a range of programs where: (1) the language is taught as a subject in school; (2) the language is the medium of instruction, or (3) the language is taught to prepare students for life in a new country, higher education or the workplace. Many of the teacher learners have experience teaching outside of Canada in various contexts.

The Goals of Autobiographical Creation

Since the autobiographical creation is a requirement of a course for teachers, the goal underlying this assignment is to support the development of their knowledge of self while allowing them to experience being creative.

Our Conceptual Frameworks

On the one hand, the knowledge base for teachers – which includes the knowledge of self – is an important conceptual framework underpinning the autobiographical creation. Turner-Bisset (1999) asserts that:

> If teaching is a profession in which the self is a crucial element, which demands a heavy investment of the self and in which the self in evaluation and reflection plays an important part, knowledge of self is an important knowledge base and should be added to the categories of knowledge for teaching. (p. 46)

Figure 1, adapted from Turner-Bisset (2001, Chapter 4) Knowledge Bases for Teaching: The Model, illustrates the place of "knowledge of self" alongside seven other knowledge bases that together comprise pedagogical content knowledge.

Maria Liakopoulou (2011, p. 69) describes the knowledge of self "a basic qualification of teachers, related to their views on their role, responsibilities, training and qualifications, rights and professional development, working conditions, values, and philosophy, etc." Turner-Bisset (2001, pp. 131–141) suggests that what separates excellent teachers from merely competent teachers is the ability of a teacher to make connections between these various knowledge bases and, in particular, be aware of themselves and the way that their own experiences, beliefs, and values affect them as teachers.

In his latest book entitled *Language Teacher Education for a Global Society*, Kumaravadivelu (2012) proposes a "Recognizing Module" focused on teacher identity, values, and beliefs. He explains that teacher knowledge is "filtered" through their beliefs and values. He further specifies that their beliefs and values guide them

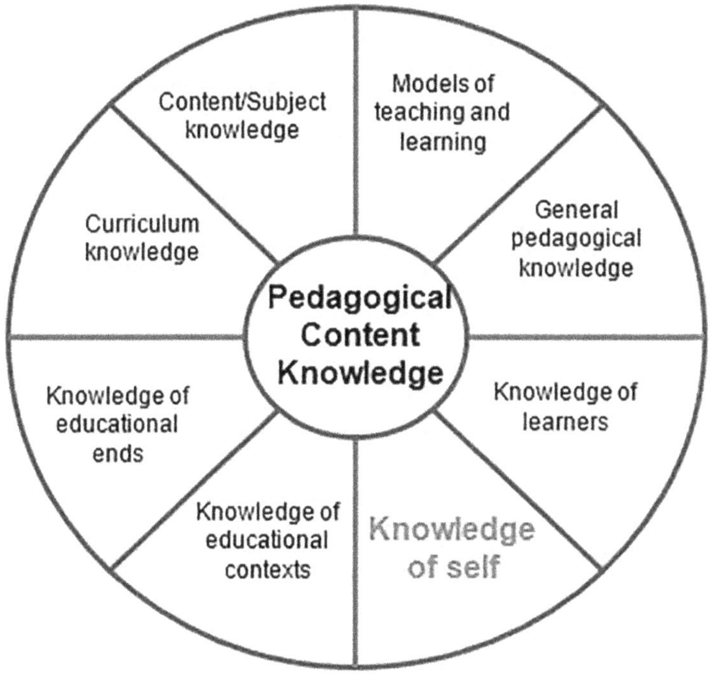

Figure 1. Knowledge of self within Turner-Bisset's 2001 knowledge bases for teaching

as they make choices about what and how to teach as well as how they make sense of what happens in their classroom. Kumaravadivelu suggests that teacher education should provide opportunities for teachers to become aware of their beliefs and values and then, analyze them through critical reflection. He underlines that teacher education can lead to identity transformation at personal and professional levels. He reminds us of the transformative power of teacher narratives and autobiographical reflections.

Autobiographical Creation and Creativity

Sir Ken Robinson has played an important role in helping both educationists and the public alike to understand how creativity in education can help ensure a strong future for all our children. Initially, in 1999 he chaired a task force which generated a report entitled *All our Futures: Education, Culture and Creativity*. In this report, creative teaching and teaching for creativity are defined and contrasted. Creative teaching involves a teacher using a variety of interesting strategies and resources to engage his/her students and motivate learning. Teaching for creativity involves teaching to support creative thinking or behaviour among learners. The report explains that teaching for creativity involves teaching creatively. Students are more likely to develop creative abilities if they have a teacher who is engaged in creative pursuits both inside and beyond the classroom. When teachers have suppressed their own creativity, they are not likely to be able to support the development of creativity among their students.

When teachers teach for creativity, they encourage their students, help them to identify their strengths and to foster them. Most importantly, the teacher must encourage students to believe in their creative potential, help them to imagine the possibilities while inspiring in them the confidence to take risks. Teaching for creativity involves strategies to stimulate curiosity while nurturing students' self-esteem and confidence as well as helping them to find their creative strengths. The goals of teaching for creativity include developing self-confidence, independent and critical thinking so that students are able to effectively handle future problems and objectives while learning more about themselves and the world beyond.

In the course in which the autobiographical creation assignment is embedded, we have attempted to *teach creatively* and *teach for creativity*. Some of the reading response strategies used to engage teacher learners are described in another article in this volume as they illustrate some aspects of our creative teaching.

To allow the teacher learners to discover their creative potential and develop the confidence to take "creative" risks, we have embedded various tasks into each week of the course that require they use various technological applications as well as explore various writing genres. Each task is a building block that they can integrate into their autobiographical creation. For example, in the first week of the course, they are asked to generate metaphors for teaching and in the fifth week they share maxims. In addition, throughout the 12-week course, they are asked to reflect critically on various aspects of their development as teachers using different media.

Autobiographical Creations and Reflection on the Creative Process

The students created a wide range of multimodal autobiographical creations. Although many of them held full-time teaching positions and led very busy lives, they were excited and relieved at the prospect of being able to "create" something as opposed to writing a term paper. However, many stated that they initially had mixed feelings about sharing their life stories with their peers. As they got to know each other, they became comfortable with this novel idea.

Many teacher learners built their autobiographies on their strengths and interests. They embraced the use of an array of production tools and genres to highlight key aspects of their lives in their multimodal and multisensory creations. Their autobiographies included websites and blogs, composing the words and music for a song, voice over *PowerPoints*, presentations on *Prezi*, an animated presentation on *PowToons*, e-portfolios, a scrapbook made of letters, fables, storybooks, comics, and a silkscreen patchwork consisting of the student's art to depict her multiple identities as a language learner and teacher. Teacher learners also had to write a reflection on the process of creating their autobiography to submit along with their creation. Figure 2

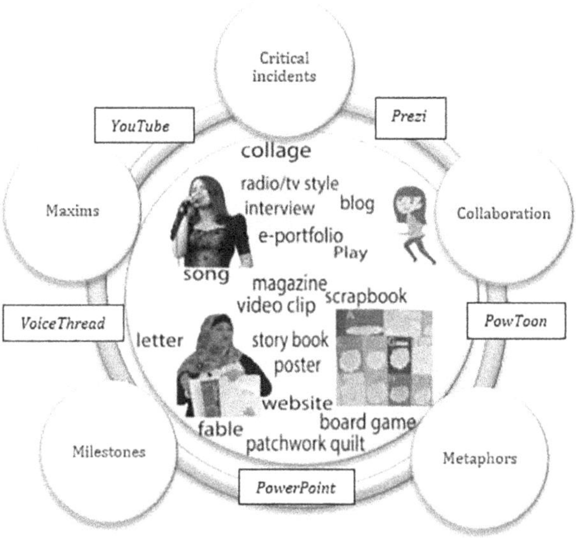

Figure 2. A myriad of formats and genres integrated into the autobiographical creations

provides a graphic summary of the varied production tools and genres used by teacher learners as well as some of the key elements of the autobiographical creations.

The figures below illustrate the wide range of autobiographical creations.

This student created Plasticine illustrations that were inspired by her favourite illustrator Barbara Reid to accompany her own narrative. She also borrowed some to include as she discovered how time consuming it was to create such visuals.

While many students built their creations to their strengths, they took this opportunity to "stretch" themselves. They explored new technologies, media and genre. One student who was a silkscreen patchwork artist (Figure 4) coupled her creation with a blog which was a new technology for her. Another student who was a professional singer had just started to learn to play the piano. She used this opportunity to accompany her song on the piano. One student who wrote a children's story stated that it was something she wanted to do for a while, but did not have the confidence to do so. She used this assignment to try out her creative writing and drawing skills. While many initially had mixed feelings about the "creative" aspect of the assignment, they embraced the opportunity to be creative and stretch themselves. Their creations were evidence of the multiple ways in which autobiographies can be created.

Two Teacher Learners' Reflections on This Assignment

Two former students, Marlon and Sreemali, describe their autobiographical creation and reflect on how it influenced some important professional choices made in the four-year period since completing this assignment.

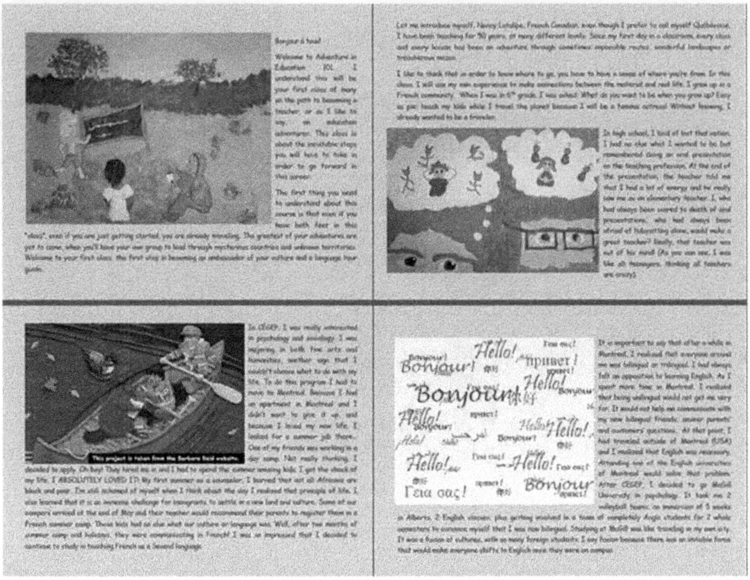

Figure 3. A children's storybook on being bilingual

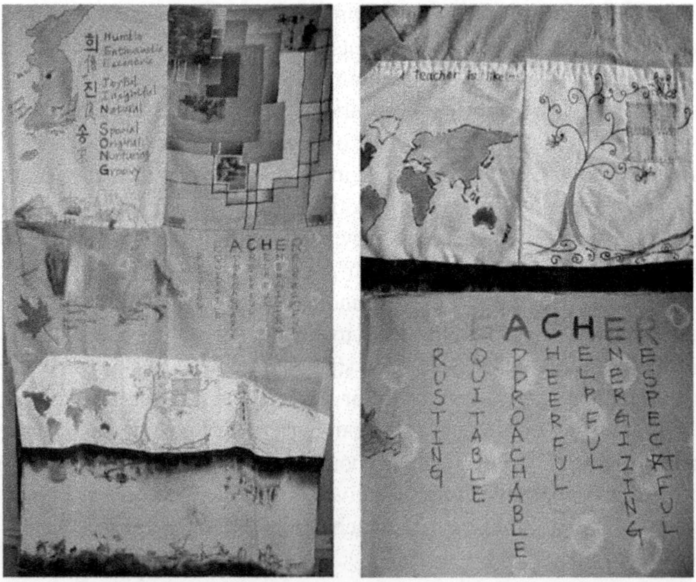

Figure 4. Patchwork quilt of silkscreen art showcasing a teacher's multiple identities as language student and a language learner. (The figure on the left shows the whole quilt, while the two figures on the side are macros of some of its interconnected pieces)

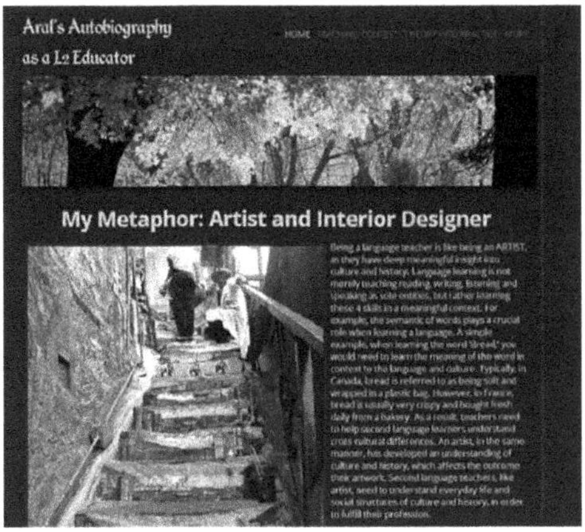

Figure 5. A website that depicts the student's life as a language teacher and a teacher educator

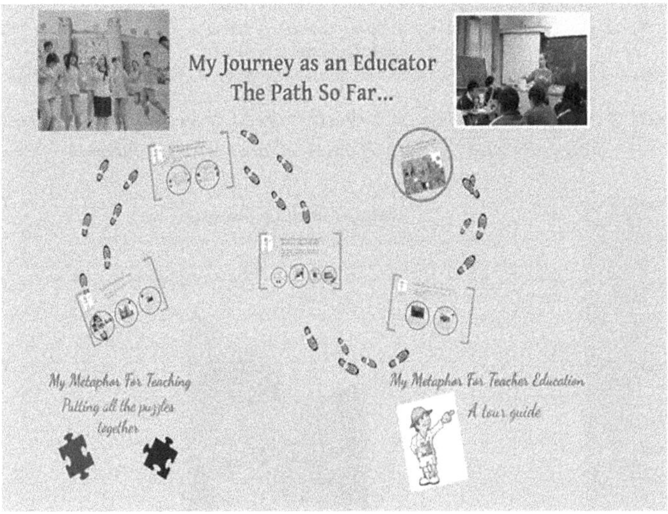

Figure 6. Footprints of an educator's journey on Prezi

An E-Portfolio: Sreemali's Autobiography. I used the e-portfolio function that is available for University of Toronto students to create my autobiography. I was introduced to the e-portfolio in another class I took with Antoinette, and I decided to "stretch" myself by using the e-portfolio to create my autobiography. In my autobiography I presented my multiple professional and familial identities as a student, language teacher, emerging teacher educator, researcher and a new mother. The e-portfolio function allowed me to integrate pictures, photographs, cartoons, audio and video files to my narrative.

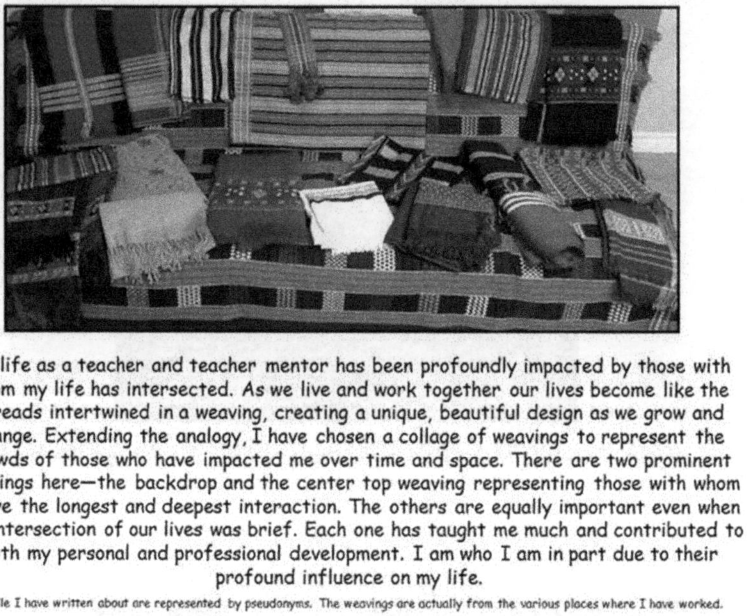
My life as a teacher and teacher mentor has been profoundly impacted by those with whom my life has intersected. As we live and work together our lives become like the threads intertwined in a weaving, creating a unique, beautiful design as we grow and change. Extending the analogy, I have chosen a collage of weavings to represent the crowds of those who have impacted me over time and space. There are two prominent weavings here—the backdrop and the center top weaving representing those with whom I have the longest and deepest interaction. The others are equally important even when the intersection of our lives was brief. Each one has taught me much and contributed to both my personal and professional development. I am who I am in part due to their profound influence on my life.
The people I have written about are represented by pseudonyms. The weavings are actually from the various places where I have worked.

Figure 7. A collage of weavings in a PowerPoint to describe how a teacher's life intersects with the lives of many of those who she has met

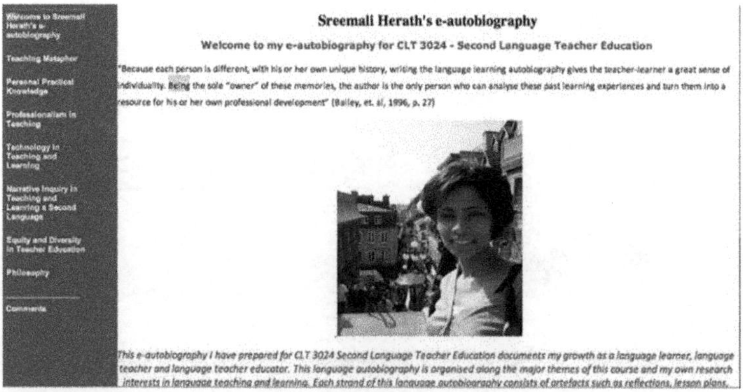

Figure 8. Welcome page of Sreemali's e-autobiography

This assignment, and its emphasis on the centrality of the self and the pivotal role of being creative in teaching and learning, had a more lasting impact on my own teaching and my doctoral research. At the beginning of my English for Academic Purposes (EAP) classes, I now get my students to create self-portraits. Although I find it difficult to get students from diverse sociocultural backgrounds to talk about themselves and share personal stories with their classmates, creating autobiographies has helped me to create a stronger sense of community and collaboration.

The personal experience of creating an autobiography has also influenced my doctoral research. In my research on post-conflict teacher preparation with pre-service teacher candidates in Sri Lanka, my primary data collection tool was life history narratives. In these narratives I elicited autobiographical information about my participants' lives as language learners, teacher candidates and as emerging teachers against the backdrop of a civil war. My participants' life history narratives were further complimented with Identity Portraits (IPs), which consists of a silhouette of a human figure in which my participants depicted their sociocultural identities using various visual semiotic resources.

Second language teacher education and homebrewing: Marlon's Autobiography. For my autobiography, I created a 12-minute video clip on Windows Movie Maker which I subsequently shared on YouTube. I had already created videos with this application, but this time I wanted to try a different approach to produce a richer video. I started with a PowerPoint with photos to create slides that I could later add voice to and background music. I built on the metaphor assignment introduced at the beginning of the course and brought two of my passions together: Homebrewing and language teaching. Thus, in this short video, I discussed my teacher journey and drew parallels to the process of crafting a homemade beer. Figure 9 shows the different milestones I discussed in my video.

This autobiography assignment allowed me to engage in a retrospective reflection of my language teaching career which helped me learn how every milestone I had achieved involved some type of "stretching". One example of this is how I felt two of my current identities overlapped and seemed conflicting at first when I moved to the U.S. as a Spanish teacher, which happened right after earning my second language teacher degree in ESL/EFL in Colombia. As a recent graduate, not only did I feel proud about my training, but I also felt knowledgeable and capable as a language teacher ready to take any challenge. Therefore, I was very excited about having received a scholarship to be a visiting Spanish language teacher at a Community College in Washington State. However, teaching my native language turned out to be really challenging because I had been trained to teach ESL and not Spanish as a second language (L2).

This particular situation allowed me to reflect on how my salient English teacher identity was challenged when I was "assigned" (Varghese, Morgan, Johnston, & Johnson, 2005) the identity of a Spanish teacher. This made me feel like an impostor because I felt my ESL teacher education made me inadequate to claim this new identity. This is a particular example of how I soon realized that this autobiographic assignment could be used as a powerful data collection tool in my international comparative doctoral research focused on how pre-service teachers of English and French develop their professional teacher identities in Canada, Chile, and Colombia.

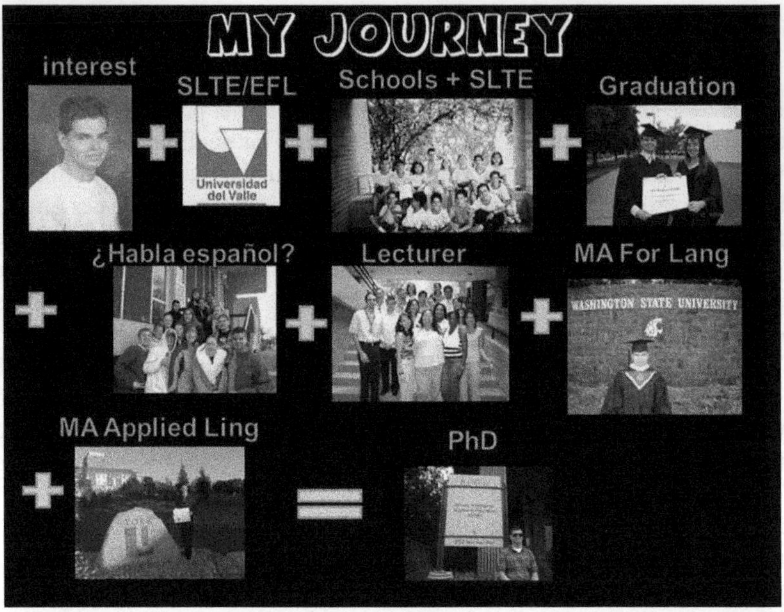

Figure 9, Marlon's Multiple Professional and Academic Identities: Language teacher, MA in Spanish Literature, MA in Applied Linguistics, and PhD in Language and Literacies

Consequently, one of my data collection tools, that not only my pre-service teacher participants but also I himself completed, is a multimodal autobiography in which all teachers' multiple salient identities are showcased on VoiceThread, a web 2.0 tool.

Pedagogical Implications

As knowledge of self is an important component of teachers' pedagogical knowledge, it is crucial to create multiple spaces in teacher education programs or courses, so all teachers, no matter what their career stage, have the opportunity to reflect on who they are and how this impacts their practice. As shown in the several examples provided, this autobiography assignment and the "stretching" required to complete it, act as catalysts for teacher learners to better understand how their multiple identities intersect and how these are constantly renegotiated across personal and professional landscapes.

Creating a safe and inclusive learning environment is a necessary prerequisite to autobiographical creation, in which so much personal information is revealed. Such an environment is a by-product of "teaching for creativity" where the development of the autobiographical creation is scaffolded by tasks requiring the teachers to explore various tools and genres while sharing little "bits" about themselves over the period of the course.

To sum up, the words of several of the teacher learners reveal the power of the autobiographical creation assignment and the need to make space for the "creative" self in teacher learning:

> The experience of completing this assignment definitely influenced how I designed my doctoral research. I incorporated the idea of "identity texts" as a method of data collection. Since I experienced creating my own autobiography, I realized that my participants will benefit by creating their own.
>
> I didn't know that autobiographies can be a powerful tool of boosting one's creativity. I found so much originality in writing an autobiography because it is about my self – it's one way of formulating a theory about one self.
>
> This activity made me realize the importance of the 'self' and 'being creative' in teaching and learning. The experience of creating my autobiography made me realize that.
>
> I think my teaching has changed ever since. I now give my teacher students more opportunities to reflect on their experiences.
>
> This was an excellent learning experience. It affirmed my creativity and proved that I am a reflective practitioner.

REFERENCES

Alvine, L. (2001). Shaping the teaching self through autobiographical narrative. *The High School Journal, 84*(3), 5–12.

Benesh, S. (2012). *Considering emotions in critical English language teaching: Theories and praxis.* New York, NY: Routledge.

Borg, S. (2006). *Teacher cognition and language education: Research and practice.* London: Continuum.

Brumfit, C. (2001). *Individual freedom and language teaching.* Oxford: Oxford University Press.

Carter, K., & Doyle, W. (1996). Personal narrative and life history in learning to teach. In J. Buttery & E. Guyton (Eds.), *Handbook of research on teacher education* (pp. 120–142). New York, NY: Simon and Schuster.

Contreras, G. (2000). Self-storying, self-understanding: Toward a narrative approach to EFL teacher education. *TESOL Journal, 9*(3), 24–27.

Crookes, G. (2009). *Values, philosophies and beliefs in TESOL: Making a statement.* Cambridge: Cambridge University Press.

Edge, J. (2011). *The reflexive teacher educator in TESOL: Roots and wings.* London: Routledge.

Edwards, D. (2009). Tracing literacy journeys: The use of the literacy autobiography in preservice teacher education. *Australian Journal of Teacher Education, 34*(4), 51–61.

Freeman, D., & Johnson, K. (1998). Reconceptualizing the knowledge base for language teacher education. *TESOL Quarterly, 32*(3), 397–417.

Jaatinen, R. (2001). Autobiographical knowledge in foreign language education and teacher development. In V. Kohonen, R. Jaatinen, P. Kaikkonen, & J. Lehtovaara (Eds.), *Experiential learning in foreign language education* (pp. 106–140). London, UK: Longman – Pearson Education.

Johnson, K., & Golombek, P. (Eds.). (2002). *Narrative inquiry as professional development.* New York, NY: Cambridge University Press.

Johnston, B. (2003). *Values in English language teaching.* Mahwah, NJ: Lawrence Erlbaum.

Kumaravadivelu, B. (2012). *Language teacher education for a global society.* New York, NY: Routledge.

Liakopoulou, M. (2011). The professional competence of teachers: Which qualities, attitudes, skills and knowledge contribute to a teacher's effectiveness? *International Journal of Humanities and Social Science, 1*(21), 66–79.

Palmer, P. (1997). *The courage to teach.* San Francisco, CA: John Wiley and Sons.

Raya, M. J. (1999). Contributions of autobiography to knowledge growth in student teachers. In P. Faber, W. Gewehr, M. J. Raya, & A. Peck (Eds.), *English teacher education in Europe. New trends and developments.* Munich: Peter Lang.

Robinson, K., Minkin, L., Bolton, E., French, D., Fryer, L., Greenfield, S., & Green, L. (1999). *All our futures: Creativity. Culture and education, Report for the Secretary of State for.*

Senior, R. (2006). *The experience of language teaching.* Cambridge, UK: Cambridge University Press.

Turner-Bisset, R. (1999). The knowledge bases of the expert teacher. *British Journal of Education Research, 25*(1), 39–56.

Turner-Bisset, R. (2001). *Expert teaching: Knowledge and pedagogy to lead the profession.* London: David Fulton Publishers.

Varghese, M., Morgan, B., Johnston, B., & Johnson, K. (2005). Theorizing language teacher identity: Three perspectives and beyond. *Journal of Language, Identity, and Education, 4,* 21–44.

Antoinette Gagné
University of Toronto

Sreemali Herath
University of Toronto

Marlon Valencia
University of Toronto

APPENDIX

Autobiographical Creation – Assignment Description

You may submit your autobiography using a genre and a medium of your choice. Although it is difficult to specify length, it may be helpful to think about your autobiography being no longer than 10 pages or the equivalent if you submit in a medium other than writing. Your submission should include a prologue and a brief reflection on the process of preparing your autobiography.

In preparing your autobiography as a second language teacher and teacher leader /educator, you should consult the pieces that you will be asked to write online throughout the term. These will most probably include:

- your metaphors of second language teaching and second language teacher education
- illustrative examples of your use of negotiation with second language students or within the context of second language teacher education
- your reflections on what it means to be successful as a second language teacher and teacher leader/educator
- 2 or 3 maxims that reflect your beliefs about second language teaching and/or second language teacher education

- milestones that are in some way linked to your work as a teacher and teacher educator
- critical incidents that reflect turning points in your teaching
- a reflection on the quality of your practicum experience and other practicum experiences
- a description of one or more partnerships that you have been linked to and a consideration of the strengths and weaknesses of the partnership
- a description of the various strategies you have adopted to improve you own language skills
- a description of one or more situations where you have mentored and/or supervised another teacher either in an official capacity or not and a consideration of the role you played and the choices you made
- a reflection on the teacher development strategies that you prefer as a teacher/learner and teacher leader/educator and an explanation of your preference
- a reflection on what type of facilitator you are

Sentence Starters

Complete two or more of these sentence starters to provide feedback to your colleagues.

- Your autobiography made me feel…
- Your autobiography reminded me of…
- What I enjoyed the most about your autobiography was…
- Your autobiography has motivated me to…
- The aspect of your autobiography that was the most surprising for me was…
- The aspect of your autobiography that resonated the most for me was…
- Your autobiography gave me a great idea….

ELIZABETH ASHWORTH AND KATHY MANTAS

12. ART MATTERS

An Advocacy Experience for Teacher-Candidates

INTRODUCTION

A Call for Advocacy

On a snowy day in March 2010, university administrators informed us that our art education classrooms and offices would be moved to another part of the campus. That news, in itself, was not bad. We liked our two classrooms for their sunny locations and shared storage space but had been having difficulty teaching 40-plus class sizes in rooms designed for populations of less than 35. We dreamed of the perfect location: perhaps a northern exposure overlooking the pond and bush area behind the main campus, or a move across the road to join the Fine Arts department in their treed setting by the escarpment? Unfortunately, our dreams were not fulfilled. We were shown a small, windowless room in an older part of the campus and told that this was our new art education classroom (one room, not two). As well, we were informed that our budget was cut. We could not believe we were losing a classroom, natural light, storage space, and half of our funding. We were dismayed, we were angry, but we were motivated to continue to advocate for our visual arts education program as well as for arts education in general. In the following paper, we describe how we dealt with these issues creatively, starting with our understandings of advocacy, how our "Art Matters" assignment evolved from those understandings and our teaching context, the assignment's implementation and assessment details, and its implications for curriculum and pedagogy.

Advocacy for Art Education

As former high school art teachers, we had encountered a lack of respect for our subject area's specific learning and teaching needs. Both of us had dealt with learners, colleagues, and communities who did not understand how art education can help teach specific art making skills and foster what Nussbaum (2010) called "essential… democratic understanding" (p. 107) through the capacities of play, empathy, and expression. Art, for example, plays an important role in student engagement. It can also provoke reflection and/or critical thinking, elicit dialogue, inform others about issues, and create a sense of community in the process. Despite providing a venue to

J. B. Cummings & M. L. Blatherwick (Eds.), Creative Dimensions of Teaching and Learning in the 21st Century, 131–138.

nurture these skills and capacities, we were aware, from first-hand experience and research, that art is often considered a "frill" in comparison to other subjects.

According to Chapman (2005), Clark (2006), Davis (2008), and Sabol (2010), art has been a staple of public education in North America since the 19th century but has diminished in importance since the 1950s. Chapman (2005) and Sabol (2010) suggested art education in the United States was affected negatively by the "No Child Left Behind" (NCLB) policies. Davis (2008) added the launch of *Sputnik* caused educators, and the general public, to raise the importance of math, science, and technology above the humanities. Closer to home, Clark (2006) argued the problem had more to do with Canadian universities focusing on general curriculum studies instead of research involving specific subject areas. From our experience, we found art education suffered the most during times of financial crises within educational institutions. By defending art education in our own contexts, and with the help of professional organizations (e.g., Ontario Art Education Association, Canadian Society for Education Through Art, National Art Education Association, International Society for Education Through Art), we learned proactive advocacy strategies to help raise the stature of art education from "frill" to "fundamental".

Although the word "advocacy" is not new to visual arts education, here we use it to refer to one of the roles that art educators have to play in schools and at all levels of education (e.g., art teacher as advocate). According to Bobick and DiCindio (2012), "the…goal [of advocacy is] increasing public awareness on the importance of art in individual lives and in society…In K-12 organizations, the focus of arts advocacy is more on the importance of arts education in schools and the role of art in students' lives" (pp. 20–21). Since we teach in a university, and this is the community we are trying to reach through our "Art Matters" assignment, we stress increasing the importance of art at all levels of education.

A Creative Plan

As teacher-educators working in a university environment, we thought that we had moved beyond trivialization and ignorance of art education, until our program relocation, and reduction of space and funding, showed us that art advocacy continues to be necessary at all levels of education. We help prepare teacher-candidates (TCs) for their future classrooms by broadening their art experiences, combining that knowledge with short and long-term planning, and teaching assessment and evaluation practices. From this assault on our program, we realized we needed to not only add advocacy to the mix but also model a creative, proactive approach.

First, we negotiated a different classroom location (one with windows) and two nearby storage rooms to house our supplies and exemplars. Next, we designed the classroom ourselves and dictated where counters, cupboards, and equipment would be, including the necessity of taking down a wall to enlarge the space to accommodate classes of 40-plus TCs comfortably. Last, we had all of our display boards moved from our former classrooms and hung not only within the new room but also in the hallways leading to and from that space. These bulletin boards became the front line for our advocacy campaign and extended our teaching space beyond the walls of our classroom.

Once settled, we turned our attention to our shared course: the Intermediate visual arts teachable. This course is designed to expose TCs, who are visual arts specialists learning to teach art from grades 7 to 10, to visual inquiry (an art-based research method) and long-term planning. As well, it focuses on encouraging future art educators to take on leadership roles in their pre-service and in-service school and community contexts. In order to stress the importance of advocacy in their future roles as art educators, we created the "Art Matters" assignment with three main goals in mind. First, it could teach art education appreciation and its importance in the curriculum and society to our university community and beyond. Second, it could provide an opportunity for TCs to apply their knowledge of art education theory and practice in a collaborative way. Last, it could help these art specialists prepare for advocacy issues they could face in their future in-service environments.

Assignment Implementation

We placed the "Art Matters" assignment near the beginning of the course. Prior to its introduction, the TCs participated in a review of elements and principles of design, plus a discussion about art advocacy, to "set the stage" for the project. They self-selected into small groups, each responsible for choosing a bulletin board, researching a topic, followed by planning, creating, and maintaining their display about that topic for the school year.

Each bulletin board/display area focused on one topic or theme related to art education awareness (e.g., promotion of visual arts, an art event, a local artist, art careers, art education as therapy, alternative teaching spaces for art, art from around the world, children's or seniors' art, community art, focus on one medium, connections with service learning). We encouraged the TCs to make their bulletin boards as educational and engaging as possible, and suggested they pay attention to how well they were communicating information through their displays. As well, a discussion of what factors lead to an effective display took place, followed by several hours of in-class work time.

Working on an assignment like this early in the course created a space for dialogue about creative collaboration. We felt that it was important for the TCs to be not only skilled themselves with group tasks but also know how to create a collaborative environment for their future students. We, therefore, included a discussion on how to work, and teach, collaboratively; for example, how to identify all tasks, how to share the work, how to oversee it for the school year, and how to instill best group practices among learners.

Assessment criteria for the assignment included knowledge/understanding of the topic, planning, application, and communication. As well, we emphasized process as well as product and asked the TCs to submit planning items for assessment (e.g., brainstorming notes, internet resources, reference materials, e-mails). Together, we conferenced with each group before, during, and after the creation of the displays, and had the opportunity to discuss each one before completing the final rubric and providing verbal and written feedback.

Educating Our University Community

The finished works were excellent displays informing not only our practice as teacher-educators but also the wider university community (e.g., students, staff, faculty, administration, visitors) as to art's place in education and beyond. Most TCs chose to create traditional bulletin boards on various topics related to art advocacy and one group built a series of site-specific art works on the university grounds and nearby trails using materials found in the natural environment (see Figures 1 and 2). Some displays were created merely for information transmission whereas others were interactive in nature.

Figure 3, for example, shows a "tree" on which a bucket of paper "apples" is attached. Viewers were invited to write on these "apples" their thoughts about how art matters to them, and then add their "message apples" to the "tree". Others provoked reflection and/or invited dialogue. Figure 4 shows a bulletin board focused on art careers and displays the question, "Why does art matter?", in order to encourage

Figure 1. "Natural Instincts" board is step one in a multi-site display

Figure 2. A "Natural instincts" outdoor display

Figure 3. 'Art Helps Us Grow" interactive bulletin board

viewers to not only answer it but also obtain more information about art careers using the Quick Response (QR) code attached to the board. All advocacy displays were in place for an entire school year and generated positive verbal and written feedback from the university community.

Through the "Art Matters" assignment, we shared what we do in an effort to begin a dialogue about art education. In doing this, we moved our curriculum from the privacy of our classroom to the public space of our high-traffic hallways. Our TCs built their displays in these hallways so the process (the mystery that often encompasses creativity) and the final products were visible for all to see. In essence, this assignment invited the viewer to have an encounter with art, one that encouraged reflection and dialogue, and, potentially, raised questions about what art is or is not, what knowledge is, and/or what kind of knowledge matters.

Figure 4. "Why does art matter?" board invites reflection and interaction

Implications for Curriculum and Pedagogy

As teacher-educators and arts-based researchers, we learned much from this assignment and plan to include it in future courses, both with art education specialists and generalists. It could reinforce what the former already know regarding the value of visual arts and may help the latter understand better why art education is important for learners, schools, and communities. We found some specialists struggled with creating visual communication for a general audience; for example, clarity of art terms and how much to say. Future displays, therefore, could include an overview outlining the purpose of the assignment to viewers and/or a series of guiding questions to promote reflection (e.g., What do you see? What is being communicated here? Is it communicated effectively?).

The assignment has been done with two different classes, over two school years, and has evolved in the process. To add more creative challenges for the TCs, all displays must now be interactive and, in an effort to integrate environmental considerations into the advocacy message, be created out of recycled materials, where possible. Figure 5, for example, shows how TCs offer invitations to viewers to add drawings and quotations to the boards, plus how they included a variety of recyclable materials (e.g., plywood, cellophane, paper cups, used picture frame) when creating their displays. As well, after the assignment is complete, there is now more follow-up discussion as to its purpose and extensions; for example, how TCs could have their own students do something similar on a smaller scale and/or involve parents/parent councils.

The impetus for this assignment was our classroom relocation, loss of space, and budget cuts. We still have one art education room and limited storage space; however, perhaps due to the visibility of the bulletin boards and positive feedback from our university community, our budget was not only reinstated but also increased for this academic year. The interactive nature of the bulletin boards has encouraged viewers

Figure 5. Interactive board created out of recycled materials

Figure 6. "Art Matters" work on the cover of a holiday card (copyright O'Connor, 2013) reproduced with permission

to add messages (mainly positive) about art education directly to the displays. Members of our university community told us the bulletin boards are a great way to brighten the hallways and miss them when they are taken down during the transition between one school year and the next. As well, one of the outdoor displays was photographed recently for the cover of the university's latest holiday card (see Figure 6). Although we appreciate the positive feedback and support, we know that advocacy is an ongoing necessity. We, therefore, look forward to continuing this assignment with future TCs in an effort to educate and inspire.

REFERENCES

Bobick, B., & DiCindio, C. (2012). Advocacy for art education: Beyond tee-shirts and bumper stickers. *Art Education, 65*(2), 20–23.

Chapman, L. (2005). Status of elementary art education: 1997–2004. *Studies in Art Education, 46*(2), 118–137.

Clark, R. (2006). Art education in Ontario, 1950–2000: Unlimited potential and unfulfilled promise. In H. Pearse (Ed.), *From drawing to visual culture: A history of art education in Canada* (pp. 200–220). Montreal, QC: McGill-Queen's University Press.

Davis, J. H. (2008). *Why our schools need the arts.* New York, NY: Teachers College Press.

Eisner, E. W. (2004). What can education learn from the arts about the practice of education? *International Journal of Education and the Arts, 5*(4), 1–12.

Nussbaum, M. (2010). *Not for profit: Why democracy needs the humanities.* Princeton, NJ: Princeton University Press.

Sabol, F. R. (2010, February). *Summary of findings from NCLB: A study of its impact on art education programs.* Retrieved from http://www.arteducators.org/research/NCLB_Proj_Report_2-10.pdf

Elizabeth Ashworth
Nipissing University

Kathy Mantas
Nipissing University

GEOFF LAWRENCE

13. INTEGRATING THE "HUMAN FEEL" INTO ONLINE SECOND/ADDITIONAL LANGUAGE TEACHING APPROACHES

INTRODUCTION

The nature of our communication processes, daily interactions, and as educators our educational tools and learning environments, are increasingly technology-mediated (Stanley, 2013). In many ways, technology use has become a normalized part of life in the 21st century (Stanley, 2013; Sykes, Oskoz, & Thorne, 2016). As Judy Brown (2012) stated in her keynote address to the 2012 Distance Teaching and Learning Conference, we North Americans check our mobile devices approximately 150 times/day, on average every 6.5 minutes. Information and communication technologies (ICTs) are having an exponential impact on the way we connect, the way we use language and the way we learn. ICTs are dramatically transforming the way we communicate and increasingly, the way we can engage with second/additional (L2) language teaching and learning.

Languages can now be taught through a range of delivery modalities. Teachers can use web-enhanced, flipped classroom or blended approaches to offer learners an individualized, self-paced approach at working with language. This can maximize face-to-face (F2F) classroom time for spontaneous interactions, corrective feedback and interpersonal connections. Language programs can be delivered completely online, meeting the needs of learners with scheduling constraints, offering varied learning pathways while engaging learners in interpersonal interactions through videoconferencing or chat. In addition, teachers can use an array of technology-mediated tools and applications to enhance language learning while also building transferable digital literacies. This can include asynchronous (self-paced) tools like email, discussion forums, blogs, wikis, twitter, podcasting or synchronous (same-time) tools like chat, video or audioconferencing or tools that combine both such as google docs, learning management systems and social networking.

There are also a full range of language e-learning tools and approaches that educators can use in their practices. For example, screencasting can enable teachers to provide personalized, nuanced forms of corrective feedback to learners. Mobile apps like Kahoot or Socrative can be used to create formative and summative assessments engaging learners with content. Video and audio podcasts can be used to provide multimodal authentic language input and learning management systems

J. B. Cummings & M. L. Blatherwick (Eds.), Creative Dimensions of Teaching and Learning in the 21st Century, 139–149.

like Moodle or Blackboard can be used to organize online learning for students and teachers and to provide learner analytics to guide teaching.

Research into the effectiveness of Computer Assisted Language Learning (CALL) has found increases in student-centred interaction, enhanced written production, improved confidence in language use, attention to linguistic form and overall engagement (Brennan, 2009; Kern, 2006; Kessler, Bikowski, & Boggs, 2012; Lawrence, 2014). A number of language learning benefits have been attributed to the self-paced multimodal language-and-culture input that technology can offer learners (Holmberg, Shelley, & White, 2005; Hurd, 2005; Kern, 2006; Kohn, 2001; Levy & Stockwell, 2006; Stockwell, 2012). A multimodal approach can offer learners individualized pathways, engaging diverse learning styles and presenting language in varied formats which can ultimately enhance language acquisition (Stockwell, 2012). Brennan (2009, p. 4) notes that learners who can see and hear content simultaneously are reported to remember 75% of this content versus 20% if they simply see it and 40% if they hear it. For example, research on captioned video-based listening activities has shown to increase learner attention, improve processing, reinforce previous knowledge to facilitate learning outcomes (Winke, Gass, & Sydorenko, 2010).

Adopting CALL approaches can also help learners refine the digital literacies needed in today's world where authorship has changed and learner autonomy has increased through computer-mediated communication (CMC) and multimedia (Garrett, 2009; Reinders & White, 2016; Sykes, Oskoz, & Thorne, 2016). ICTs have transformed communicative norms and teacher and learner roles, where knowledge emerges out of group interaction and less from an expert/novice relationship (Brennan, 2009; Lam & Lawrence, 2002; Sykes, Oskoz, & Thorne, 2016). In fact, approaches using CMC can fuel more recent conceptualizations of student-centred language learning approaches such as communicative language teaching or task-based language teaching (Salaberry, 2016). For example, English language learners can work on action-oriented tasks using Google Docs in intense collaboration to prepare a group presentation on a learner-centred topic. Students can use technology-based tools for extensive reading, writing, listening and now speaking in the target language with an audience well beyond the instructor. When producing language for their peers, students can get an extended sense of audience that can fuel investment in linguistic form to impress others and communicate a clear message (Lawrence, Young, Owen, & Compton, 2009). Such investment in the communication process has the potential to intensify noticing and language acquisition (Swain & Lapkin, 1995). The potential of enhanced autonomy, individualized learning combined with the perceived relevance of developing transferable digital and language skills can enhance overall engagement in the language learning process (Stockwell, 2012).

However, the key to learning outcomes in CALL environments depends on a number of factors that prioritize pedagogy: how a teacher integrates and uses specific technological tools within her/his teaching practice and context. As Stockwell (2012) notes, language education technologies offer various affordances, but these affordances greatly depend on the way practitioners adopt specific technologies into their L2 practices. The same technology used by different individuals may be experienced in very different ways. After all, technology can (and continues to) be used in very traditional, teacher-centred ways to teach languages. Fully online courses are plagued with higher attrition rates than F2F or blended programs often attributed to issues around motivation, a high cognitive load, the need for self-regulation and the perceived lack of interpersonal interaction (Tyler-Smith, 2006). This latter point is particularly salient in language education as online teaching and learning is often designed around self-paced, asynchronous communication that can create a depersonalized learning environment. Such environments can be demotivating for language learners who want, and need, to interact with others and build connections with new communities.

There is a human, interpersonal nature inherent in language-and-culture learning that does not always easily transfer into online environments. It is often challenging for teachers used to F2F classroom learning to appreciate how online environments will meet the psycho-social and language learning needs of their students. For example, a study examining the feasibility of e-learning in community-based English-as-a-Second (ESL) language programs in Ontario that will be discussed later in this chapter interviewed students, administrators and teachers about their beliefs, uses and visions of ESL e-learning approaches (Lawrence, 2014; Lawrence, Haque, & King, 2013). A number of instructors warned of the depersonalized nature of online learning like this instructor.

> A lot of our students feel isolated to begin with, and if you start doing online learning entirely, you're isolating them more because they're not making friends, they're not meeting people and this just increases their isolation. (Lawrence et al., 2013, p. 101)

This chapter will discuss the crucial role of social and teacher presence in CALL programs and will outline examples of successful language teaching approaches from this ESL e-learning feasibility study (Lawrence, 2014; Lawrence et al., 2013). These examples will detail features of successful online pedagogy. The chapter will conclude with a summary of pedagogical strategies that can be used to enhance CALL approaches in a range of language teaching contexts.

The Crucial Role of Social and Teacher Presence

In online learning the factor that has often inhibited engagement, learning and teacher interest (in online approaches) has been a diminished sense of social presence and the perception of an impersonal, isolating online learning environment where social distance feels great. Social presence is ubiquitous in classroom contexts but often challenging and crucial to create in online environments (Lehman & Conceiçao, 2010). Social presence reduces isolation, increases engagement (Bangert, 2008; Cortese & Seo, 2012; Cui, Wang, & Xu, 2010), interpersonal trust, enhanced participation, learner performance (Wei, Chen, & Kinshuk, 2012) and satisfaction

(Cui, Wang, & Xu, 2010; Wei, Chen, & Kinshuk, 2012). But the question for many educators exploring online approaches is what is *online* social presence and how do we facilitate this in L2 learning?

In his discussion of online learning, Garrison (2007, p. 63) describes social presence as "the ability to project one's self and establish personal and purposeful relationships". Garrison (2007) notes that social presence is characterized by effective and open communication and group cohesion. This has been reinforced by research identifying factors such as mutual attention and support, affective connectedness and open communication that contributes to a sense of community in online spaces (Lehman & Conceiçao, 2010). Dörnyei (2007) writes that group cohesion is built on group connectedness, the "we" feeling of a group (p. 271), developed through interactions that build shared goals and experiences. Garrison, Archer and Anderson (2000) developed the Community of Inquiry framework that describes three interconnected factors, social, teaching and cognitive presence, that contribute to meaningful asynchronous online learning in higher education. Their research has found that teaching presence facilitates social presence which in turn contributes to cognitive presence and learning.

In many ways teaching presence in online learning is the catalyst that fosters social and cognitive presence. "The consensus is that teaching presence is a significant determinate of student satisfaction, perceived learning, and sense of community" (Garrison, 2007, p. 67). Teachers need to provide learner-centred curriculum design and effectively model facilitation strategies and guide students. As online language learning environments are often new to learners, teachers must be explicit negotiating and modeling online communicative norms, time management and online learning strategies. Teachers' online facilitation strategies have a direct relationship with a sense of community and learning (Garrison, 2007, p. 67).

In addition, Garrison (2007, p. 63) notes that social presence does not remain static but needs to shift as a course of study evolves. At the beginning of an online program, teachers need to facilitate open communication and network learners so learners develop a shared understanding of each other so that the group feels secure enough to coalesce around shared learning goals that will facilitate cognitive presence and sustain the community (Garrison, 2007; Garrison & Arbaugh, 2007). In online environments, the curriculum design and instructional strategies need to consciously work at building group cohesion through a supportive teacher presence, interactive activities and social presence (Dörnyei, 2007; Swan & Shea, 2005).

Examples of Informative and Exemplary CALL Practices

As noted above, research outlined in Lawrence (2014) summarizes details of a government-funded study examining the feasibility of e-learning in community-based ESL programs in Ontario. This study (Lawrence, 2013a) researched and outlined a number of exemplary online English language training programs that will be detailed here. Descriptions of the program designs will be summarized along with a number of reported learning outcomes. These programs are characterized by methodical design, strategically leveraging the affordances of specific technologies and illustrating the power of facilitative instructional strategies that support social presence, learner autonomy and learning communities. A summary of pedagogical strategies that can be used in L2 teaching contexts will follow.

An Innovative Blended English for Work Redesign

This first program was the redesign of an English for Work community-based F2F curriculum that was developed for blended delivery (50% online and 50% F2F) to offer learners more flexibility with scheduling and learning (Lawrence, 2013a, p. 69). This 400-hour program was redesigned by a small team of instructors within this non-profit agency over a six-month period using Moodle and a range of technologies. To engage learners and meet the workplace communication outcomes of this program, the curriculum design team integrated skill-building work and autonomous communicative practice using e-learning tools and mostly asynchronous communication tasks to afford learners flexibility. Online activities include webquests, writing tasks on a wiki or in discussion forums, and listening and responding to dialogues. The program was divided into modules and activities that developed a range of workplace communication skills.

One unique characteristic of this program is that it runs on continuous intake accepting new students every Monday. As a result, the design team established a peer mentoring system where new students would be mentored by seasoned learners who had undergone a short leadership program in orienting new students. This mentorship program was a great success as it took the workload off instructors, helped orient new learners into the community and provided a personal connection for these new students to help build digital literacies, online learning strategies and answer questions. It also helped build social connections within the learning community that helped compensate for the focus on asynchronous communicative tasks that can sometimes be disconnecting (Kramsch & Thorne, 2002).

To explicitly thread learning between the online and F2F sessions, instructors used a smartboard in the F2F class to orient learners to online work, discussing online writing/editing strategies and how to use the various technologies. The F2F classes were also used to consolidate and expand on communication topics covered in the online learning segments. In the online sessions, learners complete tasks each week alone and sometimes collaboratively that correspond to units of study. The design team ensured learners had options to choose from in the online sessions, recognizing that choice and autonomy are crucial in engaging adult learners (Reinders & White, 2016).

Anticipating concerns about online attrition and engagement, the team developed a student accountability system where each module has a checklist of approximately ten core tasks or outcomes that a student must complete in the online and F2F classes. These assessed tasks provide content for student-controlled portfolios where learners document their learning. The accountability system also leveraged Moodle analytics to show learners and teachers the time, frequency of online participation, the completion dates of online work. In addition, students could add reflections on their progress that instructors would use to inform feedback and lesson planning.

Initial results from the program showed learner improvements in writing, speaking and listening on exit tests over learners in F2F classes. Employment-specific document use, computer use and online reading/searching skills improved. An instructor noted how online work is very relevant to today's workplace contexts, so these learners not only develop language skills, they develop workplace, teamwork and transferable digital literacies. One instructor noted this model "gives learners a sense of ownership, they must solve problems online, like work….it gives them a safe, motivating environment" (Lawrence, 2013a, p. 71). In order to sustain program development using this blended model, a significant barrier in e-learning, the program developed a continual contribution system with instructors. Each month instructors were responsible for uploading two to three items (lessons, activities, readings) to the Moodle repository where they are indexed and searchable for other instructors to use. This continual contribution system keeps the program current and helps ease instructors' search for learning materials. In an effort to stem teacher resistance and build comfort with the blended model, the design team also set up structures that allowed other teachers to lurk in these new environments and see what was happening. The design team noted that this collaborative approach is crucial to help instructors adopt a "collaborative, shared culture" to program development and delivery (Lawrence, 2013a, p. 72).

A 'Connected' Distance Listening and Speaking Course

This next program was the final project in a series of three curriculum design initiatives that one curriculum design team did over the course of a two-year span. These programs were geared to college-level adult learners in English-for-specific purpose (ESP) contexts. Before designing this final program the team had experiences redesigning two courses, a F2F ESP course for blended delivery based on an existing curriculum and a second brand new blended ESP course. The first blended course had disappointing results as the online work was selected from the existing F2F curricula and adapted into self-paced tasks, done alone as homework. Learners felt there was "too much alone work" (Lawrence, 2013, p. 63) and they reported generally preferring the face-to-face class. In the second program, the team had used an outcomes-based design approach, methodically planning how specific learning outcomes could be supported by various e-learning tools and/or F2F interactions. Online sessions engaged students in small group, action-oriented tasks where activities built social presence and learner-centred interactions that were then debriefed in the F2F sessions. Reactions from students and instructors in this blended course were very positive. Learners felt the course maximized their learning time in efficient ways and allowed them to explore occupation-specific communication skills deeply in an individualized manner. The mixed results of these two design efforts proved to be valuable for the team as the curriculum design refined this outcomes-based approach for the design of their final course.

The third course this team developed was a redesigned distance education ESP course to enhance listening and speaking skills among professionals (Lawrence, 2013a, p. 65). An existing F2F curriculum was used only as a guide as now the team recognized the need to fully rework the curriculum for this type of program delivery. Again, the team used an outcomes-based design approach, matching specific outcomes with the affordances offered through specific technologies. For example, the journal in Moodle was used for self-reflective activities that documented individual learning and an opportunity for instructor feedback, but not for peer feedback in writing that are better done through discussion tools or on a wiki.

A big challenge with this course design was the focus on speaking and listening skills delivered at a distance (Lawrence, 2013a, p. 65). Course objectives emphasized the need to develop soft skills for a range of internationally educated professionals that required work on pronunciation and nuanced speaking and listening skills that were challenging goals when done remotely. To enable this, the delivery model integrated a mix of weekly synchronous online videoconferencing sessions and small group tasks that used both asynchronous and synchronous forms of communication. The course design emphasized interactive activities, small group project-based work and individualized feedback from the instructor. Sample tasks included conducting Internet searches on occupation-specific information, delivering group presentations on Voicethread. Pairs gave each other feedback when practicing telephone communication skills using Vocaroo (an online recording tool). Small groups developed teamwork skills through video analysis/discussion and the peer-practice of job interview skills that were then debriefed in all-class videoconferences. This task-based approach encouraged learners to pool resources, build knowledge collaboratively and to negotiate meetings and forge interpersonal connections.

The first class began with a synchronous videoconferencing session where the course goals, schedule and communication processes were reviewed, technologies and learning strategies were introduced and learners began to get to know each other. This explicit discussion of communicative norms is particularly important in these types of often new online environments as there often is a need to clarify expectations around participation so there is no ambiguity (Kramsch & Thorne, 2002). The instructor paid explicit attention to learners at the beginning of the course, orienting them to course activities, to autonomous learning strategies and checking in with them when necessary. The instructor sent reminders to help students complete tasks by deadlines and to check in on absences. Weekly office hours via Google+ hangouts were scheduled. These were "so popular, there was a waiting list and the instructor had to kick people out" (Lawrence, 2013a, p. 66). The curriculum design lead added, "the teacher's presence was crucial in this online delivery model" (Lawrence, 2013a, p. 66), reinforcing the need for a facilitative instructor presence to provide instructional support, guidance, follow-up and feedback. The instructor for the pilot of this course was completely new to online learning and teaching, so when stumped with the technology, the instructor asked learners for their help, transforming learners to active agents in the teaching/learning community (Potts, 2005).

While the instructor felt that higher level learners fared best in this delivery model, analytics from the learning management system showed that the learners often spent extensive time on specific tasks like listening to a podcast or recording a professional introduction or voicemail message. Tracking tools indicated that some learners listened to a specific podcast 15 times and voicemail messages were made perfect through drafts, feedback and rerecording. This intensified language practice and language learning processes.

Student evaluations from the piloted version of this course revealed that learners were "evangelical in their enthusiasm" about this delivery model (Lawrence, 2013a, p. 67). In the final evaluations, many learners thought all ESL courses should be delivered like this. The only learner attrition in the pilot resulted from two learners who found employment, one relocating back home to India. This learner pleaded to remain in the course even after moving back home.

Implications and Strategies to Guide CALL Practices

As detailed above these two redesigned programs leveraged the affordances of specific technologies and delivery modalities to facilitate specific learning outcomes. They were designed using a pedagogically mindful, interactive and often outcomes-based approach at blended and online learning that adopted instructional practices to explicitly foster social presence through a supportive instructional practice. Below are some strategies highlighted in these examples that can help guide effective CALL program development and delivery in a range of language learning contexts.

Online/Blended Design Strategies

- Adopt action-oriented task-based approaches that leverage the affordances of specific technologies and/or delivery modalities to meet specific learning objectives.
- In blended delivery mindfully thread the online and F2F components to create synergies between delivery modalities (i.e., orient learners to online work and debrief successes and challenges in the F2F class where strategies and common experiences can be shared).
- Integrate multimodal language-and-culture content to engage different learning styles and deepen language acquisition.
- Incorporate small group collaborative action-oriented learning where learners report back to the class; this builds shared experience and intermember relationships with classmates, deepening connections (Dörnyei, 2007).

- Factor in time to 'play' with new technologies and time to network with classmates in a series of icebreaking activities, particularly in distance learning environments; this can allow learners to get to know each other more personally and forge connections.

Online/Blended Instructional Strategies

- Plan time at the beginning of online components to help orient learners, to provide strategies/feedback, to help with digital literacies and to assess learning/participation and offer guidance (i.e., through a regular instructional videopodcast).
- Spend time explicitly negotiating/discussing communication/interaction norms and expectations so learners know exactly what participation is expected in online environments; highlight successes early on and offer learner-centred strategies to maintain effective participation as the course evolves.
- Exploit video/audio podcasts, and video introductions to allow learners to ideally see and hear each other as this will help build group connections, social presence and intermember acceptance.
- Mix asynchronous and synchronous communication to afford learners the time to position their contributions and language use and to also build interpersonal connections and practice spontaneous language use.
- Offer learners choice in activities/learning options to enhance autonomy and engagement.
- Actively use student resources and knowledge to facilitate learning (i.e., use student produced language to inform teaching practice, to highlight successes or to focus on fluency or linguistic form).
- Use students as digital guides to help other learners and to negotiate the strategies/tools used in the course; employ peer mentoring strategies to help students share and build digital literacies and metacognitive awareness.
- Exploit learner analytics when available to help assess online participation and offer guidance and to inform teaching practices.
- Develop a supportive teacher presence that mentors and guides online learning, connects learners and builds classroom community.
- Encourage a community of practice among teachers working online to share strategies, develop a continual contribution system as detailed above and build collaborative creative practices.

Concluding Thoughts

Salaberry (2016) notes that computer-mediated communication (CMC) is transforming instructional methodology in two ways: generating technological tools to provide a range of interactive methodologies and by focusing teachers' perspectives on a learner-centred approach to teaching (p. 131). Salaberry argues that technology and specifically CMC are not facilitating a transformative shift as much as providing the tools needed for a learner-centred, interactive approach.

In the ESL E-Learning Feasibility Study (Lawrence, Haque, & King, 2014, p. 55), teachers, students and administrators expressed a strong preference for blended learning, not wanting to lose the "human feel" offered through F2F language learning. However, as this distance learning program above demonstrates, the technologies and instructional strategies now exist to develop and maintain social presence in completely online environments and simultaneously offer learners a range of pathways for L2 learning. As discussed above, a key to these online language teaching practices includes a supportive teacher presence that facilitates social interactions, fosters identity investment (Lawrence et al., 2009) and builds social presence that in turn sustains learning and engagement (Garrison, 2007). As noted in the 2011 *TESOL Technology Standards*, social presence is at the heart of creating an online learning community…the teacher's role is to set up structures and the climate for a successful learning environment (Healey, Hanson-Smith, Hubbard, Ioannou-Georgiou, Kessler, & Ware, 2011, p. 166).

REFERENCES

Bangert, A. (2008). The influence of social presence and teaching presence on the quality of online critical inquiry. *Journal of Computing in Higher Education, 20*(1), 34–61.

Brennan, C. (2009). Realizing the benefits of computer-assisted language learning (CALL) in English language learning classrooms. *Interfaces, 3*(1), 1–28.

Brown, J. (2012, August 8–10). *Learning in hand with mobile technology* (video). Distance teaching and learning, Madison, WI. Retrieved from http://ics.webcast.uwex.edu/Mediasite7/Play/0486235c41cf45119e072c6d985d1ff81d

Cortese, J., & Seo, M. (2012). The role of social presence in opinion expression during FtF and CMC discussions. *Communication Research Reports, 29*(1), 44–53.

Cui, N., Wang, T. & Xu, S. (2010). The Influence of social presence on consumers' perceptions of the interactivity of web sites. *Journal of Interactive Advertising, 11*(1), 36–49.

Dörnyei, Z. (2007). Creating a motivating classroom environment. In J. Cummins & C. Davison (Eds.), *International handbook of English language teaching* (Vol. 2, pp. 719–731). New York, NY: Springer.

Garrett, N. (2009). Computer-assisted language learning trends and issues revisited: Integrating innovation. *The Modern Language Journal, 93*, 719–740.

Garrison, D. (2007). Online community of inquiry review: Social, cognitive, and teaching presence issues. *Journal of Asynchronous Learning Networks, 11*(1), 61–72.

Garrison, D. R., & Arbaugh, J. B. (2007). Researching the community of inquiry framework: Review, issues, and future directions. *The Internet and Higher Education, 10*(3), 157–172.

Garrison, D. R., Anderson, T., & Archer, W. (2000). Critical inquiry in a text-based environment: Computer conferencing in higher education. *The Internet and Higher Education, 2*(2–3), 87–105.

Healey, D., Hanson-Smith, E., Hubbard, P., Ioannou-Georgiou, S., Kessler, G., & Ware, P. (2011). *TESOL technology standards: Description, implementation, integration*. Alexandria, VA: TESOL.

Holmberg, B., Shelley, M., & White, C. (Eds.). (2005). *Distance education and languages: Evolution and change*. Clevedon, UK: Multilingual Matters.

Hurd, S. (2005). Autonomy and the distance language learner. In B. Holmberg, M. Shelley, & C. White (Eds.), *Distance education and languages: Evolution and change* (pp. 1–19). Clevedon, UK: Multilingual Matters.

Kern, J. (2006). Perspectives on technology in learning and teaching languages. *TESOL Quarterly, 40*(1), 183–210.

Kessler, G., Bikowski, D., & Boggs, J. (2012). Collaborative writing among second language learners in academic web-based projects. *Language Learning & Technology, 16*(1), 91–109.
Kohn, K. (2001). Developing multimedia CALL: The TELOS language partner approach. *Computer-Assisted Language Learning, 14*(3–4), 251–267.
Kramsch, C., & Thorne, S. (2002). Foreign language learning as global communicative practice. In D. Block & D. Cameron (Eds.), *Language learning and teaching in the age of globalization* (pp. 83–100). London: Routledge.
Lam, Y., & Lawrence, G. (2002). Teacher-student role redefinition during a computer-based second language project. *CALL, 15*(3), 295–315.
Lawrence, G. (2013a). *E-Learning and non-credit adult ESL/EAL education: A research and best practices report.* Toronto, Canada: The Toronto Catholic District School Board.
Lawrence, G. (2013b). A working model for intercultural learning and engagement in collaborative online language learning environments. *Intercultural Education, 24*(4), 303–314.
Lawrence, G. (2014). A call for the human feel in today's increasingly blended world. In H. M. McGarrell & D. Wood (Eds.), *Contact research symposium, 40*(2), 128–141.
Lawrence, G., Young, C., Owen, H., & Compton, T. (2009). Using wikis for collaborative writing and intercultural learning. In M. Dantas-Whitney & S. Rilling (Eds.), *Authenticity in the adult language classroom* (pp. 199–212). Alexandria, VA: TESOL.
Lawrence, G., Haque, E., & King, J. (2013). *Rationale and recommendations for implementing E-Learning in Ontario Non-Credit Adult ESL programs: A feasibility report.* Toronto, Canada: The Toronto Catholic District School Board.
Lehman, R. M., & Conceiçao, S. C. O. (2010). *Creating a sense of presence in online teaching.* San Francisco, CA: Jossey-Bass.
Levy, M., & Stockwell, G. (2006). *CALL dimensions: Options and issues in computer-assisted language learning.* New York, NY: Routledge.
Potts, D. (2005). Pedagogy, purpose, and the *Second Language* learner in on-line communities. *Canadian Modern Language Review, 62*(1), 137–160.
Reinders, H., & White, C. (2016). 20 years of autonomy and technology: How far have we come and where to next? *Language Learning & Technology, 20*(2), 143–154.
Salaberry, M. R. (2016). A theoretical foundation for the development of pedagogical tasks in computer mediated communication. In G. Kessler (Ed.), *Landmarks in CALL research* (pp. 129–159). Bristol, CT: Equinox.
Stanley, G. (2013). *Language learning with technology.* Cambridge, UK: Cambridge University Press.
Stockwell, G. (2012). *Computer-assisted language learning: Diversity in research and practice.* New York, NY: Cambridge University Press.
Swain, M., & Lapkin, S. (1995). Problems in output and the cognitive processes they generate: A step towards second language learning. *Applied Linguistics, 16*(3), 371–391.
Swan, K., & Shea, P. (2005). The development of virtual learning communities. In. S. R. Hiltz & R. Goldman (Eds.), *Asynchronous learning networks: The research frontier* (pp. 239–260). New York, NY: Hampton Press.
Sykes, J. M., Oskoz, A., & Thorne, S. L. (2016). Web 2.0, synthetic immersive environments, and mobile resources for language education. In G. Kessler (Ed.), *Landmarks in CALL research* (pp. 160–183). Bristol, CT: Equinox.
Tyler-Smith, K. (2006). Early attrition among first time elearners: A review of factors that contribute to drop-out, withdrawal and non-completion rates of adult learners undertaking e-learning programs. *Journal of Online Learning and Teaching, 2*(2), 73–85.
Wei, C. W., Chen, N. S., & Kinshuk. (2012). A model for social presence in online classrooms. *Education Technology Research Development, 60*, 529–545.
Winke, P., Gass, S., & Sydorenko, T. (2010). The effects of captioning for foreign language listening activities. *Language Learning & Technology, 14*, 65–86.

Geoff Lawrence
York University

MATTHEW E. POEHNER

14. THE ZONE OF PROXIMAL DEVELOPMENT AND THE TWIN POLES OF TEACHING AND ASSESSING IN VYGOTSKY'S DEVELOPMENTAL EDUCATION

INTRODUCTION

During the late 19th and early 20th Centuries, the continued exploration of the natural world centered in large part around the goal of reaching the North and South Poles. This same period was marked by equally compelling explorations of the psychological world, where one of the great achievements was L. S. Vygotsky's discovery of the *Zone of Proximal Development* (ZPD). Just as the race to the Poles advanced scientific knowledge in fields such as electromagnetism, the investigations of the ZPD undertaken by Vygotsky and his colleagues led to remarkable insights into the potential for educational activity to guide learner development. Today, in the early 21st Century, the natural sciences have already reaped many of the benefits from the exploration of the magnetic poles, but psychology and particularly education continue to confront challenges similar to those that Vygotsky's research aimed to address. Central to these challenges are two metaphorical poles, assessing and teaching. Vygotsky's account of the ZPD compels us to understand these poles in relation to one another, such that assessments of learner development must include teaching if they are to take account of the full range of learner abilities while teaching that seeks not merely to impart knowledge but to lead learners to new ways of thinking and acting is necessarily predicated upon a diagnosis of their abilities.

In what follows, a brief overview of the ZPD is provided that traces how the concept was described in Vygotsky's writings in relation to both assessing and teaching. Two key terms are then introduced, Dynamic Assessment and Mediated Development. These emphasize, respectively, the assessing and teaching poles that are inherent in ZPD activity. The origin of these terms is explained, with particular attention to the research of Reuven Feuerstein, whose practical work with learners with special needs may be regarded as a continuation of Vygotsky's own interventions for at-risk learners (Miller, 2011). As a prelude to this discussion, however, a brief excerpt is provided from an interaction between a teacher/assessor, referred to as a *mediator*, and a learner. Their exchange contains certain of the principles that are characteristic

J. B. Cummings & M. L. Blatherwick (Eds.), Creative Dimensions of Teaching and Learning in the 21st Century, 151–161.

of the ZPD and its integration of assessing and teaching. As such, it provides readers a reference point for the subsequent discussion.

Mediator-Learner Interaction and Second Language Development

The following interaction[1] occurred in the context of a standardized, multiple-choice test of reading comprehension for learners of French as a second or foreign language (L2). Learners were presented with short texts to read in French and then asked to respond to a series of questions according to their understanding of the reading. Unlike most standardized tests, however, a mediator was present to offer interaction when learners answered incorrectly. The purpose of the interaction was twofold: to determine the knowledge and reasoning behind learner responses to test questions but also to identify whether, with a degree of engagement with the mediator, learners were able to arrive at the correct answer. This latter point is especially important because, as will be explained later, the extent of support provided by the mediator provides important diagnostic information concerning learner development. As the activity was intended as an assessment, it is that pole that is brought to the fore. Nonetheless, as will be clear, teaching played an integral role as well. The exchange here is adapted from a study reported by Poehner and van Compernolle (2011) and was part of a larger project to develop computerized versions of the tests in which forms of support were built-in to the program and accessible to learners[2]. We enter the exchange when the learner has completed reading a passage arguing for reforms to the rules of professional soccer. In responding to a question about the writer's main point, the learner initially selected an incorrect response (soccer is simply a business like any other). The correct answer is that the author expresses the view that (d) soccer must be better regulated, suggesting that this is crucial if the sport is to gain greater recognition and professionalism and maintain its popularity on the world stage. Identifying this point requires following the rhetorical line of reasoning and comprehending sometimes complex grammatical and discursive structures.

Following the learner's incorrect answer, the mediator intervenes in Turn 1. His first move is to take stock of the task by verbalizing that there are three remaining options, which he reads aloud. This move creates a shared orientation to task and begins the process of thinking together with the learner:

Mediator:	so + we have these three. ((pointing to response options)) soccer should be de<u>re</u>gulated? soccer players should be professionals for ten years? and to maximize both the sporting and financial side of soccer it must be <u>reg</u>ulated.
Learner:	okay.
Mediator:	so. it is + in this + second paragraph. ((indicating paragraph in text with both hands)) okay? um and

	++ what I want you to <u>con</u>centrate on? is starting <u>*here*</u>, ((pointing to text)) *mais l'erreur + serait de le considerer.* ((‘but the mistake would be to consider it’)) okay? and see if you can't figure it out from that. ((19.0 seconds pass)) ((re-reading text and response options))
Learner:	oh. ++ I think it's D? it must be regulated + because
Mediator:	mhm, right,
Learner:	+ it + needs to be regulated for the maximization of the ( ) of sports? ((pointing to text with pencil and translating sentence))
Mediator:	<u>*yep*</u> that's it.

In Turn 3 the mediator employs both verbal and non-verbal means to focus the learner's attention on the particular portion of the text where the relevant information may be found. As an assessment, this move explores how much of the passage the learner was able to comprehend; it is clear that she did not fully comprehend the text, but by delimiting the search space, some of the cognitive demand is reduced as the learner has less information to sift through. In this case, the learner is successful in reaching the correct answer (Turn 5) and she even provides a justification for her response by translating a relevant detail (Turn 7).

The view that emerges of the learner's comprehension of French from this interaction is certainly more detailed than it would have been without the mediator's presence. Indeed, most conventional assessments are able only to determine whether or not a learner is successful while functioning independently. The approach followed here extends this to another question: to what extent are learners able to be successful and under what conditions? For other learners participating in this project, for example, the mediator needed to do far more than point them toward a specific portion of the text; in some cases, vocabulary help was required and complex sentences needed to be translated. For some learners, even such extensive intervention from the mediator was insufficient for them to comprehend the text.

Finally, and in addition to the nuanced assessment information that this kind of cooperative interaction yields, there is the inherent instructional component. The vocabulary that was sometimes introduced to aid learner comprehension and the explanation of grammatical points and translation of phrases were moments of teaching and learning that arose spontaneously during this activity that was ostensibly focused on assessment. Moreover, as Poehner and van Compernolle (2011) explain, learners sometimes were able to select the right answer to a test question through partial comprehension or through a test-taking strategy. In these instances, mediator-learner interaction took on a decidedly teaching focus as they jointly examined the text and discussed pertinent cultural and linguistic issues after the right answer had been identified. This co-presence of teaching and assessing that we have seen will be helpful to bear in mind as we now turn to a reading of the ZPD as activity undertaken cooperatively between mediators and learners.

Zone of Proximal Development as Dialectical Activity

Lantolf and Poehner (2014) argue that to fully appreciate Vygotsky's conceptualization of the ZPD as well as his scientific enterprise more generally, it is important to understand that he was foremost a dialectical thinker. Full discussion of dialectical logic and its intellectual tradition that Vygotsky drew upon is beyond the scope of this chapter, and readers are referred to Lantolf and Poehner (2014) for an in-depth treatment of the topic. Briefly, dialectics stands in contrast to the traditional or formal logic that was developed in Greek philosophy and that has remained largely unchallenged as the dominant form of reasoning in the natural and social sciences since the Enlightenment (Novack, 1971). Among the premises of formal logic is that any object or phenomena must always be equal to itself (expressed symbolically as A = A). Furthermore, a thing can never be unequal to itself, such that if A and B are distinct objects or phenomena then A must always equal A and can never equal B. As Il'yenkov (1977) explains, this mode of reasoning proved advantageous to Enlightenment scientists as they delineated the objects of their inquiry and formulated methods for studying them. However, the inherent dualism also introduced problems that philosophers have long struggled to overcome. For the present discussion, what is most relevant is that the dualism necessarily imposes limitations on how phenomena may be understood, with the result that complex processes, for example, may be reduced to such a degree that important features become difficult to comprehend.

Dialectics offers one way of overcoming the dualism. Dialectical logic is concerned with understanding how seemingly contrary processes and phenomena may be regarded as together forming a unity. Novack (1971) explains that rather than accepting the bifurcation of A and B, dialectics takes the position that A and B are mutually interdependent and form a more complex whole. It is the dynamics of their interrelation that is of interest. Lantolf and Poehner (2014) offer the everyday object of a pencil as an object that contains elements of a dialectic, particularly as it is employed in the activity of writing. They note that a pencil comprises two ends, one containing graphite and the other an eraser. The former, of course, produces text by adding marks to a page while the latter can remove those marks. The two ends, or poles, stand in contrast to one another and could be understood as performing opposite functions. From a dialectical perspective, both poles together constitute the pencil. More important, both poles are essential to the activity of writing, as this involves the production but also the revision of text.

As a dialectical thinker, Vygotsky (1987) sought to understand the human mind through the processes of its formation. He reasoned that just as our physical activity in the world is not direct but is mediated through the use of physical tools, our psychological activity is similarly mediated. Thus, in contrast to animal psychology, which can be understood through responses to stimuli in the immediate perceptual field, human psychology is a process of appropriating symbolic tools and exercising them to gain intentional control over our thinking. Language, counting systems, art, and conceptual knowledge are all examples of symbolic tools that transform our understanding of and action in the world. Central to Vygotsky's account of how individuals appropriate symbolic forms of mediation is the ZPD.

Most of what we usually think of as "psychological" is only one dimension of our functioning, and Vygotsky (1978) termed this the *intrapsychological*. Here, individuals rely upon symbolic mediation they have already appropriated to regulate their thinking. They may appear to operate independently, but their thinking is still mediated by virtue of their history of engagement in activities with others. It is this social character that is brought to the fore in what Vygotsky described as *interpsychological functioning*. In this case, psychological processes occur on an "external" plane of interaction between mediator and learner. Interpsychological functioning enables learners to perform beyond the limits of the abilities they have already developed; that is, they exceed their *Zone of Actual Development*. During interpsychological functioning, learners draw upon mediation they have appropriated while also benefiting from mediation that is external and made accessible to them through cooperation.

Vygotsky (1987) expressed the importance of this idea with the example of two children, whom he reported appeared very similar when asked to solve problems independently. Both were able to successfully complete problems at an eight-year-old level. However, when allowed the opportunity to engage cooperatively with a mediator, in which they benefitted from prompts, hints, leading questions, feedback, and models, one of the children was able to complete problems at the level of a nine-year-old while the other advanced all the way to a twelve-year-old level. In Vygotsky's dialectical analysis, the two children are simultaneously the same and different; they are the same with regard to their Zone of Actual Development but different in terms of their Zone of Proximal Development.

With his career cut tragically short, Vygotsky himself did not conduct many studies on ZPD activity. Before concluding this section, it is worth describing one educational project he did undertake in which the ZPD figured prominently and that highlights its importance for diagnosing and promoting learner development. Van der Veer and Valsiner (1991) report a lecture Vygotsky gave sharing the results of an investigation into changes in children's IQ scores during their first year of schooling. Specifically, some children were found to gain IQ points whereas others made no progress or even earned lower scores. Vygotsky hypothesized that the school curriculum was promoting the psychological development of some but not all children. To understand how this was happening and why only some children were benefiting, he developed an alternate measure to IQ, one that included interaction between examiner and child. When a child failed to produce a correct response to a test item, the examiner began a process to offer mediation and in this way the measure sought to capture both their current and emerging abilities.

The results of a large-scale study comparing children's performance under the two conditions (traditional IQ test and ZPD measure) led to two important findings. First, and as predicted, children differed in terms of their responsiveness to mediation during the ZPD assessments. More important, degree of responsiveness did not correspond to a low or high IQ score, with some learners yielding a low score but high responsiveness, others a high score and lower responsiveness, and so on. In other words, the ZPD and IQ measures appeared to reveal different dimensions of learner abilities and, consequently, led to different predictions of children's academic success. The second, and related finding, was that the ZPD proved a more accurate predictor of learner performance in school. It was their responsiveness to mediation rather than their IQ score that correlated with learner progress during their first year of schooling. The significance of this finding is that it suggests a learner's future level of functioning cannot be adequately predicted on the basis of his/her current independent performance. If it could then there would be little point to including the ZPD in assessment. The ZPD affords an empirical prediction of the future as emerging abilities are externalized during cooperation with a mediator. Of course, another lesson from this study is that the future that is glimpsed in ZPD is contingent upon learner access to appropriate forms of mediation. Indeed, Vygotsky (in Van der Veer & Valsiner, 1991) argued that learners who performed well on the assessments at the beginning of their first year of school and did not make any gains when retested had spent a year receiving instruction that was aligned with what they could already do rather than their emerging abilities. They did not reap the developmental benefits of the school environment because the instruction did not function as mediation to promote their abilities. This conclusion echoes what Vygotsky elsewhere (1998) described as the great practical significance of the ZPD for education: identification of abilities that are in the process of forming and tailoring instruction accordingly so as to optimally guide development.

Dynamic Assessment and Mediated Development

Decades after Vygotsky's death, as his ideas became known by communities of scholars around the world, his writings on the ZPD led to the formalization of a range of procedures for administering tests that included mediator-learner interaction and that aimed to capture a broader picture of learner abilities than conventional assessments (Poehner, 2008b). Collectively, these procedures are referred to as Dynamic Assessment (DA). To date, they have been applied with populations including learners with special needs, learners from low socio-economic backgrounds, immigrants, ethnic and racial minorities, gifted learners, prison inmates, L2 learners, and adolescents and adults studying specific academic subjects (Haywood & Lidz, 2007; Lidz & Elliott, 2000). Poehner and Rea-Dickins (2013) explain that much DA work carries a commitment to advocating for learners whose abilities may be underestimated by other measures and who, by consequence, are more likely to have their access to educational opportunities restricted. As those authors explain, concern over equity and access in education has been a part of DA beginning with Vygotsky's own efforts to appropriately diagnose and remediate learners with special needs (for discussion see Kozulin & Gindis, 2007). According to Haywood and Lidz (2007), the assessment side of the dialectic has taken priority in most DA work, with the result that often the insights into learner abilities obtained through the procedures do not always translate to instructional plans to meet learner needs. They explain that this is because DA is frequently conducted by psychologists but that day-to-day instruction is the responsibility of classroom teachers, who often lack the knowledge needed to interpret DA outcomes and align their instruction accordingly. As will be explained, the preeminent exception to this has been the work of Reuven Feuerstein in cognitive and special education as well as the recent framework of Mediated Development in the field of L2 education. As the term DA encompasses a much broader range of approaches to mediating learners, more will be said about it.

Haywood and Lidz (2007, p. 11) offer a useful discussion of mediation that clarifies how it differs from other interactions involving assistance. They distinguish between common mediation "strategies" and the relative "depth" of intervention in learner psychological processes. "Strategies" is perhaps not the best descriptor as it refers to both specific behaviours on the part of the mediator as well as the intent behind them. These may be more aptly termed *mediator moves*. "Depth" of intervention differentiates mediator moves that serve to orient learners to the task at hand and maintain their engagement from those that involve teaching of concepts and principles that transcend a given task and represent new ways of thinking. "Deeper" interventions are clearly situated near the teaching pole of the ZPD dialectic, and thus while they may certainly occur during DA as part of an effort to diagnose learner abilities, they are brought out strongly in Mediated Development. Examples of mediator moves noted by Haywood and Lidz (2007, p. 12), arranged from lesser to greater depth, include: focusing learner attention on specific dimensions of a task; clarifying task directions and expectations of learner performance; indicating the overall correctness or acceptability of a learner's response; maintaining engagement in completion of the task; providing specific forms of assistance to help with task completion (e.g., explaining vocabulary items); pointing out specific dimensions of learner performance where errors occurred; posing leading questions; helping learners to regulate their response to the task (e.g., controlling frustration, inhibiting impulsivity); prompting learners to apply concepts and principles they have already learned; and teaching new concepts and principles.

Lantolf and Poehner (2004) further propose that the quality of mediation in DA may be distinguished according to approaches that favour scripting mediator moves in advance and then administering them in a standardized manner from those that advocate open-ended dialogic interaction between mediator and learner. They describe these, respectively, as *interventionist* and *interactionist* DA. The work of Anne Brown and colleagues (Brown & Ferrara, 1985) in a DA model they call the Graduated Prompting Approach is illustrative of the latter. In this approach, which was developed for the purpose of diagnosing children's readiness for primary school math and reading curricula, hints or prompts relevant to task completion are arranged from most implicit (e.g., inquiring whether a learner is certain of a response) to most explicit (e.g., revealing the task solution and explaining the principles involved). Prompts are administered to learners one at a time until a learner either correctly completes the task or the final prompt is given. The number of prompts a learner required is interpreted as an indication of his/her proximity to more independent functioning. Interactionist DA, in contrast, is highly individualized, with mediator moves aligned with learner responsiveness. This approach has been vigorously pursued in the L2 field. Poehner and van Compernolle (2011) refer to this as co-regulated functioning to emphasize that the interaction comprises learner responsiveness to mediator moves but at the same time mediator moves reflect an interpretation of learner needs as these emerge moment-to-moment. Close analysis of DA interactions has shed light on the range of learner behaviours, which may include for example actively soliciting specific forms of support from the mediator, posing questions, imitating the mediator's approach to the task, and refusing mediator offers to help (Poehner, 2008a; Poehner & Ableeva, 2011).

As mentioned, one of the most influential proponents of DA was Reuven Feuerstein, who developed a framework known as *Mediated Learning Experience (MLE)* (Feuerstein, Falik, Rand & Feuerstein, 2003; Feuerstein, Feuerstein, & Falik, 2010). Feuerstein developed his approach over many years, beginning with his work to rehabilitate children who had survived the Holocaust and were relocated to Israel. As a result of the extreme circumstances of their early experiences, many of the children did not have the kinds of formative interactions crucial for early psychological development and that are important for subsequent learning. Following an interactionist approach to mediating learners, MLE imposes no limits on the interaction as the intent is to determine the forms of support that are most effect in stimulating a response from an individual learner. In general, Feuerstein eschewed requiring learners to undergo a pre-test, insisting that such a move would only reinforce learners' negative academic experiences and self-perceptions. Instead, an initial session serves as a DA diagnosis of development, with mediation offered to learners as soon as difficulties arise. Learners are also prompted to verbalize the reasons behind their answers in order to further understand their orientation to tasks.

An additional point concerning Feuerstein's approach is that of all DA models, it offers perhaps the greatest integration of teaching and assessing. Just as the MLE is defined by an atmosphere of cooperation, with instruction tailored to learner needs as an essential feature of diagnosing development, the work of mediators and learners continues in an *Instrumental Enrichment Program*. While the program aims to "enrich" learner psychological functioning, the term "instrumental" refers to specially designed materials that are introduced to achieve this goal. The materials teach principles, concepts, and forms of reasoning to promote abilities that are often underdeveloped in Feuerstein's target population, such as understanding analogies, identifying patterns, and recognizing spatial relations. According to Kinard and

Kozulin, (2008), who have extended Feuerstein's approach to mathematics education, diagnosis is ongoing throughout Enrichment as mediators continually monitor learner responsiveness to the materials, how they are orienting to tasks, problems that arise as they attempt to think in new ways, and challenges they experience as they reflect on their performance and evaluate their own progress.

With the introduction of DA to the field of L2 education, which already had a robust tradition of research informed by Vygotsky's ideas, consistent effort has been made to integrate mediator-learner interaction as a feature of all instructional activity rather than reserving it for instances of assessment. Feuerstein's model of MLE, along with continued analysis of Vygotsky's discussions of the ZPD, has guided the design of both L2 DA approaches, recently, the elaboration of Mediated Development. The term development is preferred here to learning because it resonates with Vygotsky's position that not all learning promotes development but this should be the goal of education. Moreover, L2 Mediated Development has been undertaken in conjunction with a Vygotsky-inspired program known as *Systemic Theoretical Instruction*, which re-organizes curricula according to abstract conceptual knowledge. In this form of instruction, learners encounter the concepts through verbal explanations but, more important, through material representation of the concepts such as models and images. These are incorporated into activities as tools for learners to draw upon to regulate their thinking. Mediated Development thus emphasizes cooperation between mediator and learner focused upon the introduction of concepts and principles, their integration into activities, and their use as psychological tools (Poehner & Infante, 2016). In this way, DA and Mediated Development operate in tandem, emphasizing the same principles of mediator-learner joint engagement in ZPD activity. While they tend toward, respectively, the assessment or teaching pole, both elements of the dialectic are necessarily implicated in the activity.

CONCLUSION

Although Vygotsky was active more than eighty years ago, his understanding of schooling as the essential driver of psychological development needed for participation and opportunity in industrialized societies has perhaps even greater relevance in the globalized, post-industrial Twenty-First Century. If we charge schools not merely with the task of imparting knowledge to learners but with guiding them toward ways of thinking and acting, then Vygotsky's insights cannot be overlooked. The understanding of the ZPD he articulated offers a coherent approach to diagnosing and promoting learner development. The range of procedures generated under the rubric of DA point educators toward the dimension of learner development that are not captured by most assessments, namely the range of abilities that are still in the process of forming. As should be clear, existing DA protocols may be applied by classroom teachers wishing to trace learner development over time relative to their mastery of curricular goals, but DA is equally suited to more formal and even large-scale assessment contexts. Mediated Development, drawing from both Vygotsky's recommendations for the teaching of abstract concepts and Feuerstein's commitment to enriching learner functioning through specialized materials, is currently being pursued by L2 researchers to better understand how the curriculum itself may be organized to provide learners access to new tools for thinking. As mentioned, work such as Kinard and Kozulin's (2008) program in mathematics establishes that the value of Mediated Development is not limited to any particular content area. If one accepts that academic disciplines each represent specific ways of thinking, then the expansion of DA and Mediated Development across the curriculum could realize Vygotsky's vision of schooling that promotes development of all individuals.

Note

Transcription conventions are as follows:

+	short pause
++	long pause
.	full stop marks falling intonation
,	comma marks slightly rising intonation
?	question mark indicates raised intonation (not necessarily a question)
(word)	single parentheses indicate uncertain hearing
(xxx)	unable to transcribe
((comment))	double parentheses contain transcriber's comments or descriptions
underline	underlining indicates stress through pitch or amplitude

NOTES

1 For explanation of transcription conventions, see NOTE following the Conclusion.
2 See Poehner and Lantolf (2013) for details.

REFERENCES

Brown, A., & Ferrara, R. A. (1985). Diagnosing zones of proximal development. In J. V. Wertsch (Ed.), *Culture, communication and cognition. Vygotskian perspectives* (pp. 273–305). Cambridge: Cambridge University Press.

Feuerstein, R., Falik, L., Rand, Y., & Feuerstein, R.S. (2003). *Dynamic assessment of cognitive modifiability*. Jerusalem: ICELP Press.

Feuerstein, R., Feuerstein, R. S., & Falik, L. H. (2010). *Beyond smarter: Mediated learning and the brain's capacity for change*. New York, NY: Teachers College, Columbia University.

Haywood, H. C., & Lidz, C. S. (2007). *Dynamic assessment in practice. Clinical and educational applications*. New York, NY: Cambridge University Press.

Il'yenkov, Ė. (1977). *Dialectical logic*. Moscow: Progress Press.
Kinard, J. T., & Kozulin, A. (2008). *Rigorous mathematical thinking. Conceptual formation in the mathematics classroom*. New York, NY: Cambridge University Press.
Kozulin, A., & Gindis, B. (2007). Sociocultural theory and education of children with special needs: From defectology to remedial pedagogy. In H. Daniels, M. Cole, & J. V. Wertsch (Eds.), *The Cambridge companion to Vygotsky* (pp. 332–361). Cambridge: Cambridge University Press.
Lantolf, J. P., & Poehner, M. E. (2004). Dynamic assessment: Bringing the past into the future. *Journal of Applied Linguistics, 1*(1), 49–74.
Lantolf, J. P., & Poehner, M. E. (2014). *Sociocultural theory and the pedagogical imperative in L2 education. Vygotskian praxis and the research/practice divide*. London: Routledge.
Lidz, C. S., & Elliott, J. G. (2000). *Dynamic assessment: Prevailing models and applications*. Amsterdam: Elsevier.
Miller, R. (2011). *Vygotsky in perspective*. New York, NY: Cambridge University Press.
Novack, G. (1971). *An introduction to the logic of Marxism*. Atlanta, GA: Pathfinder Press.
Poehner, M. E. (2008a). Both sides of the conversation: The interplay between mediation and learner reciprocity in dynamic assessment. In J. P. Lantolf & M. E. Poehner (Eds.), *Sociocultural theory and the teaching of second languages* (pp. 33–56). London: Equinox Publishing.
Poehner, M. E. (2008b). *Dynamic assessment: A Vygotskian approach to understanding and promoting second language development*. Berlin: Springer.
Poehner, M. E., & Ableeva, R. (2011). Dynamic assessment. From display of knowledge to engagement in the activity of development. In D. Tsagari & I. Csépes (Eds.), *Classroom-based language assessment* (pp. 15–28). Frankfurt: Peter Lang.
Poehner, M. E., & Infante, P. (2016). Mediated development as interpsychological activity. *Language and Sociocultural Theory.*
Poehner, M. E., & Lantolf, J. P. (2013). Bringing the ZPD into the equation: Capturing L2 development during computerized dynamic assessment. *Language Teaching Research, 17*(3), 323–342.
Poehner, M. E., & Rea-Dickins, P. (Eds.). (2013). *Addressing issues of access and fairness in education through dynamic assessment*. London: Routledge.
Poehner, M. E., & van Compernolle, R. A. (2011). Frames of interaction in dynamic assessment: Developmental diagnoses of second language learning. *Assessment in Education: Principles, Policy and Practice 18*(2), 183–198.
Van der Veer, J., & Valsiner, J. (1991). *Understanding Vygotsky: A quest for synthesis*. Oxford: Blackwell.
Vygotsky, L. S. (1978). *Mind in society: The development of higher psychological processes*. Cambridge, MA: Harvard University Press.
Vygotsky, L. S. (1987). *The collected works of L. S. Vygotsky. Volume 1: Problems of general psychology, including the volume thinking and speech* (R. W. Rieber & A. S. Carton, Eds.). New York, NY: Plenum.
Vygotsky, L. S. (1998). The problem of age. In R. W. Rieber (Ed.), *The collected works of L. S. Vygotsky. Vol. 5. Child psychology*. New York, NY: Plenum.

Matthew E. Poehner
Pennsylvania State University

JOANNA BLACK

15. *DIGI*ART AND HUMAN RIGHTS

New Media Visual Art Integration for Teacher Candidates OR Avoiding the Information, Communication Technology (ICT) Vacuity Using Visual Art Education Infusion

A NEW MEDIA VISUAL ART INTEGRATED PROJECT FOR TEACHER CANDIDATES

It has been found that educators in all disciplines are confused with what to do with digital technology (Buckingham, 2007; Cuban, 2001; Roland, 2010; Watts, 2008). What is crucial to education is the merging of effective, meaningful pedagogy with suitable and valuable technological infusion (Buckingham, 2007; Buckingham, Willett, & Pini, 2011; Mullen & Rahn, 2010; Palfrey & Gasser, 2008). The question is, how does one do this well? Many teachers approach the integration of technologies from a '*technicist*' (technical) rather than from a creative, artistic perspective (Roland, 2010; Watts, 2008). Put simply, they are perplexed about *what* to teach, and *how* to teach it. One reason for this is that teachers tend to teach the way they have been taught (Greb, 1997; Roland, 2010).[1] Some educators simply give up and let computers sit unused (Cuban, 2001; Palfrey & Gasser, 2008). If teachers do use technology in classrooms they primarily use it in boring, unimaginative ways, repeatedly making use of it for retrieving or showcasing information: in short, teachers habitually employ computers as glorified chalkboards, digital libraries, or simple notepads (Buckingham, 2007; Cuban, 2001; Roland 2010). The body of research is still evolving in this area and far more is needed in order to learn ways in which to creatively integrate digital technologies into curricula while underscoring effective pedagogy (Bell & Bull, 2010; Castro & Grauer, 2010; Shin, 2010; Watts, 2008).

Writers increasingly have argued that visual art and digital technologies have a natural affinity (Bastos, 2010; Gouzouasis, 2006; Sweeney, 2010; Watts, 2008). Gouzouasis (2006) advocates for all educators to view the arts as the foundation when teaching digital technologies in order to foster our youths' imaginations and creativity. He writes that, "If we are to venture beyond the vacuum of ICT contexts, it is urgent that artists and arts educators begin rethinking the role of the arts and all forms of technologies" (p. 9). In addition to this, Buckingham, a seminal researcher in cultural and media studies, strongly advises all teachers to adopt the visual art education model because he envisions the crucial importance of art studio production

J. B. Cummings & M. L. Blatherwick (Eds.), Creative Dimensions of Teaching and Learning in the 21st Century, 163–173.

(hands-on art making). Art educators teaching studio typically nurture students' self-expression and imaginations through the exploration of different art forms and themes (Buckingham, 2007, pp. 163–164). Why not do this with digital art as well? Hence, both Gouzouasis and Buckingham specifically point to the value of approaching digital technology infusion in other subject areas with an art education focus. The intention is for students to deal with artistic themes in the "digital studio", hence nurturing youths' self-expression, promoting curious minds, and encouraging creative explorations.

Gouzouasis (2006) postulates that technology must be informed by the arts to make it meaningful. Even though many art educators resist using digital technologies (Bastos, 2010; Choi & Piro, 2009; Peppler, 2010; Roland, 2010) and teach outdated concepts, antiquated content, and old forms of delivery (Roland, 2010, Watts, 2008), there are indeed some who are advocating change and a few who are integrating newer technologies into their curriculum in imaginative and creative ways (Castro & Grauer, 2010; Castro, Sinner, & Grauer, 2010; Lachapelle, 2010; Lin, Castro, Sinner, & Grauer, 2011; Rahn, 2010; Roland, 2010). For this chapter the author has sought to add to this body of knowledge by writing about a unique project combining digital technologies, human rights education, and art education.

The Project

For over ten years the author has taught a class called "*Teaching Senior Years Art.*" Teacher candidates training to teach art in high schools are required to take this course in their second year of a Bachelor of Education Program at the University of Manitoba, located in Canada. The curriculum the author has designed and implemented is entitled, "'*digi*ART': A New Media Visual Art Integrated Project" and has been a major assignment since 2003. As a result of *digi*ART, teacher candidates not only learn about teaching traditional art but also newer digital art forms. What better way for students to acquire an understanding of effective pedagogy in teaching new media than by modeling it? What better way for students to develop rich curricula than by having them actually experience it?

During 2011–2012 and 2013–2014 the author selected the theme of human rights for the *digi*ART project. Human rights is an effective and engaging subject as corroborated by other scholars' findings, (Chung, 2010; Darts, 2004, 2006; Delacruz, 2009a, 2009b, 2009c). A subject such as human rights is worth studying intensely. Palfrey and Gasser (2008) write, "Most digital creativity is of the unspectacular sort. What stands out to us is not the absolute (and relatively small) percentage of Digital Natives [youths who are comfortable using digital technologies] doing the most creative things online, but the extent to which this creativity represents an opportunity for learning, personal expression, individual autonomy, and political change... This trajectory is particularly important for how we ought to be educating our kids in a digital era" (p. 113).

Many of the students in pre-service education use technology in their everyday lives as "*consumers*" or users of digital art. In *digi*ART, however, they are asked to become "*prosumers*" or "*digital art creators.*" Many challenges arose in their new, creative role: (1) some teacher candidates had not experienced making digital art; (2) many had not been challenged to create thoughtful, digital artworks[2] and (3) not all had been asked to examine art making in relation to new media curricula development and the exploration of appropriate pedagogical approaches.

Explanation of the Framework and the Goals of the Curriculum Project

"*digi*ART" has as its foundation the inspiration from the art historical movement of Intermedia. Students were taught about Fluxus artists like Dick Higgins in the 1960's who, consistent with the core principles of this movement, blurred the boundaries between visual imagery, audio texts, written words, and/or moving imagery. Thus, the amalgamation of texts creating interdisciplinary works began over half a century ago, and has become increasingly more relevant in our era of visual/digital culture, in which multimodal art is increasingly common; and so, key to the *digi*ART approach, is the notion that images enhance the meaning of digital texts.

In the area of content, for the *digi*ART project, students were exposed to Human Rights Education (HRE). Such issues as relocation/dislocation, poetics of occupation, narratives of war, and social justice were discussed in the light of professional artists' works ranging from Francisco Goya (1746–1828) to Shirin Neshat (1957–)[3].

The goals of the *digi*ART project are described as (1) modeling a novel integrated new media curriculum, (2) experiencing digital artworks, (3) fostering an understanding of visual art history, theory, appreciation, and production in relation to digital art, (4) experiencing a pedagogical approach to teaching digital technologies; and (5) developing an appreciation of digital multimodal art education. The outcome of the *digi*ART project is the production of interactive, creative digital art that has been and continues to be shared with others in the academic and school communities.

Teaching Approach

"*Digi*ART" is constructed so that teacher candidates undergo the process of creating new media, drawing upon a project based, open-ended inquiry model typically used in art education (Bates, 2000). The model is a humanistic, interdisciplinary one in which problem-solving is fostered, and imaginative skills are developed in order to promote creativity and critical thinking. Over the years the author has varied the type of media students use (such as digital video, photography, multimedia,) as well as the subject matter students explore: themes ranging from self-identity and community to human rights issues. Consistent with educators in technology, a multifaceted pedagogical approach is employed, drawing upon diverse teaching styles from lecture (*sage on the stage*) to using constructivism in the classroom.[4] Final artworks emerge from (1) student's personal interests, and concerns, (2) comprehensive study, (3) critical research, (4) idea progress using art journals, (5) rich skill development, (6) careful thought, and (6) thorough planning.

Utilizing the traditional studio approach also applies to studio projects in new media. Students undergo an intense, nine-stage process in making digital art, involving a (1) study of prior professional artworks regarding human rights themes. Teacher candidates then proceed to (2) selecting a human rights theme that is of personal interest to them, and subsequently (3) researching contemporary artists and the ways in which they handle not only digital media but also themes applicable to those selected by students. Following this, teacher candidates are required to (4) research more intensively their human rights topic in order to be well versed in this specific area. They then proceed to (5) work out possible artworks in their journals and (6) decide along with the instructor and peers a course of direction to develop their new media art. Teacher candidates generally adhere to this course, using it as a guide, as each student has developed a different direction pertaining to what he/she intends to create as an artwork. The next step in the process is to (7) make the art, and finally (8) disseminate it in a class critique. During this last stage, the artwork is constructively criticized and supportively discussed. In addition, students are asked to articulate the way in which the experience of making new media sheds light on their own future teaching and their subsequent students' learning. Finally, when the new media art is thoroughly critiqued and finished, many of the students (9) used Web 2.0 to disseminate their works on-line. Unique to this last academic year, was the fact that students were selected by the Faculty of Education at the University of Manitoba to present their *digi*ART experience at an educational conference called WestCAST 2014. During this presentation, all of the teacher candidates in the class shared their reflections of the *digi*ART experience, collectively stating that:

> We put ourselves in the place of [our] students in order to better understand what we'd be asking of our students. Each of us teacher candidates chose a human rights subject that we are personally connected to, and also explored various technological media including, PowerPoint, digital collage, video, photography, and blogging… As art educators our goal is to increase our students' digital literacy by exploring it further through art. The art classroom is a place of self-discovery, intuitive learning, self-expression; moreover our students are developing communication skills and their problem-solving skills so these conditions are ideal for our students to develop their knowledge of technology and to push the boundaries, and to possibly use technology in ways that they never thought possible… We are showing our students the value of technology as a medium in order to convey ideas and to explore themes (Gragasin, Norberg, Unrau, Van Damme, & Wilson, 2014).

Themes the students selected ranged from LGBTQ issues, invisible disabilities, and racial bias/stereotyping, to the immigrant experience of dislocation/relocation.

Example of a Student's Process and Art

Candace Unrau, a teacher candidate, based her artwork on social injustices in Canada using animation as her digital medium. She created moving imagery using the simple, ubiquitous, and inexpensive PowerPoint. At the beginning stage Candace examined thirty articles located at "The Universal Declaration of Human Rights"[5] (UDHR) website. She was inspired to pursue this topic as a result of the building, development, and ongoing controversy of the Canadian Museum for Human Rights (CMHR), a federally funded museum located in Winnipeg, Canada, which opened in 2014 and is located about twelve kilometers from the university. Its purpose is to highlight discrimination that Canadians have experienced in the past; a noble mission. Yet, recently it has attracted controversy due to contentiousness and rancorous public debate regarding what to include and, more contentiously, what to exclude from the exhibitions, a question that has in effect ostracized large community groups within Winnipeg and beyond. The CMHR recently produced a video entitled, "An Animated Declaration"[6] inspiring Candace to re-examine what has changed since the initial UDHR document was initiated, and reminds us that, even though UDHR was created in the 1940s, still much needs to be addressed in the way of human rights in our era, over half a century later. During the WestCAST conference Candace conveyed the following idea through animation, which she recorded on a screen during the public presentation at this conference:

> Canada is a very diverse country. We are considered the land of the mosaic. Our past is a rich story of immigrants and refugees from around the globe… Everyone that is in Canada brings a belief, language and culture. However, ethnocentric views have caused racism, prejudice, and discrimination across the country. Many cultural groups have been ostracized when they came to Canada… I believe that the UDHR is still not followed today. The rights and freedoms of multiple cultures are still being crushed. As a society, we are becoming better at recognizing discrimination of the past; however, we are not looking at the current human rights violations. I hope to expose some of the violations through a video production based on the UDHR. (Gragasin et al., 2014)

In Candace's artwork, which can be found on YouTube (Candace Unrau, 2013), she uses simplistic, boldly coloured imagery, reminiscent of Keith Haring's artistic style. She plays with the text and pictures to create a witty, wry dialogue relying on clever word play and uncomplicated imagery. The idea we need to address in order to uphold the UDHR is conveyed through images of weapons being taken away from people and other imagery simply being crossed out, as in Figure 1.

Candace reflected that she likes PowerPoint because it can easily be used in cross-curricular areas. Moreover, it can be employed to make other digital media like video and graphic novels if the teacher employed the scaffolding technique.

Katie Norberg, another teacher candidate, was inspired by the courage of the young girl, Malala Yousafzai, who was nominated for the Nobel peace prize for her heroic resistance to the Taliban: she not only fought for children's rights to education but also for women's rights in Pakistan. Malala retaliated against the Taliban voicing her opinions publicly on the BBC as well as through all other media at her disposal

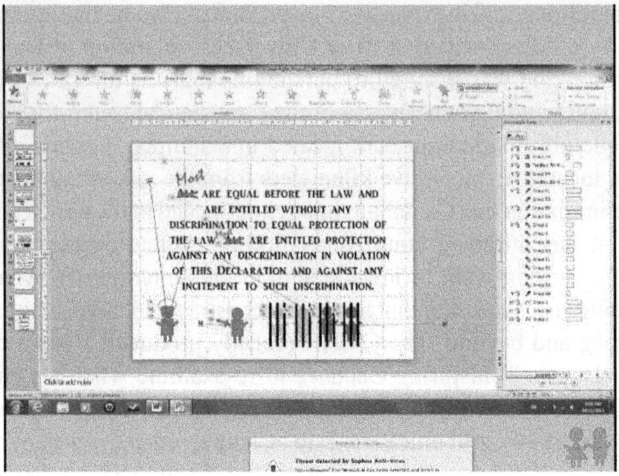

Figure 1. Screen shot of Candace Unrau's digital animation shown during the WestCAST presentation

(print, radio, and television news venues) and by means of her personal blogsite. The consequence of her open actions was that she was shot in the face by the Taliban in 2012 in a failed attempt to assassinate her. Malala survived the ordeal and because of her heroic opposition, has inspired other women in Pakistan and on the international stage to resist sexual discrimination and dictatorial authoritarianism (Sawari, 2014). Katie's final work is a digital collage/animation posted on YouTube (Katie Norberg, 2013, Figure 2). At the presentation Katie reflected:

> Involving students in a project like this engages them on every level of Bloom's Taxonomy and really pushes them to engage with and grapple with and take ownership of their own ideas in creating something new. You don't have to actually be on the cutting edge of technology to do it… I created multiple collages using Photoshop and I used PowerPoint to animate them and make a visual narrative. I sought to represent Malala's struggle herself and the symbol she has become for girls around the world. (Gragasin et al., 2014)

Katie is dealing with a timely theme as more and more cases are coming to light of escalating violations again Pakistani women. The so called "*honour killing*" of Farzana Parveen, is a recent example, who married for love and was consequently stoned to death at the hands of her family in front of a court house in broad daylight, to the spectacle of shocked witnesses. Sawari (2014, p. 1) writes, "This is what Pakistan is increasingly becoming now – a country of 180 million or so onlookers. The papers reveal one violation of human rights after another, and women are mostly the targets." Babar and Ahmed, not surprisingly (2014) conclude that in comparison to other countries globally, Pakistan's violence against women is one of the greatest human right violations occurring today.

Figure 2. A screenshot of Katie Norberg's final digital collage posted on YouTube

Katie conducted research about Malala, her past, and her beliefs regarding the "power of the pen", the power of the written word, the power of dialogue, and the power of education. A focus of the inquiry was specifically on Malala's identity forged over the last few years. Katie decided to challenge herself by using Photoshop (a media she had never used before) to make a digital moving collage. An image of Malala was collaged together with a schoolroom, hands holding a pen, and a stairway in a school. In her final work Katie merged 14 moving images together, working with the dualities of darkness/lightness; sharpness/blending; dissolving/formulating; and multiple layering using transparency/clarity. At first she attempted to make a gif (a graphics interchange format), then a video, but decided upon using a PowerPoint animation because it served her initial ideas well. Katie's artwork can be viewed on her public blogsite link (Norberg, 2013). In her final collage, one views the animation in four parts.[7] Firstly, Malala stands with a background of the school classroom, collaged against the Pakistan sky. The collage then proceeds to darken and a focus is placed upon Malala with a background of sky. Emerging from this image, appears a desk and an image of hands with pen, symbolic of Malala's belief in education and the tools with which she uses to fight. Finally, the desk and hand fades and the image brightens onto the image of Malala herself, standing against dark hills and a cloudy yet sunlit sky indicative of hope for the future. The art is not the only message on Katie's blogsite: she has also placed posts of Malala talking, being interviewed by media, and videos highlighting the political situation regarding the human rights issues in Pakistan. Additionally, in the blogsite, Katie provides texts and includes a biography of Malala as well as a description of her own digital collage, her intentions regarding her artwork, and her perceptions pertaining to Malala herself.

Conclusions and Recommendations

In this chapter, an example is provided of a way to teach new media to future art educators using digital technologies as a creative medium to explore human rights issues. Students involved in *digi*ART stated that the project focuses on promoting a strong pedagogical approach with inspiring curricula (Gragasin et al., 2014). During the WestCAST presentation (Gragasin et al., 2014), the student teacher, Katie Norberg, stated that: "Access to technology in our classrooms has become an invaluable and sought after resource but is it really being used to expose potential in our classrooms? We tend to rely on technology as a tool for research and [practical] communication but actually not a lot else. It is really a one-dimensional view of what technology can offer us as teachers and our students as learners" (Gragasin et al., 2014). The heart of *digi*ART is on the art making process and technology is the artistic medium. The project is constructed so that personal exploration, self-discovery, thematic exploration, intuitive learning, problem-solving and self-expression are fostered. These elements are crucial in promoting creativity (Milbrandt & Milbrandt, 2011). Students involved in this digital curriculum are exposed to and work with new ideas about shaping contemporary artistic subject matter resulting from strong research, experimentation, exploration and development of technological skills. Tillander (2011, p. 46) writes, "…I imagine possibilities of calling attention to the potential of problem finding and problem-solving for restructuring and enhancing transformations of creativity, technology, and pedagogy in art education". *Digi*ART is an example of such an approach.

There are many reasons why the *digi*ART assignment is so important. Explanations include the importance of (1) integrating digital technologies with art education to train students for 21st century art education; (2) keeping up with contemporary professional art practices and artworks; (3) developing teacher candidates' multimodal literacies; (4) fostering their ability to infuse technology in visual art curricula; and (5) modeling an effective way in which to teach digital technologies so that students are better prepared in their own future teaching to integrate technologies effectively in art and in cross-curricular areas. Further, there are three major recommendations.

During the WestCAST conference (Gragasin et al., 2014), student teachers voiced their viewpoint that *digi*ART was an important learning experience. The author has found that teaching *digi*ART over the last decade corroborates this view. Moreover, as other researchers in art education, media education, and educational technology have suggested, we have few models such as *digi*ART: we need more (Bell & Bull, 2010; Buckingham, 2007; Castro & Grauer, 2010; Watts, 2008). It is therefore recommended that more curricula similar to *digi*ART be developed in art education both for secondary level and higher education students. Furthermore, teacher candidates stated that this approach can be well integrated with other subject areas both at the secondary level and in higher education. The author has met with success when integrating *digi*ART into other subject areas both for high school students and in Bachelor of Education teacher training courses.[8] Consequently, it is suggested that the art education model be used as a foundation to extend the *digi*ART type of approach to other curricula areas. The author recommends that these creative approaches teaching new media need to be disseminated at conferences, in written academic texts, and posted publicly using Web 2.0 to inform others interested in this type of model. Finally, if students in teacher training programs can have positive experiences with new media curricula, these future teachers will be more interested and open to incorporating new media in their own classrooms because, to repeat the old adage, teachers often do indeed teach as they have been taught. It would be wonderful to envision a time in the near future when all educators foster creativity using digital technologies.

ACKNOWLEDGEMENTS

The author would like to thank Ms. Candace Unrau and Ms. Katie Norberg for graciously consenting to share their artworks and the processes involved in the making of it for this paper. The works were also publicly shared at the WestCAST Conference, on blogsites and on YouTube. The author greatly appreciates the use of that material generously made available.

NOTES

1 For a more detailed discussion of the reasons why educators shy away from using technology refer to Black and Browning's (2011) article, Black's thesis (2002) and Delacruz's article (2004).

2 Much has been discussed of the proliferation of digital texts posted on Web 2.0 software done by *digital natives*; but, it has been talked about that even though there is plenty of digital technology being made it is poorly done, often unimaginative, misguided, mechanical and narrow. Bielicky (2008) refers to it as a '*cultural pollution*'. For a further discussion of this refer to Buckingham (2007).

3 For a more extensive discussion of the art historical teaching refer to the article by Black and Cap (2014).

4 Cuban, an educational technologist, in his seminal work (2001), discusses his findings that most teachers who infuse technology in their curriculum effectively use a variety of pedagogical approaches.

5 The Universal Declaration of Human Right's website can be found at http://www.un.org/en/documents/udhr/

6 This video can be found at the Canadian Museum for Human Rights at http://humanrights.ca/explore/animated-declaration#.U4jo_xYQg1M

7 Katie's final animation can also be found on YouTube at https://www.youtube.com/watch?v=Io1FMYjimOY

8 The author had taught at the secondary level working with other high school teachers in many different curricula areas using a similar model to *digi*ART. Also, an example of incorporating other subject areas using the digiART model in higher education is Cap and Black's articles (2012, 2014), that is a description of integration of art with human ecology and educational technology.

REFERENCES

Babar, Z., & Ahmed, M. (2014, May 10). Husband of "honour killing" victim killed his first wife. *The Globe and Mail*, p. A9.

Bastos, F. (2010). New media art education. *Art Education, 63*(1), 4–5.

Bates, J. K. (2000). *Becoming an art teacher.* Belmont, CA: Wadsworth.

Bell, L., & Bull, G. (2010). Digital video and teaching. *Contemporary Issues in Technology and Teacher Education, 10*(1), 1–6.

Bielicky, M. (2008). Media golem: Between Prague and ZKM. In M. Alexenberg (Ed.), *Educating artists for the future: Learning at the intersections of art, science, technology and culture* (pp. 193–202). Bristol, UK: Intellect Books.

Black, J. (2002). *Topsy-turvy teacher-student relationships: An examination of digital multimedia teaching and learning* (Doctoral dissertation, University of Toronto, 2002). *Dissertation Abstracts International, 63*, 6.

Black, J., & Browning, K. (2011). Creativity in digital art education teaching practices. *Art Education, 64*(5), 19–24, 33–34.

Black, J., & Cap, O. (2014). Human rights, information, and communication technology (ICT): A case study of art education teacher candidates. *The International Journal of Civic, Political and Community Studies, 11*(2), 31–46.

Buckingham, D. (2007). *Beyond technology: Children's learning in the age of digital culture.* Cambridge, England: Polity Press.

Buckingham, D., Willett, R., & Pini, M. (2011*). Home truths: Video production and domestic life*. Ann Arbor, MI: The University of Michigan Press.

Canadian Museum of Human Rights (CMHR Webpage). Retrieved from https://humanrights.ca/

Cap, O., & Black, J. (2012). Digital comics in human ecology: Exploring learning possibilities using ICT with teacher education students. *International Journal of Learning, 18*(9), 27–44.

Castro, J. C., & Grauer, K. (2010). Structuring democratic places of learning: The Gulf Island film and television school. *Art Education, 63*(5), 14–21.

Castro, J. C., Sinner, A., & Grauer, K. (2010). New media arts education: How community based programs can reshape teaching and learning in the age of Web 2.0. In G. Sweeny (Ed.), *Inter/actions/inter/sections: Art education in a digital visual culture* (pp. 80–89). Reston, VA: National Art Education Association Publication.

Choi, H., & Piro, J. M. (2009). Expanding arts education in a digital age. *Arts Education Policy Review, 110*(3), 27–34.

Chung, S. K. (2010). Cybermedia literacy art education. In G. Sweeny (Ed.), *Inter/actions/inter/sections: Art education in a digital visual culture* (pp. 63–71). Reston, VA: National Art Education Association Publication.

Cuban, L. (2001). *Oversold & underused: Computers in the classroom.* Cambridge, MA: Harvard University Press.

Darts, D. (2004). Visual culture jam: Art pedagogy, and creative resistance. *Studies in Art Education, 45*(4), 313–327.

Darts, D. (2006). Art education for a change: Contemporary issues and the visual arts. *Art Education, 59*(5), 6–12.

Delacruz, E. (2004). Teachers' working conditions and the unmet promise of technology. *Studies in Art Education, 46*(1), 6–19.

Delacruz, E. M. (2009a). Art education aims in the age of new media: Moving toward global civil society. *Art Education, 62*(5), 13–17.

Delacruz, E. M. (2009b). From bricks and mortar to the public sphere in cyberspace: Creating a culture of caring on the digital global commons. *International Journal of Education in the Arts, 10*(5), n5. Retrieved from http://www.ijea.org/v10n5/v10n5.pdf

Delacruz, E. M. (2009c). Old world teaching meets the new digital cultural creative. *International Journal of Art and Design Education, 28*(1), 261–268.

Gouzouasis, P. (2001). The role of the arts in new media and Canadian education for the 21st century. *Education Canada, 41*(2), 20–23.

Gragasin, D., Norberg, K., Unrau, C., Van Damme, N., & Wilson, D. (2014, February). *digiART and human rights: A new media, arts integrated project.* Paper presented at the annual WestCAST Conference, Winnipeg, MB, Canada.

Greb, D. (1997). New technologies in the classroom. In D. C. Gregory (Ed.). *New technologies in art education: Implications for theory, research, and practice* (pp. 13–21). Reston, VA: National Art Education Association.

Lachapelle, R. (2010). Fading in: Strategies for teaching video editing. In C. Mullen & J. Rahn (Eds.), *Viewfinding: Perspective on new media curriculum in the arts* (pp. 83–106). New York, NY: Peter Lang Publishing Inc.

Lin, C., Castro, J. C., Sinner, A., & Grauer, K. (2011). Towards a dialogue between new media arts programs in and out of schools. *The Canadian Art Teacher, 9*(2), 24–37.

Milbrandt, M., & Milbrandt, L. (2011). Creativity: What are we talking about? *Art Education, 64*(1), 8–13.

Mullen, C., & Rahn, J. (2010). Introduction. In C. Mullen & J. Rahn (Eds.), *Perspective on new media curriculum in the arts* (pp. 1–10). New York, NY: Peter Lang Publishing Inc.

Norberg, K. (2013, October 30). *I am Malala* [blog post]. Retrieved from www.onebookandonepen.blogspot.ca

Norberg, K. (2013, October). *Malala presentation with final slide* (video). Retrieved from https://www.youtube.com/ watch?v=Io1FMYjimOY

Palfrey, J., & Gasser, U. (2008). *Born digital: Understanding the first generation of digital natives* (pp. 111–130, 223–254). New York, NY: Basic Books.

Peppler, K. (2010). Media arts: Art Education for a digital age. *Teachers College Record, 112*(6), 2118–2153.

Rahn, J. (2010). Video sketchbooks: Curriculum theory, assignment and resources. In C. Mullen & J. Rahn (Eds.), *Perspective on new media curriculum in the arts* (pp. 31–56). New York, NY: Peter Lang Publishing Inc.

Roland, C. (2010). Preparing art teachers to teach in a new digital landscape. *Art Education, 63*(1), 17–24.

Sawari, A. (2014, May 29). Farzana Parveen's killing must trigger change for women in Pakistan. *The Guardian.* Retrieved from http://www.the\.com/commentisfree/2014/may/29/farzana-parveen-killing-change-women-pakistan-human-rights-honour-killings

Shin, R. (2010).Taking digital creativity to the art classroom: Mystery box swap. *Art Education, 63*(2), 38–42.

Sweeny, R. (2010). Technology always and forever. In G. Sweeny (Ed.), *Inter/actions/inter/sections: Art education in a digital visual culture* (pp. ix–xvii). Reston, VA: National Art Education Association Publication.

Tillander, M. (2011). Creativity, technology, art and pedagogical practices. *Art Education, 64*(1), 40–46.

United Nations. (1948). *The universal declaration of human rights.* Retrieved from http://www.un.org/en/documents/udhr/

Unrau, C. (2013). *Human rights digiART project* (video). Retrieved from https://www.youtube.com/watch?v=u-XMrSEoex0

Watts, J. K. (2008). *Teaching digital media as an art class: A search to define a curriculum* (Doctoral Dissertation). Available from ProQuest Dissertations and Theses database (UMI No. 3341339).

Joanna Black
University of Manitoba

PETER LILJEDAHL

16. CARD TRICKS DISCOVERY LEARNING AND FLOW IN MATHEMATICS TEACHER EDUCATION

INTRODUCTION

Although contemporary thinking on the teaching of mathematics calls for an abundance of teacher orchestrated collaborative discovery learning, the reality is that most mathematics classrooms are dominated by healthy doses of direct instruction, teacher led exemplification, followed by the assignment of homework. This results in students coming to see mathematics as a collection of rules to be memorized and routines to be mastered. It also leads many students to become disenfranchised with mathematics as a field, as well as a school subject. From these ranks of largely disenfranchised students come our future teachers of mathematics – secondary teachers from those few who thrive in this system and elementary teacher from the many who do not. Regardless, both groups are destined to recapitulate the one model of mathematical instruction that they have had experience with (Lorti, 1975; Ball, 1988).

Given that this model of teaching mathematics is *so far* from the ideals of contemporary research and curriculum edicts how do we, as teacher educators, begin to move pre-service and in-service teachers towards a new way of being? How do we give teachers a glimpse of what discovery learning can look like?

One Possibility

Consider the following arrangement of five cards.

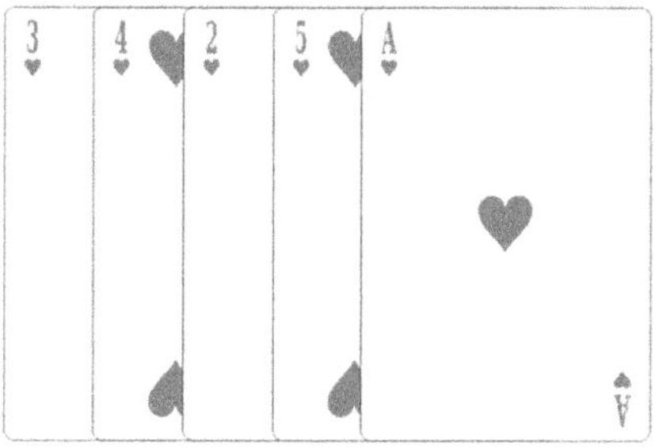

Figure 1. Initial arrangement

J. B. Cummings & M. L. Blatherwick (Eds.), Creative Dimensions of Teaching and Learning in the 21st Century, 175–179.

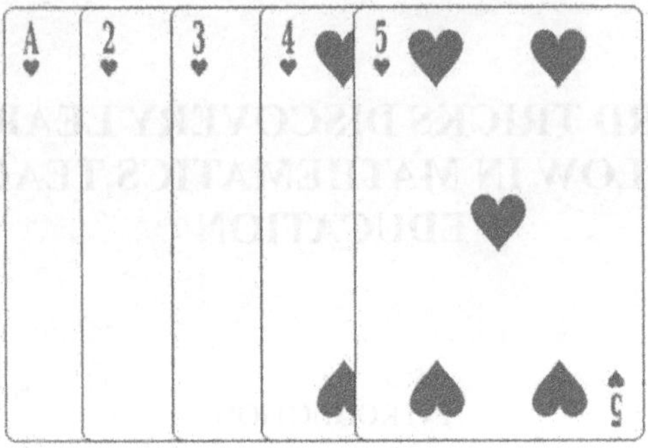

Figure 2. Final arrangement

Now, holding the cards in this order (see Figure 1) take the top card and place it face up on the table. Take the next card and move it to the bottom of the pile of cards in your hand. Repeat this process, each time placing the top card on the table (to the right of the previous one) and moving the next card to the bottom until all the cards are arranged on the table. What makes the above arrangement special is that once the above recursive process is complete the cards on the table are arranged in an ascending order (see Figure 2).

The task is now to arrange the cards from ace to six so that the same ascending order is produced when following the iterative process of placing one card on the table and placing the next card on the bottom of the pile. Then ace to seven … and so on … until the whole deck can be arranged to produce the desired result.

This trick, which I call *Place One – Kill One*, comes from a family of card tricks wherein the solution to the *trick* lies in a person's ability to arrange a deck of cards correctly. On the surface, this seems like a relatively simple task. Indeed, the solution for six cards is soon found. However, this solution does not extend well into seven cards. Regardless, the arrangement for seven cards is eventually found … and then one naturally moves on to eight cards … and so on. At each stage the trick evolves to provide new challenges at each level, enticing the solver to persist in order to move to the next number of cards. In short, this trick has all the elements necessary to occasion, what Csikszentmihalyi (1990) would call, *flow*.

The Flow Experience

> An artist works in his studio. For many hours he works on a painting or a sculpture. Time has no meaning as he loses himself in his task – a labour of love. Even bodily needs such as hunger and sleep are absent from his mind as he works away late into the evening.
>
> A group of students are collaboratively working on an activity set by their teacher. From all visible signs these students are very interested in the activity.

They are animate in their discussions and focused on the tasks at hand. They seem to be enjoying their experience – even seem to be happy. They are not distracted by the other goings on in the class and even when the recess bell rings, they don't break from their activity.

We are familiar with both of these experiences. As an artist or a model builder or a scrapbooker we have experienced getting lost in our hobby, in our passion. Likewise, as teachers we recall times when our students have been so engrossed in their work that it is difficult to tear them away from it. Csikszentmihalyi (1996) calls these experiences *flow experiences* and defines them as the pleasurable state that a person may find himself or herself in when doing an activity. It is a state where one's actions are "automatic, effortless, yet it is also a highly-focused state of consciousness" (p. 110), and enjoyment and engagement are at a maximum. He has identified nine key elements in people's descriptions of such states.

- There are clear goals every step of the way.
- There is immediate feedback on one's actions.
- There is a balance between challenges and skills.
- Attention is focused on one's actions.
- Distractions are excluded from consciousness.
- There is no worry of failure.
- Self-consciousness disappears.
- The sense of time becomes distorted.
- The activity becomes satisfying in its own right.

The last six of these are aspects of the internal experiences of flow and are not subject to control. The first three elements, however, are the external conditions present in a flow situation and, as such, provide us with the prescriptive conditions necessary to occasion a flow experience. These are also the exact elements that are afforded by the *Place One – Kill One* card trick above. At each step there is a clear goal – to arrange a number of cards in a set order. There is immediate feedback as to whether or not a proposed solution is accurate as they test it. These are secondary, however, to the importance of having a balance between challenge and skill.

Such a balance is very delicate. If the challenge exceeds the skill then anxiety or frustration ensures (see Figure 3); likewise, if the skill exceeds the challenge the student gets bored (see Figure 3 also). It is only when the two are in balance that a person is in the *flow channel* (Csikszentmihalyi, 1996). But being in flow channel is a dynamic process. As a person's skills increase they are at risk in popping out of this channel and become frustrated. That is, unless, along with their growing skill, the activity evolves to provide greater complexity. The aforementioned card trick provides this dynamic balance. As a person progresses through each level their knowledge increases and their solution strategies improve. In tandem with this growth, however, they also move onto the next level which provides them with new and more complex challenges.

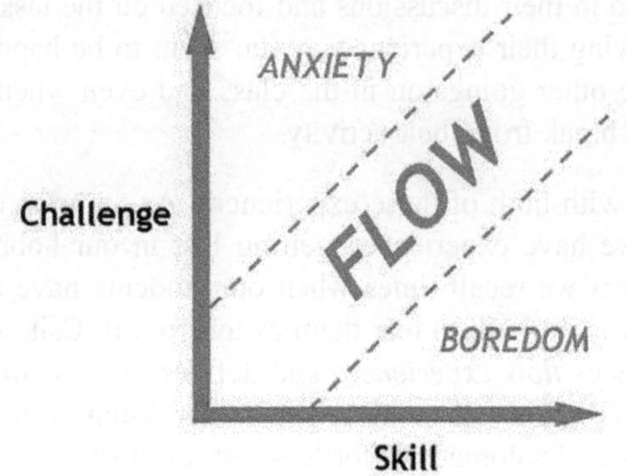

Figure 3. Flow channel (Batista, 2010)

Discovery Learning

The aforementioned card trick is more than a flow occasioning task, however. It can also, by its very nature, be seen as an example of discovery learning (Bruner, 1961; Dewey, 1913, 1916). Indeed, when the task is given to a class of mathematics students to work on in small groups, their problem-solving behaviour is indistinguishable from the ideal behaviours of students working in a discovery learning environment. They start with no knowledge of the solution or how to proceed to find the solution. They try some things and get feedback for their efforts. Soon they begin to collaboratively construct hypothesis of how to solve it and they test these through the iterative process of placing the cards on the table and at the bottom of the deck. The results of these tests provide the feedback that allows them to keep exploring and discovering new ideas.

Teachers' First Person Experience

Taken together, the *Place One – Kill One* card trick models *discovery learning* AND has a high likelihood of creating a *flow* experience. As such, it is the ideal tasks for allowing teachers to experience what discovery learning can look like in the classroom – first as students in their mathematics teacher in-service or pre-service classes and then as teachers administering the trick in their own classrooms. Their own experiences with this task as learners becomes, for many, the first time that teachers of mathematics have experienced discovery learning in its purest form (Ball, 1998). The added engagement they feel with the task provides them with an affective charge that is transformative for them in their thinking about what mathematics is and what mathematics teaching and learning can look like (Liljedahl, 2005; Liljedahl, Rolka, & Rösken, 2007).

As teachers in their own classrooms, the use of this task is likewise transformative (Liljedahl, 2010) in that they get to experience their own students engaging in discovery learning. This is very different from reading about the theories of discovery learning, hearing about others' experiences, seeing it in action in someone else's classroom, even seeing it in action in your own classroom at the hands of someone else. The first person experience of having orchestrated a discovery learning experience for their students motivates teachers to learn how to create more such experiences (Liljedahl, 2010), thereby entering into their own cycle of (professional) discovery learning.

REFERENCES

Ball, D. (1988). Unlearning to teach mathematics. *For the learning of mathematics, 8*(1), 40–48.

Batista, E. (2010). *Happiness, excellence, and boundaries: A framework for leaders*. Retrieved from http://www.edbatista.com/2010/09/happiness.html.

Bruner, J. S. (1961). The act of discovery. *Harvard Educational Review, 31*(1), 21–32.

Csikszentmihalyi, C. (1996). *Creativity: Flow and the psychology of discovery and invention*. New York, NY: HarperCollins Publishers.

Dewey, J. (1913). *Interest and effort in education*. New York, NY: Houghton Mifflin.

Dewey, J. (1916). *Democracy and education*. New York, NY: Simon and Schuster.

Liljedahl, P. (2005). Mathematical discovery and affect: The effect of AHA! experiences on undergraduate mathematics students. *International Journal of Mathematical Education in Science and Technology, 36*(2–3), 219–236.

Liljedahl, P. (2010). Noticing rapid and profound mathematics teacher change. *Journal of Mathematics Teacher Education, 13*(5), 411–423.

Liljedahl, P., Rolka, K., & Rösken, B. (2007). Affecting affect: The re-education of preservice teachers' beliefs about mathematics and mathematics learning and teaching. In M. Strutchens & W. Martin (Eds.), *69th NCTM yearbook: The learning of mathematics* (pp. 319–330). Reston, VA: National Council of Teachers of Mathematics.

Lortie, D. (1975). *Schoolteacher: A sociological study*. Chicago, IL: University of Chicago Press.

Peter Liljedahl
Simon Fraser University

BELINDA JAMIESON

17. IMAGINING ALBERTA'S FIRST NATIONS

For many years, the education of children has been a standardized procedure by which teachers implement curriculum developed by governing bodies. Occasionally, allowances are made for learning styles and learning environments, however, across this diverse country many classrooms look the same. Dr. Kieran Egan, the director of the Imaginative Education Research group founded by Dr. Egan and the Faculty of Education at Simon Fraser University, has theorized that there is something missing in this form of educating. According to Egan (2008) there are areas of children's cognition that are superior to adults and need to be encouraged and developed. Children are not dominated by rational, concrete, definite thought; they are imaginative and full of intellectual energy. He believes that engaging students' imaginations is crucial to their learning and as a result he has founded a movement aptly named Imaginative Education. This chapter will detail the Imaginative Education approach, provide a rationale for using it in my teaching, and demonstrate a lesson plan I developed to implement Imaginative Education within my own teaching practice.

The key distinctions of the Imaginative Education framework are the emotional engagement of students and their cognitive development according to socio-cultural exposure. Other educational theorists have stated that children experience innate stages of development based on their age but Egan (2008) argues that this can vary from child to child based on their socio-cultural tools, resources and experiences. Egan takes a unique approach to curriculum because he believes that the primary purpose of education is to maximize the cognitive tool kits which learners acquire. He proposes that an engaging way for learners to obtain these is through story. Before instruction a teacher should ask the question "What is the story?" about their topic of study. By looking at a topic through the element of story, learners are emotionally engaged and they will be able to connect their imaginations with the knowledge in the curriculum to enhance the power of their brain resulting in increased learning.

It is also important to note that children are engaged more when listening to an oral story as told by an adult. Too often children of today's society watch television, movies, and video games, and only hear stories read from books. These methods do little to instill the importance of generating images from words, which Egan deems is critical to developing cognitive tools.

As learners proceed through the stages of obtaining cognitive tools by acquiring language, they engage their brains in higher levels of thinking and understanding. Egan (2008) identifies the stages as follows: *somatic, mythic, romantic, philosophic,*

J. B. Cummings & M. L. Blatherwick (Eds.), Creative Dimensions of Teaching and Learning in the 21st Century, 181–187.

and *ironic*. Egan believes "Seeing education as a process of maximizing our cognitive tool kit is to see it as a process of enlarging our understanding as far as possible give the tools our culture has developed" (220, 0. 4). I have decided to concentrate on two of Egan's primary cognitive tools – mythic and romantic. The Imaginative Education Research Group (IERG) states: "It is at this phase of life that the child is no longer limited to making sense of the world through direct physical experiences. In mythic understanding the child relies on language to discuss, represent, and understand even things not yet experienced in person by using oral language" (www.ierg.net, 2010). While I do think that some of the fourth grade students I teach will have begun to master literacy and would be prepared to work with the next tools that Egan identifies as the romantic framework, the majority would benefit most from instruction within the mythic framework.

The administration at my school strongly encourages implementing differentiated instruction in our teaching practices to reach and challenge all learners. For the more advanced learners who are at an advanced stage, I attempt to incorporate elements of the romantic framework. At this stage students are becoming "increasingly fluent in reading and writing and are beginning to learn about the world around them, seek information about how extensive the reality is, what are its limits and what is most dramatic and wonderful about it" (2008, p. 64).

Students "romantically" associate with those who seem to be best able to overcome threats and constraints. These people are the heroes that embody transcendent human qualities. For today's generation of learners, they are most often from pop culture but they can be found in (and should be presented to students from) literature and great historical role models. To implement the improvement goals of my school, I utilize elements of both the mythic and romantic levels to allow for differentiated instruction.

The goal of this lesson will be to follow the framework of IE as Egan (2005) presents in *An Imaginative Approach to Teaching*. The basic framework for teaching is as follows:

- Identify Importance – What is most important about this topic? Why should it matter to students? What is the "story" of the topic?
- Find Binary Opposites – What binary opposite best shows the importance of the topic? What are the opposing forces in the story?
- Organize content in story form – What images best represent the importance of the topic and its binary opposite?
- Conclusion – What is the best way of resolving the conflict between the binary opposites? What new questions emerge about the topics?
- Evaluation – How can we know if the topic has been understood, its importance grasped, and the content learned? (pp. 40–41).

In my current teaching practice, I follow many of these steps. My training in the Understanding by Backward Design method (Wiggins & McTighe, 2005) has prepared me to look for the Big Idea, identify the importance of the lesson or unit being taught and begin with statement of desired results as detailed by Ornstein and Hunkins (2013). I felt the challenge in the IE method would be in identifying the binary opposite of the topic. Egan (2008) states: "…we have a powerful tendency to construct our conceptual grasp on the world in terms of opposites" (p. 16). He goes on to provide examples that humans equate such as good to bad, big to little, safe to dangerous. These examples are quite obvious but when considering the topics in the fourth-grade Alberta program of studies, I struggled to come up with binary opposites that are as concrete. I felt reassured when I read the fictional example of the student Sarah, in Egan's book *The Future of Education*, who is taking a training module in IE. In Sarah's journal, she also reflects on the challenge of finding the binary opposite and her instructor assures her by saying "there were no right answers to choosing binary opposites; it's just that some were more potent than others" (2008, p. 101). The instructor goes on to explain what she means by "potent" and I believe she is referring to making it engaging and meaningful to students. Students will identify and connect more to a story that they are fascinated with. Upon considering this step within the entire Imaginative Education framework, I have concluded that the binary opposite at the somatic level of cognitive development would be quite different than at the ironic level. Within my own teaching practice I will work to identify binary opposites at the level of my students and within the contexts of their learning.

Using a story framework was a new format for me but with some imagination and research I knew I could achieve this. The final steps of the IE framework are currently a part of my teaching practice, and I conclude a lesson with reflection and complete evaluation to determine if the students have gained an understanding of the content taught.

The curriculum aim I selected for this lesson is from the subject of Social Studies. In the grade four Program of Studies (Alberta Education, 2005, p. 2) students learn about the people, places and stories of their province to develop a sense of place, identity and belonging within Alberta. Students are encouraged to recognize the presence and influence of diverse Aboriginal peoples as inherent to Alberta's culture and identity.

It is important to celebrate the culture of the first people who lived in our province and create awareness among all students. I believe in the significance of this unit as many of my students in Northern Alberta identify themselves as First Nations and I feel this should be an area of recognition for them. Unfortunately, many of these students struggle academically and have unstable family lives. My goal is to showcase and celebrate their unique cultures and customs. After reading more about Imaginative Education I feel that this approach would help me to reach my objectives and students would have a more in-depth understanding of the First Nations rich history and meaningful way of life.

In her article on transformative education for First Nations communities, Jessica Ball (2004) acknowledges the importance of providing culturally aware and engaging learning opportunities. The First Nations populations in Canada represents 2.5 percent of the total population and are underrepresented in all professional and academic fields (Ball, p. 454). Ignas (2004) reports that difficulty in motivating First Nations students is most often cited as a reason for their underrepresentation. Also, Hare (2012) details how First Nation's children do not experience the same success in literacy as their non-indigenous counterparts. These disheartening facts are largely due to the suffering of First Nations communities as a result of enforced residential schooling, child welfare services and other organizations who attempted to provide what they thought was suitable help and assistance. Ignas (2004) credits the legacy of a colonialist educational system and its under representation of First Nations knowledge is a key factor that limits the future of First Nations.

The current population trends show that the majority of First Nations people are very young (the average age is 25.5 years), therefore educators are provided with a unique opportunity to develop meaningful and engaging learning opportunities that encourage the skills of youth academically as well as celebrate their rich heritage (Ball, 2004, p. 54). I believe that there is something for all of us all to learn about the traditions and customs of First Nations people, most specifically from their relationship and respect for the environment. Whether we teach in a First Nations community, or have these students within our own classroom community, it is critical to be sensitive to their needs and perspectives.

Furthermore, it is important not to perpetuate stereotypical views of First Nations culture. First Nations knowledge should be regarded as a legitimate source of knowledge not simply anthropological curiosity or entertainment. Hare (2011) identifies the need to bridge connections between First Nations people, communities, and schools to improve their educational outcomes, future success and wellbeing. Strong-Wilson (2007) discusses how First Nations people teach and learn by sharing legends, stories of ancestry, stories about the land, ceremony, survival and family stories. According to Strong-Wilson (2007), creation stories comprise the majority of First Nations reading material and carry great authority. Hare (2012) implores that this knowledge should be respected and honoured if children and families, particularly those from diverse cultural and linguistic communities are to bridge the gaps between home and community and school.

In my lesson plan I connected the framework of Imaginative Education with Alberta's Program of Studies. I also attempted to incorporate the topic of First Nations into another subject area beyond Social Studies so that students could make further connections and develop greater knowledge. The idea of creating an overarching story that connects different subjects also appears to be a useful concept of Imaginative Education. By fully engaging students within a story they are able to apply their content knowledge of one concept in various forms. This topic and lesson meets outcomes of the Social Studies, Science and Language Arts curriculum. Students already had prior knowledge of the lifestyle and traditions of First Nations people, as well as the requirements for growth and the parts of a plant. The objective of my lesson was for students to write their own creation stories based on the style and oral traditions of Alberta's First Nations people. They were to select a plant of their choice and imaginatively write about its creation. The lesson began by identifying the importance and answering the question: "Are plants important to First Nations people?" As prompting questions I asked: "What did First Nations people eat? Use for medicine? Where did they live?" The binary opposite to this idea is: "What would First Nations people do without plants?" This lesson implemented the Imaginative Education cognitive tools at the mythic level by creating stories and at the romantic level by connecting stories to people with heroic qualities. I read aloud the following plant creation story that I wrote titled *How the Spruce Tree Grew its Needles.*

> Many years ago, there was a tribe of First Nations people who lived off the land. They followed the great buffalo in their hunting season because the buffalo provided many things for the people. When a hunter caught a buffalo the tribe would feast. There would also be materials for clothing, tools and toys. The tribe would celebrate.
>
> One year, the great creator sent a particularly cold winter to the people. The cold winds snapped at their faces and blankets of snow fell on their teepees. Although the tribe had prepared for the winter by preserving food and pemmican, their supplies were running low and the winter raged on. One boy, who was not a great warrior or hunter, gathered up the courage to leave his tribe in search of food. Many people thought he was foolish for leaving the safety of his teepee within the tribe. He was brave and wanted to save his people from hunger.
>
> The boy left his tribe early one morning, wearing strong moccasins and heavy cloaks of buffalo hide. He hiked far across the land without spying any other footprints, human or animal, in the snow. As the sun began to set in the west he wondered how he would survive alone in the cold night. For the first time on his journey the brave boy became scared.
>
> In the distance, he could see a group of barren trees and he decided to reach them and spend the night there. If the trees were dry enough he could start a fire with their branches. Unfortunately, when he reached the trees he could see they were covered with snow and too damp to start a fire. The young boy wept tears because he thought this would be the end of him, and his people. As the tears fell to the snow at the base of the tree trunks, small green needles began to sprout from the branches. Before the boy's very eyes the creator turned the trees into lush, green soft boughs. The trees provided warmth for the boy. He finally had shelter from the cold wind and falling snow. That night he slept peacefully among the trees.
>
> In the morning, he woke to a shining sun and the snow had stopped. He emerged from the trees with new energy. The trees had spruced up his spirits and he was

ready to continue his search. He did not have to walk for long that day before he came upon a small buffalo. With his bow and arrow, he shot the buffalo and carried it with him back to his people. When his tribe caught sight of the brave boy they cried out joyfully – they would be saved! He told his people of the magical warm green trees, which he called spruce trees. His people later found these trees throughout the land and they provided warmth and shelter in the cold winter for the rest of their days.

Following the story telling, students collaboratively brainstormed different types of plants and each selected their own. Students then followed the writing process to write their own creation story of how this plant came to exist. They were reminded to include details about the type of environment their plant grew in and its requirements for growth.

My students responded with stories of all varieties. They were all imaginative but some students got carried away with their ideas and neglected to include their knowledge of plants. Also, some stories closely resembled the example that I wrote and shared. This is always a risk when sharing an example with students but I wanted them to know that if I could write an imaginative story they could too! I believe that with further implementation of Imaginative Education practices in my daily curriculum, my students would become more familiar with the process and their imaginations would flourish.

Planning this lesson was an extensive learning experience for me. I considered topics I have been teaching for a few years via new approaches and I experience increased student (and teacher) engagement and learning as a result. The process was not difficult, however, I believe in order to implement Imaginative Education you would have to constantly modify your lessons and units based on specific student needs, abilities and their level of cognitive development. This is something that the majority of educators do on a continual basis and is a reflective of good teaching practices regardless of the guiding frameworks.

There are many existing curriculum approaches to explore. After reflecting on the various methodologies, I feel that Imaginative Education offers a unique, meaningful and engaging approach. The educational vision of Kieran Egan identifies that "The aim of Imaginative Education is much more knowledgeable students who are able to think flexibly, creatively, and with energy about the knowledge they gain about the world and experience" (2005, p. 9). This focus is resonant of my personal teaching philosophy. I look forward to implementing my new awareness for the importance of encouraging imagination and the use of stories in further lessons.

REFERENCES

Alberta Education. (2005). *Social studies kindergarten to grade 12*. Retrieved from https://education.alberta.ca/media/159595/program-of-studies-gr-4.pdf

Ball, J. (2004). As if indigenous knowledge and communities mattered: Transformative education in first nations communities in Canada. *American Indian Quarterly, 28*(3/4), 454.

Egan, K. (2005). *An imaginative approach to teaching.* San Francisco, CA: Jossey-Bass – A Wiley Imprint.
Egan, K. (2008). *Imaginative education.* Retrieved from http://ierg.net/
Egan, K. (2008). *The future of education: Reimagining our schools from the ground up.* New Haven & London: Yale University Press.
Hare, J. (2012). "They Tell a Story and There's Meaning behind That Story": Indigenous knowledge and young indigenous children's literacy learning. *Journal of Early Childhood Literacy, 12*(4), 389–414.
Ignas, V. (2004). Opening doors to the future: Applying local knowledge in curriculum development. *Canadian Journal of Native Education, 28*, 49–58.
Ornstein, A., & Hunkins, F. (2013). *Curriculum: Foundations, principles and issues.* Toronto: Pearson Publishing.
Strong-Wilson, T. (2008). Turtles all the way: Simulacra and resistance to Simulacra in indigenous teachers' discussion of indigenous children's literature. *Children's Literature in Education, 39*(1), 53–74.
Wiggins, G. P., & McTighe, J. (2005). *Understanding by design.* Alexandria, VA: ASCD.

Belinda Jamieson
University of New Brunswick

LESLIE JULIA BREWSTER

18. THE IMPORTANCE OF ART IN CHILDREN'S WRITING EDUCATION

INTRODUCTION

"We have a huge vested interest in education because it is education that's meant to take us into this future that we can't grasp" (Robinson, 2006). This statement made by Sir Ken Robinson points to what should be a universal concern to make education our most important societal coping strategy. He highlights especially the need for arts education if we are to nurture the creative and critical thinkers necessary to move into the future. Robinson discusses the amazing creativity and talents inherent in all children, and expresses his concern that schools "squander" these talents "pretty ruthlessly" (Robinson, 2006). I agree with him that "creativity is as important in education as literacy" (Robinson, 2006). Consider how children with ADHD are often thought of as having reduced potential in school, when the opposite could well be the reality. There is research pointing to the idea that students with ADHD may have untapped creative potential. Research was conducted by the University of Michigan and Eckerd College in Florida giving creativity tests to college students: "Young adults with attention deficit hyperactivity disorder showed more creativity compared with those who did not have ADHD" (Wadley, 2011). Co-author Priti Shah suggests: "Individuals who are not succeeding as well academically may benefit from understanding that there may be tradeoffs associated with ADHD. With extra motivation to overcome difficulties in planning, attention, and impulsivity, they may be able to take greater advantage of their creative strengths" (Wadley, 2011). These results support Sir Ken Robinson's plea that we should place more importance on nurturing students' creativity to get the best potential for all students.

In elementary school, we can help nurture creativity in our students by recognizing the importance of art in children's literacy education. We should consider the significance of children's early scribbles, some of the benefits of allowing children to express themselves through pictures as well as words, and some ways exposure to the work of visual artists contributes to children's literacy education. I include a few strategies that I have found successful to help incorporate art into the classroom. As Bob Steele believes in the preface to his book, *Draw Me a Story,* "when a child scribbles on a sheet of paper or makes crude chalk pictures on the side walk, a language is beginning to emerge" (Steele, 1998, p. vii).

J. B. Cummings & M. L. Blatherwick (Eds.), Creative Dimensions of Teaching and Learning in the 21st Century, 189–195.

The Significance of Children's Scribbles

The contribution that children's early drawing makes to their emergent literacy has been emphasized in Susan Sheridan's (2002) article *The Neurological Significance of Children's Drawing: The Scribble Hypothesis*. Sheridan's abstract states:

> evidence that very young children's scribbling serves four critical purposes: (1) to train the brain to pay attention and to sustain attention; (2) to stimulate individual cells and clusters of cells in the visual cortex for line and shape; (3) to practice and to organize the shapes and patterns of thought; and (4) through an increasing affinity for marks, to prepare the human mind for a consciousness organized by literacy. (p. 1)

According to Sheridan those children who are encouraged to draw will demonstrate an affinity for geometry, and "will think more connectedly and unpredictably, or creatively" (Sheridan, 2002, p. 2). This is crucial for children's development, and Sir Ken Robinson believes that "we need to radically rethink our view of intelligence, that many highly talented, brilliant, creative people think they're not, because the thing they were good at school wasn't valued, or was actually stigmatized" (Robinson, 2006). Art needs to be valued as a method of story-telling, not as a reward activity or afterthought. Author Bob Steele (1998) also recognizes the essentialness of drawing to children's education, "I advocate an approach to home/school education that would free children to use all their "innate capabilities of mind". This would be done by shifting drawing from the periphery of the art class to the core of the curriculum as a language medium. In effect, I envisage the use of three languages: words alone, drawings alone, and drawings and words in collaboration" (p. 3). Implications for teaching should take into consideration neurobiological research that shows "that brain systems, including the two hemispheres are complimentary, suppressing each other for functions the other does best to maximize the brain's capabilities" (Sheridan, 2002, p. 2). To maximize brain activity, drawing and writing should be used "in complimentary mode as an educational strategy", taking note that "Scribbling is the tangled matrix where drawing and writing begin" (Sheridan, 2002, p. 2). To emphasize the connections between scribbling and reading Susan Sheridan states: "Children's scribbles are intelligible to them! Their marks carry meaning. The scribbling child can talk about her marks. Talk about marks is the beginning of reading" (Sheridan, 2002, p. 2).

Building on this relationship, teachers can help enhance and expand children's literacy by making use of the natural relationship between art and literacy. In *Children as Illustrators,* Susan Thompson (2005) says: "The attitudes developed during childhood about creativity and artistic ability carry over into adolescence and adulthood, dramatically influencing interest in art and creating it throughout life. Thus, it is important for young children to have opportunities to express themselves freely and experience positive feelings and success in art abilities" (p. 1).

A Classroom Strategy: "Creation Station"

Students are given a multitude of art and craft supplies and are given enough time to create/invent/build their creations. Here students work independently or in teams to create their ideas being limited only by their own imaginations and the available materials. Ideas are often sparked by each other's work and student interaction is key. The conversations that students have while working this way will lead to valuable vocabulary to be used in writing. Following the creative making process students then write the procedures they followed as instructions for anyone to repeat the process. For this writing centre students and teacher can create a special word wall for the materials they use (markers, crayons, construction paper, string, egg cartons, ribbon etc.). I have had students who chose to make kites, boomerangs, windmills, greeting cards, pencil holders, puppets, and wallets – just to name a few. Their writing is loaded with specific details about how to make their creations.

Children's natural creativity is also at the core of Sir Ken Robinson's discussions. "We're all born with immense natural talents" (Robinson, 2009). He paraphrases an idea from Picasso, "all children are born artists. The problem is to remain an artist as we grow up" (Robinson, 2006). Artistic opportunities will enhance the flow of learning for children since we know that: "Learning takes place when children make connections between new experiences and what they already know – knowledge already learned at school or experiences they bring with them from home" (Thompson, 2005, p. 12).

A Classroom Strategy: Art for Descriptive Writing

Over the past few years I have had a lot of success helping my students become excited about writing by incorporating art into their writer's workshop. For example, after reading a couple of stories about snowmen in art class, each child makes a portrait of a snowman in pastel. The subject is assigned, but the students choose how they want the snowman to look. Once the portraits are complete students then write detailed descriptions of their snowmen. With all of the portraits on display students take turns reading their descriptions aloud to another class to see if others can match the descriptions to the portraits. This strategy can be done with a multitude of subjects; I have used monsters, houses, various animals, cars, etc. Children become excited to write and "play the guessing game". This activity has the added bonus of inspiring students to become more focused creatively on both their writing and their art. Students become more purposeful. While they work through the writing process students tend to revise both their writing and their artwork as they seek to create clear descriptions of their art.

Some Benefits of Allowing Children to Express Themselves through Art as Well as Words

Story-telling is an essential literacy tool that can build on children's strengths and engage the whole child. "Drawing contributes greatly to self-expression and writing.

It provides a context for children and their writing and a framework for children's thinking as they write stories or relate experiences. Children use drawing as a way to organize their thinking and the information they want to write about" (Thompson, 2005, pp. 23–24). Artistic expression allows children a way of telling their stories more fully than they may be capable of in writing. In *Draw me a Story* Bob Steele (1998) comments: "Drawing could make the acquisition of literacy skills more pleasurable and more efficient" (p. vii). Grauer and Irwin (2005) use the same line of thought in their book saying that:

> using both visual and verbal modes of understanding and representing could actually enhance children's expression. By using the unique aspects of knowing represented by visual as well as verbal thinking, children have the opportunity to experience deeper and richer forms of communicating their ideas and appreciate these capacities in others. (p. 113)

Susan Thompson (2005) comments: "Drawing contributes greatly to self-expression and writing. It provides a context for children and their writing and a framework for children's thinking as they write stories or relate experiences. Children use drawing as a way to organize their thinking and the information they want to write about" (Thompson, 2005, pp. 23–24). She says further that: "Drawings can also be wonderful springboards for children, affording them a space to work out their ideas and stories through illustration before writing their text. Their writings, discussions, and dramatizations can develop from these drawings as children add more details and gain confidence in their work" (Thompson, 2005, p. 24).

In my classroom, I have used a resource by Lucy Calkins (2003), *Firsthand: Units of Study for Primary Writing*. This resource offers a series of writing lessons, and places much emphasis on the importance of allowing children to draw their stories before asking them to write them in words. Following the model of this resource enables teachers to instill in children the idea that writing is never done. We can always add to the picture, add to the words or start a new story. Lucy Calkins recognizes the importance of allowing children to tell their stories through pictures, and recognizes that like the written word we can always continue our visual stories by adding details to enhance meaning. I would expand on Ms. Calkins' ideas by allowing students larger paper for their pictures to encourage greater detail. Susan Thompson (2005) also makes it clear that young children who are not yet reading can express their stories or ideas through drawings; they recognize that both drawing and writing are ideas on paper. "When children are in literacy-rich school and home environments, they learn early that stories can be read, acted out, and written down", and also "told with pictures alone" (p. 32).

A Classroom Strategy: The Picture Worth a Thousand Words

The original idea behind this successful technique is from *The Writing Teacher's Strategy Guide* by Steve Peha (1995–2010). Here students are asked to draw a small moment, story, or event using quick, simple drawings and outlines. I have found that a helpful basis for this is to open student choices up to include any medium (not just drawing) and to allow a lot of time for the development of the art story before embarking on the writing. Students also include one- or two-word labels for every item, or parts of items, in their picture as well as captions where helpful. The labels really help to bring out very descriptive vocabulary in the final writing as the students are better able to visualize details and in turn create the same picture in the minds of their eventual readers. It is important that students work on a larger surface, this allows them more freedom to include details. The more work that goes into the art the more details students will have for their writing. Again, the abundance of details these young students are capable of writing has continued to be astounding and impressive. This can be a great way to introduce dialogue as well. The strategy also adapts nicely when students begin to write imaginative narratives or fairy tales. I have found that giving students the time to work out their tales in pictures (here it usually takes students more than one picture to tell a story) naturally develops their sense of beginning, middle, and end. Asking students to "show what happens next" and then write it seems to give young writers the opportunity to envision deeper storylines than I have seen without the extensive art time.

Learning Literacy through Exposure to Many Works of Art

The skills and knowledge acquired through the examination of multiple artists and illustrators provide children with many ideas for their writing and illustrations. That kind of learning also has the effect of broadening children's understanding both of what an artist is and of themselves as being artist. How gratifying for the children to discover new tools to tell their stories (Thompson, 2005, p. 55)!

Being exposed to many artists can ignite and inspire children to write or draw their own stories. This also enables them to make interpretations of what a particular artist "writes". Children benefit from such exposure to master artists and can be asked to "write about what they see visually in the art and what emotions are evoked" (Batycky, 2001, p. 34). In the article *Beyond the Curriculum: Creating Connections Through Art*, Jennifer Batycky discusses her use of reproduction postcards to invite children to "be moved to make new interpretations of the paintings, the word, and of themselves" (2001, p. 34). Ms. Batycky's finding is that in this context "children tend to employ a great deal of metaphoric language and write often in a free style poetic format. It seems that in finding a picture that "speaks" to them, the students are able to make an emotional connection and find their own voice in writing" (Batycky, 2001, p. 35). In contrast to a focus on technical skills, Batycky finds that offering children an inspiration for their writing through art is producing more descriptive writing that:

> is richer than writing focused simply on their technical skills. I have also noticed that the children's ability to write rich descriptive passages serves them

> well when they later learn to write in other genres. Working with the visual arts cultivates sensitive perception, develops insights, fosters imagination and places a premium on well-crafted form. (Batycky, 2001, p. 35)

A Classroom Strategy: Reading Pictures

Our children live in a world of communication by visual image. They should spend time in their regular schedules looking at images and making sense of them or trying to imagine the stories behind the images. I was introduced to a technique for inspiring writing during my education degree that involved students using an assortment of works of art to springboard a narrative. Presenting students with 5 or 6 prints, they are then asked to develop a storyline incorporating at least 4 of the pictures. I have used this technique many times in the classroom with wonderful results. This is a great technique for helping students to develop inferences from what they can see in a picture. I have used both large prints and the postcard sized prints of famous art works, photographs that students bring to school, as well as asking students to trade their own art work with their classmates. This allows students to enhance their skills in so many ways. Their ability to make predictions, to visualize, and to comprehend, all can come from practicing to "read pictures".

In her paper, *The Visual Arts and Qualitative Research,* Veronica Stephen (1996) says:

> What one views, sees, and observes in an art piece serves to create a relationship, much like the one that occurs between the reader and the text. With the visual arts, their processes of receiving conceptual images and later forming reactions to such images are inexorably bound to higher order thinking skills and numerous aspects of creativity. (p. 12)

In his article, *The Picture of Reading: Deriving Meaning in Literacy Through Image,* Joseph Piro (2002) says that children can benefit greatly by learning "the strategy of 'reading' a picture; part by part, using it as text aligned with other curriculum areas" (2002, p. 127). There are many similarities between the reading of text and the reading of a picture. Children possess numerous strategies for processing their environment including ways to make sense of both linguistic and non-linguistic stimulation. As Piro says: "By looking at pictures to determine how they communicate and elaborate a story's message children make a smooth transition from image to language" (p. 128).

If we think about what we really can observe about young children, it seems so natural that art be integrated in teaching writing. "We think about the world in all the ways we experience it. We think visually, we think in sound, we think kinesthetically, we think in abstract terms, we think in movement and in many other ways, too" (Robinson, 2006). Adults (parents and educators) must appreciate and value children's art right from its beginning "scribbles". Drawing is essential to children's literacy. Teaching the writing process is easily matched with artwork as students go through the same steps for each: brainstorming, rough plan/ draft, revising, editing, and publishing. We need to expose children to master artists, and allow them freedom to enter into the world of art in all of its forms, linguistic and non-linguistic. Their own art, their conception of visual images, and their ability to formulate responses to those images are all connected to higher-order thinking. Children have many stories and dreams to tell. As teachers we need to allow children all avenues of expression to help nurture their creativity as a path to their true potential; we must be careful not to "educate it out of them". "Every day, everywhere, children spread their dreams beneath our feet. And we should tread softly" (Robinson, 2010).

REFERENCES

Batycky, J. (2001). Beyond the curriculum: Creating connections through art. *Canadian Children, 26*(1), 33–37.

Calkins, L., & FirstHand (Firm). (2003). *Units of study for primary writing: A yearlong curriculum.* Portsmouth, NH: FirstHand.

Grauer, K., & Irwin, R. L. (Eds.). (2005). *Starting with...* (2nd ed.). Kingston, Ontario: Canadian Society for Education through Art.

Peha, S. (1995–2010). *Teaching that makes sense inc.: The writing teacher's strategy guide.* Retrieved from http://www.ttms.org/

Piro, J. (2002). The picture of reading: deriving meaning in literacy through image. *Reading Teacher, 56*(2), 126–134.

Robinson, K. (2006). *Ken Robinson: How schools kill creativity* (video). Retrieved from http://www.ted.com/talks/ken_robinson_says_schools_kill_creativity

Robinson, K. (2009). *How schools stifle creativity.* Retrieved from http://www.cnn.com/2009/OPINION/11/03/rob

Robinson, K. (2010). *Ken Robinson: Bring on the learning revolution* (video). Retrieved from http://www.ted.com/talks/sir_ken_robinson_bring_on_the_revolution

Sheridan, S. (2002). The neurological significance of children's drawing: The scribble hypothesis. *Journal of Visual Literacy, 22*(2), 107–128.

Steele, B. (1998). *Draw me a story portage: An illustrated exploration of drawing-as language.* Winnipeg: Portage and Main Publishing.

Stephen, V. P. (1996, February 24–28). *The visual arts and qualitative research: Diverse and emerging voices.* Paper presented at the Annual Meeting of the Association of Teacher Educators, St. Louis, MO.

Thompson, S. C. (2005). *Children as illustrators: Making meaning through art and language.* Washington, DC: National Association for the Education of Young Children.

Wadley, J. (2011, February 10). *Michigan news.* Retrieved from http://ns.umich.edu/new/releases/8258

Leslie Julia Brewster
New Brunswick

CYNTHIA WALLACE-CASEY

19. DE-CONSTRUCTING CABINETS OF CURIOSITY

Learning to Think Historically in Community History Museums[1]

INTRODUCTION

Community history museums provide powerful sites for learning about the past. Although those of us actively involved in museum education intuitively know this, in Canada we now have figures from the recently published national survey, *Canadians and their pasts* (Conrad et al., 2013), to support such claims. Their findings show that, currently, the largest proportion of adult Canadians (30%) rate museums most highly, as the single most trustworthy source of historical knowledge. By contrast, only 6% consider school teachers to be most trustworthy (Conrad et al., 2013, p. 53). This is not surprising. A similar survey, conducted nearly 20 years ago in the United States, revealed similar findings there: Americans place more trust in history museums than in any other source of information about the past (Rosenzweig & Thelen, 1998, p. 91).

Indeed, my own case study research (Wallace-Casey, 2015) suggests that most seventh-grade students also place their highest level of trust in museums. Within my sample group (n=23), when asked the same set of questions as in the *Canadians and their pasts* survey, the largest proportion of students (54%) stated that they trusted museums more than any other source of information about the past. Their primary reasoning for this was that museums present "real things" or "artifacts," and safeguard "knowledge" or "proof" about the past (Wallace-Casey, 2015, pp. 109–111).

J. B. Cummings & M. L. Blatherwick (Eds.), Creative Dimensions of Teaching and Learning in the 21st Century, 197–207.

By contrast, only 8% considered school history teachers to be most trustworthy. Such compelling percentage distinctions have led me to ask three essential questions about teaching practices in history education: How might educators build upon this trust to enable more creative understandings about the past? How can history museums play a more central role in students' formal history education? Can history museums empower middle-school students to think historically about the narratives they encounter in museums? This chapter explores these questions by demonstrating how formal classroom instruction, adopting concepts for historical thinking, enabled seventh grade students to think historically about the collections they encountered within their community history museum. It supports the premise that students can be empowered to look beyond the authority of the museum narrative – to create their own interpretations about the past and (in so doing) become active members of the museum's community of inquiry.

Historical Thinking in Museums

Historical thinking, although not new to the international discourse surrounding history education[2], represents an approach to exploring the past that is grounded in the discipline of history. The pedagogy is based upon cognitive research originating from the British Schools Council Project "History 13–16" (Schools History Project, 1976; Shemilt, 1983; Stearns et al., 2000; Wineburg, 1996), which emphasizes a procedural approach to history education. In Canada, the historical thinking paradigm has been spearheaded by Seixas (1996) and others, who (along with many international scholars) have found that through adherence to formal methods of historical inquiry, students can be enabled to use procedural meta-concepts to arrive at substantive narratives about the past. The end result is believed to be a deeper understanding of the past: an understanding that is both student-centered and creative in its approach to using multiple perspectives, historical concepts, primary sources, evidence, and ethics to interpret the past (Lévesque, 2011; Osborne, 2006; Sandwell, 2005; Seixas, 1996).

As an offshoot of this historical thinking paradigm, the national survey *Canadians and their pasts* (2013) has helped to bring museums into the forefront of discussions around history education in Canada (Clark, 2011; Conrad et al., 2013; Seixas & Morton, 2013; Trofanenko, 2014). In addition, several scholarly researchers have found that students within this age group (and younger) are very capable of deconstructing the narratives they encounter within museums. In particular, as Nakou (2001, p. 93) has observed, from the moment students enter a museum, they inevitably formulate a multitude of open-ended questions about the past, and decode meaning from museum artifacts beyond the intended historical narrative. Likewise, Trofanenko (2006) has clearly demonstrated that students do not blindly accept the narratives they encounter within museums. Instead, when tasked with the opportunity to enter into a dialogue with museum collections, Trofanenko has shown that fifth-grade students are very capable of questioning historical interpretations, analysing evidence, and examining sources.

In light of these findings, however, the question remains: how might museum educators enable middle school students to think historically about the narratives they encounter within community history museums? Certainly, Wineburg (2001) has clearly demonstrated that by making historical narratives *unnatural* (that is to say, less easily consumable), students will become more intellectually engaged. Such acts of historical thinking, however, as Seixas and Morton (2013) have emphasized, also require specific procedural and conceptual criteria that are unique to the discipline of history. Yet, this poses a dilemma for museum education, since one of the central difficulties associated with adopting discipline-based criteria for historical thinking within museums rests with the discipline of history itself. History museums are not like other history learning resources. This is because museums are primarily keepers of three-dimensional (material) artifacts. As *material historians*, museum curators employ a unique set of procedural and conceptual criteria – that are based upon the discipline of *material history*. Such a distinction poses theoretical problems for historical thinking within museums because the domain-specific knowledge that museum curators employ is unique to the three-dimensional nature of artifact sources. As a result, artifacts require that historians be able to "read" much more than words.

To this end, there are various procedures for analytical inquiry that museum curators have adopted. One of these was developed by graduate students at the University of New Brunswick in the early 1980s (Elliot, 1994; Smith, 1985), and was based upon the theoretical perspectives of Fleming (1974) as well as Prown (1982). By adopting a similar framework for material history inquiry, I have argued that middle school students can be enabled to think historically about the three-dimensional sources they encounter within history museums (Wallace-Casey, 2015, pp. 314–321).

This case study espouses such a material history framework. Over the course of my research, participants were asked to adopt a series of scaffolding tools, designed to engage students in museum history domain knowledge. These tools supported the premise that students could be empowered to look beyond the authority of the museum narrative by *doing* material history as museum curators do; but that such a scenario would require first learning how to "read" and critically analyze museum artifacts for the evidence that they contained.

Case Study Method

The single-case study design (Yin, 2009), was bounded by the context of time (7 weeks within one unit of study); as well as by the formal arrangement of a classroom (one seventh grade social studies class); and a specific community history museum. Over the course of the study, students visited the museum four times (as a class). In addition, over the same time period, four of the museum curators visited the classroom three times. During the case study, students engaged in historic space mapping of the museum exhibits; they posed questions and documented their visits through photography; participated in "think-alouds" with the museum curators; and adopted a material history framework for artifact analysis. Students also completed two written assignments. These were marked against assessment criteria for historical thinking that evaluated their ability to describe, compare and contextualise museum artifacts as sources of evidence.

Learning to Do History Like a Museum Curator

To begin, students were first introduced to the concept of material history inquiry, through a simple classroom activity that involved "reading" (and interpreting) a shoe.[3] While all seemed to enjoy this activity, students' responses were nevertheless very simplistic, and did not seem to reflect the level of critical inquiry to which the historical thinking paradigm is dedicated (Seixas & Morton, 2013; see also Denos & Case, 2006; Gini-Newman & Misfeldt, 2008; Mandell & Malone, 2007). This classroom activity was then followed by a brief introductory lesson in differentiating between evidence and sources – leading students to re-consider museum artifacts as not just interesting objects, but as valid sources of evidence about the past. The next day, students visited their local community history museum for the first time, and received a standard (45 minute) guided tour.

Assignment I

After this first museum visit, students were asked to write about their impressions of what life was like in the 1800's (based upon what they had learned from their initial guided tour). The results of this first assignment demonstrated very few examples of historical thinking: most of the students (65%) organised their narrative responses around a then-versus-now argument, citing how lifestyles in the past were very "different" compared to the present. Only two of the students, adopted a strategy of drawing evidence from the museum artifacts to support their narrative claim; and several (30%) simply appropriated versions of the narratives that they had encountered

Figure 2. Students engaged in Historic Space Mapping. Image credit: Author

during their museum visit. In addition, many students (39%) integrated narratives from other secondary sources that were obviously not present within the museum setting.

Historic Space Mapping

Subsequently, over a series of five weekly classroom lessons, organised around a strategy for learning how to differentiate between artifact sources and evidence, students became more familiar with distinctions between the two. In addition, they also participated in classroom exercises in historic space mapping, as a way of visually identifying (and de-constructing) the narratives they encountered within the museum. This strategy was adapted from the research of Cutrara (2010; see also Leinhardt & Gregg, 2002; Seixas & Morton, 2013; Van Drie & Van Boxtel, 2003), and involved creating conceptual "mind maps" of the historical narratives students encountered (Figure 1). This technique proved to be very beneficial over time, since it enabled students to revisit their museum experience (in the classroom), as well as to engage in group dialogue and to enter into the mindset of the curators who had originally developed the exhibits.

Posing Questions

In preparation for their second museum visit, a portion of class time was dedicated to an introductory lesson about recognising different types of questions: information questions; opinion questions; and probing questions (Case & Wright, 1997). Then, working in their research groups, and using the museum historic space map as a point of reference, students were tasked with developing three questions (each) to pose to the museum curators the next day. In this way, they were prompted to engage in historical thinking on three levels: socioculturally – with the artifact that attracted their personal attention; internally – with the artifacts exhibited on the museum map; and externally – with other students within their group.

Photography

Subsequently, upon arriving at the museum, students were given free rein to explore the collections, photograph artifacts of interest, and pose questions to the museum curators. This visit, although limited to 45 minutes, proved to be very engaging. It was obvious that the students had arrived "with a mission", and they knew where they were going. They seemed to be enjoying the experience. They also seemed to be very focused upon their historical inquiry objective.

Think-Alouds

Following their second museum visit, students were introduced to a modified version of The McCord Museum's (2013) *Interpreting Artifacts* worksheet,

Doing History with Objects – Material History Analysis Grid

Research Topic:

Name: ______________________ **Date:** ______________________

Analysis Steps	What	Where	When	Who	Why
Step 1: Observable data *(What can you see?)*					
Step 2: Comparable data *(How does it compare?)*					
Step 3: Contextual data *(What can you add?)*					
Step 4: Summary *(What can you infer?)*					

What are you still uncertain about?

Figure 3. A material history framework for artifact analysis

which involved examining an artifact for the "5 W's" of what, where, when, who, and why. This mediational tool served as a detailed supplement to the material history analysis framework (Figure 3), which was the focus of the case study. The next day, all four of the museum curators visited the classroom, to provide curatorial insights about students' chosen artifact (using the *Interpreting Artifacts* worksheet as their mediational tool). In this way, both curators and students were prompted to "think aloud" about the artifacts – and thus model historical thinking.

When the class commenced, students were asked to break down into research groups (according to exhibit themes), with their research folder (one per group, containing artifact images that they had collected from their last museum visit), and modified *Interpreting Artifacts* worksheet. The remaining class time was then devoted to one-on-one discussions, with the students posing artifact-based questions to the museum curators. The resulting group discussions unfolded very naturally, and students appeared to be very engaged. Through interaction with the curators, it was noticeable that students were beginning to perceive themselves as active members of a community of inquiry, and they were becoming more familiar with the questions historians ask about the past. They were also becoming more aware of the problematic nature of historical inquiry, realising that historians often do not possess a great deal of information with which to construct knowledge about the past.

Material History Framework for Artifact Analysis

Upon returning to the museum for a third visit, students were highly motivated in their "mission" to fill in gaps in the research information they had gathered to date. In so doing, they were expanding their inquiry beyond the descriptive '5W's', by examining artifacts more carefully; looking for comparative sources of evidence; and drawing inferences from the museum setting (Figure 2). Ample opportunities were also made available to gather more images, and to ask more questions of the museum curators. As a result, students were now fully in charge of their own inquiry, and were entering into deeper levels of dialogic learning: socioculturally – with the context of the museum exhibit; internally – with the artifact and the information that it revealed; and externally – with the museum curators. In the process, they were also realising how historians make inferences about the past through close examination and corroboration of sources.

This third visit represented a significant advance in students' ability to think historically about the three-dimensional sources they encounter within the museum. By now it was apparent that their attention was clearly focused upon the artifacts; they were confident in their actions, and seemed to be drawing from prior knowledge in historical inquiry (acquired from previous classes). In effect, they were digging much deeper than in previous visits. They were asking more probing quesions, comparing their artifact source against the museum's narrative claim and making full use of the 45- minute time limitation.

Flipping the Museum

Students returned to the museum for their fourth (and final) visit the following week. As part of their second assignment, the task for this day was for everyone to provide an oral presentation about their artifact. In this way, organisers were reversing roles of authority within the museum (in essence "flipping the class"), enabling students to be the curatorial "experts" and lead the museum visit. In preparation, each of the students had created an artifact photo card, containing "5 W's" descriptive information on the reverse side. These served as organising prompts for their presentations. As a result, students became the tour guides, leading the class through the museum; while along the way, each individual provided a brief oral presentation about their artifact. This final museum tour proved to be very rewarding since students now seemeed very confident in their actions as museum "experts".

Assignment II

Upon completion of the museum fieldwork experience, students were asked to create their own artifact label (50–90 words), using pieces of evidence that they had drawn from their material history artifact analysis (and addressing the inquiry question of

What, Where, When, Who and Why). Responses to this second assignment were significantly different from the previous. All of the students were now focussing their attention upon a specific artifact source, and drawing evidence from that source. Their narratives were no longer "then-versus-now" first impressions, but were focussed upon the artifact – as a source of evidence to support their narrative claims. Moreover, students were employing a combination of description, inference, and comparative processes to formulate these claims. Clearly, what they had appropriated from the museum experience was information drawn from observing their artifact, questioning the curators, and sifting through artifact accession records. These findings are significant because they demonstrate ways in which students were becoming active members of the museum's community of inquiry by thinking historically about the artifact sources they encountered within the museum. In so doing, they were de-constructing the museum's official narrative, to re-create their own personal meaning.

Implications and Recommendations

This case study has demonstrated how seventh grade students can be enabled to think historically within community history museums. As the findings suggest, however, while museums can provide powerful learning environments for understanding the past, scaffolding tools are also required to enable students to carefully examine the socially constructed narratives that they encounter. In order to achieve this, students must arrive at the museum with a clear mission and purpose that relates to a specific topic of inquiry in history. Students also require ample amounts of free choice in the museum, and need to be able to undertake repeat visits.

In this instance, sequential visits (both to the museum as well as the classroom) enabled students to become active participants in the museum's community of inquiry. This was achieved by adopting a material history domain knowledge approach to historical thinking that was student-driven and supported student-choice through asking questions, comparing evidence, drawing personal meaning, and making connections to broader aspects of history. Interestingly, these student-driven choices were based primarily upon visual interest and curiosity – which suggests that museums hold great potential for inspiring students to explore historical topics that are outside of their zone of familiarity.

Students in this inquiry also particularly enjoyed role reversal activities in which they became the experts and adults simply listened. Through student-driven inquiry, students were found to adopt more complex narratives for remembering the past. These findings suggest that museums have much to offer the field of history education, in providing students with ample freedom to carefully examine and ask critical questions about the narratives they encounter in learning about the past. To achieve this, however, students require time for wonder and discovery, as well as access to real artifacts and other primary sources. They also require ample time, after the initial museum experience, to conduct follow-up research, consult with alternative primary and secondary sources, and re-visit the museum experience in a variety of creative ways. This means that a single museum visit is by no means sufficient. As evidence from this case study suggests, students require ample time to think about the narrative, ask probing questions, engage with the artifacts, compare sources, and re-examine their evidence. Such sophisticated levels of in-depth analysis cannot be gained within the framework of a single fleeting visit. More empirical research is required in this area to enable creative ways for re-visiting the museum experience while also engaging in historical thinking.

In comparing the results of assignment I against assignment II, it is evident that – over time – all of the students became intellectually engaged with the community history museum. By the end of the seven-week inquiry, students possessed a significant level of skill and knowledge around de-constructing the historical narratives they encountered within the museum, and understanding how such narratives can/should be based upon evidence that is drawn from artifact sources. Likewise, by adopting a material history framework for historical inquiry, students became more focussed upon the museum collection as a valid source of evidence about the past; they in turn adopted formal methods of historical inquiry to arrive at their own unique narrative claims about the past – claims that were supported by thoughtful evidence, rather than simple then-versus-now first impressions.

CONCLUSION

Overall, the experience of learning to think historically within a community history museum was found to help students realise the problematic nature of historical inquiry. By *doing* material history in a community setting, students encountered (first-hand) how historians piece together the past from (seemingly) minute bits of evidence. They also came to perceive themselves as active members of a community of inquiry. By adopting these teaching practices, educators can build upon students' trust of museums to enable more creative understandings about the past. In this way, museums can play a more central role in supporting social studies instruction in the classroom. At the same time, students can be empowered to think more critically about the historical narratives they encounter in living their lives outside of the social studies classroom.

NOTES

1 This research has been supported by The Social Sciences and Humanities Research Council (SSHRC) of Canada, the University of New Brunswick, and The History Education Network/Histoire et éducation en réseau (THEN/HiER).

2 For a discussion on the various manifestations of historical thinking in North America over the 20th century, see Osborne (2003, 2006).

3 An activity adopted from The Bata Shoe Museum (2013).

REFERENCES

Case, R., & Wright, I. (1997). Taking seriously the teaching of critical thinking. *Canadian Social Studies, 32*(1), 12–20.

Clark, P. (Ed.). (2011). *New possibilities for the past: Shaping history education in Canada.* Vancouver: UBC Press.

Conrad, M., Ercikan, K., Friesen, G., Létourneau, J., Muise, D., Northrup, D., & Seixas, P. (2013). *Canadians and their pasts.* Toronto: University of Toronto Press.

Cutrara, S. (2010). Transformative history: The possibilities of historic space. *Canadian Social Studies, 44*(1), 4–16.

Denos, M., & Case, R. (2006). *Teaching about historical thinking.* Vancouver: The Critical Thinking Consortium.

Elliot R. (1994). Towards a material history methodology. In S. M. Pearce, (Ed.), *Interpreting objects and collections* (pp. 109–124). New York, NY: Routledge.

Fleming, E. M. (1974). Artifact study: A proposed model. *Winterthur Portfolio, 9*, 153–173.

Gini-Newman, G., & Misfeldt, C. (Eds.). (2008). *Exemplars in historical thinking: 20th century Canada.* Vancouver: The Critical Thinking Consortium.

Leinhardt, G., & Gregg, M. (2002). Burning buses, burning crosses: Student teachers see civil rights. In G. Leinhardt, K. Crowley, & K. Knutson (Eds.), *Learning conversations in museums* (pp. 139–166). Mahwah, NJ: Lawrence Erlbaum Associates.

Lévesque, S. (2011). What it means to think historically. In P. Clark (Ed.), *New possibilities for the past: Shaping history education in Canada* (pp. 115–138). Vancouver: UBC Press.

Mandell, N., & Malone, B. (2007). *Thinking like a historian: Rethinking history instruction.* Wisconsin, WI: Wisconsin Historical Society Press.

Nakou, I. (2001). Children's historical thinking within a museum environment: An overall picture of a longitudinal study. In A Dickinson, P. Gordon, & P. Lee (Eds.). *International review of history education: Raising standards in history education* (Vol. 3, pp. 73–96). London: Woburn Press.

Osborne, K. (2003). Voices from the past: Primary sources: A new old method of teaching history. *Canadian Social Studies, 37*(2). Retrieved from http://www2.education.ualberta.ca/css/Css_37_2/CLvoices_from_the_past.htm

Osborne, K. (2006). 'To the past': Why we need to teach and study history. In R. W. Sandwell (Ed.), *To the past: History education, public memory, & citizenship in Canada* (pp. 103–131). Toronto: University of Toronto.

Prown, J. (1982). Mind in matter: An introduction to material culture theory and method. *Winterthur Portfolio, 17*(1), 1–19.

Rosenzweig, R., & Thelen, D. (1998). *The presence of the past: Popular uses of history in American life.* New York, NY: Columbia University Press.

Sandwell, R. (2005). The great unsolved mysteries of Canadian history: Using a web-based archives to teach history. *Canadian Social Studies, 39*(2).

Schools History Project. (1976). *A new look at history: Schools history 13–16 project.* Edinburgh: Homes McDougall Ltd.

Seixas, P. (1996). Conceptualizing the growth of historical understanding.

Seixas, P., & Morton, T. (2013). *The big six historical thinking concepts.* Toronto: Nelson Education Ltd.

Shemilt, D. (1983). The devil's locomotive. *History and Theory, 22*(4), 1–18.

Smith, S. (1985). Towards a material history methodology. *Material History Bulletin, 22*, 31–40.

Stearns, P., Seixas, P., & Wineburg, S. (Eds.). (2000). *Knowing, teaching & learning history: National and international perspectives.* New York, NY: New York University Press.

The Bata Shoe Museum. (2013). *How to read a shoe* (generic). Retrieved from http://www.allaboutshoes.ca/en/chronicles/index.php?sub_section=202&target_table=chronicles_teachers_resources

The McCord Museum. (2013). *Interpreting artifacts.* Retrieved from http://www.mccord-museum.qc.ca/en/eduweb/interpret/

Trofanenko, B. (2006). The public museum and identity: Or, the question of belonging. In A. Segall, E. E. Heilman, & C. H. Cherryholmes (Eds.), *Social studies – the next generation: Re-searching in the postmodern* (pp. 95–109). New York, NY: Peter Lang.

Trofanenko, B. (2014). On the museum as a practised place: Or, reconsidering museums and history education. In R. Sandwell & A. Von Heyking (Eds.), *Becoming a history teacher: Sustaining practices in historical thinking and knowing* (pp. 269–282). Toronto: University of Toronto Press.
Van Drie, J., & Van Boxtel, C. (2003). Developing conceptual understanding through talk and mapping. *Teaching History*, *110*, 27–31.
Wallace-Casey, C. (2015). *Deepening historical consciousness through museum fieldwork: Implications for community-based history education* (Unpublished doctoral dissertation). University of New Brunswick, Fredericton.
Wineburg, S. (1996). The psychology of learning and teaching history. In R. C. Calfee & D. C. Berliner (Eds.), *Handbook of educational psychology* (pp. 423–437). New York, NY: Macmillan Library Reference USA, Simon and Schuster.
Wineburg, S. (2001). *Historical thinking and other unnatural acts*. Philadelphia, PA: Temple University Press.
Yin, R. (2009). *Case study research design and methods*. Los Angeles, CA: Sage.

Cynthia Wallace-Casey
University of New Brunswick

SUSAN GALBRAITH

20. CULTIVATING CREATIVITY

INTRODUCTION

Picture a group of middle-aged businessmen and women wandering around a room with coloured dots on their foreheads. They try to find out what group they belong to without seeing the dots. Later, these same professionals try to pat their heads with their left hands while hopping on their right feet, and whistling the Love Boat theme. These are some of the scenes described by Karen von Hahn in her article "Welcome to the Cult of Creativity" (von Hahn, 2009). The activities took place at a three-day creativity camp designed to help these professionals think outside the box. Von Hahn asserts that the current economic downturn, and the desire for businesses to take new innovative approaches, have created a "cult of creativity". According to her article, creativity is a new movement, and has become a big business in itself (von Hahn, 2009).

21st Century Learning emphasizes the importance of creativity in education. Everyone seems to agree that it is a good thing, but this article made me question what we mean by creativity.

Creativity, particularly in business, is often thought of as problem-solving. As Ken Robinson puts it, "Problem-solving is a feature of creative processes. But it would be wrong to equate creativity only with problem-solving. Creativity can be as much a process of finding problems as solving them" (2009, p. 114).

A day doesn't go by when we don't hear someone from big business or government stressing the need for creativity and innovation to help solve the economic and environmental problems we are facing today. Companies send their employees to creativity workshops like the one described in von Hahn's article in hopes that they will become more creative. But can creativity be taught in a weekend retreat? The exercises described by von Hahn are just that – exercises. The participants who do them are playing games – pretending to be creative. The exercises might get people to loosen up and to interact differently, but this is not creativity. How can you be creative without creating something? It has become apparent that many people do not distinguish between these types of so-called creativity exercises and actual creative acts. I find it disheartening that we attempt to compensate for the lack of creative experience by participating in things like weekend retreats. Perhaps we are underestimating the logical place to increase creativity – our children's schools.

J. B. Cummings & M. L. Blatherwick (Eds.), Creative Dimensions of Teaching and Learning in the 21st Century, 209–218.

What Is Creativity?

In her 2009 TED lecture presentation, author Elizabeth Gilbert mused about how the ancient Greeks and Romans viewed creativity. Creativity was seen as a "divine attendant spirit that came to human beings from a distant and unknowable source" (Gilbert, 2009). The Greeks called these spirits *daemon*, and the Romans called them a *genius*. The Romans saw this genius as a separate entity that lived within the artist's studio walls and came out to assist the artist with their work. Gilbert argues that this separation of humans and creativity protected the artist against narcissism and failure.

The idea of creativity being a God-given gift was widely accepted. In his biography of artists, "The Great Masters", Giorgio Vasari (1986) writes the following about Leonardo da Vinci:

> The greatest gifts are often seen, in the course of nature, rained by celestial influences on human creatures; and sometimes, in supernatural fashion, beauty, grace and talent are united beyond measure in one single person, in a manner that to whatever such an one turns his attention, his every action is so divine, that, surpassing all other men, it makes itself clearly known as a thing bestowed by God (as it is), and not acquired by human art. (1986)

Eventually, humans went from having a genius to being a genius, and had to accept responsibility for their own creativity. Yet, this ancient idea of creativity as a gift, that some of us have and some of us don't, remains with us. Parents and colleagues frequently ask me who my artistic or creative students are. They often pass judgment on their own children as not being creative or, sometimes just as detrimental, as being very talented. The students who have been told for years that they are not creative lack confidence; the ones who have been told that they are sometimes feel they have nothing more to learn. I pose the theory that they all have tremendous creative potential that can be nurtured and trained. But, what is creativity?

Torrance (1967) listed specific kinds of behaviour that he thought were indicators of creative talent. These included the ability to: occupy time without being stimulated; go beyond assigned tasks; ask questions beyond the single why or how; come up with different ways of doing things; and not fear trying something new (Lowenfeld & Brittain, 1987). Von Hahn (2009) poses the questions, "[Is creativity] merely permission to let your mind wander? Is a refreshed mindset really the same thing as creativity? Certainly the word 'create' implies some sort of end result". Creativity must involve doing something, whether it is painting, dancing, mathematics, engineering, writing, or making bread. Ken Robinson makes a clear distinction between imagination and creativity, noting that creativity needs to have tangible outcomes. He suggests that we wouldn't think of someone as particularly creative if they just lay around and imagined without doing things. He also states that to be creative, you need to be original and do things that are of value in your culture. He defines creativity as "imaginative processes with outcomes that are original and of value" (Robinson, 2001, p. 118).

The Contradiction

The current call for creativity in education is contradicted by the trend towards standards and high-stakes testing. This emphasis on achievement and standards has led to an imbalance of curricular offerings with an overemphasis on reading, writing and mathematics (Ornstein & Hunkins, 2009). High stakes testing and accountability preoccupies teachers at the elementary level. Test scores now drive the curriculum. The arts are not tested, so they can be easily neglected (Eisner, 2000). The pressures on teachers to improve test scores in literacy are so great that many of them are reducing or eliminating time for arts instruction in order to provide more literacy instruction. In the United States, the arts may be listed as a core subject in the *No Child Left Behind* Act (Bush, 2001), but they are not one of the subjects that is tested. Experience has shown, what is tested is what is taught.

While politicians are paying lip service to the need for more creativity and innovation in the curriculum, they are actively working against it.

How Can We Nurture Creativity?

To be truly creative in business, science, the arts, or any field, the opportunity to experiment, to explore, to make mistakes, and to learn from them, is vital. So much of what children are exposed to in school is contrary to this. Standardized tests do not measure exploration, experimentation, or discovery. They measure the ability to perform to a predetermined benchmark. Students are rewarded for conformity, and punished for any deviation from it. Lowenfeld cites several studies that show that teachers don't like the creative child and reward the conforming child, to the disadvantage of the development of imagination and creative thinking (Lowenfeld, & Brittain, 1987).

A 2011 research report by Kyung Hee Kim showed a continuous decline in creativity among American school children over the last two to three decades. In his book, *Freedom to Learn*, Peter Gray (2012) attributes this to the fact that

> …we are subjecting children to an educational system that assumes one right answer to every question and one correct solution to every problem, a system that punishes children (and their teachers too) for daring to try different routes. (n.p.)

If we want to foster creativity in school, we must provide our students with more opportunities to explore. All subjects have the potential to foster creativity.

The Arts are particularly well suited to this task as they nurture skills and provide opportunities for students to build their creative self.

The leading writers on creativity and education insist that everyone is born with the capacity to be creative. It is important to nurture and feed this creativity in our students, rather than teach it out of them (Robinson, 2001, 2009; Eisner, 2002; Egan, 1999). A strong Arts program can provide students with a wealth of creative skills that are transferable to other subjects, and to their lives beyond school. Theatre, Music, and Dance all have much to offer students, but since my area of expertise is Visual Arts, I will focus on the creative skills students can gain from this.

In a 2008 study of visual arts classrooms in Boston area schools, Winner and Hetland, identified eight "studio habits of mind" that arts classes taught. Reading through the list, I was easily able to make connections with my own students and my classroom practices. The obvious habit that the arts classes taught was the development of artistic craft. The second habit they list is persistence (the ability to work on projects over sustained periods of time and persevere through frustration). My grade 12 students just finished a major portrait project that they spent close to three weeks on. Several times through the process, a student would hit a wall, or feel that the image wasn't coming together. What is interesting is that none of them abandoned the project. They all saw it through to the end, despite the fact that they weren't always pleased with how things were going.

Figure 1. Learning to be an artist means learning to see. (Grade 11 students work on their observation skills using a wide variety of subjects)

Figure 2. The Visual Arts allow students freedom to explore, to fail, to try again. This permission to make mistakes can lead to remarkable innovation. (Grade 11 students use pieces of popcorn as inspiration for abstract pastel drawings)

Figure 3. To be truly creative the opportunity to experiment, to explore, to make mistakes, and to learn from them, is vital. Developing creativity requires an investment of time and the freedom to explore without the pressure of always having a successful product

Figure 4. Arts classes teach the development of artistic craft, but they also develop persistence – the ability to work on projects over sustained periods of time and persevere through frustration

Figure 5. Students study how artists use their skills to make social comments and they are challenged to do the same. Portrait of Bob Dylan by a grade 122 student, Ryan, uses Dylan's lyrics to add layers of meaning to the image

Figure 6. The arts not only allow students the opportunity to develop skills, but also to seek a visual representation of the visible and invisible worlds. Engraving by Grade 12 student, Morgan. In this multi-layered portrait the artist explored the world of make-up, costume, photography, and engraving

Figure 7. The arts allow students to make connections between seemingly disparate elements. This costume design by Grade 12 student Jaime uses only recycled defunct technology

Figure 8. Allowing time for exploration of materials and techniques can lead to remarkable innovation. Students experiment with poured and dripped paint to see the range of effects that are possible

The next habit listed is expression. The project that my students just finished was a portrait of their favourite writer. The way they drew the writer went beyond the demonstration of technical skills, and incorporated their interpretation of this person and their words. The style of the drawing allowed each student to make an emotional, atmospheric depiction of a voice they admire.

Winner and Hetland's fourth habit is making clear connections between schoolwork and the world outside the classroom. In every art project we tackle, connections are made to contemporary art, historical art, art from other cultures, or, in the case of the portrait project, other arts (literature, song writing, performance, etc.). Studying Visual Arts means we are looking at cultures and societies and examining how they function. Students study how artists use their skills to make social comments and they are challenged to do the same.

The next four habits are noted by Winner and Hetland (2008) as having particularly broad value in life and learning. They are: observing, envisioning, innovation through exploration, and reflective self-evaluation.

Learning to be an artist means learning to see. On the first day of classes, I tell my students seeing is the most important skill they will tackle. This means going beyond expectations, presumptions, and stereotypes, and really observing what is before them. The ability to see clearly is valuable in a multitude of areas, from science to journalism to police work. Historian Amy Herman, conducts workshops for New York City Police Detectives at the Metropolitan Museum designed to improve their skills in observation, recounting, and description (Hirschfeld, 2009). She has also given formal art observation training to medical students at the Frick to improve visual diagnostic skills.

Envisioning is a valuable skill for artists and scientists alike. Both "seek a visual representation of the visible and invisible worlds" (Robinson, 2001). The ability for art students to envision is beautifully illustrated in Sir Ken Robinson's story of the little girl who told her teacher she was painting a picture of God. When her teacher pointed out that no one knows what God looks like, she answered: "They will in a minute" (Robinson, 2006).

Much of what children do at school has desired, predicted, and expected outcomes. If the outcomes aren't met, the student has failed. The Visual Arts allow students freedom to explore, to fail, to try again. This permission to make mistakes can lead to remarkable innovation. When my students are learning to build with clay they spend the first class experimenting, trying different techniques. If the clay collapses, nothing is lost. Usually we have a good laugh about it, and the students take what they learn from that experience and apply it to their next attempt. Robinson (2001) writes:

> Creative environments give people time to experiment, to fail, to try again, to ask questions, to discover, to play, to make connections among the seemingly disparate elements. This experimentation or research may not lead to an artistic product or scientific application for many years, as all original ideas and products spring from an initial period of experimentation or fooling around. (p. 195)

Reflective self-evaluation is key to Art production. Students are assessing what they and others are producing throughout the creative process. These reflections are both verbal and non-verbal. Sometimes they are quiet one-to-one activities and sometimes they are formal group discussions. Winner and Hetland (2008) observed frequent self-evaluation in the classes they studied: "[The students] were asked to step back, analyze, judge, and sometimes reconceive their projects entirely" (p. 31)

Elliot Eisner (2002) echoes many of Winner and Hetland's points in his writings. He adds that the arts teach children important creative skills, such as the fact that problems have more than one solution, and that small differences can have large effects.

CONCLUSION

We are all born with the ability to be creative. The common misconception that creativity is a gift bestowed only on the chosen few does an injustice to those who are not grouped among the chosen. It also discredits the hard work and perseverance that goes into developing one's creativity.

Having grown men and women hop up and down on one foot while whistling the Love Boat theme does little to foster true creativity. There are ways that creativity can be fostered in business and in government that include establishing environments that allow for experimentation, failure, and innovation, and capitalizing on the creative skills that exist, rather than trying to invent new ones.

To be creative, one needs to create. Taking guitar lessons, painting workshops or cooking classes will do more to foster creativity. It is unfortunate that so many people reach adulthood feeling that they are not creative. Our job in education should be to make sure that this doesn't happen, and to do so requires that we embrace subjects, like the Arts that do so much to nurture our students' creative selves.

REFERENCES

Bush, G. W. (2001). *No child left behind.* Retrieved from http://files.eric.ed.gov/fulltext/ED447608.pdf

Egan, K. (1999). The arts as "the basics" of education. In K. Egan (Ed.), *Children's minds talking rabbits & clockwork oranges.* New York, NY: Teachers College Press.

Eisner, E. (2000, January). Arts education policy? *Arts Education Policy Review, 101*(3). Retrieved November 17, 2008, from Academic Search Premier database.

Eisner, E. (2002). *The arts and the creation of mind.* New Haven, CT: Yale University Press.

Gilbert, E. (2009). *A different way to think about creative genius* (video). Retrieved from www.ted.com/index.php/talks/elizabeth_gilbert_on_genius.html

Gray, P. (2012). Freedom to learn. *The Many Benefits, for Kids, of Playing Video Games. Psychology Today, 7.*

Hirschfeld, N. (2009). Teaching cops to see. *Smithsonian, 40*(7), 49–54.

Kim, K. H. (2011). The creativity crisis: The decrease in creative thinking scores on the Torrance tests of creative thinking. *Creativity Research Journal, 23*(4), 285–295.

Lowenfeld, V., & Brittain, W. L. (1987). *Creative and mental growth* (8th ed.). New York, NY: Macmillan Publishing Company.

Ornstein, A. C., & Hunkins, F. P. (2009). *Curriculum: Foundations, principles, issues* (5th ed.). Montreal: Pearson Education Inc.

Robinson, K. (2001). *Out of our minds: Learning to be creative.* West Sussex: Capstone Publishing Ltd.

Robinson, K. (2006). Do schools kill creativity? *TED Talks* (video) Retrieved from http://www.ted.com/talks/ken_robinson_says_schools_kill_creativity.htm

Robinson, K. (2009). *The element: How finding your passion changes everything.* Toronto: Penguin Group.

Torrance, E. (1967). The Minnesota studies of creative behavior: National and international extensions. *The Journal of Creative Behavior, 1*(2), 137–154.

Vasari, G. (1986). *The great masters: Giotto, Botticelli, Leonardo, Raphael, Michelangelo, Titian* (M. Sonino, Ed.). China: Hugh Lauter Levin Associates.

Von Hahn, K. (2009, April 4). Welcome to the cult of creativity. *The Globe and Mail.*

Winner, E., & Hetland, L. (2008). Art for our sake: School arts classes matter more than ever – But not for the reasons you think. *Arts Education Policy Review, 109*(5).

Susan Galbraith
New Brunswick

IAN FOGARTY AND CHRISTOPHER LEE RYAN

21. STEM AND A FRAMEWORK FOR LEARNING

INTRODUCTION

The purpose of teaching and schools is in the midst of change. In the past, transmission of knowledge was of utmost importance. Knowledge meant power and opportunity. We observe that "…new realities demand people with different competencies than those … in the agrarian and industrial era. Multi-literate, creative and innovative people are now seen as the drivers of the 21st Century and the prerequisites to economic success, social progress and personal empowerment" (C21 Canada, p. 4). Perhaps it is not knowledge itself that is important but rather skills for being able to find a missing piece of information and using it to solve a problem.

We do not consider ourselves as only teachers of Science content knowledge. Rather, we specialize in using science curricula to challenge students and provide instances to grow their brains. There is a subtle but important difference.

Over the past seven years we have dramatically changed the way we teach the New Brunswick Physics curriculum. We were exposed to research from Guskey and Bailey (2001), O'Connor (2007), Reeves (2000, 2004, 2011), Marzano (2010), and Stiggins, Arter, Chappuis, and Chappuis (2007) that was challenging the system in which we worked. We recognize that today's students have different needs than those ten years ago.

This chapter describes research that informs our practices and how it manifests in our classes based on our *Guiding Thoughts*. We also document a small sample of our students' success.

Research That Has Changed Our Pedagogical Framework

We have adopted these *Guiding Thoughts* in order to inform our teaching of secondary science.

- Our content is not as important as the skills that we teach using the content.
- It does not matter when they learn "it" so long as they do by the end of the semester.
- Some content is essential. Some skills are essential. Teachers need to identify what is essential.
- All students must master all essential skills and content in order to pass a course.
- Students need to find their own real life problems to solve. Teachers need to point students in the right direction, keep them out of too much trouble, and get out of their way.

J. B. Cummings & M. L. Blatherwick (Eds.), Creative Dimensions of Teaching and Learning in the 21st Century, 219–227.

- Not everyone expects to become a physicist (or scientist). Different students take physics for different reasons such as post-secondary requirements, personal interest, or needing a credit to graduate; all students are in the same class.
- One of the best ways to learn about science is to act like a scientist or engineer.
- Students achieve more when they take ownership of their learning and can be creative in defining their direction in challenging problems.

The reader must understand that current research has helped to mold these themes as research informs teaching practice. The conversation around the research which informs our teaching has spanned six years and draws on a number of writers and researchers. This research has informed our use of essentials, our assessment, and our instruction. It also explains why we push students to work outside of curriculum and why our students do not experience anxiety when encountering our challenging and novel final exams.

Students will need to be proficient in the 21st Century Skills of "Critical thinking and problem-solving; communications, information and media literacy; collaboration, teamwork, and leadership; creativity and innovation; computing and ITC literacy; career and learning self-reliance; and cross-cultural understanding" (Trilling, 2009, p. 176). Pairing this with the need to trim curriculum down to essential learnings as explained by DuFour and colleagues (2010), the need to balance curricular topics with teaching these skills becomes apparent.

When forming our assessment practices, a number of factors led us to our *Guiding Thoughts.* We expect students to achieve mastery level of the essential learnings. This aligns with O'Connor (2007, p. 63): "In a standards-based system we would have two levels of performance only – proficient and not proficient." For essentials required for the next level of learning and transferable to other concepts and skills, we accept only a high level of performance. Reeves (2000) explained: "The consequence for a student who fails to meet a standard is not a low grade but rather the opportunity, indeed the requirement – to resubmit his or her work" (p. 11). In order to make this a possibility for our students, we embrace that when "students are acquiring new skills, knowledge, and understanding, they need a chance to practice. This is the learning process" (Davies et al., 2008, p. 2). Taking these two ideas together we recognize that students need multiple opportunities to practice and are expected to prove mastery learning by course end. This means students attempt assessments multiple times over a course.

Students are engaged in multiple ways through "effective questioning strategies [that] can trigger situational interest and help foster maintained situational interest" (Marzano et al., 2011, p. 11). As well, "students work with teachers to define what learning is and what it looks like, they shift from being passive learners to being actively involved in their own learning" (Davies et al., 2008, p. 5). Students are more engaged when they are solving novel problems that are within their grasp. This approach is developed throughout the course culminating in final projects where students select a real-life problem to solve and spend a significant amount of time creating a solution.

Students entering post-secondary studies or careers in sciences need to have experiences as scientists. This insight has been developed through informal classroom-based action research examining student engagement and problem-solving abilities as well as conversations with past students. These students have identified that their greatest learning came from participating in student-directed problems.

Practical Implementation

While the above themes are noble ideas, the challenge is to implement them in classrooms and have them exist in synergy with established policies and curriculum. We teach in a public high school of 1100 students with over 85 teachers and support staff.

We teach about 100 Physics students per year. Many of these students go to STEM careers that involve physics related courses (e.g., medical fields, technicians, machinists). Some continue to further science-based studies such as physics, engineering, and flight school. Some follow paths with nothing to do with physics content but require 21st Century Skills. All students need to develop analytic and problem-solving abilities. We use Physics content to teach these skills at a wide variety of levels. The provincial curriculum requires us to teach Physics according to curriculum guidelines (Government New Brunswick, 2003). We chose to grow cognitive problem-solving abilities and 21st Century Learning Skills through physics content.

Because students have a wide set of interests and a wide range of future career paths, we have established global essentials. These are taught and assessed over the span of the entire course where students have multiple opportunities to demonstrate mastery learning of these essentials. These global essentials are largely skill-based and transferable to other disciplines. Our students need to:

- be able to collect and interpret data;
- be able to create a mathematical expression based on a real-world situation;
- be able to communicate effectively through technical writing;
- be able to solve challenging and novel problems;
- be able to demonstrate understanding and apply Newton's three laws.

Most Physics teachers would argue that this list is light on content. We agree. These are the essential skills – core ideas in our courses which students need to be successful with for what lies ahead. We continue to teach the content-based outcomes using these skills.

What Does This Look Like in Our Classroom?

At first glance, untrained observers would see a traditional Physics class. If that observer watched for a little bit longer they would see a subtle, but important, difference.

Traditional classes aim to have students solve discrete sets of problems. Teachers present content scaffolded from the last few classes, show students a new problem, and solve the problem. This showing and solving is repeated a few times followed by students working on similar problems to practice. This approach produces students who know how to do a particular type of problem very well. This is useful for repetitive, non-cognitive work.

In contrast, one of our goals is to have students to be able to solve novel questions. We start the class with a novel question; little content scaffolding; no lead up. We expect students to struggle a bit relying on their peers to collaboratively work through concepts that are a near transfer of previous skills and content. After students struggle with problems for a short time, we give a hint or solve the problem. We recognize that it is important for students to see our solution to model how experts think. It is also important for students to process information in a variety of ways so we build teacher solutions through students' contributions to the process. This activity is repeated for each proceeding topic. This takes some training in puzzle solving and grit. Eventually, some students learn that they enjoy solving challenging problems. Others appreciate that we push them to learn in a new way.

Observers might note that we do far fewer problems than a similar class. This means that we cover slightly less content and do fewer examples. We do not consider this a problem because of *Guiding Thought* number one.

A similar process occurs in our labs. We want students to think like scientists. In order to do this we come up with problems to solve and give them purposefully vague instructions, such as:

> Over the next three days you are going to do a lab. Your objective is to calculate the speed of sound. You probably want to use a large space, like the football field, have some way of making noise and have some sort of time recording device. I would suggest that you spend time today thinking about how you will design your lab and what supplies you need. Tomorrow you should experiment. The third day should be spent analyzing your data and starting to write your report. You should also think about what we talked about yesterday regarding accuracy of measurement and experimental design.

Feedback on labs focuses on design quality and result validity. We teach the correct answer while delineating a clear distinction between good lab skills and understanding physics.

A foundational element of this work is the establishment of essential content that students must master. These are specific physics topics that we could not, in all good professional conscience, let a student enter a science degree program without knowing. These topics are discussed in detail during lectures and reinforced in labs. These are specific content items that transfer to other domains and help students better understand their world. They are drawn from about thirty to fifty percent of our curricular outcomes.

When it comes to assessments, we want students to achieve mastery level understanding of essentials and when they do this, they receive a passing grade. This is done with a formal test that includes only essential content and skills. Achieving more than a passing grade requires students to complete some extension work ("extensions"). Part of the purpose for extension work is to give students opportunities to demonstrate physics comprehension and solve challenging problems.

Extension work comes in three forms: extension tests, extension labs, and an engineering problem. Extension tests are a collection of word problems and theory questions that build on essentials tests. They are challenging and novel questions. Most students will accomplish about half of the problems and a few will attempt all of them. Early in a semester students feel anxious when they have not completed the entire test and need to be reminded that this is part of the extensions. Students come to understand that they have a bank of essentials points "in their pocket" that are added to this test to create their mark. Once they experience this a few times, anxiety dissipates and they focus on individual learning. Students that struggle through the course realize that the majority of their effort needs to focus on the essentials. Students seeking scholarships and entrance to physics – based careers know that they also need to grasp the extensions.

When writing the essentials test, students complete it, hand it in to be marked, and receive their marked test back within one period. While students are waiting, they work on extension questions for the coming extensions test. Students who respond correctly to each question continue to work on extension material. Students who respond incorrectly to one or more questions correct their work, at which point they can access their class notes, a textbook, or work with a peer. Students then conference with their teacher on corrected questions where they are asked a follow-up question to ensure they truly understand the content. Students unable to answer the question are required to continue this process through reading and discussions until they prove their understanding of every question. This continues until they have answered every question correctly and may take several conferences for more challenging fundamental concepts.

This process often extends into day two of the testing block. Students conference with the teacher until they have completed the essentials. The second thing that happens on day two is that we give students challenging questions that are similar in difficulty to the extension test. Students who have completed the essentials, or are waiting to conference, work on these problems as practice.

Our formal final exam is the most challenging and least stressful portion of the course. This exam has a drastically different tone than a typical exam because it is aligned with our *Guiding Thoughts*. *Guiding Thought* 2 and 4 motivating us to have an "essentials" exam. This is an assembly of "essentials" tests that most students will have already passed. The objective is to ensure that students retain knowledge and to give a final chance to prove that they have the skills and knowledge to warrant a pass. This exam is administered three weeks before the end of classes, marked, and returned as soon as possible. Students have the remaining three weeks to complete any faults. This three week period is also used to cover content areas that are not deemed essential, to give students a chance to work on their major projects (see below), and to practice novel questions in preparation for the "extensions" exam, which is written during the formal exam block and has the same format as extension tests.

A small number (five to eight) of extension labs are used to further the lab aspect of the course and individual student learning. These labs are optional and earn students marks above a pass. Students are expected to complete these labs outside of instructional time in teams of two to four over the semester. They are informally marked pass/fail through a short conference.

We want students to tackle large problems using analytic and problem-solving skills practiced through the course. We give challenging tasks to high achievers but we avoid forcing struggling students to take on more than they can handle. To meet both of these objectives we ask students to come up with a problem to solve. These problems often start with a kernel of Physics discussed in class mixed with student interest in ways that we cannot initially predict. Students work in pairs or triads to start the project by mid-semester understanding that they will have a block of class time at the end of the semester to complete the project. Our role during this project phase is to act as a coach. We guide students by helping them overcome large obstacles such as content gaps or design flaws. This leads students away from our aptitudes and to questions that we cannot answer. Some of the most intriguing projects we have seen include a computer visualization of the inner planets' motion as the sun consumes the last of its fuel, a power generator that uses the wind passing around a moving vehicle to charge a cell phone, a full-sized electric powered motorcycle made from two-by-four, and a fully functional electric drum kit. Each of these projects was accompanied by a full explanation of the underlying physics students learned and obstacles that the group overcame in creating the final project. These projects also allow students to explore areas beyond the physics curriculum, such as engineering, graphic design or computer science.

RESULTS GATHERED FROM STUDENT FEEDBACK

The implementation of essentials and extensions changed the way that students interact with the content and it impacts their lives after school physics. Here are some of our favourite examples.

Applications in Business

"Essentials" are meant to provide useful skills and knowledge to all students, including those who will be pursuing physics and those that will not. One such skill is creating a graph in Excel and providing interpretation. One student took our class and went on to pursue Business Studies at an elite Canadian university. On her Christmas break, she barged into a Physics class exclaiming "Thank you!" in an excited and loud voice, interrupting the class to thank us for spending so much time with graphs and Excel. Because she was able to use software to make graphs and interpret them, it took her less time to complete her assignments than other students who had taken Advanced Placement and International Baccalaureate courses. This resulted in her ability to focus on the content and to follow the ideas of her business classes rather than being distracted by what a graph was showing.

Building an Electric Motorbike

Essentials provide space for project work and opportunities for students to behave like an engineer, a trade person, or a scientist. However, it is difficult to predict or measure what students will learn in a project while still providing freedom for creativity. Because students have a solid foundation from our "essentials", we worry less about the details of what students are learning as long as it is creative and has depth.

Three young men decided to build an electric wood-framed motorcycle. They built the frame, wheels, axels and gear system. These were completely new skills for these students. At one point, well into the project, they figured out that their electrical plan was insufficient. The solution required some expensive equipment. A local automotive store suggested that they purchase the equipment, do their project, and take advantage of the store's 30-day return policy to get their money back as long as the equipment was not damaged. While assembling the batteries, inverters, and motors their helpful older brother welded some of the parts together. The bike worked for a couple of feet but they were stuck with $300 of unreturnable materials. What a great series of lessons in Physics, construction, electrical engineering! One learned that he wanted to be an electrical engineer and the other decided that sciences were not his thing. These are equally valid lessons.

A Guitar for Love

"Essentials" also create space for struggling students to work on projects. Too often, enrichment is designed so that only high-end students have time to work on the projects while the struggling students spend more time on the very thing which they find difficult. Perhaps it is these students who need enrichment more in order to engage with physics or learn about themselves. This might be the most compelling reason to include large projects.

Two girls worked hard to make it to the last month of physics by passing all of their "essentials" and faced the next section: electricity. Increasingly pleasant weather was starting to decrease our seniors' focus on the lessons. Thinking that they would probably not perform as well if we assigned notes, labs or word problems about series and parallel circuits as if we assigned them to solve a new problem, and since their "essentials" were done, students could either work on word problems or do a project. Two girls were given a disassembled electric guitar and tasked with putting it back together. They knew little about electricity or guitars. They were particularly motivated because that guitar was scheduled to be used by a middle school boy to profess his love to a girl at the end-of-year concert. It was the girls' task to allow young love to happen.

The two students identified what kind of guitar it was, downloaded electrical diagrams, and learned how to read them, found YouTube videos tutorials about soldering, and learned about how the different electrical components impacted sound. They were so engaged but so slow, that they continued to work on the project even after exams. The day of the prom they came into the school to show off the guitar as a detour to their hair and makeup appointments. They had worked on physics during their graduation celebrations and found out that they don't need a teacher or a class to show them how to learn.

CONCLUSIONS

Having "essentials and extensions" changes the way that students behave and learn. This includes students who will be studying physics for the rest of their lives and those whose study of physics finishes with our exam.

Since not all students take physics with the same end in mind we are able to tailor their learning with the use of essentials. Students who are seeking high marks and entrance to prestigious post-secondary programs have more content to cover and more challenging tasks to accomplish. This means that increasingly higher grades require an exponential amount of work. Over the last four years we cut our failure rate from 30% to 5% at the same time as reducing the number of students scoring +95% by 50%. While struggling students have a more reasonable task to complete, gifted students experience a more challenging program of study.

REFERENCES

C21 Canada. (2012). *Shifting minds: A 21st century vision of public education for Canada.* Retrieved from http://www.c21canada.org/wp-content/uploads/2012/05/C21-Canada-Shifting-Version-2.0.pdf

Davies, A., Herbst, S., & Reynolds, B. P. (2008). *Leading the way to making classroom assessment work.* Canada: Connections Publishing.

DuFour, R., DuFour, R., Eaker, R., & Many, T. (2010). *Learning by doing: A handbook for professional learning communities at work.* Bloomington, IN: Solution Tree Press.

Government New Brunswick. (2003). *Atlantic Canada science curriculum. Physics 11.* Retrieved from https://www.gnb.ca/0000/publications/curric/physics11.pdf

Guskey, T. R., & Bailey, J. M. (2001). *Developing grading and reporting systems for student learning.* Thousand Oaks, CA: Corwin Press.

Marzano, R. (2010). *Formative assessment & standards-based grading: Classroom strategies that work.* Bloomington, IN: Solution Tree.

Marzano, R. J., Pickering, D. J., & Heflebower, T. (2011). *The highly engaged classroom.* Bloomington, IN: Marzano Research Laboratory.

O'Connor, K. (2007). *A repair kit for grading: 15 fixes for broken grades.* Portland, Oregon: Educational Testing Service.

Reeves, D. B. (2000). Standards are not enough: Essential transformations for school success. *NASSP Bulletin, 84*(620), 5–19.

Reeves, D. B. (2004). The case against the Zero. *Phi Delta Kappan, 86*(4), 324–325.

Reeves, D. B. (2011). *Elements of grading: A guide to effective practice*. Bloomington, IN: Solution Tree.
Stiggins, R. J., Arter, J. A., Chappuis, J., & Chappuis, S. (2007). *Classroom assessment for student learning: Doing it right – using it well.* Upper Saddle River, NJ: Pearson Education, Inc.
Trilling, B., & Fadel, C. (2009). *21st century skills: Learning for life in our times*. San Francisco, CA: Jossey-Bass.

Ian Fogarty
New Brunswick

Christopher Lee Ryan
University of New Brunswick

MATTHEW ROGERS

22. CONCEPTUALIZING AND IMPLEMENTING CRITICAL FILMMAKING PEDAGOGIES

Reflections for Educators

INTRODUCTION

The popularity of new media tools amongst young people, and the proliferation of inexpensive video-making technologies, has inspired many teachers to consider integrating filmmaking pedagogies (Klopfer, Osterweil, Groff, & Haas, 2009). As Quin (2003) explains, the resulting school-based media studies programs are often celebrated as a way to engage students who resist traditional approaches. Paradoxically, however, these practices seldom involve having students engage the world critically as a way to generate counter-hegemonic discourses that challenge systems of oppression. In addressing this tension, this chapter explores the conceptualization and implementation of an educational participatory filmmaking praxis I have been exploring with teachers and students in New Brunswick, Canada. I have conceptualized these works as critical filmmaking pedagogies (Rogers, 2010). Whereas the term may be somewhat novel, filmmaking, critical film theories (Aaron, 2004; Fitzgerald, 2012; Giroux, 1991; Lapsley & Westlake, 2006; Thornham, 1999; Waugh, Baker, & Winton, 2010), and participatory video methods (Lunch & Lunch, 2006; Milne, Mitchell, & de Lange, 2012; Mitchell & de Lange, 2011; Mitchell, Stuart, de Lange, Moletsane, Buthelezi, Larkin, & Flicker, 2010; Shaw & Robertson, 1997; Warf & Grimes, 1997; Waugh et al., 2010; White, 2003) have long been concerned with addressing social justice issues and mobilizing counter-hegemonic discourses. In this chapter, I add to conversations in these fields by exploring the possibilities, limits, and complexities of taking up the praxis with youth in secondary schools.

For the last six years, I have been working collaboratively with teachers in four mainstream schools in New Brunswick as they carry out critical filmmaking projects with students. Through the initiative, which is called the *What's up Doc?* program, students decide on themes for explorations and generate social commentary on a range of social justice issues. Since the project's inception, students have produced over 50 films that have explored how power operates in social and institutional practices, structures and discourses. When the program concludes each year, the films are shared with large audiences at the annual *What's up Doc?* film festival. The program was the basis of my doctoral research (Rogers, 2015). With teachers, I have

J. B. Cummings & M. L. Blatherwick (Eds.), Creative Dimensions of Teaching and Learning in the 21st Century, 229–237.

been learning how to negotiate critical filmmaking pedagogies while navigating the expectations, and constraints, of mainstream school systems. My work is intended to contribute to conversations that push educational video projects toward theories and methods from critical pedagogy, arts-based inquiry and participatory video.

To begin, I explore how these theoretical and methodological foundations inform my work. I then identify four elements I see as pivotal to critical filmmaking pedagogies. Through this discussion, I also show how, although we maintained critical intentions, problematic discourses and power relations continued to be in operation through critical filmmaking pedagogies. To conclude, I raise a series of questions intended to entice reflection on what it means to take up critical filmmaking pedagogies with youth in school contexts.

Critical Pedagogy

Put simply, critical pedagogy draws on critical social theories (Agger, 1998) to combat systems of oppression, marginalization and violence in, and through, the ideologies, discourses and structures of education. Adopting a critical pedagogy requires questioning the widespread, yet taken-for-granted, thinking that schools are neutral social entities (Giroux, 1981; McLaren, 2009). From a critical perspective, schools are implicated in both perpetuating and challenging social inequalities along lines of class, gender, sexuality, race, ethnicity, and ability (Giroux, 2007; Kincheloe, 2008). Rather than seeing schools as sites of oppression, critical educators understand that schools are politically contested spaces. For Dei (2006), schools "are not simply sites of domination and subordination … it would be a mistake not to see schools as agents of change or sources of transformation" (p. 66). Often drawing on the work of Freire (1970), critical educators use classroom spaces to explore how power operates through social practices, policies and institutions. Many critical educators take-up Freire's critique of "banking" education, which challenges the notion that teachers should be considered proprietors of knowledge while students should only be encouraged to "receive, memorize, and repeat" (p. 58). According to Freire, without the agency to raise questions or shape their education, students are expected to accept the same ideologies that maintain unequal distributions of power. Challenging this model requires renegotiating power relations and fostering *Conscientização.* As Darder, Baltodano and Torres (2009) explain, *Conscientização* (i.e., critical conscientization), is "the process by which students, as empowered subjects, achieve a deepening awareness of the social realities which shape their lives and discover their own capacities to recreate them" (p. 14).

While Freire's work, and critical pedagogy, are instrumental to critical filmmaking pedagogies, I am alert to insightful critiques of the field by scholars from a range of theoretical contexts. Marxist scholar McLaren (1997) warns that "critical pedagogy has often been domesticated and reduced to student-directed learning approaches devoid of social critique" (p.1). For him, beyond participation, structural criticism and political activism are vital. Feminist scholars have highlighted critical pedagogy's historical patriarchal character, and relative lack of focus on women's experiences (Luke & Gore, 1992; Weiler, 2001). Feminist poststructuralist scholars, like Ellsworth (1992) and Lather (1991, 1992), draw attention to the notion that empowerment is an incredibly complex concept. Power does not simply cease to operate just because of critical efforts. Further developments in critical pedagogy stem from the development of queer, anti-racist and dis/ability theories. Queer theories focus on how power operates through essentialized understandings of gender/sexuality and heterosexist/homophobic social constructs (Butler, 1990). Anti-racist theories explore racialized oppression, discrimination, racialization and institutional racism (Dei, Karumanchery, & Karumanchery-Luik, 2004), and draw attention to how taken-for-granted white middle-class bias is embedded in all theories – even those claiming to be critical. Critical dis/ability theories question deficit discourses of ability and disrupt the ability/disability binary (Albrecht, Seelman, & Bury, 2001). Many of these theories push critical educators to consider multiple sites where power is exerted and groups are oppressed.

Arts-Based Inquiry and Participatory Video

Generally speaking, arts-based inquiry explores the possibilities of artistic expression as a mode of knowledge production and dissemination (Irwin, Beer, Spriggay, Grauer, Xiong, & Bickel, 2006). Advocates suggest that these methods engender diverse ways of knowing and acting in the world (Kerry-Moran, 2008). As Cole and Knowles (2008) argue, the arts also provide possibilities to construct knowledge that is "generative rather than propositional" (p. 67). Barone and Eisner (2012) expand on this potential: "the major aim of arts-based research is not to have the correct answer to the question or the correct solution to a problem; it is to generate questions that stimulate problem formation" (p. 171). For them, arts-based works can bring forward divergent perspectives and the complexities of issues/problems, rather than proposing the discovery of concrete truths, answers, or solutions. This generative possibility can entice action for social change (Eisner, 2008).

The particular form of arts-based inquiry that informs my ideas about critical filmmaking pedagogies is participatory video. Participatory methods and pedagogies, inspired by the work of Freire (1970) and building on participatory action research (Whyte, 1991), involve grassroots groups in knowledge-production activities (Torres, 1995). Participants are intricately involved in: identifying issues, designing and carrying-out research processes, and disseminating knowledge. Feminist scholars, in particular, have embraced participatory research and pedagogical approaches – doing so to challenge power relations and the politics of knowledge production (Lykes & Hershberg, 2012). In this spirit, participatory video focuses on collaborative media production to mobilize the subjugated knowledges of marginalized groups (Foucault, Bertani, Fontana, Ewald, & Macey, 2003). As Kindon (2003) suggests, providing a venue for marginalized voices can encourage political dialogue; possibly leading to change and more equitable political decisions and societal practices.

In my work with students and teachers, I conceptualized critical filmmaking pedagogies with an assumption that an intersection of critical pedagogy, arts-based inquiry, and participatory video can provide pathways for exploring social issues with youth in schools (Finley, 2005; Waite & Conn, 2011). I was inspired by the idea that participatory approaches have potential as democratic tools that can help students address specific social/political issues at a discursive and structural level. In this spirit, the *What's up Doc?* program attempts to engage youth in building and mobilizing knowledge from their perspectives; exploring power relationships between individuals, institutions, and societies; generating important societal and institutional critique; and spurring and mobilizing reflection, dialogue, and informed social action. At the same time, however, I have been inspired by the important critiques mentioned above, and have incorporated this thinking into my work with youth.

Conceptualizing Critical Filmmaking Pedagogies

While concept building is ongoing, my ideas about critical filmmaking pedagogies rest on four key theoretical and methodological pillars. In discussions below I show how these four elements were supported, and exemplified in, student and teacher work during the *What's up Doc?* program. Whereas the list I provide is not meant to be exhaustive, it does offer foundation for discussions of what critical filmmaking pedagogies look like in practice.

Primarily, I conceptualize critical filmmaking pedagogies as participatory media practices that embrace questions of power and its renegotiation or resistance. Attuned to McLaren's (1997) warning mentioned above, critical filmmaking pedagogies are not simply a manifestation of student-centered learning approaches. The *What's up Doc?* program has sparked conversations about taken-for-granted power relations embedded in social practices, discourses, ideologies and institutions. The participatory film work has enticed reflections on issues of power, marginalization, oppression, discrimination and violence. For example, *Family: A Series of Smart Films*, resists marginalizing constructs that privilege certain kinds of intelligence in schools. To do so, students focused on stories about young people who are intelligent in ways that are not traditionally considered valuable in school contexts (e.g., crafts, sports, art). In this way, the film problematizes institutional practices and binary understandings of intelligence that rigidly construct which abilities are to be valued. The work acted as an entry point into critical dialogues about power relations. Students address marginalizing aspects of, or unexamined assumptions embedded in, social discourses, practices and policies in their school.

Connected to the intentions addressed above, another element of critical filmmaking pedagogies is that they move beyond *individualizing discourses to incorporate discursive, ideological, institutional and/or structural analysis.* Drawing on Freire's concept of conscientization, teachers and I have implemented the praxis as a way to avoid victim-blaming discourses and draw attention to the ways that individual "issues" are symptomatic of much broader social, ideological or institutional structures or power relations. The film I mentioned above, as well as others over the past six years, have taken up this approach to explore ways that discourses, ideologies, and institutional structures influence marginalizing conditions. *Slow Moving River*, for example, accents how youth vandalism in a rural community is connected to economic issues; especially a decline in the logging industry and the lack of social and vocational opportunities for youth. Another film, *Pressure to be Perfect*, also exemplifies conscientization by showing how a student's marginalization at school is validated by dominant gendering practices/discourses. The film chronicles the story of a young woman as she prepares for school and attempts to follow the cultural representations of beauty as depicted in the fashion magazines that cover her walls. Rather than arguing that the violence the young woman is experiencing is only a result of an individual bully's behaviour, the filmmakers address broader social discourses that validate harmful objectifying gendered expectations.

Embracing the position that critique and social action are vital components of critical pedagogy, the third element of critical filmmaking pedagogies is that they incorporate an intersection of multiple forms of critical social analysis. Engaging with critical filmmaking pedagogies means providing spaces for students to explore how social practices, ideologies, discourses and institutions (including schools) can perpetuate social stratification and inequalities along lines of class, gender, sexuality, race, ethnicity, and ability. Like all critical pedagogies, this praxis can be strengthened by drawing on an intersection of the insights of Marxist, feminist, anti-racist, post-colonialist, dis/ability studies, and queer critical social theories. Without this positioning, the theoretical tools needed to name and resist power would be lacking. Although working through critical theories with students may be difficult, and dangerous (Roman & Eyre, 1997), engaging with these perspectives is vital. Various films highlight possibilities for critical social analysis. *Challenging the Norm*, for example, draws on feminist critical theories to accent how inequitable gendering discourses are perpetuated, and enforced, in educational contexts. Through four mini-documentaries, the film troubles essentialist gender discourses and ways that young people, who do not conform to gendered expectations, are marginalized in schools.

The fourth element of critical filmmaking pedagogies is that they confront ethical issues, complexities and intricacies. As Mackenzie and Moore (2008) explain, arts-based practitioners have a responsibility to ensure that their practices "take account of a range of unwanted and unintended outcomes that may arise" (p. 454). This means that it is vital that practitioners adopting critical filmmaking pedagogies engage with, and not shy away from, tensions and complexities inherit in the praxis. As critical filmmaking pedagogies are based on an ethos of participation, attention must be devoted to potential unintended implications. Because the films focus on sensitive topics, students could experience fallout at school, at home or with their peers based on the perspectives they shared in these films. While it is vital to take precautions, ethically it is also important to respect students' "intelligence, political savvy, and agency" (Eyre, 2009, p. 55). Any kind of intervention sends a message to participants that coordinators presume to know what is best for all those involved. Paternalistic and authoritative presumptions can easily be patronizing, condescending and demeaning to students, reinforcing the same societal power structures that the praxis is intended to combat.

Furthermore, while critical filmmaking pedagogies can entice students to engage in societal critique, they can also perpetuate problematic representations, thinking, and discourses. This means that the praxis, while encompassing a spirit of social justice, might not escape from broader societal power structures. The film *Step Back: Move Ahead* accents this complexity. While critiquing economic practices that contribute to rural economic disparities, the film tacitly perpetuates gender hierarchies (Connell, 2005). Character choices and discourses in the film position males positively as powerful, intelligent, and rational, and females as irrational, plot devices, or objects for men. For example, one scene is about two teens (one male and one female) who make plans to go on a date. The boy is depicted as confident, collected, and calm. He says "hey babe, wanna go out with me tonight?" While he is presented as cool-headed, the young woman's demeanor is quite different. She hangs up the phone and screams in excitement, "He's coming at eight!" to a friend. As Giannina and Campbell (2012) explain, media texts are often fashioned to entice males by constructing women as if they "appear to crave … [the male protagonist's] acknowledgment, as if they are empty vessels unless and/or until he notices them, fills them with his presence, and makes them the object of his gaze" (p. 62). In the vignette, the girl's reaction suggests that she is benefiting from the prospect of the relationship. The boy, on the other hand, acts as if the whole situation is insignificant to him. This taken-for-granted representation has the potential to validate problematic discourses that suggest that young women's value is only related to their relationships with young men.

Reflections

In introducing the concept of critical filmmaking pedagogies, and offering discussions of some inherit complexities, this chapter is intended to contribute to conversations that locate participatory pedagogical filmmaking in critical terrains. In my experiences over the last six years, I have learned that simply adopting this approach does not ensure projects support social justice. My encounters with this complexity has encouraged me to engage in constant reflexive questioning when engaging with the praxis. In this spirit, I close with a series of questions aimed to entice reflection:

- How can educators navigate the social, discursive and institutional factors that shape and constrain the potential of critical filmmaking pedagogies;
- What are the consequences of avoiding broader socio-contextual issues;

- How can a balance be struck between education, agency and social action;
- What responsibilities do practitioners have to intervene to ensure that films do not perpetuate oppressive discourses and marginalizing representations?
- What has to be done so that interventions do not undermine a participatory ethos; and,
- How can students be informed about potential dangers of critical filmmaking and what precautions can be implemented?

These kinds of questions have helped me see the importance of conceptualizing critical filmmaking pedagogies with what Kincheloe and Berry (2004) call an "elastic clause" (p. 74), i.e., as a fluid and reflexive praxis that is constantly being renegotiated. Perhaps the ideas and questions raised in this chapter can also prove helpful for those who may be already, or are interested in, working to support social justice with youth through their classroom practices. My hope is that this chapter contributes to important conversations amongst teachers, and educational administrators, policy-makers and teacher educators about what it means to pursue social justice with youth through arts-based participatory pedagogies.

REFERENCES

Aaron, M. (2004). *New Queer cinema: A critical reader*. New Brunswick, NJ: Rutgers University Press.

Agger, B. (1998). *Critical social theories: An introduction*. Boulder, CO: Westview Press.

Albrecht, G. L., Seelman, K. D., & Bury, M. (2001). *Handbook of disability studies*. Thousand Oaks, CA: Sage.

Barone, T., & Eisner, E. W. (2012). *Arts based research*. Thousand Oaks, CA: Sage.

Butler, J. (1990). *Gender trouble: Feminism and the subversion of identity*. New York, NY: Routledge.

Cole, A. L., & Knowles, J. G. (2008). Arts-informed research. In J. G. Knowles & A. L. Cole (Eds.), *Handbook of the arts in qualitative research: Perspectives, methodologies, examples, and issues* (pp. 55–70). Thousand Oaks, CA: Sage.

Connell, R. W. (2005). Hegemonic masculinity: Rethinking the concept. *Gender & Society, 19*(6), 829–859.

Darder, A., Baltodano, M., & Torres, R. D. (Eds.). (2009). *The critical pedagogy reader* (2nd ed.). New York, NY: RoutledgeFalmer.

Dei, G. J. S. (2006). *Schooling and difference in Africa: Democratic challenges in a contemporary context*. Toronto, ON: University of Toronto Press.

Dei, G. J. S., Karumanchery, L. L., & Karumanchery-Luik, N. (2004). *Playing the race card: Exposing white power and privilege*. New York, NY: Peter Lang.

Eisner, E. W. (2008). Art and knowledge. In J. G. Knowles & A. L. Cole (Eds.), *Handbook of the arts in qualitative research: Perspectives, methodologies, examples, and issues* (pp. 3–12). Los Angeles, CA: Sage.

Ellsworth, E. (1992). Why doesn't this feel empowering? Working through the repressive myths of critical pedagogy. In C. Luke & J. Gore (Eds.), *Feminisms and critical pedagogy* (pp. 90–119). New York, NY: Routledge.

Eyre, L. (2009). Research on/with/for youth? The im/possibilities of youth peer research in creating a context for education, resistance, and agency in young women's lives. In L. Loutzenheizer & D. Kelly (Eds.), *Fostering critical dialogues in gender studies and youth studies in education* (pp. 49–60). Papers presented at the CASWE 7th Biennial Institute, June 4, 2008, UBC, Vancouver, BC.

Finley, S. (2005). Arts-based inquiry: Performing revolutionary pedagogy. In N. K. Denzin & Y. S. Lincoln (Eds.), *The Sage handbook of qualitative research* (3rd ed., pp. 681–694). Thousand Oaks, CA: Sage.

Fitzgerald, J. (2012). *Filmmaking for change: The films that transform the world.* Studio City, CA: Michael Wiese Productions.

Foucault, M., Bertani, M., Fontana, A., Ewald, F., & Macey, D. (2003). *Society must be defended: Lectures at the Collège de France, 1975–76.* New York, NY: Picador.

Freire, P. (1970). *Pedagogy of the oppressed.* New York, NY: Herder & Herder.

Giannina, S. S., & Campbell, S. B. (2012). The reality of the gaze: A critical discourse analysis of flavor of love. *International Journal of Humanities and Social Sciences, 2*(3), 59–68.

Giroux, H. A. (1981). *Ideology, culture & the process of schooling.* Philadelphia, PA: Temple University Press.

Giroux, H. A. (1991). *Postmodernism, feminism, and cultural politics: Redrawing educational boundaries.* Albany, NY: State University of New York Press.

Giroux, H. A. (2007). Democracy, education, and the politics of critical pedagogy. In P. McLaren & J. L. Kincheloe (Eds.), *Critical pedagogy: Where are we now?* (pp. 1–8). New York, NY: Peter Lang.

Irwin, R., Beer, R., Spriggay, S., Grauer, K., Xiong, G., & Bickel, B. (2006). Rhizomatic relations of a/r/tography. *Studies in Art Education: A Journal of Issues and Research in Art Education, 48*(1), 70–88.

Kerry-Moran, K. J. (2008). Between scholarship and art: Dramaturgy and quality in arts-related research. In J. G. Knowles & A. L. Cole (Eds.), *Handbook of the arts in qualitative research: Perspectives, methodologies, examples, and issues* (pp. 493–502). Thousand Oaks, CA: Sage.

Kincheloe, J. L. (2008). *Critical pedagogy: Primer.* New York, NY: Peter Lang.

Kincheloe, J. L., & Berry, K. S. (2004). *Rigour and complexity in educational research: Conceptualizing the bricolage.* Maidenhead, UK: Open University Press.

Kindon, S. (2003). Participatory video in geographic research: A feminist practice of looking? *Area, 35*(2), 142–153.

Klopfer, E., Osterweil, S., Groff, J., & Haas, J. (2009). *Using the technology of today, in the classroom today: The instructional powers of digital games social networking simulations and how teachers can leverage them.* Cambridge, MA: The Education Arcade, Massachusetts Institute of Technology. Retrieved from http://education.mit.edu/papers/GamesSimsSocNets_EdArcade.pdf

Lapsley, R., & Westlake, M. (2006). *Film theory: An introduction.* Manchester, England: Manchester University Press.

Lather, P. (1991). *Getting smart: Feminist research and pedagogy with/in the postmodern.* New York, NY: Routledge.

Lather, P. (1992). Post-critical pedagogies: A feminist reading. In C. Luke & J. Gore (Eds.), *Feminisms and critical pedagogy* (pp. 120–137). New York, NY: Routledge.

Luke, C., & Gore, J. (Eds.). (1992). *Feminisms and critical pedagogy.* New York, NY: Routledge.

Lunch, C., & Lunch, N. (2006). *Insight into participatory video: A handbook for the field.* Paris, FR: Insight.

Lykes, M. B., & Hershberg, R. M. (2012). Participatory action research and feminisms: Social inequalities and transformative praxis. In S. N. Hesse-Biber (Ed.) *The handbook of feminist research: Theory and praxis* (2nd ed., pp. 331–367). Thousand Oaks, CA: Sage.

Mackenzie, J., & Moore, T. (2008). Performing data with notions of responsibility. In J. G. Knowles & A. L. Cole (Eds.), *Handbook of the arts in qualitative research: Perspectives, methodologies, examples, and issues* (pp. 451–458). Thousand Oaks, CA: Sage.

McLaren, P. (1997). Critical pedagogy. *Teaching Education, 9*(1), 1–1.

McLaren, P. (2009/2003). Critical pedagogy: A look at the major concepts. In A. Darder, M. Baltodano, & R. D. Torres (Eds.), *The critical pedagogy reader* (pp. 61–83). New York, NY: RoutledgeFalmer.

Milne, E-J., Mitchell, C., & de Lange, N. (Eds.). (2012). *The handbook of participatory video.* Lanham, MD: Altamira Press.

Mitchell, C., & de Lange, N. (2011). Community-based participatory video and social action in rural South Africa. In E. Margolis & L. Pauwels (Eds.), *The sage handbook of visual research methods* (pp. 171–185). London: Sage.

Mitchell, C, Stuart, J, de Lange, N., Moletsane, R., Buthelezi, T., Larkin, J., & Flicker, S. (2010). What difference does this make? Studying Southern African youth as knowledge producers within a new literacy of HIV and AIDS. In C. Higgins & B. Norton (Eds.), *Language and HIV/AIDS* (pp. 214–232). Toronto: Multilingual Matters.

Quin, R. (2003). A genealogy of media studies. *Australian Educational Researcher, 30*(1), 101–122.
Rogers, M. (2010). *Critical filmmaking pedagogies: A disruptive praxis?* (Unpublished Master's Thesis). University of New Brunswick, Fredericton, NB.
Rogers, M. (2015). *Critical filmmaking pedagogies: The complexities of addressing social justice issues with youth in New Brunswick schools* (Unpublished Doctoral Dissertation). University of New Brunswick, Fredericton, NB.
Roman, L. G., & Eyre, L. (Eds.). (1997). *Dangerous territories: Struggles for difference and equality in education.* New York, NY: Routledge.
Shaw, J., & Robertson, C. (1997). *Participatory video: A practical guide to using video creatively in group development work.* London, UK: Routledge.
Thornham, S. (1999). *Feminist film theory: A reader.* New York, NY: New York University Press.
Torres, C. A. (1995). Participatory action research and popular education in Latin America. In P. L. McLaren & J. M. Giarelli (Eds.), *Critical theory and educational research* (pp. 237–256). Albany, NY: State University of New York Press.
Waite, L., & Conn, C. (2011). Creating a space for young women's voices: Using 'participatory video drama' in Uganda. *Gender, Place & Culture: A Journal of Feminist Geography, 18*(1), 115–135.
Warf, B., & Grimes, J. (1997). Counterhegemonic discourses and the internet. *Geographical Review, 87*(2), 259–274.
Waugh, T., Baker, M. B., & Winton, E. (2010). *Challenge for change: Activist documentary at the National Film Board of Canada.* Montreal, QC & Kingston, ON: McGill-Queen's University Press.
Weiler, K. (Ed.). (2001). *Feminist engagements: Reading, resisting, and revisioning male theorists in education and cultural studies.* New York, NY: Routledge.
White, S. (2003). *Participatory video: Images that transform and empower.* New York, NY: Sage.
Whyte, W. F. (1991). *Participatory action research.* Newbury Park, CA: Sage.

Matthew Rogers
University of New Brunswick

ELENI KARAVANIDOU

23. EUROPEAN IDEAS IN EDUCATION

INTRODUCTION

In 2010 a collaboration between a Greek and a Polish school library and a primary school from Cyprus was launched by the name of "Bookraft". The project was under the umbrella of eTwinning, which is the teacher network that functions within Erasmus+, the European Union program for youth, training, education and sport. Since its inception in 2004 launching, eTwinning counts around 179,000 schools through Europe as members and is a rapidly growing network for educators. It provides support through its portal (www.etwinning.net) and the Central Support Group (CSS) in Brussels that supervises the National Support Groups (NSS), which in turn coordinate volunteer eTwinning "ambassadors" that consult schools. It organizes online and face-to-face workshops and learning events, and holds annual conferences where the best projects receive the prestigious eTwinning award. Above all, eTwinning provides teachers across Europe with the opportunity to form collaborations that aim to foster cultural awareness and mutual respect between partners, to use Information and Communication Technologies (ICT) as pedagogical tools and make use of languages as a means for building bridges across nations (Holmes, 2013). The "twin" concept allows for similarity to coexist with diversity; the same classes across Europe may come up with different approaches for a topic. They may want to do "mirror" assignments, chain activities or they may want to follow novel or more traditional approaches, (Gouseti, 2013; Vuorikari et al., 2011) that typically coincide in a transitory era in education; after all, twins are siblings who have the same age, but don't always look alike. In the ten years of its existence, eTwinning has become a part of mainstream educational discourse in European school curricula (European Schoolnet, 2011). Teachers have embraced it because it is simple, it doesn't involve bureaucracy (Vuorikari et al., 2011) and in an effort to become cultural advocates its participants develop an awareness of "the other" as well as one's own civilization. Furthermore, it is an example of what can be achieved when educators are aided and supported, and when they are trusted to plan their own teaching goals within the general framework of their system instead of blindly conforming to a curriculum that does not always speak to their students.

Creative Practices in School Libraries

"Bookraft" was the initiative of a Greek School Library near Athens which sought other Library Teachers to join in a project that would enhance reading enjoyment

J. B. Cummings & M. L. Blatherwick (Eds.), Creative Dimensions of Teaching and Learning in the 21st Century, 239–244.

through a variety of creative activities. These pursuits would involve the old and the new notion of books as well as multimedia and the Internet, while it would allow pupils to use or discover their special talents in collaboration with their peers from European schools. The three-month program involved 15 to 16-year-old volunteer students in Greece and Poland, with the addition of a grade five class from Cyprus. The project was open to other teachers and the school community; it involved one more library teacher from Poland, parents, some school personnel and, last but not least, Aristotle, the library dog who loved to take naps in the Philosophy section. Initially the main collaborators made a plan, which was open to modification and was flexible enough to later include insights and proposals from the learning groups and engaged in an utterly enjoyable as much as exhausting project that won the 2011 best eTwinning award for its age group (11–15 years old). This brought about a second phase of work, where pupils and teachers prepared to meet in person in the annual conference-camp held that year in Budapest (European Schoolnet, 2011). For some of our pupils it was their first travelling experience and took the project to a blended learning format, which affirmed their preference for embodied learning and face-to-face interaction over online communication tools. Five years later, "Bookraft" has shown an admirable sustainability for a project of its kind due to the Lublin collaborators in Poland who have been making presentations in their country in librarian conferences and training sessions. It has attracted media attention in Poland and Greece and figures in the eTwinning Toolkit as an exemplary library project.

Each of the teachers involved in "Bookraft" had their own special goals and aims. For Greece, the project allowed pupils to take a break from the strenuous and exam-centered system, to creatively interact with other European teenagers and to bond within the diverse learning group; to engage the school community in the project and propagate the potential of libraries integrated in secondary education, a relatively new institution for the country (Bikos & Papadimitriou, 2013). For Poland, it was an opportunity to participate in a (European or other) project, as stipulated by the Polish Ministry and engage their students in library activities. The teacher from Cyprus wished to interest her students in a reading project and another Polish librarian followed as an individual member and made her own contributions. eTwinning has an encompassing philosophy that allows diverse educational systems and various nationalities to come up with a collaborative result, regardless of the methods they apply.

The spark of creativity was ignited when one day the cleaning lady, Katerina, an avid reader, stopped to open the book she was dusting in the school library. The instance brought to mind the 1910 painting by William MacGregor Paxton *Maid Reading* (Figure 1). Katerina put the duster under her arm and by doing so triggered the making of the calendar "Reading Beauties" (Figure 2), where girls in Poland and Greece dressed, posed and were photographed as famous paintings of readers in an artful version of the ingenious reading campaign "Get Caught Reading".

Motivation and excitement were heightened as ideas come flowing from each of the partner schools. Books were seen not only in the traditional light of content or

Figure 1. Paxton's 'Maid Reading' (1910) and Katerina reading (2010)

Figure 2. Polish student emulating Monet's 1872 painting 'Springtime' (2010)

even as valuable items, but actually "spoke" to us in different ways. Pupils used their titles to make poetry, they sang them instead of reading, and they entered reading marathons in specially transformed library corners, with the participation of other teachers who also brought their children. Books that would be thrown away were upcycled into art, new library furniture and book covers were designed and tiny library mascots were made out of well-known novel heroes. Audio books were collaboratively made (where Romeo speaks Polish and Juliette answers in Greek) and were illustrated by students. Theater masks of Shakespeare's plays based on our pupils' faces were printed and worn in each other's schools and the colorful drawings from Cyprus became an ebook. It was a thrill to see from how many different angles you could photograph a library in Greece and in Poland. In the meantime, students' initiative was building to the point where some – more than others – became self-directed and collaborated from their home computers, allowing for leadership qualities to develop and students to take over. They were the ones to learn each other's national dances, to write a song together about eTwinning, to share their ICT know-how with the teachers. The collaboration formed friendship bonds that hold to this day among the librarians and for some time, some of the students. Four years later, the leader of the Greek group, now an engineering student, found herself in the home of the Polish librarian, making crafts, during her visit to Lublin. It is gratifying to see that the educational system did not impair, but enhance, innate student creativity.

Learning happened horizontally and vertically with "Bookraft". The teacher-student relationship was shifted and enriched without ever crossing boundaries. Our students enjoyed the online talks with teachers in another country, anticipation was high during the Skype sessions (Figure 3) with their peers and they dutifully interacted with the younger pupils from Cyprus, in quite a different climate of mentoring. When it came to technology, our computer experts from either country were dependable and constant supporters of their digital learners: their teachers. At the end of the project the educators emerged more tech savvy, and some of the students had tried their favourite Web 2 tools in a school environment. The teachers greatly benefited from each other's expertise and in Greece, the eTwinning experience was transferred in the Comenius program of school exchanges with other European colleagues.

"Bookraft" was a project in a period of library mutation. The 21st century hybrid school libraries contain a wealth of books that users ignore for the sake of digital sources of questionable value. A school librarian's task is to foster a critical approach of transliteracy (Sykes, 2010) and a project like "Bookraft" allowed elements of

Figure 3. Pupils in Poland and Greece talk via Skype (2010)

this new approach to take place. It thus included a range of activities that involved all types of sources and aimed at bringing back the enjoyment of learning in school (Fontichiaro, 2009, p. 2). On several occasions reading was joined by crafting, following the example of El Lector, the 19th century Cigar Factory Reader in Cuba (Maatta, 2011), according to which, the cigar factory workers were read to by a hired Reader while they were working. The artifacts that resulted from the reading sessions were frequently exchanged between schools as good-will tokens. The eTwinning portal, guaranteed as a safe space for students, especially when it comes to primary school pupils, was used to upload assignments and facilitate synchronous and asynchronous communication but it was the public blog (http://etwinningbookraft.blogspot.com) that allowed students to comment, practice their "netiquette" manners (Vuorikari et al., 2011) and reflect on the project. It also served as an exhibition site and an evaluation tool. However, as ICT and speaking English were means to an end and not a goal *per se* as some may have initially expected (Gouseti, 2010), the few pupils with "technophobia" were encouraged to use some tools but were not pressured. The fact that they brought what they loved most to the project, be it music, theatre, dance or crafts kept them engaged, to the point that they came to the library in school breaks to work on an assignment or ask questions. The project's flexibility and open-endedness allowed for the divergers to select and co-decide what activities they would be interested in doing while it provided a semi-structured frame for the convergers to feel at ease. When it came to evaluating the project, the students involved emphasized that it brought out their talents, that they made friends and that it was great fun ("Bookraft" webpage: eTwinning anniversary, 2010). Their opinions reflect the definition of creativity by de Souza Fleith (2000) according to whom "a classroom environment which enhances creativity provides students with choices, accepts different ideas, boosts self-confidence, and focuses on students' strengths and interests" (p. 148). Above all, "Bookraft", according to a Polish student, showed that "libraries have an important place in education" ("Bookraft" website: Homepage, 2010), proving that 21st century libraries/multi-media centers are not archives but produce knowledge though the interaction of its users with its collection (Sykes, 2010; Bikos & Papadimitriou, 2013) and owing to eTwinning through European school collaborations.

CONCLUSION

"Bookraft" was an example of what can be achieved when teachers and school librarians are given the initiative and supported to collaborate and complete a project (Holmes, 2013). The support may manifest itself as peer and cross-generational mentoring, active support by the head of the school (or even the mere absence of barriers and hindrances), contributions from the school community and from the parents, recognition and media attention. The philosophy of eTwinning is to provide guidelines and to reward collaborations, and that, to many European educators, is what they seek in their own schools. Using technology as a means to an end permitted better results than making it one of the project's goals – at least for that learning cohort – and truly brought about the transformative potential of digital learning communities (Gouseti, 2013). Finally, our library project may have started as an extracurricular activity during school hours, but it extended beyond the initial planning or the school timetable. This was a result of the high student engagement that, in turn, motivated the teachers to put the extra work into the project proving, once again, that where there is enjoyment, there is empowerment and that creativity can and will flourish in an open and respectful environment that allows the learning community to take initiatives.

REFERENCES

Bikos, G. D., & Papadimitriou, P. (2013). School libraries in Greece turbulent past, uncertain present, doubtful future. *Procedia – Social and Behavioral Sciences, 73*, 3–80.

Bookraft Blog. (2010). Retrieved from http://etwinningbookraft.blogspot.com

De Souza Fleith, D. (2000). Teacher and student perceptions of creativity in the classroom environment. *Roeper Review, 22*(3), 148–153.

eTwinning. (n.d.). Retrieved from http://www.etwinning.net

European Schoolnet. (2011). *eTwinning final report 2011-Executive Summary.* Retrieved from http://eacea.ec.europa.eu/about/call_tenders/2012/documents/etwinning/eTwinning_Report_2011_Executive_summary.pdf

Fontichiaro, K. (2009). *21st-century learning in school libraries*. Santa Barbara, CA: Libraries Unlimited.

Get Caught Reading. (n.d.). Retrieved from http://www.getcaughtreading.org/

Gouseti, A. (2010). Web 2.0 and education: Not just another case of hype, hope and disappointment? *Learning, Media and Technology, 35*(3), 351–356.

Gouseti, A. (2013). 'Old Wine in Even Newer Bottles': The uneasy relationship between web 2.0 technologies and European school collaboration. *European Journal of Education, 48*, 570–585.

Holmes, B. (2013). School teachers' continuous professional development in an online learning community: Lessons from a case study of an eTwinning learning event. *European Journal of Education, 48*(1), 97–102. (John Wiley & Sons, Ltd.)

Maatta S. L. (2011, August 13–18). *El Lector's Canon: Social dynamics of reading from Havana to Tampa.* Paper presented at the 77th IFLA, San Juan, Puerto-Rico.

Sykes, J. (2010). *Transforming Canadian school libraries to meet the needs of 21st century learners: Alberta education school library services initiative – Research review and principal survey themes.* Digital Design and Resource Authorization Branch, Alberta Education.

Vuorikari, R., Berlanga, A., Cachia, R., Cao, Y., Fetter, S., Gilleran, A., Klamma, R., Punie, Y., Scimeca, S., Sloep, P., & Petrushyna, Z. (2011). *ICT-based school collaboration, teachers' networks and their opportunities for teachers' professional development: A case study on eTwinning* (pp. 112–121). Berlin-Heidelberg: Springer.

Eleni Karavanidou
University of New Brunswick

MARGARET SADLER

24. USING EXPERIENTIAL LEARNING TO ENGAGE ABORIGINAL STUDENTS IN THE VISUAL ARTS CLASSROOM

INTRODUCTION

My interest in cultural craft education began when I found myself a newcomer to the province of Nova Scotia where I started teaching as a visual arts specialist over six years ago. Arriving in a new community with a far more culturally diverse roster than I was accustomed to, I struggled to understand the students before me. In particular, I knew very little about Aboriginal culture and, when teaching at a school with over 70 First Nations students, I had a great deal to learn as a non-Aboriginal teacher.

Faced with increased demands to meet curriculum outcomes and my personal need to develop culturally inclusive lessons, I wanted to integrate Aboriginal craft into my visual arts teaching. My research turned first to our curriculum documents, and I found some opportunities for students to engage in cultural craft explorations. Within the visual arts documents, craft and fiber/textiles are considered elective units from which teachers can choose two out of five areas for students to study within the Art 10 curriculum (The Department of Education Public Schools Programs document, 2003–2004). This means that teachers are not required to engage students in cultural craft instruction and oftentimes, with many outcomes to meet, these teachings are overlooked. As a result, cultural craft instruction in general can remain a superficial, isolated unit rather than an in-depth exploration. To better meet the cultural needs of Aboriginal students, my school board developed a course called Integrated Fine Arts, which is sponsored by the local band and aims to help First Nations students receive the mandatory fine arts credit to graduate from high school. Still, I found very few Aboriginal students enrolled in Visual Arts 10 and proceeding to higher levels. I could only conclude that we were not addressing their needs in our classrooms.

The predicament in which I found myself is one I think many non-Aboriginal teachers can identify with when addressing the needs of Aboriginal students in their classroom. In fact, the Canadian Council on Learning (CCL), an independent, non-profit corporation funded by Human Resources and Social Development Canada, has released several reports in the last decade that confirm what educators already recognize about Aboriginal students: as they face higher dropout rates in school[1], new ways of engaging these students through culturally appropriate educational strategies must be found. Research by the CCL (2007) suggests that cultural craft

J. B. Cummings & M. L. Blatherwick (Eds.), Creative Dimensions of Teaching and Learning in the 21st Century, 245–251.

lessons that include experiential learning and merge Aboriginal and Western ways of knowing could help Aboriginal students succeed; however, sometimes current lessons, particularly those found online, can actually promote stereotypes rather than encourage cultural understanding.

Teachers seeking cultural craft lessons are often exposed to Aboriginal cultural craft lessons in the visual arts that lack depth and perpetuate stereotypes. One only needs to Google "Aboriginal Craft Lessons" to find numerous examples of lessons on making dream catchers, mini-totem poles, and drums out of tin cans. Brayboy (2003), a prominent Aboriginal educator, discusses the stereotyped activities students may experience in schools; for example, asking students to "sit Indian-style" and making "turkeys out of hands" when learning about Thanksgiving (p. 40). Similarly, students are asked to mimic the intricacy and spirituality of regalia by making a "costume" out of plain, brown paper bags (p. 41). His descriptions of current cultural lessons in schools are consistent with those of Chalmers (1996), whose pivotal book *Celebrating Pluralism. Art, Education and Cultural Diversity,* acknowledges that cultural art projects are often taught as isolated units that lack the necessary depth of understanding. He writes that "multicultural art education has typically been conceived as a few activities, a unit or two, resulting in a take-home product, but not as an 'attitude,'" (p. 46) and that many art lessons remain "little more than superficial; for example,...the totem-poles-out-of-toilet-rolls approach" (p. 2). Images of these lessons, and the experience of the students participating in them, allow for misinterpretations of the diversity and complexity of Aboriginal culture. Furthermore, craft lessons are grossly devalued when students are asked to make cultural crafts literally out of garbage.

As a further result, the cliché images created by students of Aboriginal people propel stereotypes and contribute to the visual culture of the school. For example, when Aboriginal people are only shown in full regalia, they appear as one-dimensional relics that belong in a natural history museum, or as "blood-thirsty savages" and "new-age" practitioners (Brayboy, 2003, p. 35). These descriptions are supported in a study by Battiste and her colleagues (Battiste, Bell, Findlay, Findlay, & Henderson, 2005), who use visual images as evidence of how Indigenous cultures are represented in education. Within the study, images used to celebrate Saskatchewan's centenary are critiqued. One particular image shows the first graduating class from the University of Saskatchewan. The black and white photograph, used in a campaign celebrating the province's educational history, shows a clear gender and race imbalance and represents many of the trappings of European education in the formal setting. Battiste et al. (2005) explain that the visual culture, described as "paintings, photographs, postcards, built forms" (p. 8) of the university presents a colonial view of education and negates the educational experiences of Aboriginal people. The above instances demonstrate a need for more discussion surrounding the ways Aboriginal people are portrayed and, according to visual literacy expert Eilam (2012), "textbooks and teachers should hopefully become increasingly sensitive to the representations of cultural, racial and ethnic groups and issues in their multicultural classrooms" (p. 77). The power of these images in schools should not be underestimated. Cultural craft lessons where students actively construct visual representations that marginalize Aboriginal culture, disengage Aboriginal students and perpetuate damaging stereotypes have no place in visual arts education. How can teachers seek better ways to engage all students in better understanding Aboriginal culture?

Aboriginal Education and Experiential Learning

Teachers can begin to embrace more culturally inclusive lessons by adopting experiential learning into their classrooms. The Canadian Council on Learning (2007) includes experiential learning as one of the key attributes of Aboriginal education. Experiential learning is based on the theory that people learn from their lived experiences. It is a holistic approach that encompasses experience, perception, cognition, and behaviour (Kolb, 1984, p. 21) in formal education, work and personal development (Kolb, 1984, pp. 2–4). Kolb outlines key characteristics of experiential learning based on research by Dewey, Lewin and Piaget. Most importantly, he concludes that experiential learning is a process by which "ideas are not fixed and immutable elements of thought but are formed and reformed through experience" (p. 26). The re-formation of ideas is grounded in experience and reflection, whereby "new ideas stem from their conflict with old beliefs that are inconsistent with them" (p. 28). For learning to take place, the learner must actively adapt their thinking to include new knowledge based on their experience (p. 30). Kolb also states that learning involves the authentic relationship between the learner and the environment, (p. 35) meaning that learning should take place in real life contexts.

Many of the characteristics described by Kolb (1984) are supported through research in Aboriginal education. Experiential learning for Aboriginal students is natural, fluid and grounded in reality (Swan, 1998, p. 49). It is also a holistic approach, just as Kolb (1984) describes experiential learning theory. Cajete (1994), who has worked extensively in bringing Indigenous knowledge into formal science curriculum, echoes this sentiment, stating: "Education is, at its essence, learning about life through participation and relationship in community, including not only people, but plants, animals, and the whole of nature" (p. 26). Experiential learning theory allows for the integration of all aspects of Aboriginal culture in learning within authentic contexts.

The Canadian Council for Learning (CCL, 2007) lists "learning from place" as another key attribute of Aboriginal education and experiential learning. It is defined as the exploration of "how learning of traditional knowledge, processes and practices is related to living in a particular place" (p. 6). The relationship between the learner and the environment is crucial in Aboriginal education as described by both Cajete (1994) and Swan (1998). Swan (1998) writes: "nature has always been the best teacher" (p. 49). Geography, and its cultural importance to Aboriginal people, is reflected in numerous studies. Research by Bequette (2007) and Bequette and Hrenko (2011) focus on the importance of learning from place and bringing traditional cultural knowledge into the formal education system. Through authentic and critical learning experiences, Bequette (2007) believes that the negative and stereotyped images of Aboriginal people can be dispelled. He implores teachers to look to Aboriginal communities for traditional cultural knowledge and to form meaningful, reciprocal relationships with elders and artists in the community. In his study, Bequette uses basket making as a means of tapping ecological and artistic knowledge. The natural environment holds both scientific and spiritual knowledge when seen through the lens of Aboriginal knowledge. The process of gathering and learning about materials from the environment and learning to weave creates a sense of community, passes on traditional knowledge and skills, and fosters a sense of belonging among all participants (Bequette, 2007, p. 365).

Bequette and Hrenko's (2011) Project Intersect further pursues bringing traditional Aboriginal knowledge into the classroom through a multi-disciplinary approach. The study's teacher participants were given training in integrating traditional knowledge into core subjects rather than approaching Native American education as an isolated unit of study or a brief, superficial add-on to a preexisting unit (2011, p. 101). Teachers made great efforts to access Aboriginal communities through museum visits and guest speakers, and students were encouraged to "view Native American artistry as a means for cultural continuance" (p. 108). Students engaged in making traditional art forms, such as beaded pouches and necklaces, quillwork pendants and birch bark baskets (p. 108). The study's results were successful because teachers were willing to immerse themselves in a culture other than their own and, as such, they gained a greater understanding of how to integrate meaningful traditional cultural knowledge into the classroom. It also speaks to the power of additional professional development for teachers in Aboriginal culture.

Merging ecological knowledge and Aboriginal craft is also reflected in the work of Sally Milne, (Huntley, 1998) a Cree expert on Aboriginal craft. Milne (Huntley, 1998) taught middle school children traditional techniques such as birch bark biting, moose hair tufting and fish scale art. She blended making crafts with gaining both scientific and Aboriginal knowledge of the plant and animal world by focusing on the important relationships between all materials. Through her work, she noted in particular how students had to develop patience in learning new craft skills and that craft also taught character development. This supports the theories of Kolb (1984) that claim that experiential learning spans both formal education and personal development.

Effective experiential craft instruction must seek to use authentic materials whenever possible. Both Bequette (2007), Bequette and Hrenko (2011) and MacEachren's (2006) research stresses the importance of authentic materials derived from the environment in teaching craft since the materials themselves hold spiritual importance. Cajete (1994) explains that in Indigenous cultures, all members of society create art and it serves both functional and spiritual purposes (p. 149). Art is meant to be an expression of the craftperson's spirit. MacEachren recalls the experience of collecting and using raw materials to construct a dreamcatcher and then later the experience of using store-bought feathers. The former experience allowed for a deep connection with the environment through her experience collecting materials, while the latter resulted in a commercial item that lacked the emotional power associated with dreamcatchers. MacEachren believes that craft allows for "a body-based knowledge that is dependent in the interacting through multiple-senses with the material from the land" (p. 220). When authentic materials are not used, the craftperson's spiritual connection to the environment, in making craft, is cut off.

Through experiential learning in craft education, students engage in communal learning, a valuable part of Aboriginal student's formal education (Bequette, 2007; Bequette & Hrenko, 2011; MacEachren, 2006). The traditional Talking Circle, for example, where a sacred object is passed and each person is given a chance to speak, can be a way of addressing issues and teaching new knowledge, values and culture (Wolf & Rickard, 2003). A Talking Circle establishes trust and respect for each participant and can be very valuable in experiential learning. Another way educators can establish a communal setting in education is through modeling. Swan (1998) explains how modeling has always been used to teach Aboriginal children about the world. Modeling takes place in a natural environment and encourages a student-mentor relationship in teaching new skills. For example, a student could work with an artist from the community by observing and then trying a new craft technique. Similarly, Cajete (1994) recognizes that tribal education was traditionally a "process that unfolded through mutual, reciprocal relationships between one's social group and the natural world" (p. 26). Cowan's (2005) research on reciprocal relationships between the teacher and student, while focusing more on adult learners, shows how students can be more engaged in craft when they have a direct say in the course of their studies. Her approach is pivotal, especially when the teacher is non-Aboriginal. While working with adult women in re-learning the lost art of Sanikiluaq grass basket weaving, Cowan noted the important ecological knowledge that developed through selecting materials for the baskets. Her findings are consistent with the attributes described by the CCL in merging experiential instruction, learning from place and involving the community. Elders provided rich traditional knowledge to both the students and teacher, and the community involved offered support throughout the project. Cowan (2005) described how learning took place, "through story, observation, and repeated practice," (p. 60) rather than traditional Western teacher-led instruction. While this study was conducted with adult learners, similar lessons could easily be adapted to younger students within the formal education system as prescribed by Bequette and Hrenko's (2011) research, where community members were brought into schools to teach cultural craft lessons.

Experiential learning in Aboriginal culture began as a natural mode of passing on knowledge. In the case of traditional craft, these skills, techniques and modes of self-expression are taught to children by their elders in a non-competitive, communal setting (Irwin & Reynolds, 1994). Swan (1998) asserts that formal education has corrupted these oral and experiential opportunities. She states: "Since it is the structure of education that has in part contributed to dysfunctions within the family systems due to missed learnings that are meaningful to a culture, it should be obligatory for the school to create conditions that revitalize some of these skills…" (1998, p. 55). She notes that even band-controlled schools must adhere to provincial guidelines and are limited in the interventions they can provide. Bringing traditional craftspeople into the classroom can make up for some of these lost skills, as does bringing students into the local natural environment to better understand raw materials and the spiritual connection to the land. Realistically, cultural craft practices will change with new generations, just as Kolb describes the process of learning experientially. The CCL (2007) asserts that Aboriginal education should strive to be a blend of Western and Aboriginal knowledge (p. 7) that allow for both traditional approaches and new adaptations.

RECOMMENDATIONS AND CONCLUSION

Research indicates that experiential learning is a crucial component in developing richer cultural craft education. Using authentic materials, as suggested in research by Cajete (1994), Swan (1998), Bequette (2007), Bequette and Hrenko (2011) and MacEachren (2006), provides a much deeper learning experience for students. For classroom teachers, this may seem daunting given the increased demands and diverse needs of all students in the visual arts classroom. Personally, teaching cultural art lessons requires that educators invest time and care in their approach. Students must learn in-depth and this cannot be compromised. There are ways this can be accomplished in a multicultural classroom and still meet provincial outcomes. For example:

- Students can learn experientially about aspects of their own cultural within a broader, thematic unit. All students in relation to their cultural heritage, for instance, can explore the theme of "peace," differently and in depth, and artwork made in an open media could be created around their new knowledge.
- Students can learn about an aspect of Aboriginal culture experientially and create a personalized response about their experiences. For example, students could all participate in a smudging ceremony guided by an elder and then respond personally.

Through the course of my research, I have expanded my knowledge of Aboriginal culture and gained a much greater understanding of my students. I have built stronger relationships with the First Nations community and sought advice on how to provide a more meaningful experience in my visual arts classroom. With experiential learning at the root of pedagogy, more meaningful and engaging craft lessons can be developed.

NOTE

1 According to the Labour Force Survey data for 2007–2010, the dropout rate among Aboriginal people living off-reserve aged 20 to 24 was 2.6% higher than non-Aboriginal people.

REFERENCES

Battiste, M., Bell, L., Findlay, I., Findlay, L., & Henderson, J. (2005). Thinking place: The indigenous humanities and education (M. Battiste & C. McConaghy, Eds.). *The Australian Journal of Indigenous Education, 34,* 1–19.

Bequette, J. W. (2007). Traditional arts knowledge, traditional ecological lore: The intersection of art education and environment education. *Studies in Art Education: A Journal of Issues and Research, 48*(4), 360–374.

Bequette, J., & Hrenko, K. (2011). Culture-based art education. In J. Reyhner, W. S. Gilbert, & L. Lockard (Eds.), *Honoring our heritage: Culturally appropriate approaches for teaching Indigenous students* (pp. 97–113). Flagstaff, AZ: Northern Arizona University Press.

Brayboy, B. (2003). Visibility as a trap: American Indian representation in schools. In S. Books (Ed.), *Invisible children in the society and its schools* (2nd ed.). Mahwah, NJ: Lawrence Erlbaum.

Cajete, G. (1994). *Look to the mountain.* Skyland, NC: Kivaki Press.

Canadian Council on Learning. (2007). *Redefining how success is measured in First Nations, Inuit and Metis learning.* Retrieved from http://www.ccl-cca.ca/pdfs/RedefiningSuccess/Redefining_How_Success_Is_Measured_EN.pdf

Canadian Council on Learning. (2009). *Approach to measuring success.* Retrieved from http://www.ccl-cca.ca/CCL/Reports/StateofAboriginalLearning/

Chalmers, G. (1996). *Celebrating pluralism. Art, education and cultural diversity.* Los Angeles, CA: The Getty Institute for the Arts.

Cowan, C. (2005). Re-Learning the traditional art of Inuit grass basket-making. *Convergence, 38*(4), 51–67.

Eilam, B. (2012). *Teaching, learning, and visual literacy: The dual role of visual representation.* New York, NY: Cambridge University Press.

Huntley, B. (1998). Plants and medicines: An Aboriginal way of teaching. In L. Stifarm (Ed.), *As we see it...* Saskatoon, SK: Saskatchewan University Extension Press.

Irwin, R., & Reynolds, J. K. (1994). Creativity in a cultural context. *Canadian Journal of Native Education, 19*(1), 90–95.

Kolb, D. A. (1984). *Experiential learning: Experience as the source of learning and development.* Englewood Cliffs, NJ: Prentice-Hall.

Labour Force Data Survey. (2007–2010). Retrieved from http://www.statcan.gc.ca/pub/81-004-x/2010004/article/11339-eng.htm#f

MacEachren, Z. (2006). The Educational Paths of Art and Craft Experiences. *Canadian Journal of Native Education, 29*(2), 215–228.

Nova Scotia Department of Education. (2003–2004) *The department of education public schools programs document.* Retrieved from http://www.ednet.ns.ca/pdfdocs/psp/psp_03_04_full.pdf

Swan, I. (1998). Modeling: An aboriginal approach. In L. Stifarm (Ed.), *As we see it.* Saskatoon, SK: Saskatchewan University Extension Press.

Wolf, P., & Rickard, J. (2003). Talking circles: A native American approach to experiential learning. *Journal of Multicultural Counseling and Development, 31,* 39–43.

Margaret Sadler
University of New Brunswick

HEATHER MCLEOD AND MARLENE BROOKS

25. WEB-BASED ARTS EDUCATION

Creativity in the Classroom

INTRODUCTION

In this chapter, we discuss how we encourage creativity amongst educators in *Arts Education: Creativity in the Classroom*, a Curriculum and Instruction Masters course at Memorial University and we recount the process of moving the course on-line. While many courses designed for the web are primarily text-based and merely replace oral lectures, this course involves aesthetic design (Parrish, 2007) and multimodal learning (Larson & Marsh, 2005). We are Heather, the instructor and course author, and Marlene, the instructional designer, who worked through Distance Education Learning and Teaching Support (DELTS). For this course, we achieved national recognition in the form of an award, "Excellence and Innovation in the K-12 Classroom (2013)" from *The Canadian Network for Innovation in Education*.

Creativity is a primary rationale for education (Kelly & Leggo, 2008) and in *Arts Education: Creativity in the Classroom* we take advantage of cultural artifacts, settings, and expertise in Newfoundland and Labrador to enable students to explore the concept of creativity in relation to educational practice through creative expression in the arts. This impacts their development of new strategies to create cultures of creativity concerning expression, pedagogy, curriculum theory/design and educational organizational structures.

Gardner (2000) argues that there are multiple intelligences: bodily-kinesthetic, interpersonal, intrapersonal, linguistic, logical-mathematical, musical, naturalistic, spatial and technological. However, while his theory is widely accepted by educators, most schools actually value only the linguistic and logical-mathematical intelligences. It is also recognized that students should be able to represent knowledge in many ways, yet teachers, and generalist teachers without a strong background in the arts in particular, frequently struggle to know how to discern and develop diverse forms of intelligence. This is often because they have not been taught how to support and teach the use of art forms and mediums to produce creative representations of knowledge. Thus, this course was conceived to give teachers some opportunities to work creativity through the arts, using intelligences and technologies that they do not normally use and which they want to explore.

The students in *Arts Education: Creativity in the Classroom* are mostly practicing teachers within K-12 schools. They find value in the series of course experiences

J. B. Cummings & M. L. Blatherwick (Eds.), Creative Dimensions of Teaching and Learning in the 21st Century, 253–260.

designed to increase their understanding of the theoretical underpinnings of interdisciplinary teaching through the arts and aesthetic expression, and to foster the creation of appropriate learning contexts for their pupils in all grades. The course components encourage students to explore theories of creativity, and examine the ways in which the contemporary mainstream educational system does not, as a rule, support creative exploration through the arts (Kelly, 2012). Students' experiences during the course motivate them to think about how they might work to change their own educational practice.

Students move towards understanding creative processes, exploring some of the materials, conventions and processes of the arts and experiencing artistic expression and ways of knowing, doing and thinking. They demonstrate and articulate through exploration and presentation, an understanding of expressive creativity and its educational implications. There are three assignments of which both the individual project (40%) and the small group project (30%) involve arts-based components. As well, students submit a guided reading assignment (30%) that involves them in reading analytically, identifying and justifying important ideas in the readings, identifying issues that need more consideration or research, and posing questions for further pursuit.

Creativity and Arts Education

The notion of creativity can be conceived as the capacity to produce new objects, concepts, insights or inventions, capable of being accepted as having aesthetic, scientific, social, spiritual or technological value (Piirto, 2004). However, Runco (2007) notes the ambiguity and complexity of the term, and the necessity of using it in precise and contextualized ways. Csikszentmihalyi's (1995) notion of "Big C" and "Little c" creativity which distinguishes between the few individuals who have a widespread impact on their chosen domain, and the creative acts that all human beings engage in on a daily basis has impacted creativity research. Nevertheless, Kelly (2012) notes that such vertical scaling, and, we add, such binary thinking, is not as useful for educators as a focus on how ideas are generated, developed and brought into form.

Kelly (2012) posits that some students' emotional distance from the school environment and the work related to it is a significant factor limiting idea generation and creative development. Such disassociation is related to other attributes of the learning culture predominant in many schools, which includes early closure on solutions to problems, extrinsic motivation, known outcomes, time constraints, summative assessment and the hyper-consumption of knowledge. Creativity research is currently gaining importance where art teachers and students find themselves striving to meet increased demands for conformity with known and measurable outcomes related to the standards movement in education (Freedman, 2010; Zimmerman, 2010).

Models of creativity and creative processes focus on idea generation, and because many students do not possess mature creative processes to develop their ideas independently, these should be modeled for them (Kelly, 2012). Creative people work from their interests, and art education should be based on student concerns and passions (Freedman, 2010). With the aim of inspiring student's intrinsic motivation, Kelly notes the power of mining personal histories as a thematic source for creative production. Students can play host to a quantity of ideas in a divergent phase before converging on one idea, which gives them an opportunity to mine their best concepts. Further, to enhance their understanding of idea generation and creative processes he advises educators to engage in creative practices themselves.

Towards this end both the individual project and the small group assignment in *Arts Education: Creativity in the Classroom* involve not only art making but also the application of Kelly's (2012) notion of generating many ideas in a divergent phase before converging on one best concept. It is worth noting that many students are challenged by such assignments. That is, they tend to close prematurely on one idea. This is likely because "efficiency" was valued in their past schooling and dominates their current work and learning cultures. They are therefore most familiar with approaches where outcomes are known in advance, and time constraints exert pressure so that participants seek early closure on solutions to problems (Kelly, 2012).

Designing the Web-Based Course

Online development and subsequent delivery of a web-based course can be viewed as a challenge for educators. Seeking to maintain value, as well as the successful course components and practices incorporated in the face-to-face course, Heather moved from her comfort of the face-to-face course to online delivery. While she was convinced that web-based courses are important for students in small and isolated communities, for example teachers in Labrador, who would not otherwise be able to access relevant educational experiences in the arts, she was somewhat fearful and skeptical about this transition. She wondered if the context in the face-to-face learning environment could be duplicated for online course delivery. In some ways, this fear and skepticism was justified, as duplication of the face-to-face course to the online environment was not attainable. Seating arrangements, syllabus, schedules, sequence of course content, activities, schedules, length of learning episodes, and communication opportunities had provided the foundation of the face-to-face learning environment. While some of these foundational elements could be transferred to an online environment such as a syllabus, schedules, and the sequence of course content, other elements such as the length of learning episodes, communication opportunities, and activities were achieved in new, creative and innovative ways for a web-based teaching and learning environment.

The practice of "design" in instructional design became a primary component for creating a web-based teaching and learning environment. Indeed, according to Parrish (2007) "aesthetic" course "design" is gaining importance in instructional design.

> The aesthetic qualities of learning experiences, in particular, offer a potent dimension through which to expand learning impacts (p. 2). The many elements of any artwork of quality – whether color, texture, tone, tempo, site, lighting, mood,

> or voice – are either purposefully controlled or creatively appropriated by the artist to make the experience immersive. […]. Thus, it is with instructional design. The success of scenarios in instruction may depend greatly on careful manipulation of context, including establishment of the frame, to create the alternative world and to encourage immersion and genuine participation. (Parrish, 2007, p. 7)

Below we discuss the process to design the course, the course components, and students' experience of this design.

Identifying and Achieving the Instructional Design Goals

During the initial course design process, Marlene, the instructional designer explored with Heather, the content expert and instructor, the existing course context, modes of communication, and types of activities presented in the face-to-face course. This was a time for Heather to reflect on her teaching philosophy and current practices for student success. This process can be viewed as phenomenological and hermeneutic as Marlene asked Heather questions to obtain rich descriptions of her lived teaching experience and provided an interpretation based on instructional design principles such as aesthetic design (Parrish, 2007) and multimodal learning (Larson & Marsh, 2005).

Derived from the described reflection by Heather, the collection of teaching experience descriptions, and interpretation by Marlene; the context goals for the course enable students to:

1. engage with course content through experiential learning;
2. participate in activities for self-expression and creativity;
3. interact with the instructor/teacher, peers and guest speakers.

Arts Education: Creativity in the Classroom is designed for a full semester where students have 12 weeks to successfully complete the course. There are 12 modules in the *Desire 2 Learn (D2L)* learning management system. Each module contains a brief introduction to the module topics and concepts, learning objectives, required readings and activities. Alternatively, the course can be provided to students as a six-week summer semester offering (students would have one week to complete two modules). While module introductions, learning objectives and readings are similar to those in the previous face-to-face course, the learning activities were developed to meet the context goals explored in the initial instructional design process. To meet these goals, the web-based course includes *The Rooms Virtual Tour* (an interpretive art tour), a *Virtual Art Crawl*, instructional videos of art activities, and the use of *Elluminate Live (eLive)*, a communication technology, as well as discussion areas in the *D2L* learning management system.

Goal 1: Engagement with Course Content through Experiential Learning

To meet the first goal to provide students with opportunities to engage with course content through experiential learning, multimedia components such as *The*

Rooms Virtual Tour and the *Virtual Art Crawl* were developed in collaboration with the multimedia team. Experiential learning, in this case, takes place between the learner and the web-based instructional environment. Student experience "includes the way that the learner feels about, engages with, responds to, influences, and draws from the instructional situation" (Parrish, 2007, p. 2). The virtual experiences provided by the media components enable opportunities for students to understand "creativity" through artists' lenses where particular values and ways of seeing and acting in the world are supported by participation in new and innovative activities.

The Rooms Virtual Tour: In the past students in the face-to-face course physically toured the art gallery at *The Rooms* located in St. John's, Newfoundland, during week five. In contrast, now a virtual tour is provided for students. The virtual tour consists of two video components. The first is an introduction to the gallery and the second, narrated by Jason Sellers, Public Programming Officer, *The Rooms,* offers a process of looking deeply at visual art using high-resolution gallery images on video.

Virtual Art Crawl: During week six, students virtually explore the creations of nine artists who work in or whose art is informed by Newfoundland. This course component incorporates the use of *Google Earth* and the artists' geographic locations are indicated. Each artist provided two high-resolution graphics of their art and commentary regarding the creation of the pieces. In addition, the artists included a description of themselves and their body of artistic works.

During and upon completion of the course students commented on their virtual experiences with the activities.

The Rooms Virtual Tour: "I was struck by Jason's comment to "take your time" when he described the pieces as "food for your eyes". I am usually so caught up with my hectic life that I always resist taking my time. This made me reflect upon our classrooms and the definitive number of outcomes that are prescribed for us. In our haste to get through the material, we are often guilty of weighing the possibility of a teachable moment versus unit completion."

Virtual Art Crawl: "I enjoyed the *Virtual Art Crawl* very much and loved how the work was shown after a picture of, and some information about, the artist. I also appreciated the map; giving a visual representation of each artist's geographical home. Although some may say that it would be best to view the artwork in "real life", I liked taking my time looking at the art, reading the descriptions, going back and reviewing certain pieces at my own leisure...while wearing my pajamas and drinking a cup of tea! Perhaps this is one way rural communities can expose their students to art?"

Goal 2: Participation in Activities for Self-Expression and Creativity

Activities in the course also include space for self-expression and creativity. To achieve the second goal, students create a journal and engage in art activities for the classroom.

Journal: Using the concepts from the required module readings, students reflect upon definitions of creativity and their current teaching practices to include creativity. Additionally, they may develop activities that promote creativity in their classrooms.

Art Activities for the Classroom: During weeks two and three, students create short projects through the arts that are appropriate for use in the K-12 classroom. To enhance this activity, two instructional videos were produced to illustrate how to create a watercolor bookmark and landscape painting as well as a mixed media piece (oil pastel and tempera).

A student commented on her experience with one of the instructional videos:

> I am thrilled with this bookmark. I do not consider myself "naturally artistic" in the area of visual arts, and not only am I happy with my final product…I LOVED every minute of the process. I chose to go with the "torn edge" look…I like the "rustic" appeal it gives the project. I am so inspired by this lesson that I am going to try it with a music class I have next week. It is a class of six children who each have a teaching assistant, as they have very high needs. Most of the students are non-verbal and love to express themselves in other ways…such as music…and now we'll try art! I plan on playing a piece of classical music while they paint.

Goal 3: Enable Students to Interact with the Instructor, Guest Speakers and Peers

Student activities have the potential to contribute to the development of relationships amongst students as well as between students and the instructor. Also, they can help build a sense of community. In this web-based course enhancing ways of student communication was important because there was a possibility that they might feel isolated or lost. Therefore, we built in opportunities to develop relationships with community and content experts who contribute to the student community of practitioners and learners.

The D2L learning management system and eLive provided the tools that enabled communication and interaction. In addition, the instructor was available via e-mail, phone, and chat room to assist students.

Discussion Posts and eLive Sessions: The use of the D2L and eLive technology provides the conditions for students to explore ideas, be humorous and playful and validate the contributions of others. Students explore their ideas, interests and work related to course topics. The instructor's comment below compares the strengths of each technology.

> The on-line discussion forums are tremendous. This is the best display of knowledge about content. The students make connections and offer reflections (they receive no marks for this). I tend to only answer direct questions. The comments in the on-line discussion forums show more insights than the verbal or written comments during eLive sessions (which tend to be warm, supportive and funny) perhaps because students can take their time to respond. (instructor journal, July 2013)

Aesthetic Course Design: Going Multimodal

Discussion boards and chat rooms are typical parts of the learning management system in many web-based courses. However, while *Arts Education: Creativity in the Classroom* incorporates these features it is different in that it also provides multimedia containers which house text, and visual and audio components. As well, *eLive*, a communication technology, is used. These aesthetic design (Parrish, 2007) components can be defined as multimodal (Larson & Marsh, 2005) for students' meaning making and understanding. Multimodal learning refers to learning situations, which engage students' multiple senses and require various actions by them. The teacher, as a guide for such learning, enables students to develop the skills and knowledge to navigate the course components and co-construct the knowledge. Students engage with the course components individually and in groups to interpret and produce complex text, audio, and image relationships for meaning making and understanding of what is to be learned. It should be noted that for some students learning to use the technology is a demanding part of the journey.

Aesthetic design (Parrish, 2007) of web-based courses is expensive because of the costs involved in producing video and multimedia, which include human resources, copyright issues and timelines for course development. However, based on our experience, we believe that web-based courses that go beyond "text" and enable students to engage in multimodal learning are worthy investments.

Speculations for the Future

Arts Education: Creativity in the Classroom will evolve over time. This includes the course content and evaluation as well as both the aesthetic design (Parrish, 2007) and instructional design goals. These changes will be based on students' feedback that provide insights into how the multimodal (Larson & Marsh, 2005) components afford them opportunities to complete or to create boundaries for successful completion of the course. While the course is designed for a twelve-week semester, it may be beneficial to provide students with additional time and flexibility for multimodal learning. Given that time constraints tend to work against creativity (Kelly, 2012) this suggestion is very much in line with the content of *Arts Education: Creativity in the Classroom* and would provide more possibilities for students' deep learning. Additional time to engage with content and thoughtfully interact with others could enhance the likelihood that students will master the challenges of engagement, participation, and interaction with the course as well as the associated technology learning curve.

REFERENCES

Czikszentmihalyi, M. (1995). *Creativity*. New York, NY: Harper Collins.

Freedman, K. (2010). Rethinking creativity: A definition to support contemporary practice. *Art Education, 63*(2), 8–15.

Gardner, H. (2000). *Intelligence reframed: Multiple intelligences for the 21st century.* New York, NY: Basic Books.

Kelly, R. (2012). *Educating for creativity: A global conversation.* Calgary, AB: Brush.

Kelly, R., & Leggo, C. (2008). *Creative expression creative education: Creativity as a primary rationale for education.* Calgary, AB: Detselig.

Larson, J., & Marsh, J. (2005). *Making literacy real: Theories and practices for learning and teaching.* Thousand Oaks, CA: Sage.

Parrish, P. E. (2007). Aesthetic principles for instructional design. In *Aesthetic principles, The Comet Program. Educational Technology Research & Development.* Springer, 1–18.

Piirto, J. (2004). *Understanding creativity.* Scottsdale, AZ: Great Potential Press.

Runco, M. (2007). *Creativity – theories and themes: Research, development and practice.* San Diego, CA: Academic Press.

Zimmerman, E. (2010). Reconsidering the role of creativity in art education. *Art Education, 63*(2), 4–5.

Heather McLeod
Memorial University

Marlene Brooks
Thompson Rivers University

AHMAD KHANLARI

26. PLAY AND LEARN

Build your Robot and Learn Science, Technology, Engineering, and Mathematics (STEM)

INTRODUCTION

From 2003 to 2011 I had the privilege of teaching robotics to students in different grade levels at several schools in Asia. The objective of my robotics classes was not only to teach robotics to students, but also to make students familiar with programming, mechanics, and electronics, and to help them learn scientific and technological subjects such as gears, electrical motors, levers, and mechanical advantages. During these years, I witnessed that robotics encouraged students' autonomy and self-confidence. I also witnessed that robotics, with its hands-on and visual feature, allowed students to experience trial and error process and step-by-step led them to solve problems. For instance, I observed that robotics facilitated learning of programming by providing prompt and visual feedback; students could see how their robots acted and could investigate whether their programs work properly or not, so they were able to find their mistakes, revise their programs, and load new programs. Getting quick feedback was especially helpful for bashful students who always hesitated to ask questions because they did not like to show their lack of knowledge.

A review of literature not only confirms my anecdotal experiences, but also shows that robotics attracts students to technological and scientific studies, leads students to fall in love with STEM, and facilitates learning of STEM disciplines (Attard, 2012; Bauerle & Gallagher, 2003; Jeschke, Kato, & Knipping, 2008). Along with reviewing the existing literature relating to the effects of robotics on learning STEM subjects, this chapter represents my own teaching experiences, as a robotics teacher, from which I draw incentive to continue teaching from this perspective and seek to inspire other educators.

The Existing Literature

According to the existing studies, robotics is an engaging activity that helps students to understand and learn STEM disciplines by: (1) providing visual and hands-on activities, (2) immersing students in problem-solving through Problem-Based Learning, and (3) creating authentic education.

J. B. Cummings & M. L. Blatherwick (Eds.), Creative Dimensions of Teaching and Learning in the 21st Century, 261–267.

Providing visual and hands-on activities. Robotics offers students hands-on exposure and helps them to learn a wide range of subjects, including (but not limited to) mathematics, physics, science, mechanical, electronics, computer engineering, programming language, algorithm and complexity, intelligent systems, geography, art, and biology (Eguchi, 2007; Kazakoff, Sullivan, & Bers, 2013; Klassner & Anderson, 2003; Kolberg & Orlev, 2001; Marulcu, 2010). The hands-on and manipulative nature of robotics creates an active learning environment that significantly motivates students to learn (Klassner & Anderson, 2003) and increases scientific conceptual understanding of subject contents (Adolphson, 2005; Brosterman, 1997; Carbonaro, Rex, & Chambers, 2004a). It provides a unique learning environment that facilitates students' learning, helps them to remember learned subjects, and improves their understanding of abstract concepts "with visual and conceptual ease" (Faisal, Kapila, & Iskander, 2012, p. 13). In fact, robotics provides an opportunity for students to observe the results of their design at both "abstract levels of concepts" and "concrete physical level" by directly mapping these two levels (Carbonaro et al., 2004a, pp. 45–49). Robotics is considered a new type of learning manipulative that provides physical embodiment of computation. Students receive strong visual feedback from physically experiencing their work. They explore, make hypotheses about how things work, and conduct experiments to validate their beliefs and assumptions (Brosterman, 1997; Weinberg & Yu, 2003). Therefore, hands-on robotics facilitates understanding of the subject matters and helps students in the process of learning.

Immersing students in problem-solving through problem based learning. Problem-solving is considered an effective and powerful teaching and learning method, because the most important and difficult subjects can easily be taught through problem-solving (De Walle, Folk, Karp, & Bay-Williams, 2011). Solving problems through the Problem-Based Learning (PBL) approach fosters students' positive attitudes toward the subjects and increases their higher order thinking skills (Harris, Marcus, McLaren, & Fey, 2001). Futhermore, a Problem-Based Learning approach helps students to deeply think and inquire about the reason of phenomena, to search for the solutions, to resolve the heterogeneities (Hiebert et al., 1996), to learn subject matter and not to forget what they have learned (De Walle et al., 2011).

Using educational robots provides teachers with an opportunity to integrate the curricula with "engaging problem-solving tasks" (Highfield, 2010, p. 22) and has "the potential for being combined in a creative collaborative problem-based approach" (Samuels & Haapasalo, 2012, p. 298). Lego RCX and Lego Mindstorm robots, for instance, are considered effective and exciting tools for generating and solving problems, supporting the Problem-Based Learning approach, and motivating students to develop creative problem-solving skills during the Problem-Based Learning approach (Adams, Kaczmarczyk, Picton, & Demian, 2010). Therefore, robotics is an effective approach for problem based learning that improves students' learning. (Striegel & Rover, 2002; Vandebona & Attard, 2002)

Creating authentic education. Authentic education focuses on solving real-world problems, employing interdisciplinary ways (Lombardi, 2007) and helps students in the process of learning because they "see the lesson as meaningful and relevant" (Grubbs, 2013, p. 13). Making connections to the real-world leads students to believe that the subject matters are relevant, integrated and useful, helps them to develop their understanding, and encourages their willingness to be actively engaged (Alberta education, 2007). One of the methods that can help students to make connections between the subjects and their lives is *project-based learning* (Boaler, 2002). Encouraging students to construct their own knowledge of the real life through the projects facilitates their learning, improves their achievement, and promotes problem-solving abilities (Satchwell & Loepp, 2002).

Robotics projects provide students with the opportunity to learn with the technology, in contrast to learning from technology (Carbonaro, Rex, & Chambers, 2004b). Robotics projects also contextualize the typically decontextualized abstractions that are taught in the classroom (Adolphson, 2005) and provide an opportunity for students to "connect and apply" mathematics and science concepts (Grubbs, 2013, p. 12). This connection illustrates "relevant applications of theoretical principles in everyday contexts", motivates students to study mathematics and science in an excellent platform (Bers & Portsmore, 2005, p. 60) that reduces the ambiguity of the processes and therefore facilitates learning. Robotics projects lead students at different ages to apply learned science, physics and mathematics and also to utilize concepts, skills and strategies to solve real-world and personally meaningful problems that are embedded in robotics projects; accordingly, it facilitates learning and understanding of STEM disciplines. (Bers, 2007; Dopplet, Mehalik, Schunn, Silk, & Krysinski, 2008; Faisal et al., 2012; Samuels & Haapasalo, 2012; Whitehead, 2010)

My Experience as a Robotics Teacher

A few years ago, I realized that my grade three students were struggling with learning levers and a simple machine subject, which was a part of my robotics curriculum. For the next session, I printed out a castle on a large paper and brought it to the class. I installed the castle at the corner of the class and told students a story about how soldiers in ancient Greece used *catapults* to conquer the enemies' castles. Then, I asked each group of students to build a catapult and throw a projectile to the castle. Whenever a group failed to throw its projectile to the castle, the members discussed with each other and changed the catapult's structure to examine how its structure, the length of the catapult's lever, and the projectile's weight affect the range of throw. At the end of the class, I realized that all the groups had a true perception of the levers and the parameters that affect the range of throw.

My anecdotes along with the existing literature provide a new example of constructivism and constructivist theories. Constructivism (Piaget, 1972, 1973,

1977) considers an active role for the learner and emphasizes that the learner gains an understanding of the features and constructs his/her own conceptualizations, knowledge, and solutions to problems by exploring from the environment and interacting with objects and events through personal experiences (Goldman, Eguchi, & Sklar, 2004). According to this approach, if teachers directly give information to students, immediate understanding and the ability of using the gained information do not occur (Whitehead, 2010). This approach to learning increases students' understanding of complex systems and promotes interest, engagement, and motivation for students (Jacobson & Wilensky, 2006). Robotics supports constructivism by providing an opportunity for students to generalize from their experiences and to make a connection between experiences and curriculum (Jadud, 2000).

Constructionism (Papert, 1980, 1992) stresses a hands-on aspect and the self-directed nature of learning. It emphasizes that designing and building a tangible and personally meaningful object, finding problems, and solving them is the most efficient way to learn powerful ideas. The goal of constructionism is to give "children good things to do so that they can learn by doing much better than they could before" (Papert, 1980, para.4). Learning through robotics illustrates constructionist theory in that it develops meaningful learning and understanding through hands-on and cooperative activities (Bers et al., 2002; Bers & Urrea, 2000; Rogers & Portsmore, 2004; Whitehead, 2010).

In my robotics classes, I realized that robotics is well-suited to making connections between the projects and students' lives or even their dreams. I encouraged students to think about their family members' jobs or their own favourite jobs and build robots related to those jobs; some of the students built minesweeper robots, fire fighter robots, cranes or lift trucks. Other students were asked to think about their favourite sports and build robots that play those sports (e.g. soccer robots or simple rally robots). These types of projects led students to think deeply about real-life situations and to make connections between subject matters and reality. I have witnessed that robotics, with its project-based nature, has the potential to create authentic learning environments, to encourage students to do scientific research, and to facilitate learning of difficult subjects, such as electronics, mechanics, and programming. My observations along with the existing literature complied with project-based learning; the project context allows students to learn relevant subjects in a personalized and meaningful context (Penner, 2001), links students to meaningful life experiences, engages them in complex activities, leads them to construct readily sharable artifacts, and encourages them to share their ideas (Carbonaro et al., 2004b).

CONCLUSION

21st century educators should employ modern ways of teaching that not only facilitate students' learning of subject matters, but also provide an opportunity for students to build their own knowledge. Robotics, with its hands-on and project-based nature, creates an alternative teaching method to traditional lecture-style classes in which students can experience authentic education and solve real life problems. Robotics is especially useful for teaching and learning STEM-related subjects because it has a multidisciplinary nature that integrates Science, Technology, Engineering, and Mathematics into one applied way. Based on my experience as a robotics teacher, I believe robotics is well-suited for teaching STEM-related subjects because it makes STEM fun and students can build their own knowledge while they are playing with their robots. I also believe the "play and learn" feature of robotics increases students' interest toward STEM subjects and has the potential to encourage students to pursue their education and careers in STEM-related fields. I do believe we, as educators, should pay much more attention to educational robotics in order to take advantage of its great potentials.

REFERENCES

Adams, J., Kaczmarczyk, S., Picton, P., & Demian P. (2010). Problem-solving and creativity in engineering: Conclusions of a three year project involving reusable learning objects and robots. *Engineering Education, 5*(2), 4–17.

Adolphson, K. (2005). *Robotics as a context for meaningful mathematics.* Paper presented at the 27th annual meeting of the North American Chapter of the International Group for the Psychology of Mathematics Education, Roanoke, VA.

Alberta education. (2007). *Mathematics kindergarten to grade 9.* Retrieved from http://education.alberta.ca/media/645594/kto9math.pdf

Attard, C. (2012). Teaching with technology: Exploring the use of robotics to teach mathematics. *Australian Primary Mathematics Classroom, 17*(2), 31–32.

Bauerle, A., & Gallagher, M. (2003). Toying with technology: Bridging the gap between education and engineering. In C. Crawford et al. (Eds.), *Proceedings of Society for Information Technology & Teacher Education International Conference* 2003 (pp. 3538–3541). Chesapeake, VA: AACE.

Bers, M. (2007). Project InterActions: A multigenerational robotic learning environment. *Journal of Science Education and Technology, 16*(6), 537–552.

Bers, M., & Portsmore, M. (2005). Teaching partnerships: Early childhood and engineering students teaching math and science through robotics. *Journal of Science Education and Technology, 14*(1), 59–74.

Bers, M., & Urrea, C. (2000). Technological prayers: Parents and children exploring robotics and values. In A. Druin & J. Hendler (Eds.), *Robots for kids: Exploring new technologies for learning experiences* (pp. 194–217). New York, NY: Morgan Kaufman.

Bers, M., Ponte, I., Juelich, K., Viera, A., & Schenker, J. (2002). Teachers as designers: Integrating robotics into early childhood education. *Information Technology in Childhood Education Annual, 2002*(1), 123–145.

Boaler, J. (2002). *Experiencing school mathematics: Traditional and reform approaches to teaching and their impact on student learning.* Mahwah, NJ: Lawrence Erlbaum Associates.

Brosterman, N. (1997). *Inventing kindergarten.* New York, NY: H.N. Abrams.

Carbonaro, M., Rex, M., & Chambers, J. (2004a). Exploring middle school children's problem-solving during robot construction tasks. In R. Ferdig et al. (Eds), *Proceedings of the 15th International Conference on Society of Information Technology and Teacher Education* (pp. 4546–4550). Charlottesville, VA: AACE.

Carbonaro, M., Rex, M., & Chambers, J. (2004b). Using LEGO robotics in a project-based learning environment. *Interactive Multimedia Electronic Journal of Computer-Enhanced Learning, 6*(1). Retrieved from http://imej.wfu.edu/articles/2004/1/02/index.asp

De Walle, J. A. V., Folk, S., Karp, K. S., & Bay-Williams, J. M. (2011). *Elementary and middle school mathematics: Teaching developmentally.* Toronto, ON: Pearson Canada Inc.

Dopplet, Y., Mehalik, M., Schunn, C., Silk, E., & Krysinski, D. (2008). Engagement and achievements: A case study of design-based learning in a science context. *Journal of Technology Education, 19*(2), 22–39.

Eguchi, A. (2007). Educational robotics for elementary school classroom. In R. Carlsen et al. (Eds.), *Proceedings of the Society for Information Technology & Teacher Education International Conference* (pp. 2542–2549). Chesapeake, VA: AACE.

Faisal, A., Kapila, V., & Iskander, M. G. (2012, June). *Using robotics to promote learning in elementary grades.* Paper presented at the 19th ASEE Annual Conference & Exposit, San Antonio, TX.

Goldman, R., Eguchi, A., & Sklar, E. (2004). Using educational robotics to engage inner-city students with technology. In *Proceedings of the 6th International Conference on Learning Sciences: ICLS 2004* (pp. 214–221). Santa Monica, CA: ICLS.

Grubbs, M. (2013). Robotics Intrigue middle school students and build STEM skills. *Technology and Engineering Teacher, 72*(6), 12–16.

Harris, K., Marcus, R., McLaren, K., & Fey, J. (2001). Curriculum material supporting problem based teaching. *Journal of Research in Science and Mathematics, 101*(6), 310–318.

Hiebert, J., Carpenter, T. P., Fennema, E., Fuson, K., Human, P., Murray, H., Oliver, A., & Wearne, D. (1996). Problem-solving as a basis for reform in curriculum and instruction: The case of mathematics. *Education Researcher, 25*, 12–21.

Highfield, K. (2010). Robotic toys as a catalyst for mathematical problem-solving. *Australian Primary Mathematics Classroom, 15*(2), 22–27.

Jacobson, M. J., & Wilensky, U. (2006). Complex systems in education: Scientific and educational importance and implications for the learning sciences. *Journal of the Learning Sciences, 15*(1), 11–34.

Jadud, M., (2000, October). *Teamstorms as a theory of instruction.* Paper presented at the 2000 IEEE International Conference on Systems, Cybernetics and Man, Nashville, TN.

Jeschke, S., Kato, A., & Knipping, L. (2008). The engineers of tomorrow: Teaching robotics to primary school children. In *Proceedings of the 36th SEFI Annual Conference* (pp. 1058–1061). Aalborg, Denmark. Retrieved from http://eprints.mulf.tu-berlin.de/249/

Kazakoff, E. R., Sullivan, A., & Bers, M. U. (2013). The effect of a classroom-based intensive robotics and programming workshop on sequencing ability in early childhood. *Journal of Early Childhood Education, 41*, 245–255.

Klassner, F., & Anderson, S. (2003). LEGO MindStorms: Not just for K–12 anymore. *IEEE Robotics and Automation Magazine, 10*(2), 12–18.

Kolberg, E., & Orlev, N. (2001, October). *Robotics learning as a tool for integrating science-technology curriculum in K-12 schools.* Paper presented *at 31st ASEE/IEE Frontiers in Education Conference,* Reno, NV.

Lombardi, M. (2007). Authentic learning for the 21st century: An overview. *Educause Learning Initiative.* Retrieved from http://net.educause.edu/ir/library/pdf/ELI3009.pdf

Marulcu, I. (2010). *Investigating the impact of a LEGO(TM)-based, engineering-oriented curriculum compared to an inquiry-based curriculum on fifth graders' content learning of simple machines* (Doctoral dissertation). Boston College, Boston, MA.

Neuschwander, C. (1997-2010). Sir Cumferance (Series). Charlesbridge Publishing.

Papert, S. (1980). *Constructionism vs. instructionism.* Retrieved from http://www.papert.org/articles/const_inst/const_inst1.html

Papert, S. (1992). *The children's machine*. New York, NY: Basic Books.

Penner, D. E. (2001). Cognition, computers, and synthetic science: Building knowledge and meaning through modeling. In W. G. Secada (Ed.), *Review of research in education* (pp. 1–35). Washington, DC: American Educational Research Association.

Piaget, J. (1972). Development and learning. In C. S. Lavatelli & F. Stendler (Eds.), *Reading in children behavior and development.* New York, NY: Hartcourt Brace Janovich.

Piaget, J. (1973). *To understand is to invent.* New York, NY: Grossman.

Piaget, J. (1977). *The children and reality: Problems of genetic psychology*. New York, NY: Penguin Books.

Rogers, C., & Portsmore, M. (2004). Bringing engineering to elementary school. *Journal of STEM Education, 5*, 17–28.

Samuels, P., & Haapasalo, L. (2012). Real and virtual robotics in mathematics education at the school–university transition. *International Journal of Mathematical Education in Science and Technology, 43*(3), 285–301.

Satchwell, R., & Loepp, F. L. (2002). Designing and implementing an integrated mathematics, science, and technology curriculum for the middle school. *Journal of Industrial Teacher Education, 39*(3), 41–66.

Striegel, A., & Rover, D. (2002, November). *Problem-based learning in an introductory computer engineering course.* Paper presented at the 31st ASEE/IEEE frontiers in education conference, Boston, MA.

Vandebona, U., & Attard, M. M. (2002). A problem-based learning approach in a civil engineering curriculum. *World Transactions on Engineering and Technology Education, 1*(1), 99–102.

Weinberg, J. B., & Yu, X. (2003). Robotics in education: Low cost platforms for teaching integrated systems. *IEEE Robotics & Automation Magazine, 10*(2), 4–6.

Whitehead, S. H. (2010). *Relationship of robotic implementation on changes in middle school students' beliefs and interest toward science, technology, engineering and mathematics.* (Doctoral dissertation). Indiana University of Pennsylvania, PA.

Ahmad Khanlari
OISE/University of Toronto

SYLVIE MORICE

27. BRINGING IMAGINATION AND LITERACY CIRCLES INTO THE MATH CLASSROOM

A Humanistic Approach

INTRODUCTION

Curriculum developers and teachers have long debated the best way to present mathematics to learners, and have engaged in an ongoing *math war* for decades. Traditional educators believe students should learn the algorithms and concepts created by mathematicians while progressivists prefer students explore, discover, and understand the meaning behind the rules.

These opposing forces have directly impacted the way I teach middle school mathematics in New Brunswick, Canada over a fourteen-year span. Until 2008, the Atlantic Canada mathematics curriculum philosophy and outcomes were based on those created by the National Council of Teachers of Mathematics (APEF). While this curriculum encouraged the development of problem-solving skills, it still relied heavily on algorithms and rote memorization. The Government of New Brunswick then unveiled a new curriculum adapted from the Western and Northern Canadian Protocol *Common Curriculum Framework for K-9 Mathematics* (2006). This redesigned curriculum focuses the attention "on understanding how knowledge can be constructed, deconstructed, and then reconstructed" (Ornstein & Hunkins, 2004, p. 8) for the student.

This shift in focus from a skill-and-drill format to an experience-based one was difficult for me. As a student, I excelled at a step-by-step sequence of problem-solving that culminated in a correct answer. Despite my traditional mathematics education background, I succeeded in completing a Minor in Mathematics as part of my Science degree. The first five years of my career were spent teaching the subject using this traditional approach. My students' results in the provincial Grade 8 math assessment were at or above the district and provincial average. I did not initially see the benefit of a 180 degree shift in ideology to an approach that involved connections with the real world, experience, and discovery. But after four years of professional development, peer conferencing and classroom practice I came to the realization that I had never truly understood numbers and how math works within the real world. However, by 2012 when both my students and I were comfortable with the new curriculum and how to speak in the new language of mathematics, I began to question why the district screener and provincial assessment results for our

J. B. Cummings & M. L. Blatherwick (Eds.), Creative Dimensions of Teaching and Learning in the 21st Century, 269–275.

school were not improving. With the emphasis on a deep understanding of numerical value, why weren't our efforts being reflected? After studying the works of Kieran Egan (1979, 2008), I began to wonder if the New Brunswick math curriculum was missing the humanistic aspect of learning. Does it "ignore the artistic, physical, and cultural aspect of subject matter; rarely consider the need for self-reflectiveness and self-actualization among learners; and, finally, overlook the sociopsychological dynamics of classrooms and schools?" (Ornstein & Hunkins, 2004, p. 8)

Starting with a strong, academically driven curriculum, I arrived at the realization that perhaps it is up to the individual teacher to apply the humanistic approach to the material. This paper will illustrate how Kieran Egan's "Imaginative Education practices" (2008) through literacy circles and storytelling were brought together in my Grade 7 mathematics classroom.

In 2008, the government of New Brunswick released the new Grade 7 mathematic curriculum developed by a group of classroom teachers. The result is a logical progression of mathematical concepts focused on developing numerical literacy. Despite the implementation of the new curriculum "the latest report from the Council of Ministers of Education shows […] students in New Brunswick continue to perform below the national average on standardized math tests" (CBC, 2011). Students are still struggling despite the implementation of current research into math education. The curriculum guide has clear goals and "uses models and a variety of pedagogical approaches to address the diversity of learning styles and developmental stages of students" (Government New Brunswick, 2008). What it lacks is the inclusion of the student's own formidable tool: imagination. This is what I have found as a teacher. Egan's Imaginative Education approach (IERG.ca) attempts to combine the cognitive, emotional, cultural, and psychological components of learning. The Imaginative Educator "seeks to value and build upon the way the child understands her or his experiences, rather than always focusing on the "adult" way of understanding as the measure of learning [and to do this by being] imaginative and sensitive to dimensions of learning that they may have never thought of as relevant to education" (IERG.ca). By introducing imagination into the math classroom, a teacher can merge the academic with the humanistic resulting in a deeper understanding of numbers.

For years mathematics has been about rules and applying them in certain situations. Very rarely have we asked students to understand the underlying meaning behind why a rule works. "The culture which places the utilitarianism of mathematics … above the importance of ideas and creativity will only result in the greater alienation of the majority of the population from mathematics" (Lingard, n.d., p. 16). The new curriculum demands an explanation for the rationale of every theorem by the learner. There is a major emphasis on using literacy skills developed in the ELA classroom and applying them to understanding math. An example of this is to start saying numbers in scientific language. Common phrasing when discussing temperature is to say "It's minus 19 out there today". Students are encouraged to say "It's negative 19 out there today". Another example is when dealing with decimals. All too often we will say "zero point five" when students should be saying "five tenths" or "one half". By calling a number by its true name we lead students down the path to deep understanding. We have been too lazy with mathematical language for too long. This is one of the major shifts within the new curriculum. Fortunately, the province of New Brunswick has placed an emphasis on literacy as well and the skills being promoted in ELA are serving our students well in math too. If the understanding of mathematics comes down to the cognitive tool of literacy, then perhaps the stagnation of success in math could be addressed using Egan's Imaginative Education approach. One of Egan's strategies focuses on "Learning in Depth" (LiD). The underlying idea is that "the imagination can only work with what we know and consequently learning knowledge in depth is important for stimulation of the imagination" (IERG.ca). Thus, both imaginative and emotional engagement plus a deep knowledge base are key to developing a humanistic approach.

The Grade 7 math curriculum is broken down into four general curriculum outcomes (GCO): Number, Patterns and Relations, Shape and Space and Statistics and Probability. This paper will look at an Essential Outcome from the Shape and Space strand. SS1 states students will "[d]emonstrate an understanding of circles by: describing the relationships among radius, diameter and circumference of circles, relating circumference to pi, determining the sum of the central angles, constructing circles with a given radius or diameter and solving problems involving the radii, diameters and circumferences of circles" (Government New Brunswick, 2008). I also explain how I have used Imaginative Education tools, particularly storytelling, to engage student imagination in the content and academic outcomes.

In the past, I would teach the relationship between radius, diameter, circumference and pi by writing the algorithms on the board. I even had a way to remember the formulae (see Figure 1). As long as students could remember that the horizontal line meant to divide and the vertical line to multiply, they could regurgitate the necessary algorithm required to answer the question. The problem was that I used memorization in the attempt to avoid memorization.

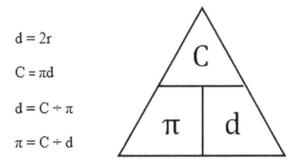

$d = 2r$

$C = \pi d$

$d = C \div \pi$

$\pi = C \div d$

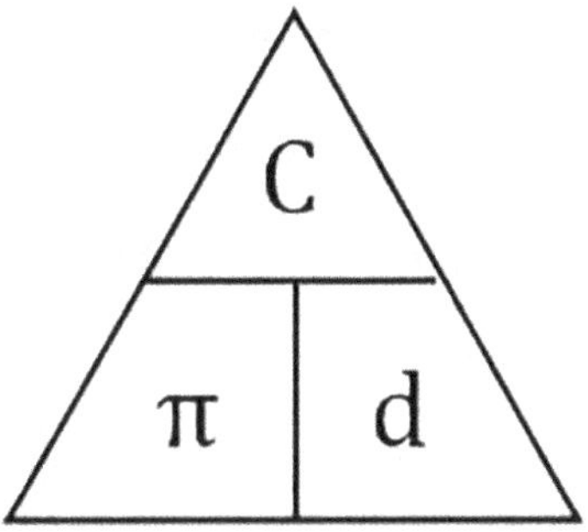

Figure 1. Relationship between diameter, circumference, radius and pi

Then I discovered Cindy Neuschwander's *Sir Cumference* series (1997–2010). In her books, Neuschwander tells the story of the boy, Radius, who solves a number of dilemmas using his logical knowledge. Radius and his mother, Lady Di of Ammeter are related both by blood and the fact that Radius is half her height. During one of his adventures, Radius discovers the distance around a pie is three times the distance across. Students respond to this story because it makes the algorithms come to life. They no longer need to recall rote fact. Instead, they have a story which both enthralls and teaches them and it becomes their personal mnemonic. Egan recommends the use of stories in any curriculum area: "Stories are the most effective tools for making their content meaningful" (1979, p. 120).

After introducing authors such as Neuschwander, I found it is logical to extend the idea to have students attempt to write their own stories. "Students tend to write following the models they have experienced. Students whose only model for mathematical writing is their textbooks tend to write word problems similar to those in the textbooks [whereas] students provided with well-written works of children's literature have a different model – one that allows them to explore math concepts through narratives" (Lauritzen, 1992, p. 6). Suddenly, the world of literature, as it has been available to them in the ELA classroom, becomes applicable to math as well. Literature in the classroom uses the imagination and engagement elements of stories to awaken the natural inquisitiveness of learners to make sense of standards-based outcomes.

Lingard believes that "[m]any children regard mathematics as a body of knowledge, and a completed one at that. It exists in books and teachers' heads, and has been there for years. There is no new mathematics; it is a dead subject" (Lingard, n.d., p. 17). The belief that math is as dead as the mathematicians who created the algorithms is one that needs to be addressed. The subject "is littered with colourful characters, intrigue, romance, passion, corruption, betrayal, adventure and more!" (Lingard, n.d., p. 17) Take, for example, Archimedes of Syracuse born in 287 BC, who is known as one of the greatest thinkers prior to Sir Isaac Newton. On his tombstone is inscribed the figure of his favourite theorem; the sphere and the circumscribed cylinder, and the ratio of the containing solid to the contained. Archimedes used his mathematical knowledge to keep Syracuse away from the Romans with the use of his war machines (Figure 2). Thirteen year old boys love strife; in fact many aspire to join the Canadian military after high school. Why not use this interest of physical aggression to introduce the Claw of Archimedes and his Heat Ray?

It is said Archimedes was killed by an invading Roman soldier as he drew circles in the dirt. "Careful, don't smear my circles!" (Čapek, 1997, p. 4) was one of his last statements. Egan (IERG.ca) would argue that a student who accumulates a vast amount of knowledge about the mathematician behind the theorem would then be motivated to learn and apply the rule with accuracy. Let us bring the "dead" mathematicians to life. Math is not ancient and stagnant; it is everlasting. Egan has illuminated an approach that bridges the gap between knowledge and imagination allowing for the success of both.

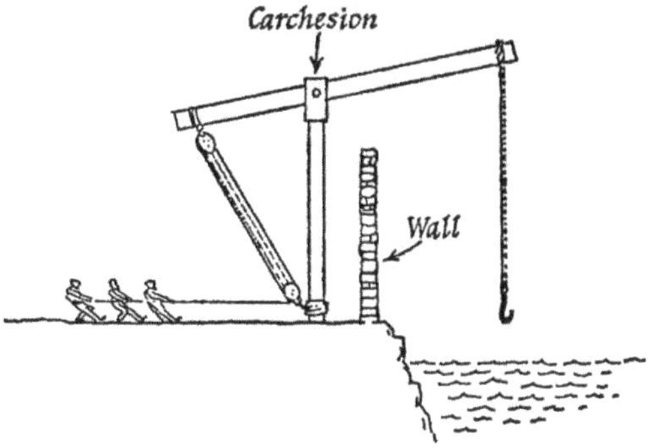

Figure 2. The claw of Archimedes[1]

The traditional method for teaching students to construct circles with a given radius or diameter is to provide them with rulers, compasses, pencil and string or geometry software within the classroom. Mathematically this concept is important because "[s]patial sense offers a way to interpret and reflect on the physical environment and its 3-D or 2-D representations. These skills are central to the understanding of mathematics" (Government New Brunswick, 2008). Students need to have a deep understanding of this knowledge in order to make the connections between the math in the classroom and its applications to the world they live in. While we typically rely heavily on the 2D world in mathematical instruction, students live in the 3-dimensional world. Connecting math to a real-life situation contributes to deeper understanding. Crop circles are becoming more frequent and student interest in extraterrestrial life is abundant. After using the traditional manipulatives in the classroom, I had the students create their own crop circles; measuring radius, diameter and circumference for all circles used. After a class vote, the winning design was reproduced in fresh snow using snowshoes. The local paper was alerted and came to report on the crop circle found in our local town. Not only did the students master the curriculum outcome, but they saw the product of their knowledge displayed in a newspaper. As Eggers states, "if it's in a published [work], no one can diminish what they've thought and said" (Eggers, 2008). This is the power of literacy in combination with mathematics.

It is well known that our students display a diversity of learning styles and interests. In his book, *Frames of Mind* (2008), Gardner states there should be "[a] commitment to convey important ideas and concepts in a number of different formats. This activation of multiple intelligences holds promise of reaching many more students and also demonstrating what it means to understand a topic thoroughly and deeply (Gardner, 2008). Egan and Gardner agree that a deep understanding of material is necessary. Egan provides an innovative method to bring imagination into a curriculum to support the required depth of knowledge. All kinds of literature can be used in the math classroom from journalistic reports, comics, short stories, songs, poems to word problems.

Figure 3. Students use snowshoes to create "crop circles" in the snow.

Figure 4. Calvin and Hobbes comic

The Calvin and Hobbes comic (Watterson, Figure 4) is one example I give my students to model how mathematics can be fun and applicable to real life. Another is the song, *Pi, Pi, Mathematical Pi,* (Ferrier & Chan) sung to the tune of *Bye Bye Miss American Pie.* The excitement of the Olympics and X Games is a hook to garner student interest. Rotations in BMX, snowboarding, skateboarding, and figure skating are all illustrations of the central angles of circles. Every year I run a school-wide Math Olympics complete with multi-age teams and medallions. Students are expected to work together to solve word problems. Tapping into students' imaginations and emotions through literature is another method of coaxing deep understanding of curriculum concepts.

I believe that "[e]very child can come to believe that he or she is capable of making sense of mathematics. Their understanding and, thus, their confidence grow as a result of being engaged in doing mathematics. To teach effectively means to engage students at their level so they can create or develop new ideas to use and understand so they can make sense of mathematics" (Van de Walle, 2006, p. 1).

Kieran Egan's Imaginative Education approach helps me promote passion for mathematics. Learners are engaged because my lessons are "tied up with feelings and images, metaphors and jokes, rhyme and rhythm, stories and wonder, heroes and the exotic, hopes, fears, and passions, hobbies and collecting, narrative and oppositions" (Egan, 2008, p. 96).

I believe I can successfully merge the curriculum with the interests of my students and their multiple intelligences by engaging their imaginations. The more diverse I am, the more my students will connect with the subject matter. Egan's Imaginative Education approach not only brings a humanistic approach to the Shape and Space Unit but provides me with yet another strategy to employ to deepen their knowledge. Literature brings math to life successfully in my mathematics classroom with the help of Egan's story telling framework.

NOTE

[1] Figure 2 from *Engineering in the Ancient World* by J. G. Landels, University of California Press, Berkeley & Los Angeles, 1978. Retrieved from https://www.math.nyu.edu/~crorres/Archimedes/Claw/illustrations.html

REFERENCES

Čapek, K. (1997). *Apocryphal tales* (N. Comrada, Trans.). New Haven: CatBird Press.

CBC. (2011, November 29). *New Brunswick students lag in math scores*. Retrieved from http://www.cbc.ca/news/canada/new-brunswick/story/2011/11/29/nb-education-math-report-940.html

Egan, K. (1979). *Educational development*. New York, NY: Oxford University Press.

Egan, K. (2008). *The future of education: Reimagining out schools from the ground up*. New Haven: Yale University Press.

Eggers, D. (2008). *Once upon a school* [Video]. Retrieved from http://www.ted.com/talks/dave_eggers_makes_his_ted_prize_wish_once_upon_a_school.html

Ferrier, K., & Chan, A. *Pi, Pi Mathematical Pi*. Song retrieved from http://www.vvc.edu/ph/TonerS/mathpi.html

Gardner, H. (2008). *The 25th anniversary of the publication of Howard Gardner's 'Frames of Mind: The Theory of Multiple Intelligences'*. Retrieved from http://www.howardgardner.com/Papers/papers.html

Government New Brunswick. (2008). *Mathematics grade 7 curriculum*. Retrieved from http://www.gnb.ca/0000/publications/curric/mathematics_nb_curriculum_grade_7.pdf

Imaginative Education Research Group (IERG). *A brief guide to learning in depth*. Retrieved from http://ierg.ca/about-us/what-is-imaginative-education/

Lauritzen, C. (1992, February). *When children write math stories*. Presented at the West Regional Conference of the International Reading Association, Portland, OR.

Lingard, D. (n.d.). *The history of mathematics: An essential component of the mathematics curriculum at all levels*. Sheffield: Sheffield Hallam University.

Neuschwander, C. (1997–2010). *Sir Cumferance* (Series). Watertown, MA: Charlesbridge Publishing.

Ornstein, A., & Hunkins, F. (2004). *Curriculum: Foundations, principles, and issues* (4th ed.). Boston, MA: Pearson Education Inc.

Van de Walle, J. A. (2006). *Teaching student-centered mathematics*. Boston, MA: Person Education, Inc.

Watterson, B. *Calvin and Hobbes*. Cartoon Strip. Retrieved from http://generationterrorists.com/quotes/calvinandhobbes.html

Sylvie Morice
University of New Brunswick

DALE VANDENBORRE

28. GLYFFIX PLAY

A Modern Image-Based Form of Language Play

INTRODUCTION

Technology in education, or *edtech* as it is often called, is an incredible trend that the world is quickly embracing. Activity in the *edtech* space abounds. More specifically, games in education continue to increase as teachers and children alike are demonstrating the value of play in learning. Play undoubtedly provides an effective method for learning by children. As David Crystal (1996) eloquently points out in his paper about language play and linguistic intervention: "language play is at the core of early parent-child interaction" and "given the amount of play in pre-school child society, a principled transition in early readers might enable children to move from a world in which language play is so important to a world where language play has been so marginalized" (pp. 340–341).

With respect to language play, I would like to introduce you to a language play solution that is modern, visual, puzzling, logical and frustratingly fun – it is called Glyffix. I am A. J. Funn, the author of Glyffix, and I have been doing language play with my children for more than 15 years.

Glyffix derives its name from hieroglyphics and is a modern day play on "words hidden in pictures". Glyffix embraces technology and *gamification* trends and wraps language play in a modern visual and playful puzzle language where "readers" and "writers" alike can communicate and learn at the same time. In its simplest form, Glyffix offers a single image or "glyf" representing a single English word or symbol. [1] In the example below, the glyfs, translated, reveal the phrase "I like you".[2]

This Glyffix example is simple, visually appealing, and arguably more engaging than reading the simple printed phrase "I like you", which, by the way, is also a set of images and symbols strung together that our minds have learned to be able to decipher quickly over the years.

J. B. Cummings & M. L. Blatherwick (Eds.), Creative Dimensions of Teaching and Learning in the 21st Century, 277–285.

Glyffix has the ability to engage learners while developing several essential skills including children's language, numeracy, computer, visual and decoding and problem-solving skills. Glyffix's mobile games have shown improvement in learners' analysis, prediction, spelling, phonics, vocabulary, and reading skills. Glyffix is visually stimulating, but the real beauty of the language is in the learning that comes with its play.

Glyffix is not a brand-new concept, but an evolutionary iteration and variation of a language play concept that has been around for many years and in many forms called Rebus. With a modern Rebus, a single visual is often designed to represent encoded phrases. Below are examples of Rebus that reveal phrases:

Answer: Top Secret *Answer: Once in a blue moon* *Answer: No Time to lose*

There are plenty of Rebus puzzles similar to this online, but my favourite Rebus resource is an automatic translator found at MyRebus.com. It is worth checking out.

While it was tempting in its creation to also achieve phrases with a single image concept, it was essential for me to embrace a "rule" that a glyf always translates into one and only one word. This helps structure the visual "language" and have words separated by spaces just as it happens with regular text. It allows for someone deciphering a phrase to know that overlapping images are part of the same word, while a space between images facilitates multiple distinct words. This can be seen in the followings example, which translates to "Good Clean Fun".

Without the "rule" of an image translating into a single English word, one might think the above example translates into "Not bad clean fun", but that *doesn't* flow very well, or make much sense. Another "rule" about Glyffix is that everything, once translated fully, makes perfect sense. In the case above, "not bad" needs to be further deciphered into a single word. What is a single word meaning "not bad"? "Good". Good clean fun.

Another key concept of Glyffix seen in the same above example above is in the glyf for the word "fun". There are attributes that can be added to images, such as pointers, text manipulation, sound symbols and more that we will learn about as we see more examples. In the example, the text below the gun suggest swapping the letter "G" for the letter "F". So, instead of G-U-N, the glyf translated is F-U-N. This text manipulation is key to being able to create almost any word in the English language. In the next example, the simple "-P" is a revealing part of the puzzle that helps immensely with deciphering. The image alone could be a cookie or a sheep. The "-P" suggests "cookie" would be the wrong word to use in this case as there is no "P" in the spelling of cookie. However, there is "P" in the spelling of "sheep", indicating that this is indeed quite likely the right translation to use for the image. As Glyffix is heavily based on phonetics, the glyf below is "she" (Sheep, minus a "P" is "shee", which phonetically is the same as "she").

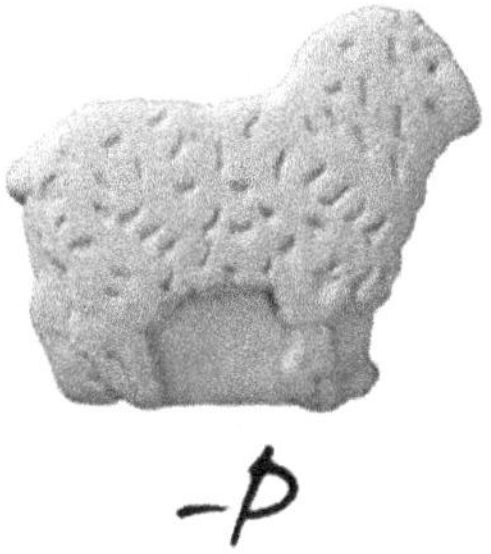

Complex or compound English words are often achieved by breaking the word into syllables. In the days of the Rebus, words would often be represented with a "+" connecting the syllables of a word. In Glyffix, instead of using a "+", we have opted just to overlap the images within the same word to save ourselves some screen and print real estate. This evolution can be seen in the following examples for "subliminal" in the old style, and "exhilarating" in the new style.

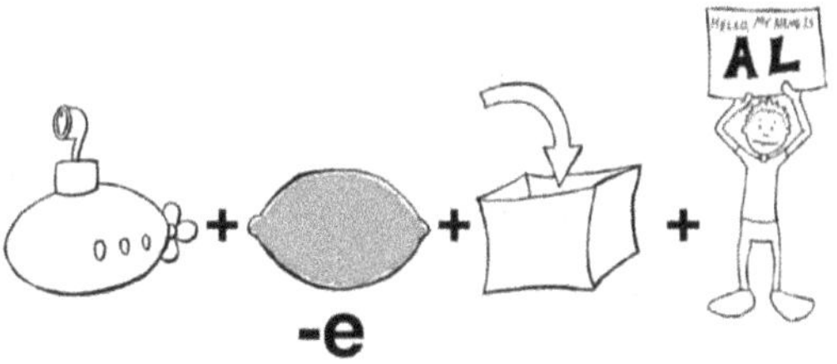

For the glyf "exhilarating" above, we can see the breakdown of syllables fairly clearly: **x + ill + r + eight + ing**. In the case of the second syllable, the decipherer might think that this is an image of a dog, but **x + dog + er + eight + ing** just does not flow right. Upon further scrutiny, the dog is sick (as water bottle and thermometer might indicate). **X + sick + er + eight + ing**. Nope – that does not flow well either. The decipherer might need to try cycling through synonyms for the images of each image if it does not make sense since a rule is, once deciphered, it clearly makes sense. A synonym for "sick" is "ill" ... Let's try that: **x + ill + er + eight + ing**. Bingo!! Phonetically this flows. Exhilarating!

Glyffix is challenging, fun and rewarding for all ages, and especially for younger children becoming literate. I experienced this with my own children by watching them work through encrypted messages hundreds of times in Christmas and birthday treasure hunts and in bedtime reading. It is rewarding to watch someone work through the logic when deciphering. It is also revealing to watch the train of thought.

Now that we have seen a few examples, let's look at deciphering a longer phrase. It can seem intimidating at first as it looks just like hieroglyphics, but, by remembering that each image is a miniature puzzle, and that the entire phrase will make perfect sense, we can conquer this.

If we look at the following two lines of Glyffix, we can see that there are multiple ways to achieve the same message. Each glyf-based phrase below translates to "I really like your dog", yet no image repeats to achieve the encoded words. Thus, there is often more than one glyf for a single English word. This keeps the language evolving and allows creators and readers alike to continually invent.

Reflecting on the literacy and learning elements we get from Glyffix the benefits are numerous:

- Phonetics – graph-feet-e translates to graffiti;
- Antonyms – "not bad" is antonym for "good", and "not me" means "you";
- Syllables – x – ill – r – eight – ing;
- Synonyms – sick versus ill;

- Logic & problem-solving;
- Spelling;
- Cultural nuances;
- A sense of accomplishment.

In addition to the above, it is important to remember that Glyffix can introduce children to pretty much any learning topic you want to teach as long it is still about reading. The message behind the pictures and puzzles eventually comes in loud and clear. As an example, my Glyffix Original book *Freeda Firefly's Fantastic Flight* is about a firefly that flies around the world. Through the play involved in deciphering this book, children also learn about and are introduced to New York, Spain, France, India, Canada, Japan and more.

How Glyffix Came to Be

Reflecting back, I can't quite recall my first exposure to language play, or what led me to pursue the development of my own visual based puzzle language as a grown man. I am sure there were many factors that contributed to the language play being "in me". I do know that I enjoyed television games such as Connection in the 1980s, and I know my schoolmates have reminded me that I used to create similar decoded messages back before I can remember. I do know that Glyffix started in my household when my daughter was only 4 years old. With both my children, it was a tradition for us to give a glyf-based riddle at Christmas time to serve as a bit of a treasure hunt for the last or main gift on Christmas morning. It was not called Glyffix in the early years, but we faithfully created treasure hunts with my rudimentary hand-drawn puzzles that would take me hours to create often late on Christmas Eve.

Then, as my daughter loved bedtime stories, it was at her request that we do Glyffix at night instead of regular old reading to "spice things up". She enjoyed the play. This was great as I grew to appreciate seeing her young mind work through my logic within puzzles. We also stretched the treasure hunts from Christmas to Easter and also to birthdays.

The only challenge was, as the children got more Glyffix play exposure, they also improved their deciphering skills, and they developed the ability to decode things rather quickly. They could read Glyffix nearly at the same pace as regular reading. My creation process was not as quick, so I would sometimes spend an hour to create a 10-minute bedtime story. But, it was always worth the effort.

One Christmas eve, I was up particularly late making a treasure hunt and I had an epiphany. I needed an English to Glyffix translator. I could type a treasure hunt or a bedtime story in English, and voila, it would automatically translate into puzzling images. Play with my daughter is the reason why my first book, *Penelope's Imagination Runs Wild*, is about a girl that lies in bed at night and lets her imagination take her places.

Today, with a translator available, anyone can create Gyffix stories. With a translator for thousands of English words, people can create their own stories in visual puzzles, post to their favourite media sites, or even chat over mobile phones and talk in encoded images versus regular text. Fun and learning at the same time.

Glyffix for Schools

It became obvious early on that the quickest and most prolific uptake of Glyffix was in the educational community. Teachers that were introduced to Glyffix fully embraced the concepts and validated the fact that there are clear educational concepts and benefits that come with Glyffix play in the classroom. I was pleased to share my books and my time with schools. In the class, in front of the children, my suspicions about this being a fun and playful way to learn were validated. Even I was surprised that when using Glyffix how quickly the children grasped the deciphering and how well the fun and engagement spanned multiple grades levels.

These puzzles, treasure hunts, stories, and language play e-games have been met with enthusiasm and requests for more by the learners and teachers with whom I tried them. I believed their worth and effectiveness needed to be pilot tested with students and their teachers to gain their feedback and input. The pilot and research is still in its early stages at this point, but has been carried out in several elementary schools in my home area with multiple classes and learners ranging from Grades 1 through 8. Teacher and student responses and ideas were extremely helpful in determining what to include, what is meaningful, what is fun, and what is educational to evolve the language.

One of the things the children always want to see is their name in Glyffix. Here are a few examples of that for a few of the more common names in my area.

Alex Jessica Kaitlyn Jordan Billy

Samples of favourite feedback that I received include quotes from both teachers and students alike.

Language Play

According to David Crystal (1996), language play is a normal and healthy part of learning about and using language – both for children and adults. Dr. Seuss, in his series of perennial favourites like *The Cat in the Hat* and *Hop on Pop*, was one of the earliest North American educators and authors to recognize and maximize the amusement and learning that children get from language play. And, Seuss has proven to provide learning across many generations for decades of readers since the 1950s!

Glyffix, like Seuss, is unique and recognizably distinct in its delivery. It tells stories without using words. Glyffix as language play develops vocabulary and decoding skills for young readers as they identify an image and the sound and word that lie "underneath" that representation in the glyf. Glyffix is more than just playing, and, it is also more than just reading. It is deciphering, then reading… or *Reading+* as I affectionately like to refer to it. After just a few quick examples are shown to reveal how the language works, children are moving from decoding a single glyf to a message in glyfs; then a whole paragraph and story; and then creating and writing their own Glyffix messages.

> Play is our brain's favourite way of learning.
> Diane Ackerman, Contemporary American Author

> Almost all creativity involves purposeful play.
> Abraham Maslow, American Psychologist

> People tend to forget that play is serious. (David Hockney, Contemporary British Painter)

CONCLUSION

For an extended period now, I have had the luxury of seeing the reactions of educators, parents and children alike as they get introduced to Glyffix for the very first time. It is always an inspiring and rewarding experience. I am always impressed and intrigued at how quickly some grasp and run with the concept and translation of complex messages while others remain frustrated with an inability to decipher what comes so easily to others.

When educators describe their perceived benefits of Glyffix play, they have described it in various ways, showing that different people take away different things from their experience with play:

- Some speak about Glyffix being all about art and creativity, and highlight, emphasize and reiterate the value of art in education.
- Others focus on the cultural aspect of Glyffix and how Glyffix play highlights ties that culture has with language.
- Many comment on the opportunity of collaborative problem-solving and believe one of the more valuable features of Glyffix is that, much like a large puzzle, it accommodates the contributions of many through its play to complete a final translation.
- Some focus on Glyffix as an important communication method that reminds us of humanity's earliest achievements in communication through pictography and hieroglyphics.

- Some focus on the puzzling nature of Glyffix, and point to the benefit of puzzles in learning.
- Ultimately, educators tend to emphasize the fun, playful and engaging nature that Glyffix play while facilitating the learning of a fundamental, core and potentially boring education subject – literacy.

As long as there are readers interested in deciphering, I will continue encoding Glyffix messages in books, web and mobile applications. Ultimately, I can only hope that children and parents, and children and teachers, from around the globe get as much reward from playing and learning together as I did doing Glyffix play with my children.

NOTES

1. In this case above, as well as for the examples in this chapter, all translations are Glyffix-English, but there is no reason this same concept cannot be applied in other languages.
2. All images are by license of Dreamstime.com.

REFERENCES

Crystal, D. (1996). Language play and linguistic intervention. *Child Language Teaching and Therapy, 12*(3), 328–344.

Geisel, Th. / Dr. Seuss. (1957–). *The cat in the hat* (Series). New York, NY: Random House Books for Young Readers.

Geisel, Th. / Dr. Seuss. (1963). *Hop on pop*. New York, NY: Random House Books for Young Readers.

Websites

Books by A.J. Funn are available at AuthorHouse.com, http://bookstore.authorhouse.com/Products/SKU-000637757/Penelopes-Imagination-Runs-Wild.aspx
Glyffix games, puzzles & treasures can be found at Glyffix.com
http://www.myrebus.com/

Dale Vandenborre
University of New Brunswick

ALLY A. ZHOU AND XIAOMIN HU

29. TUTORING SECOND LANGUAGE LEARNERS WITHIN THEIR ZONE OF PROXIMAL DEVELOPMENT

Recommendations for Changes in University Writing Center Pedagogy

INTRODUCTION

Many English as a second language (ESL) writers at the tertiary level lack contextual, rhetorical, or lexicogrammatical knowledge to meet the criteria of good writing in the academia of English-speaking countries. To improve upon these areas, they often come to university writing centers (UWCs) to seek assistance and many focus on lexicogrammatical knowledge and skills (Blau, Hall, & Sparks, 2002; Harris, 1997; Harris & Silva, 1993; Moussu, 2013; Myers, 2003; Powers & Nelson, 1995).

This focus often conflicts with traditional, yet changing (Moussu, 2013), writing center pedagogy which utilizes the collaborative, non-directive approach with a focus on improving learners' writing processes, or in North's (1984) words "to produce better writers" (p. 438). In particular, tutors are encouraged to facilitate learning through the Socratic Method (posing open-ended or leading questions pertaining to student writing). Additionally, tutors are encouraged to focus on global errors (e.g., focus, logic, organization) rather than local errors (e.g., unclear expressions, morphological and syntactical errors) (Blau et al., 2002), also commonly referred to as higher-order versus lower-order concerns (Gillespie & Lerner, 2000; Severino, 2009) or rhetorical versus linguistic errors (Harris & Silva, 1993; Taylor, 2007). This methodology, primarily process approach-based, may be ideal for L1 learners who possess native linguistic awareness; however, it does not adequately address the needs of second language (L2) learners whose lexicogrammar knowledge often adversely affects semantic content in writing. Thus, local errors may affect cohesion and coherence, thereby leading to global concerns. As such, L2 writers' needs are not adequately met through this methodology.

To address this disparity, we argue the need for providing linguistic feedback to L2 learners at various stages of their writing processes (e.g., planning, drafting, reviewing) based on relevant research in second language acquisition (SLA) and UWCs. We further recommend how such linguistic feedback should be provided to ESL writers through an innovative pedagogy that is based on sociocultural theory (SCT). This pedagogical approach allows the tutor to assess the ESL learner's needs dynamically and to subsequently provide graduated and contingent assistance within

J. B. Cummings & M. L. Blatherwick (Eds.), Creative Dimensions of Teaching and Learning in the 21st Century, 287–294.

the learner's zone of proximal development (ZPD), which helps the learner achieve self-regulation or learner independence, a fundamental tenet of writing center philosophy.

Why Should Linguistic Feedback Be Provided To L2 Learners At Various Stages of Their Writing Processes?

When working with tutees, tutors are often instructed to address global concerns before local errors. Language errors are supposed to be left to the final stage of writing or the editing stage. This method may be infeasible if it is followed rigidly when working with ESL learners. Indeed, tutors should be encouraged to address linguistic or lexicogrammatical concerns in learners' texts at the various stages of their writing processes when such needs arise.

This is because, first, the line between global and local matters is sometimes hard to draw (Blau et al., 2002; Harris & Silva, 1993). Blau et al. argued that when local errors are at the magnitude of obstructing meaning, they could become global concerns. For example, if the thesis statement of a student's writing is incomprehensible due to its lexicogrammatical errors, the main idea of the essay will likely be unclear to the reader. Thus, certain language errors cannot be left to deal with until global concerns are addressed or until the final stages of writing, particularly those that interfere with a clear understanding of the main idea and major supporting points of a written text. Tutors could, according to Blau et al. "interweave the discussion of global and local concerns" (p. 35).

Second, language constraints for L2 writers are not limited to their final draft or the editing stage. They could result from any stages of their writing – drafting (also called transcribing), revising, or editing, and their transcribing process has been found to be "more laborious, less fluent, and less productive – perhaps reflecting a lack of lexical resources" (Harris & Silva, 1993, p. 668). Indeed, ESL learners' language limitations during the writing process may not be as easily identified as errors in their texts because this process is largely social as well as private and independent, thereby limiting our understanding of their linguistic constraints during the process. Hence, the approach that emphasizes global concerns in early drafts and local errors in later or final drafts, which works well for native-speaker writers, may not work well for ESL writers.

Third, language is a resource for creating meanings. As such, it is practically infeasible to separate the discussion of form and meaning/content during one-to-one conferences. Hyland (2003) argued forcefully and succinctly against the separation of form and meaning:

> The separation of form and content is largely an artificial one, of dubious theoretical value and impossible to maintain in practice… we only successfully articulate our meanings *through* the selection of appropriate forms. Language is a *resource* for making meanings, not something we turn to when we have

> worked out what we are going to say, and the two cannot be realistically separated when responding to writing (pp. 184–185).

This comment provides a solid basis against rigid adherence to the writing center's method of addressing global concerns first and then local errors.

Fourth, because the understanding of what writing is has evolved, writing center practice and philosophy need to be in accordance with this current understanding. Writing used to be treated as simply text or composing, and it remains treated as such in some writing classrooms. The process approach flourished in the 1980s, and in the same decade, North (1984) published his oft-cited article titled "The Idea of a Writing Center." In this article, North wrote that "writing is most usefully viewed as a process" (p. 438), which indicated the close link he drew between the process approach and the writing center philosophy or practice he advocated- "our job is to produce better writers, not better writing" (ibid). Regardless of the legitimacy of his goal of producing simply better writers, given that writing is no longer considered to be solely text or composing, rather, "writing is text, is composing, and is social construction" (Cumming, 1998, p. 61), North's proposal needs modifications to reflect the current understanding of what writing is.

Indeed, is it not our job to facilitate learning and produce better writers step-by-step through guiding students to produce better writing or better texts each time they visit the writing center? If better texts are not produced, how can professors measure whether students have become better writers? In the end, in addition to becoming better writers, many students as well as their professors would also like to see better texts because as Jones (2001) argued, the notion of better writing ability is obscure and difficult to measure. At least to most professors, better texts can be an indication that their students have become better writers. Simply, subject matter professors may have no mechanism or see no need to measure their students' writing ability by documenting their progress in the planning, writing, and reviewing stages of the writing processes. Instead of having professors assess the intangible writing ability as demonstrated by improved writing processes, it is likely more feasible to have them evaluate learners' texts. Thus, the ultimate goal of improving writing processes remains to produce better texts.

It is not only necessary for tutors to provide feedback to the language of learners' texts at various writing stages when such needs arise, as indicated by the foregoing discussion, it is also desirable to do so. This is because, based on sociocultural theory (SCT), one-to-one tutoring provides an ideal learning environment for developing language proficiency in L2 learners in addition to developing their writing skills. Then what changes should be made to the current writing center pedagogy, which is non-directive and global before local errors, in order to effectively address L2 learners' language concerns?

In the rest of this chapter, we suggest an innovative pedagogical approach that is based on SCT and does not predetermine the directness of language feedback provided to learners. Rather, the tutor dynamically assesses the learner's needs for direct (i.e., explicit) versus indirect (i.e., implicit) feedback and provides assistance accordingly based a regulatory scale that moves gradually from implicit to more explicit assistance. I will explicate how this approach can be used by looking at the nature of collaboration between the tutor and tutee in this process.

An Innovative Pedagogical Approach to Providing Linguistic Feedback Based on Sociocultural Theory

Prior to this explication, I will review three concepts in SCT that are central to the discussion in the rest of the chapter: regulation, zone of proximal development (ZPD), and contingent and graduated assistance. These concepts conform to the writing center's philosophy of developing learner independence and allow tutors the flexibility to move back and forth between direct and indirect assistance. In terms of regulation, SCT states that the primary goal of learning is to achieve self-regulation or accomplish a task with little or no external assistance. In order to develop self-regulation, learners usually move through three stages. The first stage is object-regulation; that is, children or individuals use objects to regulate a mental activity in order to complete a task (e.g., using blocks to aid counting). The second stage is other-regulation; in other words, individuals receive external support from more capable others to regulate mental activities. The third stage is self-regulation, and when individuals have reached this stage, they usually can accomplish tasks independently (Lantolf & Thorne, 2007).

The second key concept is ZPD, or in Vygotsky's words, "the distance between the actual developmental level as determined by independent problem-solving and the level of potential development as determined through problem-solving under adult guidance or in collaboration with more capable peers" (in Aljaafreh & Lantolf, 1994, p. 468). This concept provides a framework that brings together a wide array of elements in the process of learning, such as the learner, the teacher or the tutor, their resources, their goals, and their social, cultural, and historical backgrounds. More importantly, learners are able to reach their potential level in collaboration with more skilled others such as teachers or peers. In other words, other-regulation is an important stage prior to actual development or self-regulation.

This other-regulation within the framework of ZPD, from the perspective of SCT, is not random; rather, it is graduated and contingent. *Graduation*, according to Aljaafreh and Lantolf (1994), requires that the skilled other moves gradually from indirect or implicit, strategic assistance to more concrete, specific, direct and explicit assistance. The appropriate level of assistance (either implicit or explicit) is determined by the response patterns of the learner in a joint, dialogic activity. *Contingency* entails that assistance be provided when required and withdrawn when the learner demonstrates signs of self-regulation or the ability to complete a task independently.

The ZPD provides a framework in which the more experienced interlocutor could negotiate orally with the learner the appropriate level of assistance needed.

Collaborative dialogue is a hallmark of writing center tutoring, and as such, theoretically speaking and also as evidenced by recent research (e.g., Aljaafreh & Lantolf, 1994; Nassaji & Swain, 2000), one-to-one tutoring in the ZPD facilitates individualized learning and develops linguistic proficiency in learners. This framework is effective and innovative because it affords the tutor the flexibility to provide both implicit and explicit feedback based on the needs of the learner and the tutor's ongoing assessment of them, not simply the tutor's procedural beliefs. When the assistance is graduated and contingent, it helps the learner to reach his or her full potential, and therefore self-regulation can be attained. To illustrate how self-regulation can be achieved in the ZPD, we use Figure 1 (based on the regulatory scale from Aljaafreh & Lantolf) to demonstrate how a ZPD could be efficiently negotiated between the tutor and the tutee by the tutor's providing contingent, implicit to gradually more explicit assistance.

The following dialogues illustrate the flexibility of applying the above steps in a typical tutoring session. In the first example, the dialogic interaction results in tutee self-regulation with minimal explicit instruction.

Example 1

1. T (utor): Please read the second sentence in this paragraph.
2. S (tudent): Okay.
3. T: Is there anything wrong with this sentence?
4. S: The spelling of *pedogogical*?

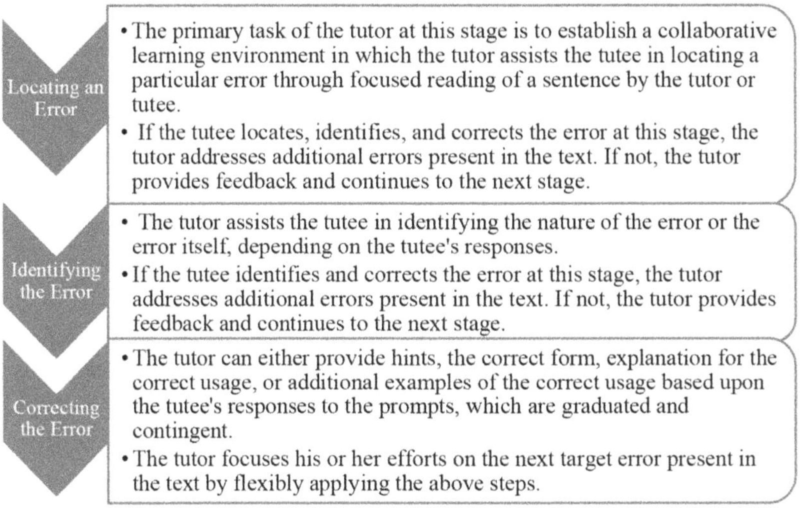
Locating an Error
• The primary task of the tutor at this stage is to establish a collaborative learning environment in which the tutor assists the tutee in locating a particular error through focused reading of a sentence by the tutor or tutee.
• If the tutee locates, identifies, and corrects the error at this stage, the tutor addresses additional errors present in the text. If not, the tutor provides feedback and continues to the next stage.
Identifying the Error
• The tutor assists the tutee in identifying the nature of the error or the error itself, depending on the tutee's responses.
• If the tutee identifies and corrects the error at this stage, the tutor addresses additional errors present in the text. If not, the tutor provides feedback and continues to the next stage.
Correcting the Error
• The tutor can either provide hints, the correct form, explanation for the correct usage, or additional examples of the correct usage based upon the tutee's responses to the prompts, which are graduated and contingent.
• The tutor focuses his or her efforts on the next target error present in the text by flexibly applying the above steps.

Figure 1. Graduated and contingent assistance in the learner's zone of proximal development

5. T: How should it be spelled?
6. S: *Pedagogical*?
7. T: Correct, but there are some other problems that we agreed to focus on.
8. S: Punctuation?
9. T: Your punctuation is correct.
10. S: *An* needs to be *a*?
11. T: You have the correct article there.
12. S: I'm really having trouble finding this error.
13. T: Look at this phrase here (pointing to the problematic text).
14. S: Okay. Hmmm, *have utilize*?
15. T: Yes.
16. S: That doesn't sound right.
17. T: What's wrong with it?
18. S: The tense isn't right.
19. T: How so?
20. S: I think that *have been utilizing* sounds better. Does it?
21. T: What do you think?
22. S: It's right.
23. T: That is correct. Let's continue with the remaining text.

However, if self-regulation is not attained with tutor assistance at the first stage (i.e., locating an error), the tutor has the flexibility to provide more explicit assistance, as demonstrated in the next example (continued from Line 15 in Example 1).

Example 2

1. S: *Have utilize* sounds good to me.
2. T: There is something wrong with the verb tense here.
3. S: I think *have utilizing* sounds better. Does it?
4. T: Not really. You can't use the word *have* with the base form of a verb or the present participle of the verb.
5. S: That's right. Sorry! I forgot. I think I can use *have utilized* or *have been utilizing. Have been utilizing* seems better.
6. T: You got it. Excellent!

In the second example, the tutee has attained self-regulation with assistance at Stage 2—identifying the error. In other words, right after the tutor identifies the error, the tutee is able to correct the error by himself or herself. In practice, some students may need more explicit assistance in correcting the error, as shown in the following example (continued from Line 4 in Example 2).

Example 3

1. S: Hmmm? You mean I should use *have utilized*? Can I use *have utilized*?

2. T: Well, you actually need the present perfect progressive form of the verb. You need something that states the teachers have used it in the past and continue to do so.
3. S: I don't know what that means exactly.
4. T: You should say, *The teachers have been utilizing a pedagogical approach that facilitates learning in an EFL setting.*
5. S: Oh. Why is *have been utilizing* better than *have utilized*?
6. T: *Have been utilizing* is appropriate here because the teachers have and continue to use the same pedagogy. With *have utilized*, you are not sure whether the teachers are continuing to do that.
7. S: I see.
8. T: Can you locate a similar example in your paper?
9. S: I should have used *have been* here because the students have and continue to demonstrate a lack of comprehension.
10. T: Good. Let's continue with the remaining text.

In the third example, the dialogic interaction may not have resulted in tutee self-regulation, even after graduated and contingent implicit to explicit instruction. Therefore, the tutor provides explicit explanations and examples of correct usage in an effort to facilitate learning.

The above vignettes demonstrate an ideal environment that offers the flexibility to apply graduated and contingent assistance, which can be either implicit or explicit based on the tutee's ZPD, to facilitate self-regulation. Problematic linguistic features are assessed by the tutor and the tutee is afforded the opportunity to self-regulate. When self-regulation does not occur at the beginning of the discussion of an error, the tutor utilizes a more explicit dialogic pedagogy. This mediated and progressively scaffolded interaction provides a means for the student to learn and thus potentially achieve self-regulation, which is different from the traditional writing center pedagogy that predetermines the directness or non-directness of feedback.

CONCLUSION

In conclusion, given the unique nature of second language writers and their writing, university writing centers must make changes to their tutoring methods – which may have worked well with native English-speaking students – and address ESL students' learning needs in the areas of both writing and language development.

As discussed previously, the benefits of the ideal learning environment offered by the UWC may not be fully realized if writing centers fail to modify their pedagogical approach to suit L2 students' needs. The incongruence between existing UWC pedagogy and the clients they serve can be rectified by implementing the above pedagogical approach that conform to current SLA theory. In particular, adopting a ZPD-centered approach throughout the tutoring session is paramount to student internalization of other-regulation and achieve self-regulation. Graduated and contingent assistance is the means to accomplish this end, which is learner independence—the primary goal of university writing center.

REFERENCES

Aljaafreh, A., & Lantolf, J. P. (1994). Negative feedback as regulation and second language learning in the zone of Proximal development. *Modern Language Journal, 78*(4), 465.

Blau, S., Hall, J., & Sparks, S. (2002). Guilt-free tutoring: Rethinking how we tutor Non-Native-English-Speaking students. *Writing Center Journal, 23*(1), 23–44.

Cumming, A. (1998). Theoretical perspectives on writing. *Annual Review of Applied Linguistics, 18*, 61–78.

Gillespie, P., & Lerner, N. (2000). *The Allyn and Bacon guide to peer tutoring*. Needham Heights, MA: Allyn and Bacon.

Harris, M. (1997). Cultural conflicts in the writing center: Expectations and assumptions of ESL students. In C. Severino & J. C. Guerra (Eds.), *Writing in multicultural settings* (pp. 220–233). New York, NY: MLA.

Harris, M., & Silva, T. (1993). Tutoring ESL students: Issues and options. *College Composition and Communication, 44*(4), 525–537.

Hyland, K. (2003). *Second language writing*. Cambridge, UK: Cambridge University Press.

Jones, C. (2001). The relationship between writing centers and improvement in writing ability: An assessment of the literature. *Education, 122*(1), 3.

Lantolf, J. P., & Thorne, S. L. (2007). Sociocultural theory and second language learning. In B. VanPatten & J. Williams (Eds.), *Theories in second language acquisition: An introduction* (pp. 201–224). Mahwah, NJ: Lawrence Erlbaum.

Moussu, L. (2013). Let's talk! ESL students' needs and writing center philosophy. *TESL Canada Journal, 30*(2), 55–68.

Myers, S. A. (2003). Reassessing the 'Proofreading Trap': ESL tutoring and writing instruction. *Writing Center Journal, 24*(1), 51–70.

Nassaji, H., & Swain, M. (2000). A Vygotskian perspective on corrective feedback in L2: The effect of random versus negotiated help on the learning of English articles. *Language Awareness, 9*(1), 34–51.

North, S. M. (1984). The idea of a writing center. *College English, 46*(5), 433–446.

Powers, J. K., & Nelson, J. V. (1995). L2 writers and the writing center: A national survey of writing center conferencing at graduate institutions. *Journal of Second Language Writing, 4*(2), 113–138.

Severino, C. (2009). Avoiding appropriation. *ESL Writers: A Guide for Writing Center Tutors, 2.*

Taylor, V. G. G. (2007). *The balance of rhetoric and linguistics: A study of second language writing center tutorials* (Doctoral dissertation). Purdue University, West Lafayette, IN.

Ally A. Zhou
Oklahoma City University

Xiaomin Hu
Oklahoma City University

ROBIN BEYEA

30. ASSESSING CREATIVITY IN THE SCHOOL CLASSROOM

INTRODUCTION

The current climate of accountability and efficiency in education systems across the Western world has pushed assessment to the forefront of the teaching practice (Volante, 2005). The data collected from standardized tests is used to measure not only student learning, but also to appraise the efficacy of teachers and schools (Government New Brunswick, n.d.). This culture of assessment has become so pervasive that classroom learning that is not directly evaluated and quantified is often seen as superfluous and even dispensable. The problem with this focus on assessment is that some learning lends itself more easily to common testing while other essential learnings are more difficult to measure. As an elementary school teacher, much of my day is spent teaching the "hidden-curriculum". Along with core curricular subjects such as literacy, mathematics and science, students at the elementary level also learn and practice many skills, attitudes and behaviours, such as teamwork, respect, self-esteem, independence, citizenship, tolerance, and conflict resolution, to name a few. These skills and behaviours are important for students as they are necessary for their continued success in school and in the larger world, but they are difficult to assess in a traditional manner.

An important skill which lies between the core and hidden curricula is creativity. Creativity is a skill that requires instruction and practice. It is critical that students from grades K-12 be instructed in creativity and creative thinking in order for them to be successful, both personally and professionally, in the larger world beyond school (Azzam, 2009). In elementary school, students should be given many opportunities to learn and practice creativity, but the assessment of their development in this area should not follow the model of standardized testing. Instead, the assessment of creativity at the elementary level should be based on qualitative observational data and self-reflection. The goal of assessing creativity at this level should be to examine an individual's creative growth rather than compare their achievement with their peers.

In the headline article of the Business Section of the *Daily Gleaner* the entrepreneurs described are representative of successful business design in the contemporary globalized economy. *Sixty-Five York* is a group of five small businesses sharing a work-space and collaborating to "provide, a range of complementary services including website design, photography, event promotion and copywriting" (Chase, 2015, p. D6).

J. B. Cummings & M. L. Blatherwick (Eds.), Creative Dimensions of Teaching and Learning in the 21st Century, 295–299.

They operate in creativity – producing images, design and story. These entrepreneurs exemplify the fundamental changes which have been occurring in the economies of developed countries over the past few decades. The purview of creativity is no longer limited to art; it is "the main engine of the innovation of economy and source of social changes in [the] contemporary world" (Karwowski, Gralewski, Lebuda, & Wiśniewska, 2006, p. 57). According to Florida (2002, p. 44), "today's economy is fundamentally a Creative Economy", where the basic elements are no longer labor and natural resources, but knowledge and innovation.

This new economic period has been labeled the "Conceptual Age" by Daniel Pink (2006). According to Pink, the Conceptual Age has come about because of the technological advances of the two previous ages: the Industrial Age and the Information Age. These advances have created our contemporary economic reality: The unskilled manufacturing jobs of the Industrial Age have largely been taken over by automation, while the more highly skilled knowledge sector careers of the Information Age have been shipped overseas. For Western businesses to survive in this new economic age, they must differentiate their products in a value-added manner. This cannot be accomplished by focusing on the skills of the past century. The skills needed to succeed in this new age will be the ability to craft, design, persuade and create. Successful individuals and organizations will need to be creative.

Traditionally, creativity was viewed as an aspect of intelligence that was innate. Individuals were either born with creative abilities or without them. Fortunately, the concept of creativity is no longer as exclusive as it was once. There is a large body of research confirming that creativity can be developed in the individual (Karwowski et al., 2006). As any other subject taught in school, the development of creativity requires direct instruction, learning time and practice.

Since creativity plays such a pivotal role in the modern economy, and since it is not an innate ability, but one that can be learned and developed, it follows that creativity can and should be taught in schools. In fact, Sawyer (2006, p. 47) states: "in today's knowledge societies, one of the key missions of the schools is to educate for creativity". While creativity and creative thinking can and should be woven across the curriculum and incorporated into all subject areas, its importance demands that it also be treated as a field of study in its own right. For creativity to be valued as an area of academic study, and for it to be taught effectively, it must also be assessed. For teachers to gauge student learning and development, and to assess if pedagogical practices are effective, then the teaching of creativity should be paired with constructive assessment practices.

The field of assessing creativity presents an exhaustive body of literature for both academic and personal use. These tests cover the assessment of many of the different elements of creativity, such as: creative thinking, problem-solving, fluency, originality, elaboration, divergent thinking, and synthesis (Barbot, Besançon, & Lubart, 2011).[1] A quick Google search reveals a wide variety of "layman's creativity tests" meant to evaluate one's own creativity. Most of the questions on these tests are either self-assessment inventories (i.e., 'I do/do not enjoy thinking of new designs for products') or divergent thinking tasks such as those developed for creativity tests in the 1960's and 70's (i.e., 'How many creative uses for a brick can you think of in 1 minute?'). These older tests of creativity, such as the Torrance Test of Creative Thinking, developed by E. Paul Torrance in 1966, the Creativity Assessment Packet, developed by Frank Williams in 1980, and the Structure of the Intellect Learning Abilities Test, developed by J. Paul Guilford in 1969, were created to measure an individual's creative potential, and largely report on divergent thinking abilities (Barbot et al., 2011; Cooper, 1991). While these tests are interesting and fun to take, they are not designed to measure learning and growth; rather, they are designed to measure "innate abilities". As such, they are not useful for classroom purposes. Unfortunately, divergent thinking is still the most common measure of creativity, and is still widely used to measure creative ability in the school system (Kaufman & Baer, 2012).

Some noteworthy examples of new approaches to assessing creativity include the Rainbow Project and the CAT-Consensual Assessment Technique. The Rainbow Project was developed as a test to enhance the SAT by adding assessments of analytical, practical and creative skills. It is based on the "triarchic theory of successful intelligence" developed by Sternberg, and is meant to broaden the range of skills that are tested on the SAT – a college readiness exam. The traditional SAT measures analytical and memory skills. Sternberg's theory goes beyond this limited measure of intelligence to also include practical and creative skills. Test items require individuals to deal with relatively novel situations that call for both convergent and divergent thinking. The Sternberg Triarchic Abilities Test (STAT) is a multiple-choice style test measuring analytical, practical and creative skills. The Rainbow Project enhanced the Sternberg model by adding open-ended performance tasks which require test subjects to use higher order thinking skills such as analysis, synthesis and evaluation in their responses while also allowing them more freedom in the expression of their thoughts and ideas (Sternberg et el., 2006).

The CAT-Consensual Assessment Technique is a very different type of test. It does not measure skills or traits that are associated with creativity. It assesses actual creative performance. All subjects are given the same basic instructions and if necessary the same materials, and asked to create some kind of product (a sculpture, a poem, a musical composition or even an experimental design). Experts in the particular domain of the creation (i.e, creative writers, poets, composers or visual artists, depending on the domain) are brought together to judge the creativity of the artifact. There are no rubrics or checklists, it is purely a subjective analysis based on the expertise of the panel of judges, and experts work independently so as not to influence each other. The judges are not required to defend or justify their ranking. Judges are asked to use their expertise in the particular domain in question to rate the individual products in relation to one another (Baer & McKool, 2009). In one example, students were given a drawing of a girl and a boy and asked to write a story where the girl and the boy were characters. There is no attempt to measure skills, attributes or dispositions that may be theoretically linked to creativity. The focus is instead on the creativity of the finished product the subject has produced as envisioned by leaders within the field.

Both the Rainbow Project and the CAT assessment demonstrate a more-multifaceted view of assessing creativity than previous tools. They both also present a manner of assessing creativity that focuses on creative products rather than creative propensity. While these assessments may be useful at higher levels of education, they do not fit the needs of elementary school teachers. The CAT assessment could be used as a measure of creativity for an end product after a unit of study in college or university, but it is not feasible in the public-school system as the judges must be experts in the domain being assessed. This type of evaluation is also not necessary at the elementary level, where students are only beginning to learn skills in many different creative domains. At this level, it is as important to provide learners with evaluative feedback regarding not only the creative product, but also the process of creation. Aspects of the Rainbow Project are also valuable for assessing creativity more broadly as an aspect of success in other fields of study, but these tests rely too heavily on verbal-linguistic skills, which are still being developed at the elementary level.

Teaching, fostering and encouraging creativity is vital to the development of children, not only for their benefit as workers in the new economy, but also for their sense of self-fulfillment and development as lifelong learners. Creativity must be seen not as an "add-on" in different subject areas, but as a subject in its own right – a discipline that is taught, practiced and *assessed.* Unfortunately, creativity cannot be assessed through standardized measures. The assessment of creativity at the elementary level must consider the process as well as the product. The actual assessment should be rubric-based, and accompanied by qualitative observational information. Each creative assignment must be paired with an assessment rubric designed specifically for the project, incorporating the creative process, use of materials, attitudes and outcomes; as well as a self-reflection portion allowing students to comment on what they liked about their work and what they might have done differently. At the elementary level, creativity should be fostered and encouraged, discussed and practiced; formal, standardized assessments do not suit these goals.

NOTE

[1] Some examples of assessments of creativity have been included in the appendix and the display.

REFERENCES

Azzam, A. M. (2009). Why creativity now? A conversation with Sir Ken Robinson. *Educational Leadership, 67*(1), 22–26.

Baer, J., & McKool, S. (2009). Assessing creativity using the consensual assessment. In C. Schreiner (Ed.), *Handbook of assessment technologies, methods and applications in higher education* (pp. 65–77). Hershey, PA: IGI Global.

Barbot, B., Besançon, M., & Lubart, T. I. (2011). Assessing creativity in the classroom. The *Open Education Journal, 4*, 58–66.

Chase, S. (2015, January 24). Creative studio Sixty-Five York thrives downtown. *The Daily Gleaner – Business*, p. D6

Cooper, E. (1991). A critique of six measures for assessing creativity. *The Journal of Creative Behavior, 25*(3), 194–204.

Florida, R. (2002). *The rise of the creative class and how it's transforming work, leisure, community and everyday life*. New York, NY: Basic Books.

Government New Brunswick-Department of Education and Early Childhood Development. (n.d.). *Provincial assessments function as a reasonable and cost-effective gauge of an individual student's or school's overall achievement.* Retrieved from http://www.gnb.ca/0000/anglophone-e.asp#e

Karwowski, M., Gralewski, J., Lebuda, I., & Wiśniewska, E. (2006). Creative teaching of creativity teachers: Polish perspective. *Thinking Skills and Creativity, 2*(1), 57–61.

Kaufman, J. C., Plucker, J., & Russell C. (2012). Identifying and assessing creativity as a component of giftedness. *Journal of Psychological Assessment, 30*(1), 60–73.

Pink, D. H. (2006). *A whole new mind: Why right-brainers will rule the future*. New York, NY: Riverhead Books.

Sawyer, R. K. (2006). Educating for innovation. *Thinking Skills and Creativity, 1*(1), 41–48.

Sternberg, R. J., & Collaborators, T. R. P. (2006). The rainbow project: Enhancing the SAT through assessments of analytical, practical, and creative skills. *Intelligence, 34*(4), 321–350.

Volante, D. (2005). Accountability, student assessment, and the need for a comprehensive approach. *IEJLL: International Electronic Journal for Leadership in Learning, 9*(6).

Robin Beyea
University of New Brunswick

APPENDIX

The Rainbow Project-Example Test Items:

1. *Cartoons*: participants were given New Yorker cartoons without their captions and asked to provide a caption for three of these. The responses were rated by 'trained' judges on cleverness, humor, and originality, These scores were combined to produce a combined creativity score (Sternberg et al., p. 327).
2. *Written Stories:* participants were given 30 minutes to write two stories based on one of the titles provided: "A Fifth Chance," "2983," "Beyond the Edge," "The Octopus's Sneakers," "It's Moving Backwards," and "Not Enough Time". The stories were similarly assessed by a team of judges in reference to originality, complexity, emotional evocativeness, and descriptiveness.
3. *Oral Stories:* Participants were given a choice among 5 sheets of paper which each contained an assortment of images linked by a common them – they were given 15 minutes to develop a short story and dictate it into a voice recorder. The oral stories were evaluated in the same manner as the written ones (Sternberg et al., p. 328).

LORRAINE LASMANIS

31. LANGUAGE ACQUISITION THROUGH PERSONAL STORY WRITING

A Learner Book Project

INTRODUCTION

To be a guide on the side, or a sage on the stage – that is the question.

This was my pedagogical guiding principle. I have come to realize that effective teachers select the approach that works best for them and for the content that they are teaching. The article titled "*From Sage on the Stage to Guide on the Side*" (King, 1993) written some twenty plus years ago has come to represent a big debate in education reform over the years. Educators still argue about the merits of traditional teaching (teacher-directed) versus constructivist (student-directed) teaching and learning approaches. I think that most educators would agree that both approaches are needed for successful learning to take place.

The Language Experience Approach (LEA) to language learning, which balances both teacher-directed and student-directed methodology, has proven to be the most effective learning and teaching pedagogy that I have witnessed while working in the classroom over many years with a variety of students at beginning stages of second language acquisition. When the book project that I am about to describe was launched in 1991, there were very limited appropriate reading materials available for English as a Second Language (ESL) learners. It was critical to provide meaningful language learning resources to develop language acquisition. Language learning materials in the form of student-generated and written stories was "an idea whose time had come". It fit the formula of the Language Experience Approach and therefore was accepted as a valid and effective teaching tool.

Background

The LEA approach is as diverse in practice as its practitioners. Nonetheless, some characteristics remain consistent (Hall, 1970):

- Materials are learner-generated.
- All communication skills – reading, writing, listening, and speaking – are integrated.

J. B. Cummings & M. L. Blatherwick (Eds.), Creative Dimensions of Teaching and Learning in the 21st Century, 301–306.

- Difficulty of vocabulary and grammar are determined by the learners own language use.
- Learning and teaching are personalized, communicative, creative.

Krashen and Terrell (1983) recommend two criteria for determining whether reading materials are appropriate for ESL learners: The reading must be (1) at a comprehensible level of complexity and (2) interesting to the reader. Reading texts originating from learners' experiences meet these two criteria because (1) the degree of complexity is determined by the learner's own language, and (2) the texts relate to the learner's personal interests.

Both criteria are of particular importance in adult beginning ESL classes, where the paucity of reading materials can be problematic. Many books written in simplified English are either too juvenile or too uninteresting to be considered appropriate reading material for adults (Taylor, 2000). These criteria guided the development of the LEA book project based on ESL learners' personal narratives that I describe below.

Personal anecdotes or short stories about us or people we know comprise an important part of our lives, and can be drawn on as a valuable resource for ESL classes. Stories involve the skills of listening, reading, speaking and writing. Storytelling allows learners to practice asking questions to elicit information, to hear the rhythm of the language and to decode the sound system, to negotiate grammar, learn new vocabulary and retell events in sequence, to infer meaning from context, predict what might happen next…all of which facilitates authentic language learning where grammar points are reinforced and follow-up skills are eagerly completed. Students are captivated by the sharing of experiences of one another in a supportive community environment, and become motivated to write and are thankful for the opportunity to share their customs and cultures, descriptions of family members, feelings about Canada, and the treasured memories they carry with them. In other words, storytelling in ESL provides an exciting medium which allows the whole language process to take place. My inspiration to publish their stories has come from the enthusiastic response of the learners. Their inspiration to write has come from the understanding that they have interesting and important things to share.

Story Telling Approach

Story telling employs constructivist methodology in which the teacher begins with asking students to recall what they already know about the subject. Then they will involve the students in an activity that will take them beyond what they currently know. The students must actively engage in the learning process by doing something. Writing a story is the perfect medium for pairing what they already know with the language they are learning, giving them an opportunity to practice and further develop their language skills.

This constructivist, student-directed learning model requires active input and cognitive effort by students and, in so doing, aids retention of new material. The role of the teacher in student-centered learning is to facilitate the students' learning by providing a framework that facilitates it – for example, projects that involve writing stories, reports, publishing web pages, creating surveys for conducting research, creating artwork, and organizing events. All of these activities were put into practice and resulted in a book of illustrated stories written by the students – ESL and literacy students – for the students. The story book was called *From Our Hearts A Collection of Personal Life Stories from the Students of St. Louis Adult Learning Centre.*

This began as a writing project that gave our creative and imaginative thinkers a vehicle in which to accomplish their goals of being able to clearly communicate in English. They could voice their ideas, their life experiences; freely express themselves in a safe and inviting environment and very practically put into meaningful practice their developing English language skills.

Description of the Writing Project and How It Was Implemented

In February 1991, the time had come to tackle the limited availability of appropriate language learning materials for literacy and beginner ESL learners. A project to publish a learner-written reader for literacy and ESL students was started. The idea was to empower students with a sense of pride and ownership while they acquired the necessary skills that would lead to functional literacy.

The project coordinator took on the responsibilities of managing the funding once the proposal was written and funding acquired from the National Literacy Secretariat. I was the project facilitator and had the pleasure of going to all of the ESL classrooms to introduce the idea of creating a book of multi-cultural stories of life experiences written by the students, which could be used as a learning resource for the students.

I entered the classrooms armed with chart paper, colored markers, and a suggested list of writing topics to which I invited the students to add their own. The topics included such themes as jobs, memories, special people in our lives, traditions, leaving home/coming to Canada, and more. The students were very excited about becoming writers, publishers and illustrators and participated enthusiastically in the writing workshops that I had initiated. The workshops continued for the next few months. The classes were divided into working groups and each group contained a story teller, one or two scribes (to compare content), a listener/questioner, and an illustrator. Once they agreed on a topic that interested them, the students wrote, illustrated, read aloud and peer edited. The more advanced ESL classes did a little more intensive work with the drafts once they were written. They read in groups to examine themes, literary techniques and writing models and vocabulary usage. The roles in these groups differed slightly with an (a) *instigator* – one who raises issues for the group to discuss based on reading, (b) *linguist* – who draws attention to interesting words in the story and discusses the meanings with the group, (c) *literary artist* – who chooses an event or mood conveyed in the reading and illustrates it for the group, (d) literary critic – who finds examples of effective use of literacy techniques in a passage and conversely passages that are problematic, (e) *questioner* – who presents puzzling issues related to personal response as well as content, (f) *re-teller* – who summarizes the reading for the group, and (g) *text-enricher* – who supports the text by bringing in other related stories or non-fiction articles. Finally, the stories and pictures were presented in groups to the class. They were received with warmth, compassion, good natured laughter and discussion.

The students took up the challenge and, for months, stories were popping up like rabbits out of a hat as teachers followed up the exercise with more writing, editing and reading practice. By April, we had received 200 written stories! A committee of students and instructors had the difficult task of choosing 21 stories and a title for the first publication *From Our Hearts*. We spent many hours with the final editing, organizing into themes and presenting a literacy-friendly layout.

Following the printing of the book of collected stories, and the ceremonial inauguration, we launched into producing an accompanying workbook in order to extend the language learning experience. The rationale for the workbook was also informed by the LEA approach, particularly the following from "Features of the Language Experience Approach" by Marcia Taylor (2000).

Extending the experience

Many language and literacy activities beyond rereading can be based on the written text. The following possibilities can be selected and adapted according to learners' proficiency levels.

With beginners, teachers can:

- have students copy the story themselves;
- have students match words with pictures or definitions;
- delete every nth word (4th, 5th, 6th, etc.) to create a cloze exercise, Have the students fill in the blanks either with or without the assistance of a word bank, depending on their literacy level;
- select words from the story for vocabulary, spelling, or sound-symbol correspondence activities;
- use the texts to review a grammar point, such as sequence of tenses, word order, or pronoun referents;
- dictate the story for learners to write;
- write the sentences in scrambled order and have students rewrite them, restoring the correct sequence;
- scramble key words and have students unscramble them.

More advanced learners can:

- use the group-produced text as the basis for individually written texts about the same topic, about a similar experience, or as a critique of this experience. Then they might read each other's texts;
- revise and edit the texts and prepare them for publication;

- read other texts related to the topic;
- generate comprehension questions for classmates to answer;
- write other types of texts-songs, poems, letters (for example, a letter to the editor), or directions for how to do something.

In a class with learners at different proficiency levels, the teacher can use the more basic activities with the learners at lower levels while the more proficient learners work on the more advanced activities individually or in groups with less teacher help.

CONCLUSION

Although the LEA was developed primarily as a tool for reading development, this technique can be used successfully to develop listening, speaking, and writing as well. This integrated approach is unique in that it begins with students' individual or shared experiences as a basis for discussion, writing, and finally reading. As students see their personal experiences transcribed into the written word, they also gain a greater understanding of the processes of writing and reading and can make the bridge to reading and writing independently (Taylor, 2000).

As project facilitator, I enlisted the talents of several teachers on staff and together we brainstormed a variety of language learning activities ranging in levels of difficulty. We took seven stories each and worked independently to compile a draft and pilot it with several ESL and LBS (Literacy and Basic Skills) classes. We used the feedback we received from the teachers and students to edit the exercises. Again, layout and presentation were major considerations as our target audience defined by our funders was the literacy learner, both LBS and ESL.

The workbook exercises were developed co-operatively by instructors and students. As a team, we were able to generate a creative variety of workbook exercises which corresponded to each of the stories. The student-written stories were our most valuable resource in terms of content and context. Both the vocabulary and the topics were relevant and appropriate for adult learners. Instructors and students had a lot of fun developing language learning activities for the stories.

The workbook included reading comprehension exercises for oral and written responses, spelling, vocabulary and grammar. Certain exercises focussed on the development of critical and divergent thinking skills as well as discussion and expression of opinions and ideas. The exercises were designed to stimulate both lower level thinking skills such as observation and recall, and the higher level interpretive, critical and divergent thinking skills.

The workbook lessons matched the order of themes in the reader, which were organized to offer an inviting blend of variety and balance in topics, length and level of difficulty. Each workbook exercise progressed from simple comprehension, grammar, spelling and vocabulary building exercises, to extended writing and discussion activities.

The greatest challenge was to create exercises which met a variety of student skill levels, interests and learning styles. In this challenge, we saw an opportunity for our learners to have a voice and ownership in the workbook as well. We decided to include adult learners in a pilot test of the exercises before publishing the workbook, inviting input and feedback. They were extremely helpful with their comments, suggestions and constructive criticism. As a result, there is something appealing or useful in each story and workbook exercise for every student, no matter how short or long, easy or advanced the story. These stories and accompanying workbook have gone on to inspire many other teachers and learners to develop their own learner stories and activities.

The learner story writing project described here and its progeny, *From Our Hearts*, are vibrant examples of Jim Cummins' advice to educators to draw on learners' own cultural knowledge and experiences to enhance literacy engagement and learning. According to Jim Cummins in his presentation about promoting literacy in multicultural contexts (2007):

> Ontario educators have demonstrated that ESL students' cultural knowledge and language abilities can be mobilized within the classroom as important tools for learning and as resources to fuel literacy engagement. (p. 4)

The *From our Hearts* book project also represents the successful implementation and outcome of *The Natural Approach: Language Acquisition in the Classroom* (Krashen & Terrell, 1983). This approach "levels the playing field", so to speak, for learners of varying aptitudes in order to achieve the goal of developing communication skills in the target language while simultaneously elevating learners' self-confidence, and validating, and recognizing their prior knowledge, identities, and experiences. As Krashen & Terrell (1983) put it: "the acquisition-oriented second language classroom minimizes individual differences in aptitude" thereby making all students acquirers of communication skills. What could be more desirable for "the guide on the side"!

REFERENCES

Cummins, J. (2007). *What works? Research into practice*. Literacy and Numeracy Secretariat, Ontario Ministry of Education. Toronto, Ontario, Canada: Queen's Printer of Ontario.

Hall, M. A. (1970*). Teaching reading as a language experience*. Columbus, OH: Charles Merrill.

King, A. (1993). From sage on the stage to guide on the side. *College Teaching, 41*(1), 30–35.

Krashen, S. D., & Terrell, T. D. (1983). *The natural approach: Language acquisition in the classroom*. Hayward, CA: Alemany Press.

Taylor, M. (2000). Features of the language experience approach. *JobLink*. Retrieved from http://www.cal.org/caela/esl_resources/digests/LEA.html

Lorraine Lasmanis
Waterloo Region Catholic School Board
Waterloo Ontario

TREVOR STRONG

32. A CREATIVE PROCESS

Using Songwriting to Develop Creativity

INTRODUCTION

Creativity is popular. Schools want to teach it; parents want their kids to have it; and businesses want to harness it, although usually under the cover of the more Darwinian-sounding word "innovation". The way ahead seems clear: we should make people creative. But how to do that? It should come as no surprise that there is no single agreed upon way to teach creativity; there isn't even a definitive meaning of the word – one group of researchers found 42 different definitions of "creativity" in the literature (Kampylis & Valtanan, 2010). So I could go down the rabbit-hole and talk about what creativity is and isn't and could be, but that would go on forever and in circles. Instead, I shall walk past the hole for now and tell you about who I am and how I approach teaching creativity.

My Creative Experience

Prior to becoming a creativity-focused educator I enjoyed (and still enjoy) a career as a writer, performer, and humorist. I'm in a group called *The Arrogant Worms* where I make and perform comedy songs. I'm the author of several very silly books; and I sing and play guitar. This experience gives me a direct and practical approach to creativity.

More recently, I returned to university and got a Bachelor of Education in the Artist in Community Education stream from Queen's University and, soon after that, a Master of Education degree (also from Queen's) where I researched the role of creativity and humor in education. This experience gave me a better understanding of how I create and how I might go about helping others be creative. Since then I've spent a lot of my time visiting classrooms as an "artist in the school." In this role, I go into classrooms and encourage students to create in the realms of humor, story, and song. These visits can be anywhere from an hour-long workshop to a unit spread over several weeks. My goal is always the same: getting students to make or create something.

Skills and Process

I view creative work as a combination of two separate, but overlapping things:

J. B. Cummings & M. L. Blatherwick (Eds.), Creative Dimensions of Teaching and Learning in the 21st Century, 307–314.

Technical prowess. This is learned skill. Sometimes it is a physical ability like the ability to move your fingers adeptly enough to play the piano and sometimes it is a mental skill like knowing musical theory.

Coming up with stuff. I am sorry to use such a… technical term, but this is really what it boils down to. You could have a great deal of technical ability and yet not be able to do anything but repeat what is given to you or what has already been done. Also, you could have no technical ability and come up with something very interesting but, technically speaking, a disaster. "Coming up with stuff" is a result of your frame of mind more than anything else. It is an ability to "play", to hold multiple meanings and interpretations simultaneously, and to see the process of creation through.

Now of course these two things aren't really separate; they overlap, interact, and affect each other and, in experienced creative folks, can become impossible to divide. Still, I find this framework helpful as my work focusses mostly on the "coming up with stuff" part of creativity, especially when dealing with learners who might not consider themselves "creative."

Conceptual Framework: Creativity as a Process

Early theories about creativity often considered it a talent, as something an individual either did or did not have, and focused mainly on creative giants such as Mozart and Einstein (Plucker, Beghetto, & Dow, 2004). This view of creativity as a fixed, unchangeable attribute has given way to the idea that creativity, although influenced by personal attributes, is best understood as a process that all people use to generate new and useful ideas (Plucker et al., 2004). Implicit in this conception of creativity as a process is that this process can be understood and taught.

The idea of creativity as a process, and the importance of teaching it, has been popularized by many writers, including Sir Ken Robinson. In his book *Out of Our Minds* he describes creativity as involving the "dynamic interplay between generating ideas and making judgments about them" (Robinson, 2001, p. 133), and stresses that "creativity flourishes when there is a systemic strategy to promote it" (Robinson, 2001, p. 12). Many schools are trying to put these systemic strategies into place. The Ontario Arts Curriculum (2009, p. 21) devotes several pages to understanding "the creative process" and the "feedback and reflection" that "take place throughout."

More directly pertinent to my teaching practice is the work of Peter Elbow (2000), a writing theorist and practitioner who advocates for a process-based approach. He believes anyone can write if given the right process is established. Like Robinson, Elbow describes creation as involving two different states of mind – both "a fertile, inventive, yea-saying" mentality and a "critical, ney-saying, skeptical" one (p. xiv). For him writing is most easily created when "we make separate arenas" for these two mentalities so they can "flourish on their own and even encourage each other" (p. xiv). Central then, to the process of writing, is how, and when, these two mentalities are used.

Teaching Creativity

I use creative writing exercises, including songwriting, to get learners to create. One advantage of using language-based exercises is that anyone who has ever used a language already has technical prowess in it. When I ask someone if they can write a simple song or a story, the limiting factor usually isn't their skill level, but their ability to make something up, to follow the process through. Some have a hard time even starting – "I can't do that. I'm not creative!"

Making a Song

To get over this hurdle, my first exercise is writing a song as a group. I've done this with little children, high school and university students, and grown-up professionals.

First, we choose a topic. I ask: "What could you write a song about?" followed by: "What are some things you like? What are some things that annoy you?" Once we all have the potential topics on the board we pick one through voting. Let's say they decide to write about "pigs", I then ask them to brainstorm any ideas about the topic. These are all written on the board. If the ideas start to slow down I'll ask some leading questions about the "Who?, What?, Where?, When?, How?" or probe for more details on a specific points. Once we have several boards full of ideas we stop.

I ask the participants what they think the song is about in as simple terms as possible and we make that the chorus. In our pig song, it could be as easy as repeating the word "pig." Or it could be more specific such as "the Mutant Pig in my Driveway" song that one class recently created.

Now that we have the chorus, I ask them for ideas on what to do next. Usually someone comes up with the idea of organizing the material into groups. "Maybe we can put all the comments about what pigs do in one verse, then all the ones about all the things describing them in another?" To accomplish this, we usually turn the lists of ideas into rhyming couplets suggested by the learners. And, just like that, we have a chorus and a couple of verses.

Then I sing the song to a tune I either make up or borrow from an existing song. We all sing it. Usually there are a couple of learners who mention, unprompted, that we should make some changes to improve it, and we will add these changes in if everyone agrees.

Everyone has now been a part of writing a song. It usually takes about forty-five minutes.

And then I show them how we did it.

A Creative Process

I try not to say "*the* creative process" because I don't want to accidentally give the impression that there's only one way to create things. So, I tell the learners that we just did was "*a* creative process." I show them the steps we used:

- Get an Idea. (Voting until we got *pig.*)
- Gather Materials. (Writing down ideas about pigs.)
- Organize. (Using the key idea as the verse and clumping like-thoughts into a chorus.)
- Assemble. (Writing down these ideas and making them rhyme.)
- Present. (Singing the song.)
- Make it better. (Making changes that improve the song in some way.)

I tell them that these steps aren't just for songwriting but can be used for creating anything: a novel, a painting, a newspaper article, a chair.

I ask the learners if following these steps exactly is how creativity always works and they (so far, anyway) say "no" – you can double-back from one step to another; you could present something and then throw the whole thing out except for one little bit that becomes the idea for a something new; you could run out of material after organizing it and then go back and gather some more, and so on. So, although I call parts of the process "steps" they're more like "stations" that can be visited in different orders. But for now, I tell them that we will follow the basic order starting with "Getting an Idea."

Where Do You Get Your Ideas?

Ideas are everywhere. Yet people think they don't have them. And that's the problem – you don't need to "have an idea," all you need to do is find one. Ideas are seldom completely new. Shakespeare based many of his plays on other works and yet he is generally regarded as a creative person. An idea is just a starting point – it is not the creation. It can be novel and exciting, or it can be absolutely mundane. And they are everywhere. Here are just a few ways to find one:

- *Be given it:* This is the easiest. Someone tells you to, "Paint a portrait of my dog," or, "Write an article about the rise in price of lemons." You don't even have to think. You can start gathering material right away.
- *Be inspired by something:* This can be something in your own life, something in someone else's life, or any type of media out there (movies, books, songs…).
- *Combining ideas:* Taking two (or more) ideas and putting them together (One current fashion for this is adding the word "zombie" to everything.)
- *Out of thin air:* In this technique you gather material first and let the idea come out of it. This is used in improvisational techniques in music and theatre, and also in free writing.

The problem then, isn't finding an idea. It's choosing which one to work on. How could you ever decide?

Write What You Feel

Writing is often portrayed as a "rational" act. We're told to write what you "know." But is knowing something enough of a reason to write about it? I know a lot about eating cereal but do I want to share that with the world? It is much easier to write what you *feel*. Feeling propels you. If you love cats, you'll have no problem writing a song about them. If bad drivers bother you, writing a rant about them will be easy. If you *really* love cereal, then by all means, make it the subject of your next opera. I often ask learners to make lists of things they either love or hate as a way to get ideas. Most discover that the things they feel most strongly about also happen to be things they know a lot about.

Be on the lookout. Ideas are everywhere, but you'll miss them if you're not paying attention. The people talking at the next table about a gallbladder operation, the little kid who says something unexpectedly funny, that idea that came out of nowhere when you were in the shower – how do you know if any of these are good ideas? Because you feel it. I tell learners to be on the lookout for ideas, and that when something strikes you, record it. You don't even have to know why – sometimes you only find out much later in the process, if at all.

Have a purpose. When I'm asked what inspires me most, I answer, "Deadlines." Deadlines give the process purpose and can propel you along. Any kind of purpose can be helpful. It is one thing to write a song because it's an exercise some guy who showed up in class one day told you to do; it is another thing entirely to write a song that you know will be performed before the whole school and parents as part of the holiday concert.

Gathering Material

Once you have an idea that you feel strongly about or that you have a compelling reason to pursue, the next step is usually to gather material. This material could be anything. In writing it is the thoughts and words about your idea. If you were making a dress it would be actual material; in a non-fiction article, it would mostly consist of research. And it is during this step that many people flounder. This is because "gathering material" requires a completely different frame of mind than all the steps that come after it. When gathering material, your mind needs to be open to possibilities, to be seeking, to be expanding, to be collecting everything that it happens upon. When this is going well you get in a groove; things flow. But if you interrupt that flow, things stop, and it can be hard to get back on track again. How do you prevent this from happening? Well, in the immortal words of Keanu Reeves in the movie *Speed*: "Don't Slow Down!" (Mark & Debont, 1994).

And what slows you down? Premature judging.

Judging (or, if you wish, evaluating) is our default mode. This is a good thing because it is the state of mind that tells us what is right and what is wrong and makes sure we don't get run over by cars, or are late for work, or put shirts on backwards. Judging is a very important part of creativity. Steps 3–6 are mostly judging, but if you do it while you're gathering material, you might just go nowhere.

Some people can't stop themselves from correcting every possible mistake. If something doesn't work right away, they're seized by the urge to correct or kill it. This stops everything. Even after I tell the learners this, some still just can't abide seeing an idea up on the board that has a spelling error or that doesn't fit into their vision of the song. They want to stop things right now to change it! But there is no need – any material you don't use will simply not appear in the final work, so fixing it is a waste of time. Also, ideas you initially feel are terrible sometimes make it into the final work in unexpected ways.

And the Rest of the Steps...

I'm not going to get into steps 3–6, because the main focus of my work is the initial process—the generation of ideas and material—and these later steps are generally more technical in nature. The key for me is getting learners to the point where they know they *can* create and I find that once they have the material in hand they're usually pretty good at the organizing and assembling part (revising takes a little more practice). That is why I use exercises that move them from step to step with as little opportunity to judge as possible, so they can experience the process and see just how easily it can flow. And, before I say "goodbye", I would like to share one of these exercises with you.

The "New Product" Exercise

I am especially proud of this exercise because it was inspired by a research paper (ideas are everywhere!). Thagard and Stewart (2011), in "The AHA! Experience: Creativity Through Emergent Binding in Neural Networks", propose that creative thinking is a matter of combining current neural patterns into new ones that are both "novel and useful," and that "such combinations arise from mechanisms that bind together neural patterns by a process of convolution rather than synchronization" (p. 2). Creativity, in this view, is not a result of different neural patterns activating each other and working simultaneously but, instead, is a result of separate neural patterns melding into each other and creating something new that might have some of the old characteristics but also has new characteristics which are not part of either of the original patterns. This is known, in cognitive-speak, as *emergent properties* (Thagard & Stewart, 2011). But to be truly creative, this emergent convolution must *also* be relevant in achieving the discoverer's goal. When this happens, it generates "the AHA! moment", an excited feeling of discovery.

I wanted to see if I could make an exercise that generated this AHA! moment so that learners would be excited by their idea and compelled into a creative process. Here's what I created. I pair learners up and ask each of them to pick one "thing" noun. I then tell them that they are going to create a new product by combining their two nouns in any way they want. So, if a pairs' words are "sweater" and "potato" they can come up with a sweater made up of potatoes, or sweater that looks like a potato, or a sweater for potatoes. The learners get very excited when they figure out what their product is – they almost always have an AHA! moment – as their new product almost always has emergent properties not associated with either of the original words and the discovery of this new product achieves a goal for them.

After they have decided on what their new product is I give them a worksheet full of questions to help them describe it ("What does your product look like?" "What is the best thing about it?"). They can even draw a picture. This is, although I don't tell them, the gathering materials phase. And because they are excited by their new product idea and because the questions are already there, they seldom stop in judgement. When they have finished answering the questions I inform them that they must now sell their new product by creating a short ad and jingle. Because they already have their raw material at hand they are able to quickly organize, assemble, and present their work. The ads are often inventive and compelling. I would have bought a dozen potato sweaters had they actually existed.

The End (and the Beginning)

I'd like to stress that the model I use to teach creativity is just that – a model. It is a greatly simplified interpretation of creativity that I use as a tool to help learners through the process of creation. Like all models, it is incomplete and focuses on some things more than others (for example, I seldom mention the potential of incubation in creativity), but I have found it to be useful, especially in demonstrating that creative work involves both imagination and evaluation and that the trick is often in the timing of the two. I intend to develop new techniques and exercises and expect that I will continue to be surprised by just how creative people – all people – really are. Even those who say they aren't.

REFERENCES

Elbow, P. (2000). *Everyone can write: Essays toward a hopeful theory of writing and teaching writing.* New York, NY: Oxford University Press.

Kampylis, P. G., & Valtanen, J. (2010). Redefining creativity—analyzing definitions, collocations, and consequences. *Journal of Creative Behavior, 44*, 191–214.

Mark G. (Producer), & DeBont, J. (Director). (1994). *Speed* (Motion Picture). USA: 20th Century Fox.

Ontario Ministry of Education. (2009). *The arts: The Ontario curriculum grades 1–8.* Toronto: Ontario Ministry of Education. Retrieved from http://www.edu.gov.on.ca/eng/curriculum/elementary/arts18b09curr.pdf

Plucker, J. A., Beghetto, R. A., & Dow, G. T. (2004). Why isn't creativity more important to educational psychologists? Potentials, pitfalls, and future directions in creativity research. *Educational Psychologist, 39,* 83–96.
Robinson, K. (2001). *Out of our minds: Learning to be creative*. Chichester: Capstone.
Thagard, P., & Stewart, T. C. (2011). The AHA! experience: Creativity through emergent binding in neural networks. *Cognitive Science, 35*, 1–33.

Trevor Strong
Queen's University

APPENDIX

A sample of student song writing

Pigs

INTRO
They're fat
They're cute
They love to eat slop too

Who?
Pigs! Pigs! Pigs!

They are good for bacon they're lovable and vicious
Lazy, crazy, innocent, and also quite delicious
Everyone's best friend, even though they stink
They snort and they're pork and they're also pink

CHORUS
Chubby, Chubby pigs
Cool down in the mud
Oink Oink Oink
Pigs are what I love

They squeal and snore and wallow and have real bad manners
These walking pork chops are not real good tanners
They're lovable and huggable with bitsy swirly tails
They float on the water and they're sorta fat like whales

CHORUS

BRIDGE
They're fat
They're cute
They love to eat slop too

CHORUS

MICHAEL BUSCH

33. FROM RESEARCH TECHNIQUE TO CLASSROOM ACTIVITY

Adapting Elicited Imitation as a Grammar-for-Speaking Task

INTRODUCTION

Among the many techniques available for researchers in studying oral language production, elicited imitation (EI) stands out due to its ease of use, reliability, and versatility. The technique consists of a second language (L2) learner who simply listens to a sentence, typically 8–15 words in length, and then repeats verbatim what he or she has just heard. The reliability of EI is well documented in the psychology, education, and health sciences research literature and has been used to investigate a variety of phenomena, such as aphasia, memory, L1 child language, and more recently L2 learning. As for its versatility, EI is highly adaptable across a range of contexts because of its minimal design requirements, which can be easily configured to accommodate any clause level language feature. Given its background and track record, the technique is worth considering for the L2 classroom. In this chapter, I describe an innovative application of EI by which it can be used to facilitate L2 classroom grammar learning. In my presentation, which is intended for teachers, I discuss its theoretical basis, design characteristics, and practical aspects of its use as an instructional activity.

Theoretical Basis and Purpose

A primary reason for using EI in the classroom is the unusual ability of the technique to tap into L2 implicit knowledge by requiring the learner to reconstruct target grammar structures. The key-construct for understanding how EI works is *reconstruction.* Learners must draw on their internalized knowledge of grammar and meaning in order to reproduce an utterance accurately. In explaining how reconstruction works, Jessop, Suzuki, and Tomita (2007) propose a three-stage cognitive process in which a learner has to first process the utterance, then reconstruct it internally, and finally verbalize the reproduction. Many studies since the 1960s (Vinther, 2002) have documented how research subjects have been able to reconstruct utterances under a variety of conditions, including prompts with incorrect grammar that were corrected by participants automatically, task demands that required a focus on meaning rather than form, and time pressure that forced participants to respond after a short delay

J. B. Cummings & M. L. Blatherwick (Eds.), Creative Dimensions of Teaching and Learning in the 21st Century, 315–320.

in order to eliminate the effect of short-term memory on reproducing utterances without awareness. In all three conditions, participants could reconstruct the prompts accurately, thus indicating underlying implicit knowledge.

More recently, a new rationale for EI has been advanced that expands on the notion of reconstruction: EI as a measure of both current implicit L2 knowledge and potential development. Poehner (2008) and others have argued that EI can be used to assess learners' unfolding abilities when they interact with a collaborator and receive assistance. This argument draws on sociocultural theory, and in particular Vygotsky's concept of a zone of proximal development where learners enter into a space of cognitive development through meditational means. When EI is performed with the collaboration of another, the task has the ability to identify and measure learning potential. This form of mediation, termed *dynamic assessment*, can be linked to reconstruction when the interaction with a more knowledgeable other assists the learner to reproduce the utterance. In practice, studies of dynamic assessment involving EI have consisted of either an interlocutor or computer-generated prompts providing additional information to assist the learner in reconstruction. The nature of the collaboration is what has attracted researchers working within a sociocultural theory framework because the assistance is viewed as an instructional activity and an opportunity to learn rather than simply being a summative assessment of grammatical accuracy or fluency.

While the rationale for using EI in a number of research contexts is well established, the most compelling reason for its use is a high correlation with implicit knowledge of L2 grammar structures, which has been confirmed by using corresponding transfer tasks (Erlam, 2009). Whatever the mechanisms or processes involved or the theoretical approach to explaining why, it seems to work. EI is a highly efficient tool for determining L2 grammar knowledge. Arguably, any reluctance to accept EI for either proficiency assessment or as an instructional activity does not come from disputes concerning empirical observations, but rather stems from its validity as a measure of free-flowing language production. EI lacks face validity because it does not involve spontaneous language production during social interaction. In other words, EI is not inherently a communicative task when administered for the purpose of assessing implicit knowledge. However, as I show in the next section, EI is such a highly adaptable technique that it is possible to convert it into a meaningful communicative activity that learners would find beneficial.

In contrast to using EI for research purposes, the reasons for using EI as a regular part of an L2 teacher's instructional repertoire differ. These reasons stem from EI's ability to facilitate L2 learning and not necessarily because of its ability to measure implicit knowledge. To be sure, EI could be used for summative assessment, but if it is designed with certain characteristics in mind, EI can facilitate *explicit* knowledge by making the learner aware of their own production while also receiving valuable feedback. In other words, the purpose of EI differs between quasi-experimental studies and classroom use in that researchers seek to measure implicit knowledge of L2 grammar while classroom teachers desire students to produce the target grammar and reflect upon their use in expectation that this consciousness – raising improves accuracy in L2 grammar production.

Design Characteristics

In order to use EI effectively for grammar instruction, teachers need to consider five characteristics that define EI: (1) *prompt length*, (2) *frequency of repetition*, (3) *comprehension response*, (4) *domain knowledge*, and (5) *location of structure*. In discussing these characteristics, I contrast methods used in research studies with recommendations for instructional use in a classroom setting.

For statistical reasons, EI research tasks have consisted of a long series of 20–75 sentences containing target structures with a *prompt length* ranging from six to eighteen words depending on proficiency level. In a classroom setting, the recommended number of prompts is a set of 10 or 15 for each task in order to maintain student interest and prevent fatigue. As with previous research studies, sentence length should be determined by learners' proficiency level and type of target grammar structure. Some structures, such as embedded clauses, require a longer sentence to represent the structure accurately. For a lower proficiency class, the target grammar structure may not require an entire sentence, so the instructor could create prompts that contain phrases rather than complete sentences.

Frequency of repetition. The number of times each sentence is read out loud until the sentence is accurately produced will depend on the instructional objectives of the EI task. If the task is intended for testing, then repeating the prompt could be limited to one repetition. However, if the instructor's intention is to create a pair work activity for dynamic assessment, then the prompt could be repeated three to four times with time allowed for intervention by the partner who offers additional assistance to help the learner until the prompt is reconstructed verbatim. Poehner and Lantolf (2013) distinguish two types of intervention, one being a dialogue between the interlocutor and learner and the second being a predetermined script with limited feedback. When pair work is used to do the EI task, the classmate serving as interlocutor would be expected to provide feedback. It is possible for instructors to create scripted assistance, but this would negate the advantages of more detailed feedback that would occur during interaction with a partner.

A *comprehension response* is needed to circumvent learners from relying on short-term memory alone to reproduce the prompt. Researchers have developed two methods to overcome this problem. In one method, learners must first answer whether the information in the prompt is true or false. The second is installing a time delay so that learners must wait three to five seconds before responding. In the classroom, these two methods are difficult to follow strictly. Students working in pairs will often ignore the protocol or forget to indicate true/false first and go directly to reading and repeating the prompt instead. Training students to follow the protocol and asking them to physically move external cue reminders, such as index cards with *true* or *false* written on them, will help students in following the protocol and complete the activity effectively.

Domain knowledge refers to the background knowledge required to understand the meaning of the sentence prompts. It is possible to create sentences with the assumption that they consist of general truths that would be understandable to anyone, but instructors cannot always assume that their students will know the information found in the prompts, especially if the topics are related to a specific domain, for example mathematics, physical sciences, or the host culture. To circumvent this potential problem, it is recommended that when creating EI tasks the teacher needs to ensure that the prompts contain information from a text that learners have been assigned to read in advance. In this way the task also becomes integrative, requiring reading as well as listening and speaking skills. EI can be used to reinforce reading texts, thus exponentially increasing its value as an instructional tool to facilitate L2 learning through multiple modes of reading, listening, and speaking. A second and equally important advantage of incorporating reading texts with specific topics is the task becomes communicative in nature rather than a rote repetition speaking drill.

Bly-Vroman and Chaudron (1994) noted in their study of EI that when the prompt had the target grammar located at the beginning of the sentence, learners were able to repeat the prompt more accurately by relying on short-term memory compared to prompts with structures located in the middle or end of the sentence. Erlam (2009), in her study of EI, decided to place structures in the middle of the prompt. However, not all grammar structures are amenable to middle or end placement. Some, such as adverbial conjunctions, appositives, or relative clauses modifying the subject of a sentence, may be required to appear in the beginning of the prompt. In designing an EI task for instructional purposes, middle or end location should not be a priority because the primary aim of the task is having learners' consciously notice the grammar.

Implementation

Applying EI in classroom settings creates a different set of conditions that researchers may find unacceptable, but that teachers would expect as part of everyday instruction. First, unlike research settings, a practice effect is a desired outcome. The more learners become familiar with the procedures of the task, the more efficient and accurate they will become in their performance. Training learners to perform the task will be necessary due to the complexity of the protocol. Once learners understand how to proceed, they will be able to do the task on a routine basis throughout the course without further direction, saving class time and increasing their ability to perform the task.

Another aspect of classroom instruction is assessment of performance for grading purposes, which can be accomplished in a number of ways. In research studies, one point is given for each accurate repetition, but this method of scoring requires a long series of prompts, as many as 75 in order to establish statistical norms.

For instructional purposes, a different method could be used in which teachers assign two points—one point for a correct true/false comprehension response and one point for accurate repetition of the prompt. Alternatively, the teacher could assign three points for each correct repetition and decrease the score by one point each time the learner fails to repeat the prompt accurately. After three attempts if the learner fails to repeat the prompt correctly, he or she receives a score of zero.

Related to repetition is the role of assistance or "coaching" which, like a practice effect, is a desirable outcome of the task. The learner's partner can help them by providing a one word hint or repeating the key grammatical structure that was stated incorrectly. From a theoretical point of view coaching is seen as a means of scaffolding learning as the learner interacts with a more knowledgeable partner. The learner becomes more consciously aware of the error and subsequently how the target structure is formed, which then leads to direct L2 learning. Coaching, known as dynamic assessment in the research literature, has been the focus of several studies in recent years and attempts have been made to map out all the possible responses, e.g. corrections, hints, and brief explanations by the interlocutor and to use these responses to build testing software (Poehner & Lantolf, 2013; Van Campernolle & Zhang, 2014).

Another practical concern for teachers is modifying the technique for lower proficiency learners. Long sentence prompts, in particular, may prove to be too difficult. As with researchers who initially do pilot testing to determine the optimum sentence length of the prompt for their study participants, teachers need to anticipate finding the correct length for their students through trial and error. Other possible modifications for less able learners include using shorter phrases rather than complete sentences, eliminating the true/false comprehension response, and increasing the frequency of repetition to four.

A final consideration in regard to practical implementation of EI for classroom use is accounting for problems and developing strategies to address them. Among the potential problems are partners who read the sentence prompt but fail to read all of the words or whose pronunciation is incomprehensible to the learner who is expected to repeat the prompt. Two ways of combatting these issues are treating the reading text that forms the basis of the EI prompts as a listening task and assigning learners to read and record themselves as they read the text out loud. Both strategies increase comprehension by fostering what is known in the psychology literature as *depth of processing* (Calderon, 2013), in which the object to be learned is cognitively processed in a variety of different ways (e.g., reading. listening, speaking, writing), thus exponentially leveraging EI into a more meaningful task for the learner.

CONCLUSION

On the face of it, EI appears to be a 1960s pattern practice grammar drill taken from a time when behavioralist psychology and audiolingualism were in their heyday (Larsen-Freeman, 2009). An observant reader may have noticed that in writing this chapter I have used the term "prompt" rather than the behavioralist term "stimulus," which is still in common use today. It is important to keep in mind that the theory underlying EI is radically different from behaviourism in that focal attention generated by conscious reflection and social interaction is believed to be the main driver for second language learning. It is also important to note that the empirical research supporting EI as a measure of L2 learning is substantial, dating back several decades. Unlike pattern practice drills, EI, if designed and executed properly, can carry communicative meaning for the learner, making the technique an effective tool in the grammar teacher's instructional repertoire.

REFERENCES

Bly-Vroman, R., & Chaudron, C. (1994). Elicited imitation as a measure of second language competence. In E. Tarnone, S. Gass, & A. Cohen (Eds.), *Research methodology in second language acquisition* (pp. 245–261). Mahwah, NJ: Erlbaum.

Calderon, A. M. (2013). The effects of l2 learner proficiency on depth of processing, levels of awareness, and intake. In J. M. Bergsleithner, S. M. Frota, & J. Yoshioka (Eds.), *Noticing and second language acquisition: Studies in honor of Richard Schmidt* (pp. 103–121). Honolulu, HI: National Foreign Language Resource Center.

Erlam, R. (2009). The elicited imitation test as a measure of implicit knowledge. In R. Ellis, S. Loewen, R. Erlam, J. Philip, & H. Reiders (Eds.), *Implicit and explicit knowledge in second language learning, testing, and teaching* (pp. 65–367). Bristol, UK: Multilingual Matters.

Jessop, L., Suzuki, W., & Tomita, Y. (2007). Elicited imitation in second language acquisition research. *Canadian Modern Language Review, 64*(1), 215–220.

Larsen-Freeman, D. (2009). Teaching and testing grammar. In M. H. Long & C. J. Doughty (Eds.), *Handbook of language teaching* (pp. 518–542). Chichester, UK: Wiley-Blackwell.

Poehner, M. (2008). *Dynamic assessment: A Vygotskian approach to understanding and promoting second language development.* Berlin: Springer Publishing.

Poehner, M., & Lantolf, J. (2013). Bringing the ZPD into the equation: Capturing L2 development during computerized dynamic assessment (C-DA). *Language Testing Research, 17*(3), 323–342.

Van Compernolle, R. A., & Zhang, H. (2014). Dynamic assessment of elicited imitation: A case analysis of an advanced L2 English speaker. *Language Testing, 31*(4), 395–412.

Vinther, T. (2002). Elicited imitation: A brief overview. *International Journal of Applied Linguistics, 12*, 54–73.

Michael Busch
Saginaw Valley State University

SNEZHANA HARIZANOVA

34. CARING FOR THE WHOLE PERSON IN THE EAP CLASSROOM

INTRODUCTION

Most educators worldwide would agree now that when we talk about second language (L2) learning, and learning in general, there are many factors to consider. We need to take into account learners' age, learning styles and strategies, aptitude, attitude, motivation, hemisphere specialization, and more (Larsen-Freeman & Long, 1991). Regarding English for Academic Purposes (EAP) in Western English language medium institutions in particular, a brief review of literature shows that some of the most discussed issues relate to (integrated) reading and writing skills and strategies development (Grabe & Zhang; 2013; McCulloch, 2013; Meyer Sterzik & Fraser, 2012; Spack, 1997), including knowledge of academic genres, registers and rhetoric conventions (Grabe & Zhang, 2013; Hyland, 2002, 2006; Spack, 1997), critical thinking (Grabe & Zhang, 2013; Hyland, 2006; McCulloch, 2013; Spack, 1997), background knowledge and L2 linguistic competence (Grabe & Zhang, 2013; Moussu, 2013; Spack, 1997), to name just a few.

Discussions on the above issues focus on a variety of cognitive and social aspects of learning and relate mostly to EAP learners' struggles in their academic endeavours. I have seen quite a few of those struggling learners myself while teaching at an international ESL school and at York University in Canada. There is an abundance of insightful research offering advice and looking for new answers. Yet, in most of it, as Meyer Sterzik (2012) points out, one important focus has been missing: the focus on the person in EAP, on the learner's psychological (and physiological) needs. Neglect of the person is an issue relevant, in fact, to all learners, but especially to international EAP students who can feel distressed from the cultural, linguistic and academic environment change, all happening at the same time. I find at least three reasons why taking into account the person in EAP is important.

First, it highlights the fact that the learner, the subject and object of all academic (EAP) discussions, is above all a human being. Failing to recognize that can impact all learning and teaching (see Lozanov, 1971, 1978b, 2009; Tarr, 1995), the role of affect in (L2) learning (Lozanov, 1971, 2009; Schumann, 1994; Swain, 2013) and the need for identity change in a new context (Hyland, 2002, 2006; Spack, 1997), which can impact classroom communication, hence learners' cognition and well-being. Furthermore, from a Suggestopedic perspective, caring for the person necessitates the need to consider also the role of art, (role)play and creativity (Lozanov, 1978b, 2009;

J. B. Cummings & M. L. Blatherwick (Eds.), Creative Dimensions of Teaching and Learning in the 21st Century, 321–330.

Lozanov & Gateva, 1981; Tarr, 1995) and of the classroom environment, both human and physical (Lozanov, 1971) in cognition. Focusing on the personhood of the learner also gives Suggestopedia a special place in current (North American) EAP discussions. Suggestopedia is about the learner, the person as a whole: the unity of his/her rational and emotional being, his/her idiosyncratic nature as influenced by and influencing the environment and, ultimately, his/her emotional well-being. Suggestopedia has been found to make learning effortless, more joyful and faster (see Bancroft, 1999; Lozanov, 1971, 1978b, 2009; Schuster & Miele, 1978; Tarr, 1995) and there is recent research from outside the field of SLA that confirms many of its claims, most importantly, its main claim that the whole brain and the whole person take part in learning (Omaha Boy, 2010). That is why I find it compelling to investigate its applicability in (North American) EAP classrooms by focusing first and foremost on the person.

What Is Suggestopedia?

Imagine a bright colourful room, plants in the corner, educational posters, pictures and art reproductions on the walls, a carpet on the floor, chairs in a circle or in a row along the walls (or regular desks if in a regular schools), all sorts of accessories, drawing materials, classical music in the background at times replaced by popular songs… There you could see how "knowledge pours in like a river, submerging the conscious mind and awakening its reserve capacities" (Omaha Boy, 2010, p. 35); how learners, immersed in a new language, laugh, joke, sing, play, act, create and live a story, and in the process learn, with less effort and faster than usual. This is how the Suggestopedic classroom has been described (see Racle, 1975, 1979; Schaefer, 1980; Tarr, 1995; Omaha Boy, 2010) and this is how I saw it while in training in Bulgaria in 2012.

Suggestopedia has been used in many countries and contexts but mostly with L2 learning beginners. It has been considered quite successful in creating a safe, inspiring and stimulating environment that can accelerate learning and transform the learning and teaching experience in exciting ways (Omaha Boy, 2010; Prichard, 1978; Racle, 1975, 1979; Schuster & Miele, 1978; Tarr, 1995). It is considered a teaching philosophy, rather than methodology, for it is not the teaching techniques but the theory and inspiration behind their use that form its essence. But how does Suggestopedia work?

Back in the 1950s Dr. Lozanov, a Bulgarian psychiatrist, psychotherapist, neurologist, brain physiologist, and, later, pedagogue, became interested in the hidden potential of the human brain, mind and personality which can manifest as increased memory, high creativity, and even control of the body. He established through various experiments that this potential could be tapped by use of (positive) *suggestion* and continued to test his theory in pedagogy to help learners tap their unused abundance of reserves and learn faster, with joy and without effort.

Lozanov's (1971) suggestion is not the clinical or manipulative type of suggestion used in psychotherapy and hypnosis. It is the "spontaneously absorbed non-manipulative suggestion" (Lozanov, 2009, p. 82) that plays a role in all communication through all verbal and non-verbal stimuli present in it. These stimuli are both external and internal and one perceives them *consciously*, but mostly *peripherally* (non-consciously and/or subconsciously), and they can have positive (or negative) suggestive influence on a person's state of mind. As such, suggestion is in essence similar to Vygotsky's concept of mediation (see, for example, Lantolf & Thorne, 2006), one major difference being that suggestion works together with *desuggestion* and is subject to control by an (adult) person's *anti-suggestive barriers*. Desuggestion, a form of suggestion, can liberate a person from previous negative influences and beliefs formed by experience or imposed by the (limiting) *social suggestive norms* which impede the use of his/her reserve potential. The three anti-suggestive barriers (the *intuitive-affective*, the *critical logical*, and the *ethical barrier*) are a person's natural defence system against such negative suggestion; they vary between individuals and a message needs to be in harmony with them in order for suggestion and desuggestion to work. Lozanov considers it essential for teachers to be familiar with how suggestion works in order to ensure communication that can stimulate a person positively.

Thus, the theory behind Suggestopedia reflects Lozanov's view on how the brain/mind receives and stores information. According to Lozanov, the brain functions as a whole and that is also how it processes information. Furthermore, analytical and synthetic processes take place simultaneously as do conscious and paraconscious (peripheral) processes. In other words, according to Lozanov (2009, p. 54), "the brain does not accept isolated stimuli" but "[t]here is always something from the environment, the atmosphere or the state of mind of the recipient, which clings to the primary stimulus". That is how connections are formed in long-term memory. Lozanov spent most of his life researching how suggestion can be effectively used in pedagogy (and all communication) through organized simultaneous use of *conscious* and *peripheral perceptions* and simultaneous stimulation of logic and emotion.

In the Suggestopedic classroom Lozanov's theory is applied by use of the following means of suggestion: *double-planeness* (harmonization of the second plane, i.e. the non-verbal stimuli, with the first, i.e. the main message); *rhythm* (of speech and in art); *intonation* (e.g., of the teacher's voice, which plays a role in the double-planeness); *prestige* of the teacher/source (the "prestige and reliability" [Lozanov, 2009, p. 103] which help create learner trust, confidence and positive expectations); "childlikeness" (Schaefer, 1980, p. 277), or what he calls *infantilization* (not in the clinical sense, but the childlike state of increased confidence and trust to the source, or of inspiration, yet with a critical attitude [see also Gateva, 1991]); and *concentrative psychorelaxation* (the state of relaxed concentration in which the brain/mind can absorb a great amount of information and one's reserves can be tapped). Suggestopedia employs a system of *didactic*, *psychological* and *artistic means* based on the theory of suggestion. In these, classical art is widely used as the highest form of (positive) suggestion and a variety of techniques to create interest and motivation. In his most recent development Lozanov (2009) translated his theory into seven laws for use by teachers to create a positive, harmonious, and effective learning environment. They will be referred to below only briefly with respect to their possible applicability in EAP (for more details see Lozanov, 2009).

The Person in Suggestopedia and EAP

As mentioned above, the person has barely been the focus in EAP literature, while in Suggestopedia the person is the main focus. This is also the central point I want to make in this chapter. The first three of Lozanov's (2009) laws relate directly to the personhood of the learner. Genuine care of and respect for the human being (the first law), freedom of choice and expression of both learner and teacher (the second law), and high teacher expectations and confidence in learners' abilities (the third law) are major contributors to successful (Suggestopedic) instruction. This clearly gives a perspective on the learner as a human being first and foremost.

The Learner Is a Human Being

Schooled in the tradition of the Bulgarian and Russian psychology of his time including the Vygotskian sociocultural view on human interaction, Lozanov (1971) also considers the person as directly influenced and influencing the environment, both human and physical. The physical environment and people with whom a person communicates can have either a positive or a negative impact on his/her psychosomatic state; likewise, the school can either heal and stimulate learning, intellect and creativity (i.e. the whole person) or cause disease and block development (Lozanov, 1971, 1978b, 2009; Tarr, 1995). Hence, from a Suggestopedic point of view, focusing on the person in EAP requires consideration of learners' emotional states as well as their classroom environments since these are related and both can directly impact learning.

Affect and cognition. There have been earlier discussions in the Second Language Acquisition (SLA) field about the positive correlation between affect and cognition (e.g. Schumann, 1994), and a renewed interest seems to be emerging (see Swain, 2013). But generally, EAP research seems to be mostly concerned with the cognitive and social factors in learning. In Suggestopedia emotion and learning have always been inseparable and "learning is facilitated through stimulation of the [positive] emotions" (Omaha Boy, 2010, p. 37). On the one hand, positive emotions cater to the learner's psychological well-being. They can help bring out the "child" in each learner and lead to concentrative relaxation. On the other, positive emotional stimuli are used through art, teacher attitude and behaviour, a comfortable and stimulating environment, singing, (role-)play, and other engaging activities, to "cluster" (on the second plane) with the main message of communication (the first plane) so the information can be sent to long-term memory. This is not simply considering the affective filter the way Krashen (1982) does, i.e. as increasing or decreasing acquisition. According to Lozanov (1971, 2009), positive affect can be empowering and can help release one's full potential, while negative affect can have a detrimental effect on the psychophysiological state of the learner. Teachers' attitudes and expectations as revealed and perceived on both planes play a major role in this. The purpose of Lozanov's science is precisely to help learners have the benefit of positive stimulation and be healed and protected from negative psychological influences. This can help them reach their hidden learning and creative potential and absorb a great amount of information (Lozanov, 2009; Dougal, 2010).

Cognitive neuroscience research has recently confirmed that information with arousal (emotion) is retained better and longer (Phelps, 2005). In psychology, positive emotions in particular have been found to improve a person's health, and to transform, and foster creativity and cognition (see Fredrickson, 2003; Gateva, 1991; Lozanov, 1971). It would follow then that we cannot ignore the emotional side of learning and the emotional state of the person(s) involved, but should instead take care of them especially in postsecondary institutions where anxiety and stress have been increasingly reported to hinder academic success (Somers & Jamieson, 2014).

Positive emotions, play and creativity in learning. One way to create positive emotions is through play (Fredrickson, 2003; Power, 2011). The role of play has been widely recognized in childhood development but when it comes to adult learning it has barely been given any serious attention (Burghardt, 2006, in Power, 2011, p. 288). Regarding L2 language learning, SLA research has mostly offered insights from foreign language settings and mostly on (pragmatic) language play (Waring, 2013).

Yet play has been recognized to contribute to (language) learning and development both from a Social Cultural Theory (SCT) and from an applied linguistics point of view (Waring, 2013). According to Power (2011), both cognitive and neurological studies have established that playfulness, an essential part of true play, can develop creativity in adults through divergent, novel thinking. In accord with Lozanov's (1971, 2009) theory, research in psychology has also established that positive emotions can broaden the mindset and make thinking more global, "more creative, integrative, flexible, and open to information" and can "undo" the effect of negative emotions (Fredrickson, 2003, pp. 333–334). Creative play can help see the relationship between the parts and the whole, which promotes meaning and understanding and brings theory and practice together (see Latta, 2001; Provenzo, 2009; Serrano-Lopez & Poehner, 2006). Such play can also help make meaning personal (Latta, 2001). It is through seeing meaningful relationships between the whole and its elements, rather than bit by bit, that the brain can best process new information, according to Lozanov's (2009) fifth law. In sociocultural terms, that is promoting higher mental processes.

Some of the research mentioned above addresses issues of EAP related to developing learners' critical thinking (i.e., the ability to assess and integrate information) and recommends explicit instruction (e.g., Grabe & Zhang, 2013;

Meyer Sterzik & Fraser, 2012). Based on the above, I would like to suggest here that creativity can also have a place in EAP since it can help develop critical through divergent thinking. Suggestopedically speaking, this could be best achieved in a safe and stimulating environment carefully organized by a teacher.

The environment. The environment in terms of physical surroundings as well as the human contribution in the classroom (i.e., the main message of communication and all the peripheral stimuli, such as decorations, comfort, intonation, rhythm, body language and appearance of the teacher) is considered a key factor in learning in Suggestopedia and the teacher is expected to ensure double-planeness. In fact, Lozanov (1971) considered it so important that even the hallways and the whole building were made to be conducive to positive suggestion at the Suggestopedic Research Institute in Bulgaria. To me this part of Suggestopedia was absolutely enlightening. I knew the environment can make a difference but I had not realized it could make such a big difference. This is another aspect not addressed much, if at all, in EAP literature which seems intriguing to investigate from a Suggestopedic perspective.

The physical environment. Aesthetics is important in Suggestopedia and not simply for style. Classical art, in all its forms, is used as decoration, background music, or textbook illustrations for example to stimulate peripheral perception. Presenting subject matter through art helps activate the whole brain and engage the whole person both logically and emotionally according to Lozanov's seventh law. Classical artworks are based on the Golden Ratio which is a sign of harmony and balance, and which, according to the sixth law, needs to be observed also in the structure of the lessons and materials in Suggestopedic instruction (for details see Lozanov, 2009). Classical music is used in the "concert séances" right after the introduction of every new unit when the teacher reads the new text with special intonation to the background of music and the students listen relaxed. Key target language features have already been introduced and the séances serve to ensure pleasant stress-free perception of the whole. Art is considered by Lozanov (1978a, 2009) and his colleague Gateva (1991) the highest form of suggestion since it provides plenty of positive stimuli to facilitate memorization and increase creativity and motivation. "Great art […] awakens feelings, thoughts and actions one does not always account for" (Lozanov, 1978a, p. 162) and can lead to inspiration and concentrative psychorelaxation and thus awaken one's full potential (Dougal, 2010; Gateva, 1991; Lozanov, 2009).

Caring for the environment in North American EAP classrooms in such a way raises at least two issues. One of them is how, if at all, classical music in particular will be accepted by all learners, especially those of non-European origin. This issue has been often raised during my formal or informal talks about Suggestopedia to Canadian audiences. It has also been discussed in the literature. Gateva's (1991) research suggests mostly positive emotional and physical reactions to the experimentally selected classical music in the concert sessions, regardless of age, background or nationality.

Yet, while some learners have never objected to it (Schaefer, 1980), there are still others who have not readily accepted it (Racle, 1975), which means this question still remains to be discussed. Another concern I foresee is that often university or college EAP classes meet once or twice a week and teachers have to share rooms with others. This can impose restrictions as to whether and how much a teacher can attend to aesthetics. Yet, while I am aware that such issues could prevent use of classical art in EAP, I feel encouraged by those who have appreciated it and by research that has confirmed its psychophysiological, intellectual and cognitive benefits (e.g., Dougal, 2010; Gateva, 1991; Lozanov, 1971), especially of music (Campbell, 2001), which according to recent brain research seems to have similar effects on the brain regardless of individual differences and preferences (see Baker, 2007; Goldman, 2013). If classical art can stimulate positively and help memorization, then its benefits for EAP are worth investigating, while respecting and slowly harmonizing with learners' preferences.

The human environment and the individual learner. In Suggestopedia teachers are expected and trained to pay special attention to each learner's individual characteristics and level of knowledge in advance in order to promote good rapport and collaboration in each group. The rationale behind that is that each learner's individual characteristics and abilities can be influenced by and can influence the learning outcomes of the whole group and teachers need to control the process (Lozanov & Gateva, 1981). At the same time, "Suggestopedia is not selective" (Loubaton, 1979, p. 101) as it caters to all needs and styles through various ways of learning and practice (e.g., from use of art, [role]play, songs, dance, games, allowing for freedom and creativity, to translation and dictation) and allows for mother tongue support (see Lozanov & Gateva, 1981). It uses an individual approach to learners who, by choosing whether to work alone or in a group, can progress at their own pace (Loubaton, 1979). This particular feature can be very helpful in North American EAP settings where students, immersed in a new culture, despite all the research informed support, often feel discouraged and isolated linguistically, culturally, and as members of their learning community (Moussu, 2013; Spack, 1997). Focus on the learner as both an individual and a member of a group also relates to issues of identity in L2/EAP learning as briefly discussed below from a Suggestopedic perspective.

Identity and role-play. Lozanov (1971, 2009) hardly talks about identity. He rather talks about a person's multiple personalities and changing states of mind (mindsets), which quite agrees with one SCT view of identity as "multiple, multifaceted and shifting" (Swain, Kinnear, & Steinman, 2010, p. 76). The issue of identity, accordingly, has been resolved in Suggestopedia through role-play. From the beginning, students are invited to adopt a new fictitious self which they create and co-create while developing a story throughout the course (Lozanov, 2009; Racle, 1979; Schaefer, 1980). Learner identity is a complex construct in EAP. I will only refer here to identity change in a new context (Hyland, 2002; Spack, 1997), which can have cognitive, psychological and social effects and thus links EAP and Suggestopedia more directly.

Spack's (1997) account of an EAP learners' identity crisis shows that it can have two different dimensions. One is the fear of expressing one's thoughts due to poor L2 competence or pronunciation. The other is related to cultural and educational differences. Interestingly, in Suggestopedia role-play serves precisely these two functions. One is to ensure pronunciation practice. The new names, professions, addresses, etc., that the students can choose from, are to contain (some of) the more typical and/or expected to be problematic sounds and sound/letter combinations of the target language. That way, while focused on acting and (co-)constructing their roles, learners practice sounds and spelling often without realizing that. The new identity also serves as "a psychological protection" under which the student can safely experiment, make mistakes or tell jokes without fear (Racle, 1975, p. 238). It helps towards an easier adjustment to a new situation (Racle, 1975) and can transform the atmosphere and increase enthusiasm and rapport as learners create, co-create and explore (Schaefer, 1980; Suzuki, 1997). These points of contact suggest that role-play may help facilitate EAP learning in ways yet to be explored.

Implications for EAP

It seems that, from a Suggestopedic point of view, caring for the person in EAP and, in fact, all classrooms can benefit cognition in different ways. A positive atmosphere fostered through a variety of aesthetic, playful and creative means may indeed be the way to tapping into learners' full potential. Much research has confirmed that Suggestopedic instruction can make both adult and child learning more joyful, faster and creative (Lozanov, 1978a, 2009; Schuster & Miele, 1978; Tarr, 1995). Such "multifaceted learning" creates memories in the whole brain and engages the whole person in a joyful experience where freedom and inspiration drive learning (Omaha Boy, 2010, p. 37). By employing affect in learning, Lozanov's (1971) theory provides important insights for both teachers and researchers in EAP.

Keeping learners' well-being in focus requires, of course, a lot more to consider and can impose certain limitations. One is related to the crucial role of the teacher. It takes a lot more than subject matter competence to organize such a safe and inspiring environment in which, according to Lozanov's (2009) fourth law, a great amount of information is expected to be taught and learnt with ease. One criticism of Suggestopedia has been precisely the great demands it puts on the teacher (Racle, 1975). Another possible limitation in an EAP context is that Suggestopedia has been developed mostly for lower level (L2) teaching and my best knowledge is that some of the most discussed issues in EAP mentioned above (e.g., critical thinking, integrated reading and writing strategy development, use of academic discourse conventions) have not been addressed explicitly in Suggestopedia. Yet, if Suggestopedia has the ability to transform positively both learners and teachers (Omaha Boy, 2010; Tarr, 1995) and is consistently validated by recent neurological research findings on how cognition works (Omaha Boy, 2010), then it holds much promise for education in general and EAP in particular. The question that remains for me to investigate is if, indeed, and then how EAP teachers in North America could apply that knowledge in their classrooms. In the process, I will be looking for insights by comparing literature on current and past Suggestopedic practices to the practices and opinions of North American (i.e., Canadian) EAP teachers themselves.

REFERENCES

Bancroft, W. J. (1999). *Suggestopedia and language acquisitions: Variations on a theme*. Florence, KY: Gordon & Breach Publishing.

Baker, M. (2007, August 1). Music moves brain to pay attention, Stanford study says. *Stanford School of Medicine News Releases*. Retrieved from https://med.stanford.edu

Campbell, D. (2001). *The Mozart effect: Tapping the power of music to heal the body, strengthen the mind, and unlock the creative spirit*. New York, NY: Quill.

Dougal, S. (2010, July 22–24). *Suggestion with a capital 'S'* (pp. 20–29). Proceedings of the International Scientific Conference on Suggestopaedia, Sliven, Bulgaria.

Fredrickson, B. L. (2003). The value of positive emotions. *American Scientist, 91*(4), 330–335.

Gateva, E. (1991). *Creating wholeness through art: Global artistic creation of the educational training process*. Accelerated Learning Systems.

Goldman, B. (2013, April 11). Study shows different brains have similar responses to music. Stanford School of Medicine News. *Inside Stanford Medicine, 5*(8). Retrieved from http://med.stanford.edu

Grabe, W., & Zhang, C. (2013). Reading and writing together: A critical component of English for academic purposes teaching and learning. *TESOL Journal, 4*(1), 9–24.

Hyland, K. (2002). Options of identity in academic writing. *ELT Journal, 56*(4), 351–358.

Hyland, K. (2006). *English for academic purposes: An advanced resource book*. New York, NY: Routledge.

Krashen, S. (1982). *Principles and practice in second language acquisition* (pp. 1982–1982). Oxford: Pergamon.

Lantolf, J., & Thorne, S. L. (2006). *Sociocultural theory and the genesis of second language development*. Oxford: OUP.

Larsen-Freeman, D., & Long, M. H. (1991). *An introduction to second language acquisition research*. New York, NY: Longman.

Latta, M. M. (2001). The possibilities of play in the classroom: On the power of aesthetic experience in teaching, learning, and researching. In E. Mirochnick (Ed.), *Lesley College series in art and education* (Vol. 4). New York, NY: Peter Lang.

Loubaton, M. (1979). A comparison of Suggestopedia and conventional learning methods. *Journal of Suggestive-Accelerative Learning and Teaching, 4*(2), 100–103.

Lozanov, G. (1971). *Sugestologia* [Suggestology]. Sofia, Bulgaria: Nauka i izkustvo.

Lozanov, G. (1978a). Suggestology and outlines of suggestopedy. In S. Krippner (Ed.), *Psychic studies* (Vol. 2). New York, NY: Gordon and Breach Science Publishers.

Lozanov, G. (1978b, December 11–16). *Suggestology and suggestopedia – theory and practice. Working document for the Expert Working Group of UNESCO*. Conference for Suggestology, Sofia, Bulgaria. (ERIC Document Reproduction Services No. ED78/WS/119). Retrieved from http://www.unesco.org/new/en/unesco/resources/online-materials/publications/unesdoc-database/

Lozanov, G. (2009). *Suggestopedia/Reservopedia: Theory and practice of the liberating-stimulating pedagogy on the level of the hidden reserves of the human mind*. Sofia, Bulgaria: St. Kliment Ohridski University Press.

Lozanov, G., & Gateva, E. (1981). *Sugestopedichno praktichesko rakovodstvo za prepodavateli po chuzhdi ezitsi* [A Suggestopedic manual for teachers of foreign languages]. Sofia, Bulgaria: Research Institute of Suggestology.

McCulloch, S. (2013). Investigating the reading-to-write processes and source use of L2 postgraduate students in real-life academic tasks: An exploratory study. *Journal of English for Academic Purposes, 12*(2), 136–147.

Meyer Sterzik, A. (2012, March). Intercultural experiences affecting language learners. In *The newsletter of the intercultural communication interest section*. Alexandria, VA: TESOL International Association. Retrieved from http://newsmanager.commpartners.com/tesolicis/issues/2012-03-06/2.html

Meyer Sterzik, A., & Fraser, C. (2012). RC-MAPS: Bridging the comprehension gap in EAP reading. *TESL Canada Journal, 29*(2), 103–119.

Moussu, L. (2013). Let's talk! ESL students' needs and writing center philosophies. *TESL Canada Journal, 30*(2), 55–68.

Omaha Boy, N. H. (2010, July 22–24). *The joy of teaching: Gloria Marie Caliendo, PhD* (pp. 30–37). Proceedings of the International Scientific Conference on Suggestopaedia, Sliven, Bulgaria.

Phelps, E. (2005). The interaction of emotion and cognition: The relation between the human amygdala and cognitive awareness. In J. A. Bargh, R. R. Hassin, & J. S.Uleman (Eds.), *The new unconscious* (pp. 61–76). New York, NY: Oxford University Press.

Power, P. (2011). Playing with ideas: The affective dynamics of creative play. *American Journal of Play, 3*(3), 288–323.

Prichard, A. (1978). An introduction to SALT/Suggestopedia. *The Journal of Suggestive-Accelerative Learning and Teaching, 3*(3), 206–210.

Provenzo, E. F., Jr. (2009). Friedrich Froebel's gifts: Connecting the spiritual and aesthetic to the real world of play and learning. *American Journal of Play, 2*(10), 85–99.

Racle, G. (Ed.). (1975). Suggestopaedia – Canada, 1972–1974. A teaching experience with the suggestopaedic method. In *Public Service Commission of Canada. Staff Development Branch. Studies Division*. Ottawa, Canada: Information Canada.

Racle, G. L. (1979). Can suggestopedia revolutionize language teaching? *Foreign Language Annals, 12*(1), 39–49.

Schaefer, D. A. (1980). My experiences with the Lozanov method. *Foreign Language Annals, 13*(4), 273–278.

Schumann, J. H. (1994). Where is cognition? Emotion and cognition in second language acquisition. *Studies in Second Language Acquisition, 16*(2), 231–242.

Schuster, D. H., & Miele, P. (1978, December 11–16). Minutes of the conference for suggestology, Sofia, Bulgaria. *The Journal of Suggestive-Accelerative Learning and Teaching, 3*(3), 211–223.

Serrano-Lopez, M., & Poehner, M. (2006). Materializing linguistic concepts through 3-D clay modeling: A tool-and-result approach to mediating L2 Spanish development. In J. Lantolf & S. Thorne (Eds), *Sociocultural theory and the teaching of second languages* (pp. 321–351). London, UK: Equinox.

Somers, K., & Jamieson, S. (2014). Stress and anxiety in (second language) learning: Using HRV biofeedback and stress management education to facilitate learning success. *TESL Ontario CONTACT Magazine, 40*(1), 29–35. Retrieved from http://www.teslontario.net/uploads/publications/contact/ContactSpring2014.pdf

Spack, R. (1997). The acquisition of academic literacy in a second language: A longitudinal case study. *Written Communication, 14*(1), 3–62.

Suzuki, M. (1997). *On a practical application of suggestopedia to English education in a senior high school* (Unpublished M.Ed. Thesis). Japan: Aichi University of Education.

Swain, M. (2013). The inseparability of cognition and emotion in second language learning. Plenary speech. *Language Teaching, 46*(2), 195–207.

Swain, M., Kinnear, P., & Steinman, L. (2010). *Sociocultural theory in second language education: An introduction through narratives*. Bristol, UK: Multilingual Matters.

Tarr, R. L. (1995). *Understanding the spirit of Georgi Lozanov's work in second language learning as informing the complex future of pedagogy* (Doctoral Dissertation). University of Minnesota, Minneapolis, MN. Retrieved from Researchgate.net

Waring, H. Z. (2013). Doing being playful in the second language classroom. *Applied Linguistics, 34*(2), 191–210.

Snezhana Harizanova
York University

ANTOINETTE GAGNÉ, SREEMALI HERATH
AND MARLON VALENCIA

35. STRATEGIES TO ENGAGE AND TRANSFORM TEACHER LEARNERS IN AN ONLINE COURSE

INTRODUCTION

The demand for online courses for teacher learners (TLs) across all disciplines continues to increase, as does the diversity of those who enroll in these courses. This diversity constitutes both a benefit and a challenge for online learning where active engagement and the creation of community are of utmost importance. Modeling strategies that reflect what works well with language learners and that can be adapted for students of different ages, levels and goals is also important when working with teachers online.

Teaching Context

The strategies described in this chapter are embedded in an asynchronous online graduate course for language teachers of English, French and other languages including Spanish, Mandarin and Korean. These teachers work across levels including primary, secondary and adult education as well as college and university. They also teach within a range of programs where (1) the language is taught as a subject in school, (2) the language is the medium of instruction, or (3) the language is taught to prepare students for life in a new country, higher education or the workplace. Many of the TLs have experience teaching outside of Canada in various contexts.

The class was facilitated through a course management system (CMS) called *Pepper* developed at the University of Toronto. This particular CMS organizes content in folders, which contain notes. These notes can be created by any community member and may contain traditional print-based text, as well as embedded media (e.g., voice recorded responses, YouTube videos, Prezis…) in addition to file attachments. Figure 1 below provides a snapshot of *Pepper*'s interface. We chose this CMS because it offers a wealth of administrative tools that allow a more accurate account of learners' engagement with the course materials (e.g., amount of time spent logged on, number of written notes, number of typed words, etc.). Both folders and notes can be shared with everyone or with a select number of community members.

J. B. Cummings & M. L. Blatherwick (Eds.), Creative Dimensions of Teaching and Learning in the 21st Century, 331–344.

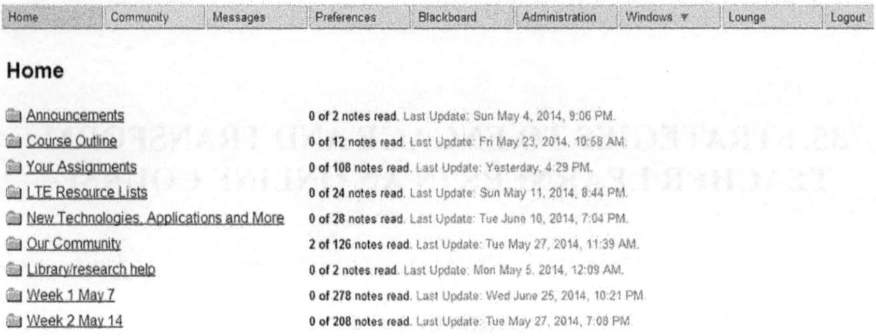

Figure 1. Pepper snapshot

The Goals of Our Approach

As our course involves teachers, the goal underlying our chosen strategies is to support the development of professional identity within a community of practice where TLs can engage actively within a multi-modal environment.

The Conceptual Framework

Singh and Richards in their 2009 article entitled "Teaching and Learning in the Course Room" suggest that the course room, and in our case the online learning environment, is a community of practice (Lave & Wenger, 1991) where TLs can grow by taking part in various activities such as the reading response activities described in this chapter while learning professional discourses via various artifacts including articles, videos, cases, peer and instructor responses, as well as their uses of multiple types of media. Singh and Richards also explain that every community of practice involves power relations which usually reflect the power structure beyond the course.

Singh and Richards describe the role for teacher educators in this situated social learning context in the following way:

> The aim is to scaffold opportunities for learning, rather than transmitting preset theories. Central to this role are modeling good instructional practice, dialogically organizing instruction, encouraging participation in multiple discourses, and setting up collaborative learning. A challenge for anyone teaching LTE (language teacher education) courses is how well the trainers' and the course's instructional practices model the kinds of learning opportunities and dispositions that are encouraged to create in their own classrooms. (p. 204)

In *How People Learn*, Bransford, Brown and Cocking (2000) highlight three conditions for effective learning including the engagement of prior understandings, the integration of factual knowledge and conceptual frameworks as well as active control over the learning process.

These ideas resonate with us and underpin the instructional choices we have made in creating and managing our asynchronous online course for TLs.

Creative Thinking and Learning

Henriksen and Mishra (2013) underline the importance of creativity in teaching and connect it to the growing research that suggests that creative thinking is an essential skill for teachers in 21st century classrooms where globalization and technology create new challenges. They also point to the various benefits of possessing creative abilities. Henriksen and Mishra interviewed a group of highly creative teachers and found that they had a number of common attributes and teaching behaviours which include: (1) connecting their interests with their teaching, (2) linking lessons to real-world learning, (3) cultivating a creative mindset, (4) valuing collaboration, and (5) taking intellectual risks.

In our course, we have tried to create an environment to support TLs in developing these attributes and behaviours through the completion of weekly activities and assignments that push them to “stretch”, which implies learning about and trying new ways of participating in the course that involve the use of technology and multimedia in addition to traditional print-based text. We have chosen to focus on some of the reading response strategies embedded in our course to illustrate how basic activity design principles can lead to activities that will support the development of creativity among TLs.

Reading Response Strategies

As experienced teachers, we were already familiar with the importance of varying the ways in which we took up readings with our students in face-to-face environments keeping in mind the need to change the pace and grouping strategies throughout our three-hour-long classes. However, working in an asynchronous online environment presented new challenges as many of our strategies did not transfer directly. So, we began to experiment by combining different requirements for the completion of various reading response activities.

The grouping strategies required to complete activities and those required for peer response vary from whole class to small groups and from pairs to individuals. The use of varied media is in some cases expected, while in others it is only encouraged. There is a course folder where there are tutorials and links to various free programs and applications that our TLs can access to learn new ways to share their responses. For now, these include: *PPT, Prezi, BitStrip,* Avatars, *Powtoon, YouTube, BrainShark, Story Jumper, WordPress, Google Docs, Pixton, Jing, VoiceThread, Screencast-o-matic*. However, we are continuously adding new links as more applications become available.[1] Table 1 below provides some examples

Table 1. Description of Reader Response Strategies

Reading Response Strategy	Grouping Strategy For Completion of Activity	Grouping Strategy for Peer Response	Multimodality in Responses
Aha! Passage / Significant excerpt *Provide a brief excerpt from your reading and explain in what way this passage is significant for you. Remember to comment on at least three of your colleagues' A has.*	Individual	TLs choose who to respond to	Encouraged
Personal Connections *After you have viewed the assigned videos and read the related article, determine the top 3 priorities for your own professional development (PD).* *In your group folder, create a note where you briefly describe your teaching context including information on location, age of learners, proficiency level of learners, type of learning environment, goals of the program etc…* *Then indicate which of the priority areas in terms of your PD and explain your choice of priority areas.* *Once all 4 or 5 student members of your group have posted, respond by noting similarities and differences across contexts and pose at least one probing question to better understand the priorities that each person has set.*	Individual	The instructor places each student in a small group	Encouraged
Note to author *Describe an experience you have had which would qualify as collaborative teacher development. Comment on your experience and reference the benefits and challenges Bill Johnston mentions in his article.* *Then, write a brief comment for Bill Johnston on the personal benefits you derived from your involvement in collaborative teacher development. I will collate these and email them to him.*	Individual	TLs choose who to respond to	Encouraged

Conversation between authors *After you complete your reading of the four chapters, we would like you to imagine the type of conversation that might occur between Kathleen Graves, Nat Bartels, Rod Ellis and John Hedgecock after a conference presentation where they participated in a panel discussion on pedagogical knowledge in second language teacher education.* *You can post your conversation in writing or in another genre. If there are friends and family members who would like to take on a role, you can audio or video record the conversation and post it*	Individual	TLs choose who to respond to	Encouraged
Discussion with author as course guest *Imagine that Paula Golombek has come to visit our class to speak to us about Personal Practical Knowledge in L2 Teacher Education. The first person to open this note will begin the presentation. Each person will add a statement or a question as though they were Paula or a graduate student in the seminar and indicate their own name in parentheses. Here is what the resulting text might look like:* *Paula Golombek (Sabia): Hello everyone! I am very happy to join you here today to discuss the importance of Personal Practical Knowledge. It was a long flight from Florida, but I'm excited to be here! Can someone here tell me what they think Personal Practical Knowledge is?* *Graduate Student A (Ben): PPK refers to the type of knowledge that is constantly reconstructed through critical reflection on a combination of a teacher's past educational and personal life experiences, and her practical teaching experiences. These knowledges and experiences allow teachers to "make sense" of their current classroom contexts.*	Whole class	No peer response is required as this is built into the actual activity	Not feasible because of constraints of the activity
Review of a resource *Form a group with two others and select a resource that interests you. Learn how to use Google Docs which will allow to collaborate more easily than sharing files via email. Explore the Tech Apps Folder to determine the best way to share your review.*	Groups of three self-selected	Each course participant is required to respond	Expected

of how we have connected reading response activities, grouping strategies and modalities.

With permission of the TLs, we have chosen several responses to illustrate how they have stretched themselves in responding to course readings using various modalities. The examples presented in Figures 2 through 10 reveal how these TLs are beginning to cultivate a creative mind-set, value collaboration, and take intellectual risks, three of the activities that characterize the very creative teachers in Henriksen and Mishra's 2013 study.

Teacher Learners' Feedback on the Process

Once the TLs had finished (1) reading and viewing, (2) posting their ideas via varied media, (3) responding to their peers and (4) exploring the instructor's responses to the group, they were invited to reflect on their learning experiences. The purpose of this reflective activity was to help TLs become more aware of the reasons for integrating various instructional strategies into the weekly tasks. The process of reflecting on their learning also revealed to us how the online learning environment as well as the weekly activities and tasks we assigned enhanced or impeded the TLs' creativity.

A recurring theme in the TLs' reflections was their concerns about preparing creative posts. Although the creative posts were meant to empower the learners and give them greater freedom to express themselves, many stated that due to their busy schedules, they did not have the time to learn new technologies and view different multimodal posts. Moreover, many felt that it was more difficult to access various multimodal posts that required Internet access and consisted of audio files and were not as easily accessible as text-based posts that they could access at any time or place. However, as the semester progressed, the TLs wrote less about feeling overstretched, and got used to the different medium of engagement. It took them a couple of weeks to become more comfortable with the concept of creative posts and develop a "creative mindset" (Henriksen & Mishra, 2013) that valued the space for creativity.

As the TLs became more familiar with the online learning environment and using creative technologies, many started to value the use of multimodal technologies to share ideas. They recognized its pedagogical value in their own teaching contexts. One TL stated: "Many of us used different ICT tools to share our ideas. These types of participation tools are also helping us to value the importance of integrating them in our teaching".

In their list of creative attributes and behaviours, Henriksen and Mishra (2013) list "valuing collaboration" as a quality that enhances creativity. Many TLs in our class reflected on how collaboration brought the learning community together. Through collaboration students found creative ways to scaffold the learning process. One TL noted:

> Whenever there is a student who continues to upload great resources, and remains honest about his/her life, other students follow in the sharing. The international presentations helped us write meaningful discussions and openly share our thoughts.

Collaboration also exposed the TLs to new technologies that were available, and innovative ways in which those technologies can be used to create and respond to posts. Many started to take risks and experiment different technologies. One TL stated:

> Having been out of the high bandwidth Internet easy world for a while, I am amazed at all the great apps and software available. I tried out the Bitstrips site after seeing Clara's work, and after seeing Annemarie's assignment, I want to check out Jing/Screencast. This type of access of colleagues' work is inspiring and enlightening.

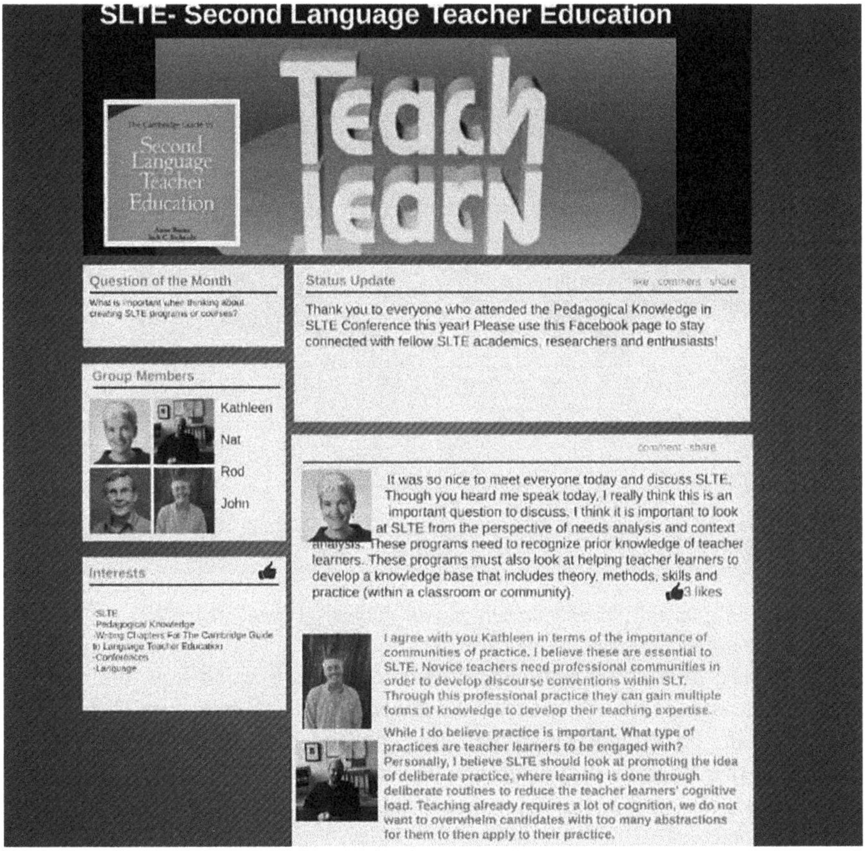

Figure 2. Personal connections

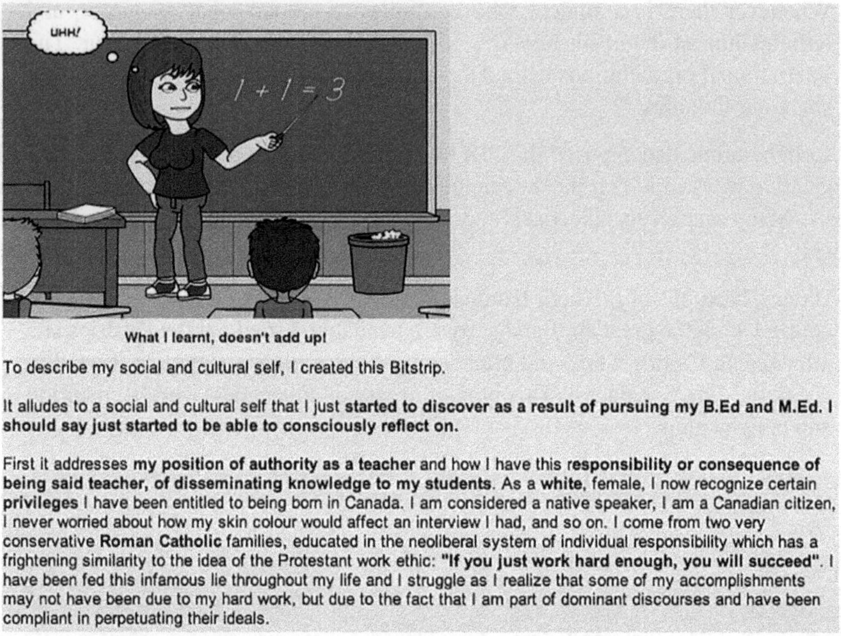
UHH!
1 + 1 = 3
What I learnt, doesn't add up!
To describe my social and cultural self, I created this Bitstrip.
It alludes to a social and cultural self that I just started to discover as a result of pursuing my B.Ed and M.Ed. I should say just started to be able to consciously reflect on.
First it addresses my position of authority as a teacher and how I have this responsibility or consequence of being said teacher, of disseminating knowledge to my students. As a white, female, I now recognize certain privileges I have been entitled to being born in Canada. I am considered a native speaker, I am a Canadian citizen, I never worried about how my skin colour would affect an interview I had, and so on. I come from two very conservative Roman Catholic families, educated in the neoliberal system of individual responsibility which has a frightening similarity to the idea of the Protestant work ethic: "If you just work hard enough, you will succeed". I have been fed this infamous lie throughout my life and I struggle as I realize that some of my accomplishments may not have been due to my hard work, but due to the fact that I am part of dominant discourses and have been compliant in perpetuating their ideals.

Figure 3. Conversation between the authors: A Facebook-style Prezi

Figure 4. Conversation between the authors: A comic strip hike

The process of reflecting on their own learning revealed how the various tasks and assignments we created enhanced the TLs' creativity. What was evident, from the TL posts was that they needed time to get used to being creative. However, once they overcame the initial hurdle of learning about new technologies, they began to enjoy exploring those technologies to share and respond to posts.

Figure 5. Conversation between the authors: A superhero comic strip

Figure 6. A conversation between the authors: A post-conference comic strip

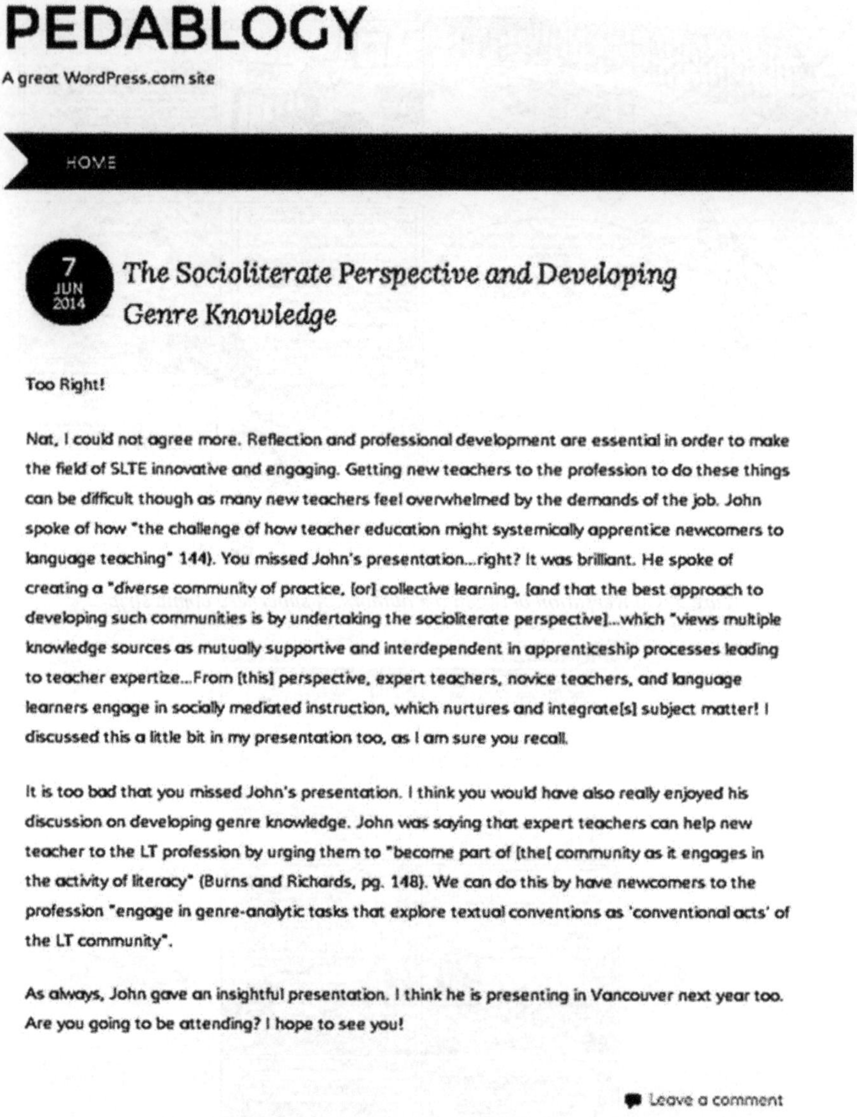

PEDABLOGY

A great WordPress.com site

HOME

7 JUN 2014

The Socioliterate Perspective and Developing Genre Knowledge

Too Right!

Nat, I could not agree more. Reflection and professional development are essential in order to make the field of SLTE innovative and engaging. Getting new teachers to the profession to do these things can be difficult though as many new teachers feel overwhelmed by the demands of the job. John spoke of how "the challenge of how teacher education might systemically apprentice newcomers to language teaching" 144). You missed John's presentation...right? It was brilliant. He spoke of creating a "diverse community of practice, [or] collective learning, [and that the best approach to developing such communities is by undertaking the socioliterate perspective]...which "views multiple knowledge sources as mutually supportive and interdependent in apprenticeship processes leading to teacher expertize...From [this] perspective, expert teachers, novice teachers, and language learners engage in socially mediated instruction, which nurtures and integrate[s] subject matter! I discussed this a little bit in my presentation too, as I am sure you recall.

It is too bad that you missed John's presentation. I think you would have also really enjoyed his discussion on developing genre knowledge. John was saying that expert teachers can help new teacher to the LT profession by urging them to "become part of [the[community as it engages in the activity of literacy" (Burns and Richards, pg. 148). We can do this by have newcomers to the profession "engage in genre-analytic tasks that explore textual conventions as 'conventional acts' of the LT community".

As always, John gave an insightful presentation. I think he is presenting in Vancouver next year too. Are you going to be attending? I hope to see you!

Leave a comment

Figure 7. Conversation between the authors: A blog

Learning Opportunities through 'Stretching'

Our online course allowed us to learn about creative and engaging uses of technology that enhanced communication and in-class participation. We achieved this through the use of software that is either free-source (i.e., Prezi or VoiceThread) or that is already available to most PC or Mac computer users (i.e., Windows Movie Maker,

Figure 8. A conversation between the authors: A Lego Movie on YouTube

IMovie). In doing this, we had to learn about these new technological tools ourselves before presenting them to our TLs. Therefore, we were able to model successful teaching and learning practices that TLs can easily incorporate to their teaching repertoires. The rich technology-mediated discussions and participation that occurred suggest a deeper level of reflection and learning in which TLs were able to connect the theory presented in course reading to their personal and professional experiences (see Figure 2 above). Moreover, the online and asynchronous qualities of the course provided TLs with greater accessibility and flexibility to participate in the class in spite of their different geographical locations, time zones, and multiple occupations.

Challenges

The multiple class activities and assignments aimed at stretching TLs' creative uses of technology and critical reflection also resulted in a significant amount of stretching on our end as instructors. Our first challenge was to develop an online presence in order to facilitate a sense of community. We had to find activities to help our TLs negotiate their multiple understandings of language teacher education and language teachers' needs. Second, providing technological support relevant to TLs' different needs while giving timely feedback was a constant challenge. One strategy we used to provide feedback involved preparing video responses to threaded discussions.

At times, a few TLs did not fully understand their instructors' scaffolding efforts, which, in some cases, resulted in reduced participation or disengagement. This was problematic because a TL's lack of engagement translated into spending less time online becoming familiar with the resources and getting to know their peers as well as ultimately not benefitting from the scaffolded "stretching" built into the course.

Imagine that Paula Golombek has come to visit our class to speak to us about Personal Practical Knowledge in L2 Teacher Education. The first person to open this note will begin the presentation. Each person will add a statement or a question as though they were Paula or a graduate student in the seminar and indicate their own name in parentheses. Here is what the resulting text might look like:

Paula Golombek (Sabia): *Hello everyone! I am very happy to join you here today to discuss the importance of Personal Practical Knowledge. It was a long flight from Florida, but I'm excited to be here! Can someone here tell me what they think Personal Practical Knowledge is?*

Graduate Student A (Ben): *PPK refers to the type of knowledge that is constantly reconstructed through critical reflection on a combination of a teacher's past educational and personal life experiences, and her practical teaching experiences. These knowledges and experiences allow teachers to "make sense" of their current classroom contexts.*

Paula Golombek (Crystal): That's a great definition. It connects well with how Clandinin defines it using similar terms such as constructed, reconstructed and dynamic. This type of knowledge is very fluid, and also touches upon moral and emotional dimensions of teacher's experiences, as Clandinin and Connelly define PPK further. Why do you think PPK became part of a robust scholarly tradition? What are the implications or assumptions that are raised by the use of PPK for further research on teacher knowledge?

Graduate Student B (Qasim): Perhaps PPK became a significant part of teacher research because scholars recognized that teachers respond to classroom situations based on their experiences as students and teachers. The academic community also realized that for teachers to make effective decisions they need to draw upon knowledge that is explicit, which is what PPK is.

Paula Golombek (Rosemary): Great points! PPK is rooted in the context of a teacher`s experiences. Indeed, teachers use PPK as a framework to make sense of their classrooms. We can think of PPK as a way to understand how beliefs and knowledge inform teachers and how their previous experiences impact their current teaching experiences. Given this importance in education, why does PPK have such scant visibility in the published literature concerning second language teacher education? In pre-service teacher education programs and in graduate programs, autobiographies, personal narratives, and reflective journals are becoming more and more present to help teachers make sense of their experiences (both prior and in the practicum), of their knowledge (as it relates teaching and otherwise), and as a reflection tool. Should these journals and autobiographies be used as data collection tools for research connected to PPK? How authentic will these journals and autobiographies be if pre-service teachers and graduate students know these artefacts will be analyzed for research purposes? Will that detract for their original intended function? In other words, how do we even conduct research on PPK without interfering with the reflection process?

Graduate Student C (Jon): These are diverse questions that you are raising about qualitative research and personal practical knowledge. Furthermore, I like your concern Dr. Golombek about "the risk of reductionism" and your concern for the portrayal of teachers as deficient who do not articulate their personal practical knowledge (2009, p. 159). I look forward to learning from our discussion of your questions.

Paula Golombek (Lauren): It's true that I do often worry about the risk of reductionism. In some cases, teachers "do not always externalize their knowledge easily or completely." There are also issues with reductionism that arise when teachers interchange terms and definitions, or minimize differences are not always beneficial when looking at the big picture. Another area that I suggest needs further examination is how teachers' "knowledge shapes and is shaped by identity." Although some factors have been examined, such as personal histories and how teachers understand their activities, *what other personal factors could shape an L2 teacher's knowledge and therefore identity?*

Graduate student D (Sarah): I know there has been some research on this but I think one of the most important personal factors that shapes our identity as language teachers is our previous language learning experience. Whether these experiences were positive or negative, easy or difficult, the pedagogy used and the context of the learning shapes how we teach, how we view language learning and how we perceive our students. Well that's my opinion as far as something that's shaped my identity and PPK but I'm sure other people in the class have different opinions on what shaped their identity as a language teacher.

Paula Golombek (Yecid): Sarah, very well said. Identity is a key factor in teachers' personal profession. I also would like to add that a good way to legitimize and articulate teacher's way of knowing is through personal teacher's stories. These encourage, empower and motivate other teachers and reframe their PPK and their classroom experiences. Personal stories help us to organize, articulate and communicate what we know about ourselves, our students, our past, present and future.

Figure 9. Discussion with the author as a course guest

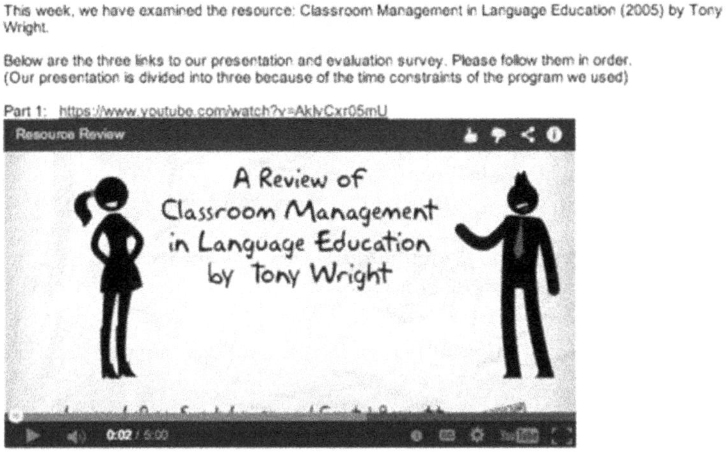
This week, we have examined the resource: Classroom Management in Language Education (2005) by Tony Wright.
Below are the three links to our presentation and evaluation survey. Please follow them in order.
(Our presentation is divided into three because of the time constraints of the program we used)
Part 1:
Resource Review
A Review of
Classroom Management
in Language Education
by Tony Wright
0:02 / 5:00

Figure 10. Review of a resource

We share our experiences in this chapter with the intention of inviting all educators to be adventurous and explore creative uses of technology. We believe it to be an important exercise to facilitate the creation of collaborative relations of power (Cummins, Brown, & Sayers, 2007) that empower all teachers regardless of their level of expertise and engagement with technology to support each other, reflect on their own practices and grow together.

REFERENCES

Bransford, D., Brown, A., & Cocking, R. (2000). *How people learn: Brain, mind, experience and school.* Washington, DC: National Academies Press.

Cummins, J., Brown, K., & Sayers, D. (2007). *Literacy, technology, and diversity: Teaching for success in changing times.* Boston, MA: Pearson.

Henriksen, D., & Mishra, P. (2013). Learning from creative teachers. *Educational Leadership, 70*(5).

Lave, E., & Wenger, E. (1991). *Situated learning: Legitimate peripheral participation.* Cambridge: Cambridge University Press.

Singh, G., & Richards, J. C. (2009). Teaching and learning in the course room. In A. Burns & J. C. Richards (Eds.), *The Cambridge guide to second language teacher education* (pp. 201–208). New York, NY: Cambridge University Press.

Antoinette Gagné
OISE/University of Toronto

Sreemali Herath
OISE/University of Toronto

Marlon Valencia
OISE/University of Toronto

APPENDIX

Links to Online Resources

Avatars and comic strips
Bitstrips: http://www.bitstrips.com/
Doppel me: http://www.doppelme.com/
Pixton: http://www.pixton.com/ca/

Collaboration, file sharing and presentations
Brainshark: http://www.brainshark.com/
Google Drive: https://drive.google.com/
Microsoft Office 365 (paid):http://office.microsoft.com/en- ca/products/?CTT=97
Prezi: Prezi.com
Powtoon: http://www.powtoon.com/
Story Jumper: http://www.storyjumper.com/
VoiceThread: https://voicethread.com/

Video sharing, captions and editing
Amara: http://www.amara.org/en/
Screencast-o-matic: http://www.screencast-o-matic.com/
YouTube: https://www.youtube.com/

Website development
Wix: http://www.wix.com/
WordPress: https://wordpress.com/

ABOUT THE CONTRIBUTORS

EDITORS

Jill Cummings develops, facilitates, and supervises faculty development programs and activities at Yorkville University (Canada) where she is the Associate Dean of Faculty Development. Jill completed her dissertation and Ph.D. in Curriculum, Teaching, and Learning at the University of Toronto. She has worked in developing, teaching and supervising teacher education at the graduate and undergraduate levels (post-secondary and K-12), particularly in the areas of methodology, curriculum development and curriculum theory, program development, assessment, technology in education, and second language education. Her research includes work related to online teaching and learning, literacy instruction and assessment, English as a second language, creativity and innovation, and mobile educational games.

Mary Blatherwick is a Visual Arts educator in the Faculty of Education of the University of New Brunswick, Canada where she teaches visual art education, creativity and curriculum development at the undergraduate and graduate levels. Her research interests include: intercultural understanding, arts-based inquiry, community-based art education, creativity and multimodal literacies. Mary has extensive experience in teacher education and presents her research nationally and internationally. She is the chair of the Atlantic Centre for Creativity which promotes interdisciplinary research and professional development in creativity and innovation in New Brunswick and regionally. Highlights of her scholarly and artistic activities include: publications on innovation in teaching art, the production of a series of short documentary films on the creative practices of New Brunswick visual artists and painting as a form of arts-based education.

AUTHORS

Elizabeth Ashworth is an Associate Professor of art education and fine arts at Nipissing University, North Bay, Ontario, Canada. Her research foci are the integration of visual arts, science, and environmental education in the classroom, along with social and political issues that impact the quality of art education in elementary schools. She is also a photographer and mixed media artist.

Robin Beyea holds a B.A. and B.Ed. from the University of New Brunswick where her studies included an honors in Anthropology and a minor in Spanish as well as a concentration on second language learning. She has been teaching French Immersion and Intensive French in New Brunswick schools since 2006. She is currently completing her Masters of Education in Critical Studies, also at UNB. Her current research interests are focused on assessment practices at the elementary school level.

Joanna Black is an Associate Professor of Art Education in the Faculty of Education and is cross-appointed as an Associate Professor in the School of Art at the University of Manitoba, Winnipeg, Canada. Her research interests are on subjects of new media in education, digital arts pedagogy, contemporary art education, and human rights issues in teaching and learning. For over thirty years she has worked as an art educator, art director, museum educator, curator, art consultant, and a K-12 teacher in formal and informal settings in Canada and the United States. Dr. Black has received awards from the Centre for Human Rights Research at the University of Manitoba, and the Provincial Affiliate Art Educator Award from the Canadian Society for Education through Art. She has recently co-written a book, along with Juan Carlos Castro and Ching-Chiu Ling, entitled *Youth Practices in Digital Arts and New Media: Learning in Formal and Informal Settings.*

Leslie Julia Brewster teaches in the small rural community of Riverside-Albert, NB. As in most small schools, Leslie wears a variety of hats – art teacher, resource teacher, and classroom teacher. She holds a Certificate in Art Media, a BA in Organizational Management, a BED with an Early Years specialization, and a Master's in Instructional Design. Leslie was brought up in an artistic environment: "I think everybody in my family studied art at one time or another". Her grandmother was especially influential: "I remember as a young child my grandmother being very upset that my homework included colouring a pre-drawn map of the country. She felt that students should be given the opportunity to do all of their own drawings, creating and involving themselves personally with their studies." This attitude toward education is at the heart of her teaching philosophy.

Marlene Brooks is a tenure track faculty of the Instructional Design Group at Open Learning Thompson Rivers University. Her previous position was at Memorial University as a senior instructional designer where *Arts Education: Creativity in the Classroom* was developed and implemented. She has over 25 years of experience working in the adult education field for private, college and university environments. Her interest and research areas include phenomenology, hermeneutics, aesthetic course design and multimodal learning environments to increase student engagement and interaction in web-based teaching/learning environments.

Michael Busch is an instructor in the English Language Program at Saginaw Valley State University. His research and teaching interests include second language grammar pedagogy, testing and assessment, and task-based instruction. He has an MA in English as a Second Language from the University of Hawai'i at Mānoa and a Ph.D. in Second Language Education from the Ontario Institute for Studies in Education (OISE) at the University of Toronto.

Jim Cummins is a Professor Emeritus at the Ontario Institute for Studies in Education of the University of Toronto. His research focuses on literacy development in educational contexts characterized by linguistic diversity. He has explored the nature of language proficiency and its relationship to literacy development with particular emphasis on the intersections of societal power relations, teacher-student identity negotiation, and literacy attainment in numerous articles and books.

Gerald Cupchik studied with Bob Zajonc at the University of Michigan, received his Masters (1970) and PhD (1972) at the University of Wisconsin with Howard Leventhal before doing postdoctoral study with Daniel Berlyne (1972-74) at the University of Toronto, where he has been a professor since 1974. Gerald collaborates with scholars from many fields, emphasizing the complementary use of quantitative and qualitative research methods and topics include responses to art, literature, and film. He was president of the International Association for Empirical Aesthetics, the International Society for the Empirical Study of Literature and Media, and Division 10 of the American Psychological Association, Psychology and the Arts.

Kieran Egan is an emeritus professor of education at Simon Fraser University in British Columbia, Canada (http://www.educ.sfu.ca/kegan/). His work has dealt with both innovative educational theory and detailed practical methods whereby implications of the theory can be applied in everyday classrooms. Various of his books have been translated into around 20 languages. He is a director of the Imaginative Education Research Group (http://ierg.ca). His recent books include: *The Future of Education: Reimagining the school from the ground up* (New Haven: Yale University Press, 2011), *Learning in Depth: A simple innovation that can transform schooling* (University of Chicago Press, 2010), and, co-authored with Gillian Judson, *Imagination and the engaged learner: Cognitive tools for the classroom* (NY: Teachers College Press, 2015).

Ian Fogarty has an honors Bachelor of Science in Chemistry and Bachelor of Philosophy in Science Methods from Mount Allison and an MSc in Organometallic Chemistry. Ian has been teaching chemistry and physics at Riverview High in New Brunswick, Canada, since 1998. He is the author of the virtual high school chemistry classes for the province and the recipient of the Prime Minister's Award for Excellence in Education (2008), the Partner's in Learning World Wide Innovative Educator Forum. He achieved 3rd place in Communication and Collaboration Strand (2010), and has received the Canadian Association of Physicists' High School Teacher Award (2011). Ian is a speaker and teacher coach about 21st Century Learning, Project Based Learning, probeware, 1:1 and interactive whiteboards in the classroom in Oxford, London, Netherlands, Jordan, South Africa, Mauritius, China, Canada, and USA, and the creator of the SMART Collaborative Classroom, of which there are now 50 copies around the world.

A. J. Funn is the pen name of *Dale Vandenborre*. Dale is the author and creator of a visual puzzle language called Glyffix. Dale has been doing Glyffix play with his children since 2001. He published his first book, *Penelope's Imagination Runs Wild* in 2013 based on the language. It is the first book that tells a detailed story without using words. He also launched his first Glyffix mobile app in 2014, and a second book in 2015. Dale has found or co-found multiple technology-based companies and teaches Technology Management & Entrepreneurship at the University of New Brunswick.

Antoinette Gagné is an Associate Professor at the Ontario Institute of Studies in Education of the University of Toronto. She has over 30 years experience in preparing teachers to work with diverse students and has supervised the research of doctoral students in related fields. As Academic Advisor for the OISE Student Success Centre from 2005 onward, she has had the opportunity to work closely with a team of doctoral candidates to meet the academic and cultural needs of undergraduate and graduate students in education. Dr. Gagné is also involved in research with immigrant teachers and learners and has explored the use of various innovative qualitative methodologies designed particularly to give voice to these diverse research participants. She has written extensively about diversity issues in education and the experiences of immigrant children, teachers and families in the Canadian education system.

Susan Galbraith was born in the Rifle Range in Saint John, N.B. She studied at Concordia University and the University of New Brunswick, and heads the Visual Arts program at Carleton North High School in Florenceville-Bristol, NB. She has run many PD sessions for high school and elementary school teachers, and has mentored many new art teachers in her classroom. She has served on the New Brunswick Curriculum Development Advisory Committees for Elementary Art and High School Visual Arts and was a leading contributor to the Visual Arts 9/10 and the Art 110 Curriculum Guides. Her program has received numerous awards, including Innovation in Education Grants (2000 & 2002), and an Innovative Learning Fund Grant (2008), and her achievement has been recognized with an ArtsNB School of the Arts prize (2008), and the Prime Minister's Award for Excellence in Teaching (2009).

Dustin Garnet completed his PhD in Art Education at Concordia University. The focus of his research forms a storied institutional history of the Central Technical School Art Department. He has published in top tier education and art education journals and has received a Social Science and Humanities Research Council Doctoral Fellowship to support his study. Dustin lives in Toronto and has taught for the past eleven years at the internationally recognized Art Centre found on the campus of Central Technical School. His research interests include contemporary art education practice, stories and story creation, architecture and educational space, and the history of education.

Snezhana S. Harizanova has taught beginning to advanced high school and university learners of English in both EFL and ESL settings. She has an M.A. degree in Linguistics and Applied Linguistics and an M.A. degree in English Philology. She is also a certified suggestopedagogue. At present, Snezhana is pursuing her doctoral degree in Linguistics and Applied Linguistics at York University in Toronto, Canada. Her research interests include explicit vs. implicit and conscious vs. unconscious teaching and learning. Her doctoral research is focused on Suggestopedia, its relevance to current (language) learning theories and cognitive science research, and its applicability in English for academic purposes.

Erika Hasebe-Ludt is a professor in the Faculty of Education at the University of Lethbridge. She teaches and researches in the areas of multiple literacies, in particular life writing and literary métissage, in the context of Canadian and transnational curriculum studies. In addition to various articles in journals and edited books, her publications include Curriculum Intertext: Place/Language/Pedagogy, Contemplating Curriculum: Genealogies/Times/Places (with Wanda Hurren), Life Writing and Literary Métissage as an Ethos for Our Times (with Cynthia Chambers and Carl Leggo) and A Heart of Wisdom: Life Writing as Empathetic Inquiry (with Cynthia Chambers, Carl Leggo, and Anita Sinner).

Sreemali Herath is a doctoral student in Language and Literacies and Education at the Ontario Institute for Studies in Education, University of Toronto. Her doctoral research, which she conducted in Sri Lanka, focused on how pre-service English language teachers are prepared to address issues of diversity in post-conflict Sri Lanka. At OISE, she provides academic and cultural support to teacher candidates and graduate students. She is a certified ESL teacher.

Xiaomin Hu is a lecturer of Teaching Chinese to Speakers of Other Languages in the College of International Education at Zhejiang Normal University. Her research and teaching interests include modern Chinese, Chinese grammar and writing, curriculum development, and teaching Chinese as a second language.

Belinda Jamieson did her Master of Education studies at the University of New Brunswick where she examined Imaginative Education approaches and the use of storytelling in teaching students with First Nations backgrounds. She has taught elementary school learners in Fort McMurray, Alberta; and, has lived and worked in Prince Edward Island, Canada.

Gillian Judson is one of the Directors of the Imaginative Education Research Group and a Lecturer in the Faculty of Education at Simon Fraser University. Her published work and teaching show how we can routinely engage students' imaginations (pre-K through graduate school) to ensure effective learning across the curriculum. She is particularly interested in sustainability and how an imaginative and ecologically sensitive approach to education can lead to a sophisticated ecological consciousness. Her most recent book is *Engaging Imagination in Ecological Education: Practical Strategies For Teaching* (Pacific Educational Press, 2015).

Eleni Karavanidou is a public school teacher of Humanities in Greece and a PhD student in Education (University of New Brunswick). She holds a BA in History and Archeology, and a BA in Preschool Education from the Kapodistrian University of Athens as well as a Master's in Adult Education from the University of New Brunswick. Eleni has spent seven years in the innovative programme of School Libraries in Greece. During the period 2012–2017 she taught at the Centre for Hellenic Studies at the UNB Department of Classics and Ancient History as a secondment instructor.

Robert Kelly, educator and author, is an associate professor at the University of Calgary where he is academic coordinator of the Creative Development in Educational Practice and Design Thinking for Innovation graduate certificate programs in the Werklund School of Education. His pioneering work in the area of creativity in education has focused on creativity in teacher education and understanding the nature of creative development in educational practice. Robert has previously edited *Creative Expression, Creative Education: Creativity as a Primary Rationale for Education* (2008). He is also associate editor for two research volumes from the International Journal of Creative Arts in Interdisciplinary Practice, Inquiries for Hope and Change (2010) and Research for Community and Cultural Change (2011). Robert is profiled on the University of Calgary's Great Teachers website and has been a featured keynote speaker nationally and internationally on the topics of creative practice and creative development in education.

Ahmad Khanlari is a researcher with the Department of Curriculum, Teaching, and Learning at OISE/University of Toronto where he studies for his PhD in educational technology and knowledge building environments. He also has obtained his 2nd master's degree in educational technology at Memorial University of Newfoundland. Prior to his study at Memorial, he was the co-owner and manager of a successful educational company which produces educational kits to teach science and modern technologies (such as robotics, astronomy, and chemistry) to students. He worked in his company as the education manager for about eight years, to design different technology-related curricula, and to hire, train, and supervise teachers/instructors to teach various curricula at schools. During these years, he also taught robotics in different grade levels. His research area lies in knowledge building environments, educational technology, educational robots, engineering education, and STEM education. He is also expert in wireless communication, wireless networks, and satellite communications, as he has obtained his bachelor's degree and his first master's degree in electrical and communication engineering.

Philip Lambert is an engineer, a businessman, an entrepreneur and a creativity researcher. After working as an engineer and production manager in advanced manufacturing, Philip became a pioneer and entrepreneur in the field of online education. It was while building online learning companies that the interplay of creativity across diverse jobs – including graphics, new media, instructional design, software development, and marketing – sparked his interest. Philip is currently the Program Coordinator for the University of New Brunswick's Technology Management & Entrepreneurship program where he mentors student entrepreneurs and teaches creativity. At the same time, he is completing a PhD in creativity. His areas of research interest include: creativity theories, assessment of creativity, enhancement of creativity, online evaluation of creativity, teaching creativity online, creativity of product development teams in startup companies, the relationship between novelty and the success of crowdfunding campaigns, and the rejection of creativity (that is, the bias against highly novel ideas and products).

Lorraine Lasmanis is an experienced teacher, administrator, and the "ultimate professional" in all things ESL and TESL. Lorraine has achieved her B.A., B.Ed. in ESL and Special Education, and TESL Certification. In addition to 25 years of ongoing professional development courses, workshops, and participation in annual TESL conferences, she has participated in ACE (Advance Consulting for Education) as a TESOL Certificate Trainer. She worked as Regional Program Manager and Administrator of Adult English as a Second Language (ESL) and Language Instruction for Newcomers to Canada (LINC) for the Waterloo Catholic District School Board in Ontario, where she planned and managed all aspects of program development and delivery. During this time, Lorraine was key to the creation of the ESL learner book project described here as the facilitator of *From Our Hearts* and the accompanying workbook. She has contributed generously to professional development and programs in TESL as a member of the Advisory Committee for the TESL Training Program (Conestoga College) and a Board of Directors executive member of TESL Waterloo-Wellington for ten years. Lorraine is also an "artist and presenter in her own right", as well as active and passionate contributor to the community and her family.

Geoff Lawrence works an Assistant Professor in ESL and Applied Linguistics at York University in Toronto, Canada. He is a teacher educator, researcher and curriculum designer interested in exploring the potential of online, blended and classroom-based English language teaching and teacher education programs. His research examines online/blended language teaching methodology, teacher beliefs towards educational innovation and intercultural learning in language and teacher education.

Samuel LeBlanc is an adjunct lecturer at the Université de Moncton in philosophy, economy, and political sciences. In parallel, he was an economist at the Canadian Institute for Research on Regional Development, and a private research firm. His studies in economics (BA, Université de Moncton, 1995; MA, Université de Montréal, 1997), philosophy, and German (BA, McGill, 2000; student Mphil, King's College London, 2002-04) were recognized with a Baxter & Alma Ricard Scholarship. Inspired by teaching, he completed an education and French studies degree (BA, Université de Moncton, 2011), and enrolled in an Education PhD program (University of New Brunswick, 2012–present), working with Dr. Ellen Rose (Faculty of Education,), and Dr. Ronald Weed (Department of Philosophy). Samuel's research—supported by the Joseph-Armand Bombardier Canada Doctoral Scholarship and New Brunswick Innovation Foundation (2014-17) – concerns the conception of the 21st century's epistemically or intellectually virtuous student.

Carl Leggo is a poet and professor in the Department of Language and Literacy Education at the University of British Columbia. His books include: *Growing Up Perpendicular on the Side of a Hill*; *View from My Mother's House*; *Come-By-Chance*; *Teaching to Wonder: Responding to Poetry in the Secondary Classroom*; *Lifewriting as Literary Métissage* and an *Ethos for Our Times* (co-authored with Erika Hasebe-Ludt and Cynthia Chambers); *Being with A/r/tography* (co-edited with Stephanie Springgay, Rita L. Irwin, and Peter Gouzouasis); *Creative Expression, Creative Education* (co-edited with Robert Kelly); *Poetic Inquiry: Vibrant Voices in the Social Sciences* (co-edited with Monica Prendergast and Pauline Sameshima); *English in Middle and Secondary Classrooms* (co-edited with Kedrick James and Teresa M. Dobson); *A heart of wisdom: Life writing as empathetic inquiry* (co-edited with Cynthia Chambers, Erika Hasebe-Ludt, and Anita Sinner); and *Sailing in a Concrete Boat: A Teacher's Journey.*

Peter Liljedahl is an Associate Professor of Mathematics Education in the Faculty of Education at Simon Fraser University in Vancouver, Canada. He is a former high school mathematics teacher who has kept his research interest and activities close to the classroom. Peter regularly works closely with teachers, schools, school districts, and ministries of education on issues of pertaining to the improvement of teaching and learning. His primary research interests are teacher beliefs, teacher education, and creativity in mathematics.

Kathy Mantas is an Associate Professor of art education and graduate studies at Nipissing University in North Bay, Ontario, Canada. Her research interests include ongoing teacher development, teacher knowledge and identity, arts education, arts-based and arts-informed inquiry, creativity in teaching-learning contexts, and women's studies. She is primarily a mixed-media and conceptual artist and her art work has been published in a women's studies book, and in several arts-based research books and publications.

Adrian McKerracher is a writer and illustrator with a PhD from the Centre for Cross-Faculty Inquiry in Education at the University of British Columbia. His research explores the pedagogical potential of metaphor, life writing, and creative problem solving. He has published literary fiction and academic research in Canadian and international journals.

Heather McLeod is an assistant professor of art education at Memorial University. Before entering the academy as a professor she taught in the public school system in British Columbia and in Nunavut. As well she worked in communications and policy development for a provincial teachers' federation and for government. Her current funded research projects include an examination of teacher dress; the documentation of an experiential museum education program for children and an exploration of how faculty members become researchers.

Kerri Mesner is an Assistant Professor in the School of Education at Arcadia University, in Glenside, Pennsylvania. Kerri is also an ordained minister with Metropolitan Community Churches, a queer theologian, a theatre performer and educator, and an activist. Kerri's dissertation explored performative autoethnography, queer theology, and anti-oppressive education in addressing religiously rooted anti-queer violence, and includes an original one-act play written and performed by Mesner. Kerri has a PhD from the Centre for Cross Faculty Inquiry in Education at the University of British Columbia, and an MA in Theological Studies from Vancouver School of Theology.

Sylvie Morice has been a teacher since 2000 most of which have been in a Middle School math classroom. She holds a Bachelor of Science from Mount Allison University and a Masters of Education from the University of New Brunswick. The ever-changing bulletin boards, hands-on activities, participation in provincial and national student math competitions and real world application of outcomes in Sylvie's classroom reflect the pace and evolution of today's mathematics. To keep math engaging, competitive and fun she runs an annual Math Olympics as described in the Spring 2013 edition of "Achieve Magazine" published by The Anglophone East School District. She is currently creating multi-leveled activities for her classrooms, aimed to meet the needs of all learners. Sylvie resides in Sackville, New Brunswick.

Burcu Yaman Ntelioglou is an Assistant Professor in the Faculty of Education, Department of Teaching and Learning at Brandon University, Canada. She completed a postdoctoral fellowship and a PhD at the Ontario Institute for Studies in Education, University of Toronto and holds a Master's in education from York University, Canada. She teaches in both the teacher education and graduate education programs. Her work focuses on the education of linguistically and culturally diverse students in contexts of migration, multiculturalism and multilingualism; second/additional language pedagogy; multiliteracies; transnational literacies; and the use of collaborative, community-based, participatory, and digital methodologies in research.

Matthew E. Poehner is Associate Professor of World Languages Education and Applied Linguistics at Pennsylvania State University. His research examines the use of Sociocultural Theory, as conceived by Russian psychologist L. S. Vygotsky, as a basis for second language educational practice. Specifically, his work focuses on mediating learner development of abilities in second languages. He approaches this primarily through three interrelated frameworks: Dynamic Assessment, Mediated Development, and Systemic Theoretical Instruction. Matthew's research has appeared in venues including The Modern Language Journal, TESOL Quarterly, and the International Journal of Applied Linguistics. His most recent book is *Sociocultural Theory and the pedagogical imperative in L2 education: Vygotskian praxis and the research/practice divide* (2014, with J. P. Lantolf). In 2008 he received the Pimsleur Award for Outstanding Research Contribution from the American Council on the Teaching of Foreign Languages.

Gail Prasad is an assistant professor in the department of Curriculum & Instruction at the University of Wisconsin – Madison. She has worked both as a classroom teacher and supporting teacher education in Canada and the US, as well as in France, Kenya and Burkina Faso. She is particularly interested in teaching and learning in culturally and linguistically diverse settings. Her research focuses on children's plurilingualism and literacies production, as well as on creative multimodal research methods for engaging children and youth in research.

Matt Rogers is a professor in the Faculties of Education and Arts at the University of New Brunswick. He is a former public school teacher and a New Brunswick filmmaker. His areas of concentration include critical pedagogy, media studies, critical literacies, social studies, and critical teacher education. His academic research involves the coordination of the documentary film programme *What's up Doc?* in high schools in New Brunswick. Dr. Rogers has directed and produced a number of short documentary and narrative films and has been internationally recognized with an award for Excellence in Cinematography at the Tampa Bay Underground Film Festival.

Chris Ryan has a Bachelor of Philosophy in Interdisciplinary Leadership from the University of New Brunswick, a Bachelor of Education in Science and Social

Studies from Saint Thomas University, and is currently pursuing a Masters of Education (Leadership and Administration) at the University of New Brunswick. He teaches Math, Physics, Economics, and Philosophy from 2006 to present at Riverview High School. He held the Supplementary Position of Responsibility for 21st Century Learning, instructional practices, and assessment from September 2010 to July 2012 and September 2014 to present. He has presented at the Learn2Learn Conference at Rothesay Netherwood 14 (July 2013) and at the STEM Symposium in Fort Collins, Colorado (2015), on the topic of using formative assessment to better inform summative assessment and rethink the relation between them.

Margaret Sadler is an educator and Visual Arts specialist within the Nova Scotia public school system, where she has been teaching for seven years. She has served on the executive for the Art Teachers Association of Nova Scotia and co-chaired the Canadian Society for Education in Art 2014 national conference. In 2013, she successfully completed a thesis-based Master's of Education in Curriculum Studies at the University of New Brunswick focusing on art education. She currently resides in Truro with her husband and two children.

Anita Sinner is an Associate Professor in the Department of Art Education at Concordia University, Montreal, Canada. She has authored numerous articles and co-edited several books concerning arts research methods, life writing, teacher culture, and community art education.

Saskia Stille is an Assistant Professor in the Faculty of Education, Centre for English Language Learning and Teaching Research at Simon Fraser University. Publications from her recent work appear in several edited books and journals, including *Language Assessment Quarterly, European Journal of Teacher Education, TESOL Quarterly* and *Canadian Modern Language Review*.

Trevor Strong is a writer, musician, and arts-educator. As a member of the Arrogant Worms he has toured the world, released 13 albums, and had a song of his played on the space shuttle Endeavour. He is interested in understanding how creativity works and in fostering it in learners of all ages. In his research for his M.Ed. at Queen's University he focused on the importance of creativity and humor in education and created Understanding Humor: a Teacher's Handbook.

Paul Syme teaches high school art and multimedia design in Nova Scotia, Canada. He also teaches part-time in the Master of Education in Curriculum Studies with a Focus on Creativity, a program he conceived for Acadia University, Canada. Paul holds a Master of Arts in art education from Nova Scotia College of Art and Design, Canada, a Baccalaureate of Education from the University of Ottawa, Canada and a Bachelor of Fine Arts from the University of Guelph, Canada. Paul's research and work with teachers applies a media ecology lens to teaching and creative development. This includes the impact of human relationships, media, spaces, and time on cultivating creativity, curiosity, and collaborative problem solving.

Marlon Valencia is a PhD Candidate in Language and Literacies Education, as well as Comparative International and Developing Education at the Ontario Institute for Studies in Education of the University of Toronto. His doctoral research focuses on how teacher educators and pre-service teachers negotiate their multiple identities in three different language teacher education programs and whether the structuring of these programs facilitates their investment in the communities and identities that they envision as professionals. Valencia's research interests also include language policy and planning, and multiliteracies. He has taught English and Spanish as additional languages in Canada, Colombia, and the United States. His work also involves pre-service language teacher proficiency assessment, and curriculum design for the teaching of both languages in colleges and universities in North America.

Cynthia Wallace-Casey has a PhD in History Education at the University of New Brunswick. She also holds a Master's degree (with a Diploma in Material Culture) from UNB. Her Master's thesis, entitled "Providential Openings," was a case study of women weavers in 19th century New Brunswick, which pieced together the (then) unrecognised contribution of female home workers to the economy of rural Queens County. Cynthia has worked in the field of public history and heritage for over twenty years. She commenced her career as curator of a local community museum; has also been curator of collections at Kings Landing Historical Settlement; and was a member of the restoration team for Government House in Fredericton, where she was responsible for the development of interpretation and education programs for this national and provincial historic site. Since 2003, she has been manager of heritage education for Heritage Branch in the Province of New Brunswick. Cynthia's doctoral dissertation was about self-constructed meaning from the past, investigating the connection between community history, museums, and classroom instruction in Historical Thinking. Her research has been supported in part by The Social Sciences and Humanities Research Council (SSHRC) of Canada, the University of New Brunswick, and The History Education Network/Histoire et education en réseau (THEN/HiER). Cynthia Wallace-Casey is now working as a SSHRC Postdoctoral Fellow with The Making History Educational Research Unit at the University of Ottawa.

Ally A. Zhou is Professor of Teaching English to Speakers of Other Languages (TESOL) at Oklahoma City University. Her research interests include second language writing, grammar for writing, English for Academic Purposes, and discourse analysis. She was the Higher Education and Applied Linguistics Chair for Oklahoma Teachers of English to Speakers of Other Languages and Associate Editor for American Review of China Studies. She currently serves on the U.S. Student Fulbright National Screening Committee and is a manuscript reviewer for the journal Language Awareness.

Lightning Source UK Ltd.
Milton Keynes UK
UKHW02f1549100918
328642UK00004B/422/P

9 789463 510455